THE BATTLE OF BULL RUN

KRAUS REPRINT CO.

Millwood, N.Y.

1977

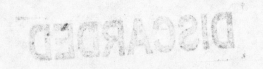

Extracted from:
U.S. Congress. Joint Committee on the Conduct of the
War. Report of the Joint Committee on the Conduct of
the War. 1863-1866.

ISBN 0-527-17553-6
LC 76-41431

KRAUS REPRINT CO.
A U.S. Division of Kraus-Thomson Organization Limited
Printed in U.S.A.

INTRODUCTION

In the summer of 1861 the cry heard in Washington was, "On to Richmond." The citizens of the north, as well as the Congress itself, believed that a single decisive battle would end the new-born Confederacy once and for all.

On July 21, President Lincoln, under pressure from Congress and his War Department, allowed General McDowell to advance against General Beauregard's forces at Manasas Junction—about thirty miles south of the capital—in the hope of claiming "one decisive battle." Under the horrified watch of spectators who had driven out to enjoy a picnic lunch and watch their boys "whip the rebels," a fierce and bloody battle ensued along a little creek called Bull Run. The resulting fight appeared at first to be a Union victory, but the tide quickly turned. Inexperienced federal troops first retreated and then panicked into a desperate race for the safety of Washington, leaving thousands of their dead and wounded behind.

Within three months federal troops again faced a Confederate force, this time on Harrison's Island—a day's march northwest of Washington—and again met bloody defeat in the Battle of Ball's Bluff. Killed during the battle was a United States Senator from Oregon, Colonel Edward E. Baker.

Congress, now under intense pressure to investigate the military disasters, attempted to develop a uniform war policy. On December 5, 1861, Senator Zachariah Chandler, a leader of western radicalism, presented a motion to create a joint Senate and House committee to determine the causes of the Union defeats at Bull Run and Ball's Bluff.

The Joint Committee on the Conduct of the War, under the chairmanship of Senator Benjamen F. Wade, held hearings and meetings from December 20, 1861, through the final days of the conflict some four years later. Although political infighting, personal prejudices, and regional differences often prevented a common understanding of military strategy, the detailed testimony and reports from the military officers and personnel directly involved with the day-to-day conduct of the war provide a unique picture of the Union's action during each critical phase of the conflict.

This monograph, extracted unedited and unabridged from the eight-volume *Report of the Joint Committee on the Conduct of the War, 1863-1866*, published by the U.S. Congress, makes available the individual reports, testimony, individual communiques, maps, and accompanying correspondence that resulted from the Committee's work. This unique monograph provides scholars and Civil War buffs with an opportunity to study and evaluate one individual segment of the Civil War.

Benedict A. Leerburger
Kraus Reprint Company

February 1977

CONTENTS

BULL RUN.

REPORT

OF THE

JOINT COMMITTEE ON THE CONDUCT OF THE WAR.

PART II.—BULL RUN—BALL'S BLUFF.

BULL RUN.

The joint committee on the conduct of the war submit the following report, with accompanying testimony, in relation to the battle of Bull Run, in July, 1861:

So long a time has elapsed, and so many important events have occurred in the progress of the war, since the campaign which ended with the battle of Bull Run, in July, 1861, that your committee do not deem it necessary to go very much into detail in their report. The testimony they submit herewith is very voluminous, and fully covers all the points of interest connected with that campaign. They therefore submit a brief report, confining their attention principally to the causes which led to the defeat of our army in that battle.

That which now appears to have been the great error of that campaign was the failure to occupy Centreville and Manassas at the time Alexandria was occupied, in May. The position at Manassas controlled the railroad communication in all that section of country. The forces which were opposed to us at the battle of Bull Run were mostly collected and brought to Manassas during the months of June and July. The three months' men could have made the place easily defensible against any force the enemy could have brought against it; and it is not at all probable that the rebel forces would have advanced beyond the line of the Rappahannock had Manassas been occupied by our troops.

The next cause of disaster was the delay in proceeding against the enemy until the time of the three months' men was so nearly expired. In that respect the movement was made too late rather than too soon, and the enemy were allowed time to collect their forces at Manassas and to strengthen the position by defensive works. The reason why the movement was so long delayed is shown, to some extent, by the testimony, to which your committee would direct the attention of those who desire to examine that point.

And when the movement was finally determined upon, much was needed to render the troops efficient. There had been but little time devoted to disciplining the troops and instructing them, even as regiments; hardly any instruction had been given them in reference to brigade movements, and none at all as divisions. When General McDowell reviewed eight regiments together—the only instance previous to the battle, so far as the evidence shows, that even that number of troops were manœuvred in one body—he was charged with desiring to make a show.

General McDowell was instructed, verbally, by General Scott, to prepare and submit a plan of operations against the enemy at Manassas. This plan was considered in cabinet meeting, and agreed to; and the 9th of July was fixed upon by General Scott as the day when the army should move.

The plan of General McDowell was to move out in the direction of Centreville, and endeavor to turn the enemy's right with a portion of his force, and destroy his communication by railroad with Richmond. He asked that a certain number of troops be given him to operate against the force which it was estimated that Beauregard had under his command. He was assured that the enemy below should be kept occupied by General Butler, who was in command at Fortress Monroe; and that the enemy under Johnston, in the Winchester valley, should be held there by General Patterson. Some days before the battle, upon expressing some fears in regard to the force under Johnston being detained by Patterson, he was assured by General Scott that "if Johnston joined Beauregard, he should have Patterson on his heels."

The movement did not commence until the 16th of July, a week later than the time first decided upon. The transportation was deficient, and General McDowell had to depend upon others to see that supplies were forwarded to him in time. The march was slow, one reason being that, since the affair at Vienna, near Alexandria, and at Big Bethel, near Fortress Monroe, a fear of "masked batteries" caused hesitation in regard to advancing upon points concerning which there was a want of information. There was some delay, on the march, in consequence of the want of complete discipline among some of the troops. They were not sufficiently under control of officers to be prevented from leaving the ranks and straggling.

The affair at Blackburn's Ford, on Thursday, the 18th, being more extensive than General McDowell had ordered, drew the attention of the enemy to that point; and, in consequence of the preparations they made there to meet any attempt of General McDowell to turn their position in that direction, it became necessary to adopt another line of operations. General McDowell determined to make the attempt to turn their right, and steps were taken to secure the necessary information. It was not until Saturday that the information which General McDowell desired was obtained.

He then issued orders for the troops to move the next morning, the 21st, some at two o'clock and some at half-past two. The division of General Tyler was in the advance, and was ordered to proceed directly out to Stone Bridge, and take up position there. General Hunter's and General Heintzelman's divisions were to follow, and when they reached a road leading to the right, about a mile in advance of General Tyler's camp, they were to turn off and proceed in the direction of Sudley's Church, and endeavor to turn the enemy's left. The movement to the right was intended to be made under cover of General Tyler's force at Stone Bridge.

But there was much delay in the movements of the troops that morning. Tyler's division did not pass the point, where Hunter's and Heintzelman's divisions were to turn off, until after the time designated. Some of the troops were delayed for three hours, affording time to the enemy to discover the movement and make preparations to meet it.

Notwithstanding these disadvantages, our forces were successful during the fore part of the day, although Beauregard had been re-enforced by some of Johnston's forces from Winchester. Our troops were very much fatigued. The day was exceedingly warm; the roads were dusty; and they had been some hours longer on the march than had been anticipated. In the afternoon additional re-enforcements arrived from Johnston's army, and suddenly attacked our right and threw it into disorder.

About the same time two of our batteries (Ricketts's and Griffin's) were captured by the enemy, and our entire force began to fall back in great confusion. In regard to the capture of the batteries, it appears by the testimony that they were ordered to take an advanced and exposed position, and were not sufficiently supported. Not long after they were placed in position, a rebel regiment appeared in their immediate vicinity. Captain Griffin states that he took them to be rebels from the first, and directed one of his lieutenants to open upon them with canister. But Major Barry, chief of artillery, coming up jus at the time, told him that they were some of our own troops coming to the support of the batteries, and directed him not to fire upon them.   The battery was accordingly turned in another direction, and, almost immediately after, this regiment of the enemy opened fire upon it, disabling the horses, and killing and wounding most of the men at the guns.   That completed the discomfiture of our troops, and the day which had opened upon our success, closed upon a defeated and retreating army.

A division, under Colonel Miles, had been stationed at Centreville, partly for the purpose of a reserve, and partly to guard against any flank attack.   The enemy did attempt a movement upon our left, but were promptly met and checked by our forces there.

The principal cause of the defeat on that day was the failure of General Patterson to hold the forces of Johnston in the valley of the Shenandoah.   He had a force of about 23,000 men; while the force of the enemy opposed to him, according to the best evidence your committee could obtain, did not exceed from 12,000 to 15,000 men.   General Patterson testifies that he was satisfied that Johnston had from 35,000 to 40,000 men, and over 60 guns.   He also states that a large number of his troops were anxious to return home; that their time had about expired, and he could not persuade them to remain.   There is considerable testimony to show that the troops became dissatisfied, and refused to remain, only when they learned that their movement from Bunker Hill on the 17th of July was a retreat, and not an advance upon the enemy; that while they supposed they were being led to the attack, little, if any, complaint was made, and they were in excellent spirits.

In reference to the orders given to General Patterson, and the object to be accomplished by his operations, there seems to be no question.   That object was to prevent Johnston from joining Beauregard before General McDowell could have an opportunity to attack the forces under the latter.   The character of the orders is indicated by the following telegram of the 13th of July (Saturday) from General Scott to General Patterson:

"I telegraphed you yesterday, if not strong enough to beat the enemy early next week, make demonstrations so as to detain him in the valley of Winchester. But if he retreats in force towards Manassas, and it be hazardous to follow him, then consider the route *via* Keyes's Ferry, Leesburg, &c."

General Scott had, the day before, conveyed to General Patterson the intimation that General McDowell would commence his movement on the 16th or July, and on the 15th General Patterson advanced from Martinsburg to Bunke-Hill, remaining there the 16th.

On the 17th General Scott telegraphs to General Patterson:

" I have nothing official from you since Sunday, but am glad to learn through Philadelphia papers that you have advanced.   Do not let the enemy amuse and delay you with a small force in front, whilst he re-enforces the Junction with his main body.   McDowell's first day's work has driven the enemy beyond Fairfax Court-House.   The Junction will probably be carried to-morrow."

There is no evidence at what time that despatch was received.   But it could not have been received before the movement from Bunker Hill to Charlestown was made by General Patterson, for that movement commenced very early in the morning of the 17th, the date of the despatch.

On the 18th General Scott telegraphs:

" I have certainly been expecting you to beat the enemy.   If not, that you had felt him strongly, or at least had occupied him by threats and demonstrations.   You have been at least his equal, and, I suppose, superior in number. Has he not stolen a march, and sent re-enforcements towards Manassas Junction?   A week is enough to win a victory."

To this General Patterson replies on the same day:

"The enemy has stolen no march upon me. I have kept him actively employed, and, by threats and reconnoissances in force, caused him to be re-enforced."

General Patterson testifies as follows:

"Question. During all this time you knew that General Scott expected of you that you should either engage and beat Johnston, or detain him in the valley of Winchester; or, in the event that he should come down by a route where you could not follow him, that you should follow him *via* Keyes's Ferry and Leesburg?

"Answer. Yes, sir.

"Question. And yet, when you were at Charlestown, you found yourself not in a condition to do either. Now, my question is: Why did you not communicate that fact to General Scott?

"Answer. There was no occasion for it, in my judgment. He knew my condition, and to have added to the information he already had would have been a waste of time and paper. I had informed him of my condition, and it was his business to order me what to do. I had asked him: 'Shall I attack?' It was not my business to say anything beyond that."

When asked if the telegram of the 18th, from General Scott, did not show that he still deemed it was of the first importance that he (Patterson) should detain Johnston there, General Patterson replies:

"I looked upon that telegraph, and so did every gentleman upon my staff, as nothing more nor less than an exhibition of bad temper."

General Patterson also testifies:

"'Question. You say you could have attacked on the 18th if ordered to do so. You knew the necessity of detaining Johnston, and you must have inferred from the telegraph of General Scott that he expected or required of you that you should do something in that direction. Why did you not do all that you could to detain him without an order?

"Answer. Because I could not go up there without fighting, as I could not fall back again. I had no reason to believe that that telegram was not written in the morning in reply to mine of that morning, [1.30 a. m., asking 'Shall I attack?'] General Scott did not fight that day, and there was no more occasion for my going up and perilling my men without an order, than of doing anything entirely uncalled for—not the slightest occasion for it. * * * * * * * If General Scott did not fight, and saw the necessity for my acting, I repeat it was his business to give the order."

In another place he testifies:

"Question. When you found you were in no condition to detain Johnston, was it not all important that that fact should have been communicated to General Scott; not the fact that you could not fight Johnston, but that you could not detain him, that your strength was insufficient for that, and that he could not rely upon his being kept back?

"Answer. I never supposed, for a moment, that General Scott believed for the fifty-fifth part of a second that I could hold him."

General Patterson further testifies:

"Question. You were not threatening Johnston at Charlestown so as to prevent his joining Beauregard at Manassas?

"Answer. No, sir. I remained there because I was ordered to remain in front of him until he left.

"Question. You knew at that time that you were not offering any obstacle to his going down to Manassas?

"Answer. Perfectly: I knew I had not the means to do it.

"Question. Why did you not communicate that fact to General Scott immediately?

"Answer. I did communicate my condition, and where I was.

"Question. When?

"Answer. On the 16th I wrote him in detail from Bunker Hill. On the 17th I wrote again. And on the 18th I gave him all the information necessary. And it was his business to order me, not my business to make any further suggestions to him.

"Question. Did you communicate to him by telegraph?

"Answer. Certainly. I sent three telegrams to him on the same day.

"Question. On what day?

"Answer. On the 18th, at half-past one in the morning, I telegraphed him my condition, and asked him if I should attack. To have sent further information to him would have been rather impertinent, and he would have so considered it.

* * * * * * * *

"Question. Why did you not inform him that you were not then in a condition to offer any obstacle to Johnston's joining Beauregard?

"Answer. I would have considered it rather a reflection on him to have told him so. He knew my condition."

General Scott testifies:

"But, although General Patterson was never specifically ordered to attack the enemy, he was certainly told and expected, even if with inferior numbers, to hold the rebel army in his front on the alert, and to prevent it from re-enforcing Manassas Junction, by means of threatening manœuvres and demonstrations—results often obtained in war with half numbers."

Instead of doing that, however, General Patterson came down to Bunker Hill, remained there over the day when he had been given to understand the advance would be commenced by General McDowell; and early the next morning, without waiting to hear how far General McDowell had advanced, or whether he had advanced at all, left the neighborhood of Winchester, where the enemy was, and turned off to Charlestown, where, as he himself says, he had no means to offer any obstacle to Johnston's joining Beauregard whenever he chose. Johnston at once took advantage of the opportunity thus afforded him, and re-enforced Beauregard in season to inflict a defeat upon our forces at Bull Run.

Johnston started the greater portion of his forces from Winchester on the 18th; some of the testimony shows that a portion started on the afternoon of the 17th. General Patterson, though only some twenty miles distant from Winchester, and under orders to prevent the enemy from re-enforcing Beauregard, did not discover that Johnston had left Winchester until two days afterwards, when he telegraphed, on the 20th, to General Scott that re-enforcements had left there.

In reference to deferring the attack upon Beauregard, when the arrival of Johnston's forces had become known, General McDowell says that the information that he received was too indefinite, mere rumor, and he could not tell how much credit to give to it. The arrival of the cars during the night preceding the battle was not certain evidence of the arrival of Johnston's forces; for it was expected that re-enforcements would be hurried up to the enemy from every direction possible. And he had been assured that "if Johnston joined Beauregard, Patterson should be on his heels."

General Scott testifies on that point:

"As connected with this subject, I hope I may be permitted to notice the charge made against me on the floors of Congress, that I did not stop Brigadier General McDowell's movement upon Manassas Junction after I had been informed of the re-enforcement sent thither from Winchester, though urged to do so by one or more members of the cabinet. Now, it was, at the reception of that news, too late to call off the troops from the attack. And, besides, though opposed to the movement at first, we had all become animated and sanguine of success. And it is not true that I was urged by anybody in authority to stop the attack which was commenced as early, I think, as the 18th of July."

B. F. WADE, Chairman.

BALL'S BLUFF.

The joint committee on the conduct of the war submit the following report, with the accompanying testimony, in relation to the battle of Ball's Bluff.

On the morning of Saturday, the 19th of October, 1861, General McCall, commanding a division in the vicinity of Washington, moved his entire command, under orders from General McClellan, to Drainesville and its immediate neighborhood. A portion of his force was moved some miles beyond Drainesville and within eight or ten miles of Leesburg, but was recalled to Drainesville, by order of General McClellan, about sunset of that day. The entire division of General William F. Smith was also sent out within supporting distance of General McCall.

General McCall testifies that he was directed to make reconnoissances in all directions, for three or four miles from Drainesville, noting particularly the character of the country. About ten o'clock on Sunday morning he informed General McClellan that he should not be able to get through his work that day, and received, in reply, " If you finish in the morning, return."

On Sunday, the 20th, General McClellan directed a telegram to be sent to General Stone, at Poolesville, of which the following is a copy furnished your committee :

" Received October 20, 1861, from Camp Griffin.

" General McClellan desires me to inform you that General McCall occupied Drainesville yesterday, and is still there; will send out heavy reconnoissances to-day in all directions from that point. The general desires that you keep a good lookout upon Leesburg, to see if this movement has the effect to drive them away. Perhaps a slight demonstration on your part would have the effect to move them.

"A. V. COLBURN,
" *Assistant Adjutant General.*

" Brigadier General STONE, *Poolesville.*"

On Sunday afternoon General Stone moved some forces to the bank of the river at Edwards's Ferry, and crossed over one or two companies to the Virginia side, but very soon recalled them.

Colonel Devens, of the 15th Massachusetts, testifies that he received from General Stone, about one o'clock on Sunday, the following order :

" HEADQUARTERS CORPS OF OBSERVATION,
" *Poolesville, October* 20, 1861.

"COLONEL : You will please send orders to the canal to have the two new flat-boats now there opposite the island (Harrison's) transferred to the river; and will, at three o'clock p. m., have the island re-enforced by all of your regiment now on duty at the canal and at the New York battery. The pickets will be replaced by the companies of the 19th Massachusetts there.

" Very respectfully, your obedient servant,
" CHA'S P. STONE,
" *Brigadier General.*

"Colonel CHARLES DEVENS,
" *Commanding 15th Regiment Massachusetts Volunteers.*"

About dark a verbal order was sent to Colonel Devens to send Captain Philbrick, of his regiment, with a small party, across the river from Harrison's island, with directions to push out to within a mile of Leesburg, if possible, without being discovered, and then return and report. Captain Philbrick accordingly crossed, with, perhaps, fifteen or twenty men, at a place where he had crossed some time previously, when he had discovered that the river at that point was not picketed by the enemy. He landed at the foot of the bluff opposite Harrison's island known as Ball's Bluff, ascended by a path that led to the top, and proceeded to reconnoitre as directed.

Before Captain Philbrick returned General Stone sent the following despatch to General McClellan, a copy of which was furnished your committee:

"HEADQUARTERS ARMY OF THE POTOMAC,
"Received Washington, October 20, 1861, from Poolesville.

"Made a feint of crossing at this place this afternoon, and at the same [time] started a reconnoitring party towards Leesburg from Harrison's island. Enemy's pickets retired to intrenchments. Report of reconnoitring party not yet received. I have means of crossing 125 men over in ten minutes at each of two points. River falling slowly.

"C. P. STONE,
"Brigadier General.

"Major General McCLELLAN."

Captain Philbrick pushed out some distance from the bluff, and then returned and reported that they had discovered a small camp of the enemy that did not appear to be very well guarded. This report was sent to General Stone.

Colonel Devens testifies that about midnight he received the following order from General Stone:

"HEADQUARTERS CORPS OF OBSERVATION,
"Poolesville, October 20, 1861—10½ p. m.

"SPECIAL ORDER NO. —.]

"Colonel Devens will land opposite Harrison's island with five companies of his regiment, and proceed to surprise the camp of the enemy discovered by Captain Philbrick, in the direction of Leesburg. The landing and march will be effected with silence and rapidity.

"Colonel Lee, 20th Massachusetts volunteers, will, immediately after Colonel Devens's departure, occupy Harrison's island with four companies of his regiment, and will cause the four-oared boat to be taken across the island to the point of departure of Colonel Devens. One company will be thrown across to occupy the heights on the Virginia shore, after Colonel Devens's departure, to cover his return.

"Two mountain howitzers will be taken silently up the towpath and carried to the opposite side of the island, under the orders of Colonel Lee.

"Colonel Devens will attack the camp of the enemy at daybreak, and, having routed, will pursue them as far as he deems prudent, and will destroy the camp if practicable, before returning. He will make all the observations possible on the country; will, under all circumstances, keep his command well in hand, and not sacrifice them to any supposed advantage of rapid pursuit.

"Having accomplished this duty, Colonel Devens will return to his present position, unless he shall see one on the Virginia side, near the river, which he can undoubtedly hold until re-enforced, and one which can be successfully held against largely superior numbers. In such case he will hold on and report.

"CHAS. P. STONE,
"Brigadier General.

"Great care will be used by Colonel Devens to prevent any unnecessary injury of private property; and any officer or soldier straggling from the command for curiosity or plunder will be instantly shot.

"CHAS. P. STONE,
"Brigadier General."

Colonel Devens commenced crossing his force between 12 and 1 o'clock at night, and about 4 o'clock in the morning had crossed his five companies. He proceeded up the bluff and formed his command on the top of the bluff, and remained there until it was light enough to find his way. Colonel Lee also crossed with about 100 men and took position upon the bluff. Colonel Devens sent out scouts to the right and left, who reported that they could find no enemy.

At the first dawn of light Colonel Devers moved his command out in the direction of the supposed camp. Upon reaching the point to which the reconnoitring party of the night before had proceeded, it was discovered that what had been taken for a camp was a single row of trees, the dim light of the moon shining between them, below the branches, presenting the appearance of a row of tents.

Colonel Devens had advanced with his force to within about a mile of Leesburg; he halted his men there, and proceeded to examine the country about his position as far as practicable. He sent word to General Stone that there had been a mistake about the camp of the enemy; that he was well posted in a wood and concealed, and waited further orders.

Not far from 7 o'clock in the morning a body of rebel riflemen was discovered to the right of Colonel Devens's position, in the direction of Conrad's Ferry; Captain Philbrick with his company advanced towards them, when they fell back until they reached a ditch, under cover of which they halted and opened fire upon our men; they were soon driven out of the ditch into a corn-field, where they obtained cover behind some stacks of corn. Another company was ordered by Colonel Devens to the support of Captain Philbrick; but before they reached him some of the enemy's cavalry made their appearance from the direction of Leesburg. The two companies were then ordered to fall back to the main body.

About 8 o'clock Colonel Devens determined to fall back to the bluff, where Colonel Lee was, which was done in perfect order. He then reconnoitred the woods to his right and left, and discovering no appearance of the enemy, moved forward to his former position.

Between 8 and 9 o'clock the messenger of Colonel Devens returned from General Stone with instructions to him to remain where he was, and he would be supported. Colonel Devens testifies that it was either then or soon after that he was told that Colonel Baker was to come over and take command. He sent word to General Stone that he was discovered by the enemy, but could still hold his old position. About 10 o'clock the messenger returned with this message: "Very well; Colonel Baker will come and take command."

Colonel Devens states that while awaiting further instructions he directed his adjutant to ascertain the amount of the force with him; the report was 28 officers and 625 men. He sent once or twice to the river to ascertain if re-enforcements were coming, and what he was to do, but he received no further order or message.

About 12 or 1 o'clock an attack was made upon Colonel Devens's force, which lasted some 10 or 15 minutes. Receiving no orders or message from the river, he fell back about 60 yards, reformed his line and made dispositions to retire still further if necessary. And in perhaps an hour he fell back to the field just in front of the bluff, where the main action afterwards took place. There he met Colonel Baker, who congratulated him upon the manner in which his men had conducted themselves.

In relation to the orders to Colonel Baker, General Stone testifies :

"I can give you all the early orders to Colonel Baker. I sent him an order, about midnight on the 20th, to send the California regiment to Conrad's Ferry, and have them there at daybreak, to await orders there; to have the remainder of his brigade roused early; have a comfortable breakfast, and be in readiness to move at 7 o'clock in the morning. Late in the night—it might have been between 2 and 3 o'clock in the morning.—I sent a cautionary order to Colonel Baker, knowing that volunteers make too much noise sometimes, to have that regiment march with silence and with unloaded guns. From that time I sent him no order."

General Stone testifies that between 8 and half-past 9 o'clock, when Colonel Baker was with him, and they had discussed the whole matter for some time, he gave him a written order to take the entire command of the right at Ball's Bluff. That order, with a communication from General Stone to Colonel Baker, sent some time later, was found upon his body after he was killed. The two papers are as follows:

"HEADQUARTERS CORPS OF OBSERVATION,
"*Edwards's Ferry, October* 21, 1861.

"COLONEL: In case of heavy firing in front of Harrison's island you will advance the California regiment of your brigade, or retire the regiments under Colonels Lee and Devens now on the Virginia side of the river, at your discrecretion, assuming command on arrival.

"Very respectfully, colonel, your most obedient servant,
"CHARLES P. STONE,
"*Brigadier General Commanding.*

"Colonel E. D. BAKER,
"*Commanding Brigade.*"

"HEADQUARTERS CORPS OF OBSERVATION,
Edwards's Ferry, October 22, 1861—11.50.

"COLONEL: I am informed that the force of the enemy is about 4,000, all told. If you can push them you may do so, as far as to have a strong position near Leesburg, if you can keep them before you, avoiding their batteries. If they pass Leesburg, and take the Gum Spring road, you will not follow far, but seize the first good position to cover that road. Their design is to draw us on, if they are obliged to retreat, as far as Goose creek, where they can be re-enforced from Manassas and have a strong position.

"Report frequently, so that when they are pushed Gorman can come in on their flank.

"Yours, respectfully and truly,
"CHARLES P. STONE,
"*Brigadier General Commanding.*

"Colonel E. D. BAKER,
"*Commanding Brigade.*"

Colonel Baker proceeded to Harrison's island, and finally concluded to send over troops to re-enforce Colonel Devens and Colonel Lee. One of the witnesses states that Colonel Baker was in doubt for a time whether to recall the troops already over, or to re-enforce them; but, upon hearing some one on the Virginia shore call out that they needed assistance, as the enemy were coming, he determined to re-enforce them, and proceeded himself to the Virginia side, and assumed command. Colonel Baker directed the forces to cross at the point where Colonel Devens and Colonel Lee had crossed with their forces.

The means of transporting troops at Ball's Bluff was exceedingly limited. Between the Maryland shore and Harrison's island were only three flatboats or scows, all together capable of crossing about 125 men at a time. On the Virginia side of the island there were at first only a Francis metallic life-boat and two small skiffs, together capable of carrying from 25 to 30 men at a time. After a time, one of the scows, or flatboats, was taken from the Maryland to the Virginia side of the island.

The landing on the Virginia side was at the foot of a very steep bluff, up which a narrow path, widening towards the top, wound its way; and on the top of the bluff was a cleared space, or field, bordered by woods, which afforded a cover to the enemy, until within a short distance of where our troops were formed.

Colonel Baker, according to the testimony, arrived on the field between one and two o'clock, and proceeded at once to form a line of battle upon the field at the top of the bluff. The amount of the force engaged upon our side was between 1,700 and 1,800 men, consisting of about one-half of the 15th Massachusetts regiment under Colonel Devens; a portion (317 men) of the 20th Massachusetts, under Colonel Lee; the Tammany regiment under Colonel Cogswell; and the California regiment under Lieutenant Colonel Wistar. The enemy's forces were about four thousand men.

The enemy began the attack—some of the witnesses say between two and three o'clock, others at three o'clock—at first, heavily, on the right of our line, then moving along towards the centre and left, where the hardest fighting took place.

Your committee do not deem it necessary to go into the details of the action. It continued for over two hours, our troops contending most bravely against greatly superior numbers. Colonel Baker fell between four and five o'clock, having been most conspicuous for his bravery and almost reckless daring. When he fell the line began to waver, and some portions of it gave way, before the destructive fire of the enemy.

After the death of Colonel Baker the command devolved upon Colonel Cogswell, of the Tammany regiment, who proposed to attempt to cut through to Edwards's Ferry, which was assented to by the other regimental commanders. Upon attempting a movement in that direction they were met by a Mississippi regiment coming from below, which opened a most destructive fire upon them. Our troops gave way, and retreated down the bluff towards the river. This was about dusk, so that our troops were somewhat concealed by the bushes on the side of the bluff. The enemy continued to fire upon them from the top of the bluff. The men attempted to escape to the island in the boats and by swimming, being exposed all the time to the fire of the enemy. The flatboat was soon riddled and sunk; the life-boat drifted down the stream, and the skiffs were lost. Many were shot while in the water; others succeeded in swimming to the island; some few, under cover of the darkness, succeeded in escaping along the bank of the river, and finally reached our lines. But the greater portion were killed or taken prisoners.

In relation to the operations at Edwards's Ferry, under the supervision of General Stone and the immediate command of General Gorman, as there was no serious fighting there, it may not be necessary to go much into detail. The crossing was commenced about daybreak by the forces under Colonel Dana, of the 1st Minnesota regiment, and was continued until some 2,500 men were crossed over that day. The means of crossing was very limited, as at Harrison's Landing, consisting of three or four flatboats or scows, propelled across by poles. The place of landing was very good, and covered by our artillery on the Maryland side. There were no important demonstrations made by our forces on the Virginia side of Edwards's Ferry. Some reconnoissances were made for a short distance, and one regiment of the enemy seen, probably the Mississippi regiment that arrived on the field at Ball's Bluff, near the close of the action there.

General McCall's division had remained at Drainesville all of Sunday and Sunday night. General McCall testifies:

"At six o'clock Monday morning I reported to him (General McClellan) that the engineers whom I had consulted reported to me that they would finish their work in two hours. I sent that express to General McClellan at six o'clock, and got his reply, dated eight o'clock, telling me to return as soon as the work was finished. I got his answer between nine and ten o'clock. I ordered the troops then to be ready to move, and as soon as the work was finished I returned to my camp under orders."

Both General McClellan and General McCall testify that the movement to Drainesville was for the purpose of reconnoitering the country in that direction. But General Stone received no intimation of the object of the movement. On the contrary, the language of the despatch of Sunday might well lead him to believe that the movement had reference to driving the enemy from Leesburg. The despatch contained no intimation that General McCall was to be soon withdrawn from Drainesville. He was directed "to keep a good lookout upon Leesburg to see if this movement has the effect to drive them (the enemy) away. Perhaps a slight demonstration on your part would have the effect to move them." General Stone made demonstrations both at Edwards's Ferry and at Ball's Bluff, and promptly notified General McClellan of what he had done. He sent that information on Sunday night, and he testifies that he received no intimation from General McClellan as to what he should do, whether to continue the demonstrations or not; and received no intimation that General McCall was not close at hand to come to his assistance until about eleven o'clock on Monday night. It was a very general impression among the officers and men at Edwards's Ferry during Monday that General McCall would come to their assistance; and General Stone testifies that he cautioned his artillery about firing upon any troops that might show themselves in that direction lest they might fire upon our own forces.

In regard to that matter, General McClellan testifies as follows:

"Question. Do you remember whether, or not, you informed him (General Stone) of the withdrawal of Smith and McCall to their former positions?

"Answer. I think I did."

General Stone, (February 27, 1863,) after stating that, upon hearing of the death of Colonel Baker, he proceeded to Ball's Bluff, where he learned the full extent of the disaster, and at once determined to withdraw the troops at Edwards's Ferry, testifies as follows:

"And then, knowing that I could go myself quicker than anybody I could send, I turned my horse and galloped down to withdraw my troops at Edwards's Ferry back to the Maryland shore. I supposed at that time that I had about 2,500 men across the river; and the reports I had heard opposite Ball's Bluff were that the army had been largely re-enforced, and they were then about 10,000 strong. I saw that there was great danger of Gorman being overwhelmed at Edwards's Ferry. I did not know whether McCall would be there to assist him or not. I was in utter ignorance in reference to him or his position.

"I at once commenced retiring my troops as quietly but as rapidly as I could, taking the precaution to have my artillery on the Maryland side so placed as to cover the troops on the Virginia side. The ground on the Maryland shore commands perfectly the ground on the Virginia shore there, and it would be an exceedingly dangerous thing for troops to advance and attack any body of men on the Virginia shore, directly at Edwards's Ferry, while the Maryland shore was well held by artillery.

"The moment I had given the orders for the retiring of those troops, I reported by telegraph to General McClellan, at Washington, that we had met with a repulse on our right, but I was doing the best I could to secure the left, and to retrieve. I am not quite sure now whether I telegraphed to General McClellan, before I went up to Harrison's island, that Colonel Baker had been killed, or whether I put that in the same despatch in which I informed him of the repulse.

"Having sent that information to General McClellan, I continued withdrawing the troops, watching carefully, so as to use the artillery for their protection, if necessary. After some time—I cannot tell how long, for one takes but little note of time under such circumstances, but apparently as soon as a message could go to Washington and an answer be returned, (being carried by a courier on horseback four miles each way from the telegraph station to Edwards's Ferry)—I received orders from General McClellan to this effect : ' Hold all the ground you now have on the Virginia shore if your men will fight, intrenching, if necessary. You will be re-enforced.' Perhaps the words ' if your men will fight' came before the rest of the despatch ; and my impression is, though I will not be positive, that the words ' at all hazards' were used in the direction to hold all the ground on the Virginia shore.

" I am sorry that I have not possession of a single paper, telegraph or otherwise, of the records connected with my division. You know the way in which I was removed from my command. 1 was ordered to report myself here, in Washington, at once; and having not the slightest suspicion of why I was required here, I left all my papers as I would have done had I been going out for a two hours' ride ; and from that time to this I have never seen a single paper of any kind I then left behind me. I make this explanation to show why it is that I cannot speak positively about the language of despatches received and sent; why I cannot, perhaps, give their exact words.

" I saw all the danger in which my troops were on the Virginia side. But I supposed at that time that General McCall was very near there, and I took it for granted when General McClellan telegraphed me to hold my position on the Virginia side at all hazards, and that I should be re-enforced, that he had the means of immediately securing me.

" I cannot state positively when it was that I telegraphed to General Banks But my impression now is, that just as I started to go up to Ball's Bluff, when the news of Colonel Baker's death reached me, I telegraphed to General Banks, requesting him to send up a brigade. When I got to Harrison's Island, and before I returned to Edwards's Ferry, I despatched a messenger to meet whatever brigade General Banks might send, and conduct it to Conrad's Ferry, instead of to Edwards's Ferry, from which my despatch to General Banks was sent.

"And my impression is, that when I returned to Edwards's Ferry, and telegraphed to General McClellan the fact of the repulse at Ball's Bluff, I sent another telegram to General Banks, that he better bring up his whole division. I know I sent General Banks such a telegram; but at what time I will not be positive.

"Some time was lost in communicating with General McClellan, by my receiving a despatch, in cipher, of which I had not the key, from him or from his chief of staff. What the contents of that despatch were I have never learned. I immediately responded to it : ' I have received the box, but have no key;' What that despatch was, I have no knowledge of whatever; but I presume that the despatches which came afterwards covered the same ground.

" I cannot state now, after so long an interval of time, at what hour I telegraphed to General McClellan, urging that the re-enforcements should be sent to Goose Creek, on the Virginia side, supposing all the time that General McCall was not far off. The response to that, which I think I received about 11 o'clock on Monday night, was the first intimation I ever received that McCall had not all the time been near me. That despatch informed me that no re-enforcements could reach me from the Virginia side, but that General Banks would re-enforce me from the Maryland side.

"Question. How far was General Banks from you?

"Answer. He was about fourteen miles in my rear.

"Question. Did that first despatch from General McClellan, promising you re-enforcements, contemplate that they should come from General Banks?

"Answer. Yes, sir; I suppose so. But at the time my idea was that McCall was close by me. And I was led into an error, late in the evening, by receiving a despatch from General McClellan's headquarters, whether signed by him or his chief of staff, I do not now recollect, asking me if there was a road from 'Darnesville' to Edwards's Ferry. Now, there is no such place as 'Darnesville;' but there is a 'Drainesville.' And having in my mind that McCall was at Draineville, I took it for granted that the operator had made a mistake, and had meant Draineville instead of 'Darnestown,' which was the name of a place in Maryland, and which proved to be the place meant. I replied to that despatch, to the best of my recollection, that there was a good road from Draineville to Edwards's Ferry. I presume that that caused some misconception at headquarters, because they undoubtedly had 'Darnestown' in their minds when they telegraphed 'Darnesville;' just as I had 'Drainesville' in my mind when I saw 'Darnesville' in the despatch. But that is not very important, only to show how errors will creep in.

"I think that by this statement I must remove any unpleasant impression with regard to my improperly exposing troops to disaster at Edwards's Ferry, since I acted under the instructions of my superior officer; and also under the impression that our forces under General McCall were near us on the Virginia side of Edwards's Ferry.

"Question. How happened it that you failed to make this statement, concerning those orders, on your former examination?

"Answer. Because I did not deem it proper to give any of the orders of my superior officer which he had not himself previously published or authorized me to use. The morning that I came before your committee I was instructed at General McClellan's headquarters that it was the desire of the general that officers giving testimony before the committee should not state, without his authority, anything regarding his plans, his orders for the movements of troops, or his orders concerning the position of troops. That covered this case.

"Question. Did you understand that to apply to past orders and transactions, as well as those to be executed in the future?

"Answer. I did; because I could not know, and did not know, what orders to others were given cotemporaneous with those I received, and I might create wrong impressions by giving the orders I had received from my commanding general, unless there were at the same time produced cotemporaneous orders given to other generals. And I presume that the chairman will remember that I stated, when giving my testimony before, that I could not give any orders from my commanding general except such as he, himself, had made public.

"Question. Did General McClellan approve of the crossing at Edwards's Ferry and Ball's Bluff, on the 21st of October, 1861?

"Answer. I received a despatch from General McClellan in reply to one which I had sent him, informing him of the crossing of General Gorman and Colonel Baker; that despatch to me commenced with these words: 'I congratulate you and your command.' I took that congratulation, on the fact of my having crossed, as an approval of the crossing; and as I had received no information whatever concerning General McCall, in my own mind I supposed that it was but a simple thing of General McClellan in connexion with any other movements he might be making.

"Question. Was General McClellan informed of your means of transportation for crossing troops?

"Answer. Some time during the day—and I think it was in the same despatch in which he asked me for information of the enemy, and I should think that that despatch must have reached me about noon—General McClellan asked what means of transportation I had. I replied to him by telegraph, stating the number and character of the boats at each crossing—at Edwards's Ferry and at Harrison's island."

General McClellan testifies in reference to the crossing of General Stone's forces into Virginia:

"I have no recollection of any order which justified the passage of the river in force; I am sure that I had no intention that he should do that."

The events that occurred subsequently to the operations of Monday—the arrival of General Banks with his forces, the arrival of General McClellan, and the final withdrawal of all our forces to the Maryland side of the river—are fully set forth in the testimony herewith submitted, and your committee do not deem any comments by them to be necessary.

In connexion with the battle of Ball's Bluff, two points remain to be considered : First, whether a crossing was justifiable under any circumstances, considering the very insufficient means of transportation at the command of General Stone. Second, whether the forces under Colonel Baker could, and should, have been re-enforced from the Virginia side of Edwards's Ferry, when it was known that the troops under his command were engaged with the enemy.

In regard to the first point, all the testimony goes to prove that the means of transportation were very inadequate. The testimony of General Stone would seem to indicate that, while he was inclined to deem it sufficient, under what he understood to be the circumstances under which the movement was made, he left much to the judgment of others; and this much can be said for him, that he received no intimation that a movement across the river would be expected from him, or would be justified, until the day before (Sunday) it was actually made. And the reasons that he had for supposing that other forces were within a short distance to render him assistance are set forth in the previous portion of this report.

In reference to re-enforcing Colonel Baker, the testimony is very conflicting. There is no question that it was known that the forces at Ball's Bluff were engaged with the enemy. The firing of musketry was distinctly heard at Edwards's Ferry, on both sides of the river. The only question is whether re-enforcements should have been sent under the circumstances, and whether there was any sufficient reason why they were not sent. General Stone testifies that he received no intimation from Colonel Baker that he needed re-enforcements; that he received little, if any, information from Colonel Baker in reference to the condition and progress of affairs at Ball's Bluff; and he also testifies that, even if re-enforcements had been needed, they could not have been sent up on the Virginia side; that the enemy had earthworks and batteries between Edwards's Ferry and Ball's Bluff, which would have made it extremely hazardous, if not impossible, to have sent any re-enforcements up by that route. Some of the other witnesses testify to the same effect. Others testify most positively that, so far as they were able to judge, there was no obstacle whatever in the way of our troops passing up on the Virginia side from Edwards's Ferry.

It cannot be denied that had re-enforcements promptly arrived at Ball's Bluff from Edwards's Ferry, the result of the battle there would, in all probability, have been greatly to our advantage, instead of being a most melancholy disaster. The evidence is so very contradictory that your committee refrain from expressing any positive opinion upon that point, but allow each one to form his own conclusion from the testimony they have been able to obtain.

One other subject remains to be considered before closing this report—the arrest and imprisonment of General Stone. Your committee would have made no reference to that subject, but have submitted the testimony without comment upon their part, had it not been for the efforts that have been made by many to hold them responsible for all that has taken place in reference to the arrest of General Stone.

In the course of their investigation concerning the causes of the disaster at Ball's Bluff they obtained testimony, most unexpectedly to them all, which, without explanation, seemed to impeach both the military capacity and the loyalty of General Stone. That testimony, as in every other instance that they deemed of importance, was brought to the attention of the proper authorities here, and the War Department was informed that, in the opinion of the committee, a prompt investigation should be instituted. First, Secretary Cameron, and afterwards Secretary Stanton, were informed that the testimony before your committee was of such a character that some explanation by General Stone was required.

General Stone was called to this city, and on the 31st of January, 1862, appeared before your committee, at the instance of General McClellan, and stated that he had been informed that certain testimony before this committee affected him in such a way as to require his explanation. He was informed that there was testimony which might appear to impeach his conduct in the Ball's Bluff affair; to show that he had had undue intercourse with the enemy, both by letter and by personal intercourse with their officers; and also that he had permitted the enemy to erect formidable fortifications and batteries within reach of his guns, and which he could have prevented. The statement was made in general terms to General Stone, and without indicating who were the witnesses who had testified, in order that they should not be called to account by their commanding general for statements made before a committee of Congress.

In reply to this general statement upon the part of your committee General Stone proceeded to make an explanation in general terms. They then reported to the Secretary of War that the testimony upon the points to which his attention had been called was conflicting. They made no recommendation as to what should be done, one way or the other; merely reported to him that the testimony was conflicting.

Not long afterwards they learned through the press that General Stone had been arrested, and sent to Fort Lafayette. The immediate cause of his arrest they did not know. They were satisfied that the information which they had furnished to the department had in all probability furnished some of the grounds upon which his arrest had been made; but they did not learn until more than a year afterwards what was the immediate cause of his arrest at the time it was made.

General Stone was arrested on the 8th of February, 1862. On the 28th of February, 1863, General McClellan testified before your committee as follows:

"About ten days or two weeks before General Stone was actually arrested the Secretary of War gave me a written order to arrest General Stone, for the reason that he had been informed by the members of the committee upon the conduct of the war that they had taken testimony going to show that General Stone had been guilty of conduct not consistent with loyalty. General Stone was removed from his command, and, I understood, appeared before this committee.

"Finally, on the very day of his arrest, a written report was made to me of the examination of a refugee from Leesburg, which, so far as such a thing could, tended to corroborate some of the charges made against General Stone. I satisfied my own mind of the sincerity of this refugee by personal examination, and then showed the statement to the Secretary of War, upon which he directed me to give the order to arrest General Stone immediately, and to send him under guard to Fort Lafayette. The order was carried into execution the same evening."

Since the release of General Stone he has been permitted by your committee, in consideration of the peculiar circumstances attending his arrest, to examine all the testimony which your committee have taken in reference to the administration of his department, and to make as full a statement to the committee as he considered necessary. That statement, together with all the testimony, is herewith submitted.

It is due to General Stone that your committee should state that it appears, from documents before your committee, that immediately upon his arrest he demanded that he should be furnished with a copy of the charges against him, and be allowed the opportunity of promptly meeting them; why his request was not granted your committee have never been informed.

B. F. WADE, Chairman.

TESTIMONY.

BULL RUN.

General J. B. RICHARDSON sworn and examined.

By Mr. Chandler:

Question. General, you accompanied the army to Bull Run, did you not?

Answer. I commanded a brigade in that action.

Question. What time did you with your brigade leave your intrenchments; that is, what time did you start?

Answer. I started from Chain Bridge the morning of the 16th of July, I think.

Question. That was Monday morning, was it not?

Answer. I believe it was; it was the 15th or 16th of July—about that time.

Question. At what time did you reach Fairfax with your brigade?

Answer. We took the direct road to Vienna alone; there we concentrated with the rest of General Tyler's division of four brigades; mine was the second brigade of his division. We stayed one night at Vienna, and then moved to Germantown, where we stayed one night; then, on the morning of the 18th, my brigade took the lead and moved on to Blackburn's Ford, on Bull Run, or Occoquan.

Question. What day of the week was that?

Answer. It was the morning of Thursday that we took the lead.

Question. And your brigade was in that first action at Blackburn's Ford?

Answer. Mine was the only one that was engaged at Blackburn's Ford.

Question. Your four regiments?

Answer. Yes, sir.

Question. What time on Thursday did you reach Blackburn's Ford?

Answer. We reached within a mile of Blackburn's Ford with the brigade, I should think, about noon. We came to a halt a mile from the ford, finding the enemy in position there at their batteries. We came on top of a hill, where we could see down the slope of a hill towards the batteries, and could see the men in the batteries.

Question. Did your brigade advance from that position nearer to the batteries?

Answer. Yes, sir. General Tyler directed me to make a movement with the brigade, in advance, to try and find the position and strength of the enemy, if possible. Accordingly I first moved on to the front a separate detachment of 160 skirmishers. At the same time two pieces of artillery (rifled 10-pounders) were brought into position on the top of the hill where we had arrived; and soon after another battery (Captain Ayres's) of 6-pounder guns and 12-pounder howitzers were brought into action. The skirmishers advanced until they came into action in a skirt of timber on this side of the run, in front of the enemy's position; and then I detached three other companies to their support, and two guns of Captain Ayres's battery, who moved up to the skirt of timber with two companies of cavalry. They commenced fire from that point to assist the skirmishers, who were in the action already. I moved up to the timber myself, and proposed to General Tyler to form the four regiments in line of battle on the outside of the timber and move in.

Question. To charge upon the batteries?

Answer. Yes, sir. The New York 12th, Colonel Walworth, was the nearest to where I was. I had it conducted in column of companies down the ravine, out of view, and near the position where I was in front of the timber, and had it deployed in line of battle in support of those that were in action already. I formed the New York 12th on the left of the battery, and directed Colonel Walworth to make a charge into the woods. I spoke a few words of encouragement to the regiment before they went on. I told them that it was a good regiment, and I expected they would do well. As soon as I had given this direction, I ordered up the Massachusetts 1st, through the same ravine, out of reach of the enemy's fire. The enemy could bring neither cannon nor musketry to bear upon them the way I brought them. I formed the 1st Massachusetts in line of battle on the right of the battery, then the 3d Michigan on the right of them, and then the 2d Michigan still to the right—all in line of battle. When I had finished putting the 2d Michigan on the line at the right, I moved back to see what had become of the New York 12th on the left. It had probably taken me as much as twenty minutes to go through with this formation. I found, on arriving at the left, parts of two companies of the New York 12th, about sixty men altogether, retreating outside of the woods, carrying along a few wounded. I asked them what the matter was, and where they were going. They said the regiment were all killed, and they were falling back; that the rest of the regiment had fallen back—those that were not killed. Says I, "What are you running for? There is no enemy here; I cannot see anybody at all. Where is your colonel?" They knew nothing about it. They knew nothing about any of their officers. I could not find any officers with the men at all, I believe. The men halted and faced around, and then fell back again. The other three regiments, at the same time, were standing firm and ready to advance; and the skirmishers, at the same time, held their ground in the woods in front. I sent an aid to General Tyler to acquaint him of the retreat of the New York 12th, and he came down to see me. I proposed to him to rally the New York 12th in the woods as a support, and move on with the other three regiments against the batteries; and I, at the same time, asked him where Sherman's brigade of his division was. They moved from camp at Germantown at the same time as we did in the morning, and we had been halted and in action at the place as much as two hours. He said that brigade had not yet arrived. General Tyler then said that it was not a part of the plan of battle to do anything more at that point than a mere demonstration—to make a reconnoissance to find the force of the enemy; and, as I understood him, it was against orders to bring on a general engagement at that place. He then ordered me to fall back with the three regiments in rear of the batteries—not to undertake to rally the New York 12th. "Let them go," he said. So I accordingly fell back with the three regiments in rear of the batteries. I took the regiments back in good order, without bringing them under the fire of the enemy's cannon at all. The enemy found that we had fallen back in rear of the batteries, and then they commenced the fire of their artillery again, which had been aimed at us to reach the woods in front. As soon as they discovered we had fallen back, they directed the fire of their artillery against our batteries on the hill again, which were in their original position.

Question. One word right here: do you think you could have captured the enemy's batteries with your force if you had not fallen back?

Answer. I think if the other brigades had come up to our support we could have done it.

Question. What number of men do you think you would have lost in capturing those batteries?

Answer. We had already lost about 60 men, and I had the idea that by losing as many more we could have taken the batteries; because some of our skirmishers had crossed the ravine, and one of them was so near that he was shot by the revolver of one of the enemy's officers; and another man killed one of the men at the guns inside the intrenchments, so he said, and the captain of the skirmishers—Captain Bernsneider—reported the same thing.

Question. Had you captured that battery on Thursday night, and a general advance had taken place promptly on Friday morning, what, in your opinion, would have been the result?

Answer. We should probably have avoided their being re-enforced; have avoided the re-enforcements under General Johnston and General Davis, that took place by railroad on Friday and Saturday nights—they both came up during those nights; we should probably have avoided altogether fighting on Sunday; at least we should have probably turned Manassas by the rear before those re-enforcements had come up.

Question. So that, in your judgment, there would not have been a severe engagement at all had you captured that battery on Thursday night?

Answer. No, sir. From what we have learned since, we find that they had probably a brigade of infantry opposed to us at first. But they continually increased their force until they had some 7,000 or 8,000 men in position.

Question. If your supports had come up?

Answer. I think we could have carried the batteries, but we might not have been able to have retained them with one brigade.

Question. Precisely, I understand that. Was it your intention, when you formed your brigade in line of battle, to capture those batteries?

Answer. Yes, sir. The musketry fire particularly was very heavy against us. After we had fallen back behind our batteries the head of General Sherman's brigade came up, and I spoke to him. He asked me how many the enemy had in front. I told him they were strong there; that they had, I thought, from 8,000 to 10,000 men, which turns out to have been nearly the case, from what we have heard since through their reports. The other three regiments of my brigade, besides the New York 12th, remained as firm as I ever saw any regiments in the war with Mexico, at any time. No man thought of going to the rear.

Question. All eager for a fight?

Answer. Yes, sir.

Question. After you had retired, as you have stated, you remained there until Sunday, did you?

Answer. No, sir; we went back to Centreville for the purpose of getting water and rations. There was no water near there that we had found then; I had found some for myself and horse in a ravine, but I did not consider that there was enough for a brigade of troops. We fell back to Centreville, and the next morning moved up again and dug for water and found it. We moved up to the same position in rear of the batteries, throwing out pickets in front of the position down towards the timber.

Question. How long did you remain at Centreville?

Answer. Over night only, and marched back at daylight.

Question. And you then remained in camp there till Sunday morning?

Answer. Yes, sir.

Question. Did you take any part in the battle on Sunday?

Answer. Yes, sir.

By the chairman:

Question. Why was it concluded to fight that battle on Sunday, without any knowledge of where Patterson and his men were, and of the position of Johnston? Did you know at the time where they were? I will ask that first.

Answer. Yes, sir; I knew General Johnston was on our right before we moved from there at all.

Question. On Sunday morning?

Answer. Before we moved from the river I knew General Johnston was in that direction from this fact: About a week before we moved towards Bull Run at all, I was ordered to make a reconnoissance from the Chain Bridge, on the road to Vienna, with a squadron of United States cavalry, to see whether it was a practicable road for artillery and wagons, for my brigade to move on to Vienna. Vienna is about eleven miles from Chain Bridge. I made the reconnoissance, and went a mile beyond Vienna, and found nothing but an abatis across the road where the enemy had been at work. It was probably a fatigue party who had gone back, giving up the idea of making an abatis there. I came back and reported to General McDowell. He told me that there was a meeting of the officers to which he read his instructions for carrying on that campaign, and wished to read me the plan which had been submitted to General Scott, and which had not been disagreed to so far. He read over to me this plan, and stated to me the brigades and divisions which were to move on such and such roads. My brigade was to move to Vienna, and there was to join the other three brigades of General Tyler's division. General Tyler was then to move on to Germantown, where other divisions were to concentrate with his, and then, on getting to Centreville, the whole army would move up on the roads to the left. He stated to me that each division was from 10,000 to 12,000 men strong, and that our division—Tyler's—would be a little the strongest, as it looked towards Johnston on the right. Johnston, he said, was in that direction. But General Scott thought that if Johnston moved towards Manassas, Patterson "should be on his heels," as he expressed it. Says I, "General, are there any cross-roads to communicate from the right of the line to the left, so that if one of these columns is attacked by two or three times its numbers, it can concentrate on any of the other columns, or any of the other columns can concentrate on it?" He said it was not known whether there were any cross-roads or not on which any troops could concentrate; but that our columns were very heavy, and would be able to protect themselves. Since then we have found that there were abundance of cross-roads all through the country where troops could concentrate, if a person had been acquainted with them.

Question. Then when that battle was fought on Sunday it was expected that Johnston would be down?

Answer. It was known that he was on our right.

Question. You expected he would participate in the battle?

Answer. I expected something all the time, for I asked General McDowell why this column of ours was stronger than any of the others—12,000 instead of 10,000—and he said because it looked towards General Johnston.

Question. Was there any insurmountable obstacle to tearing up that railroad on which Johnston was expected to come down before the battle was fought?

Answer. That was in front of our position, and we knew nothing of it. I did not even know there was a railroad there until I heard the cars running Friday and Saturday, both up from Richmond and down the other way. We heard them running all night.

Question. If you had known of the road when you first advanced, would it not have been easy for a skirmishing party to have gone out and destroyed it, so that Johnston's army could not have come down there, at least quite as conveniently as they did?

Answer. I could not answer that, because I do not know the force Johnston had there.

Question. My idea was not to encounter a force, but for a scouting party to tear up the rails and obstruct the road.

Answer. Yes, sir; but then they could have marched the distance in a day or night. They could have come down part of the way by cars, and then marched the rest of the way.

By Mr. Chandler:

Question. These re-enforcements did not begin to arrive until Friday night, I understand you to say.

Answer. Friday and Saturday we heard the cars running all night. The next morning we spoke of it, and concluded that fifty car-loads had come.

By the chairman:

Question. I asked you the question because I could not see why they came to the conclusion to fight that battle on Sunday, when they knew the disadvantages to which they were subjected.

Answer. I knew nothing about the railroads there. I knew there were railroads in the rear of Manassas that this army was intended to cut off, but where they were I did not know until I heard the cars.

By Mr. Chandler:

Question. You took part in the battle on Sunday ?

Answer. Yes, sir.

Question. Did you remain at Blackburn's Ford?

Answer. On Saturday there was a council of commanding officers of divisions and brigades, and I was called there, among the others, to hear the plan of attack for the next day. The main army was to move on the road to the right of Centreville and make their attack some three or four miles above where we were at Blackburn's Ford. These attacks the other officers would know more about than I do. My brigade was to remain in position in front of Blackburn's Ford. It was not to hazard an engagement on any account whatever. I received written instructions to that effect in addition to verbal instructions. It was not to hazard an attack at all, but merely to make a demonstration with artillery, and perhaps skirmishers, but nothing more than a demonstration. If necessary, the positions were to be intrenched by abatis or earthworks thrown up on the road according to the discretion of the commanding officers.

By the chairman:

Question. What, in your judgment, led to the disasters of that day?

Answer. I will state all I know about it, and then I can draw some conclusion afterwards.

Question. Of course; that is all I expect.

Answer. The other three brigades of General Tyler's division were detached to make an attack to my right. They were to be in action by daylight in the morning, and as soon as I heard the report of his artillery I was to commence the fire, with my artillery, on the front. At the same time my brigade was detached from General Tyler's command, and, together with the brigade of General Davies, of New York, and the brigade of General Blenker, we were constituted three brigades of the reserve under Colonel Miles, of the United States army. I was to consider myself under his command. I waited until some 8 or 9 o'clock in the morning of Sunday before I heard the artillery on my right.

By Mr. Chandler:

Question. The attack was to have commenced at daylight?

Answer. Yes, sir. I said to the officers the night before—to General Tyler especially—"It is impossible, general, to move an army of regular troops under two hours, and you will take at least that time to move volunteers; and if reveille is not beaten before two o'clock in the morning you cannot get into action at daylight; it is impossible." Said I, "If you beat reveille at 12 o'clock, with volunteer troops, you may get into action at daylight, but not before; that is the best you can do." Other officers heard me, I have no doubt, but I addressed myself particularly to General Tyler, as he had been my commanding officer. I waited until 8 o'clock in the morning before I heard a gun fired on the right, and then I commenced a cannonade on the enemy's line with my artillery. About this time Colonel Davies came up with his brigade, and inquired the date of my commission as colonel, and told me his, and found he ranked me eleven days. He took command of the two brigades. At the same time I showed him my position in front of Blackburn's Ford. He wished a good position for artillery to play. I took him to a hill some 600 yards on our left, with a ravine between, and showed him a good position for his battery to operate on a stone-house, in front of us about a mile, which was said to be the enemy's head-quarters, and which our rifled ten-pounder guns could easily reach. He immediately took up that position, which was at a log-house on this hill to our left, which was fully as high, and a little higher, than the hill we were on. We kept up a fire from two batteries of artillery until 11 or 12 o'clock in the day—perhaps until noon. About that time Colonel Miles showed himself to us. He came to a log-house where I was, near my position—for there was a log-house there also—on the top of the hill. I showed him that re-enforcements were coming in in front of us. In fact, before he came I had reported to him that some three bodies of men had already come into the intrenchments in front of us. One body was probably two regiments, and the others were one regiment each—as much as that. They appeared to come from off in a direction towards the south. That was about 12 o'clock in the day. Colonel Miles came down himself, and I showed him, with a glass I had, the bayonets of some of the men coming in front of us on the road—the last detachment. I will say here that they did not answer with cannon at all in front of us that day. Colonel Miles then went away. In the forepart of the afternoon he came back again, and said that he did not believe the enemy were in front of us. At the same time, between these two visits, we could see men moving in the direction of Manassas, up towards the attack in front, which was then going on; and about that time the enemy were also falling back. After they had advanced from Manassas, they then fell back in great disorder along the roads.

Question. That was in sight of your guns?

Answer. Yes, sir. We opened upon them with a ten-pounder rifled gun from our position. Colonel Miles at that time said that he believed they were retreating towards Manassas, and that he thought we could force the position in front of us, and that we had better go down and try "to drive them out," as he expressed it. Said I, "Colonel Miles, I have a positive order in my pocket for this brigade not to attack at all." I took it out and showed it to him. Says he, "That is positive." And he said nothing more about making an attack then; but he proposed throwing out a few skirmishers. We threw out 160 skirmishers, and I think three other companies in support of them. They moved down to the edge of the woods, and then the advance of the skirmishers were driven in by a volley of musketry right off. I then ordered the skirmishers back, satisfied that the enemy were there in considerable force. About the time that was over we could see batteries of horse artillery and bodies of cavalry and infantry moving in large force back again towards the Stone Bridge, which was some three or four miles from us. Lieutenant Prime, of the engineers, had at that time been down with a party of skirmishers to see if he could find any place where we could make a good attack in front. He came back and made the observation at that time that before night Centreville would be our front instead of our rear; as much as to say that we had got to change our line of battle; that we were beaten on the right. I had thought about noon that it might be necessary for us to repel an attack. I got together a party of pioneers, about forty, and I had about sixty axe-men detailed from the Michigan regiments, to use all the axes and spades we had. I commenced to make an abatis of heavy timber between my position and Colonel Davies, on my left. I also threw up an intrenchment across the road, with rails and dirt, to sweep the road in front of us. I knew the enemy, if they attacked our position, must go through the woods in column on our right, and would have to deploy under our fire, and move up against our battery which I had put in the road. We worked on that abatis until about two hours before night, when we had it completed, and I considered the position safe. The timber was very heavy; some of the pieces were two feet in diameter; nothing could possibly get through it. I had it completed as far as Davies's position two hours before sunset, and I took him over to look at it. It met with his views completely. About two hours before sunset I heard heavy firing of musketry, and of artillery also, near Davies's brigade, on my left. An officer came over and informed me that the enemy had made an attack with a column of infantry, some 5,000 strong, on Davies's position; that he had caused his infantry to lie down in support of his guns; that Hunt's battery had opened with canister shot, and fired some forty rounds, and that the enemy had fallen back in confusion, and that in five minutes not one man was in sight. They came across Bull Run on our left, and to the left of Hunt's battery. They came up a ravine leading towards his battery, and had come within 300 yards before they were seen. They were then a dense mass of men, and the officers were trying to deploy them in line of battle. They were within 300 yards, the most effective distance for canister shot. Major Hunt immediately opened his battery, and fired some forty rounds of canister shot, when the enemy fell back. That was reported to me about two hours before sunset. At the time this firing was going on, an officer of Colonel Miles's staff came to me and ordered my brigade to retreat on Centreville. Notwithstanding I had been ordered by General McDowell to hold this position at all hazards, still, as I was under Colonel Miles's direct authority, I could not disobey the order, and so I put the brigade in march.

Question. You had repulsed the enemy when this order was given?

Answer. Colonel Davies had repulsed them. We did not know how that had turned them. On getting within some three-quarters of a mile of Centreville with my brigade I met Colonel Davies, and asked him what the object of this movement was. He said he did not know. I asked him if the enemy had attacked him on our left. He said they had, and that he had repulsed them handsomely. But the object of this movement he knew nothing about. On getting within three-quarters of a mile of Centreville, some officer of General McDowell's staff ordered me to put my brigade in line of battle, facing both the road from Centreville to Blackburn's Ford and the road from Centreville to Union Mills, which was about four miles on the left of Blackburn's Ford, and try to hold that position, if possible. I put the brigade in position, leading from between the two roads, and on some slight hills that commanded the advance in front. While I was busy in putting my brigade in line of battle, I found that a great many other regiments of different brigades had been formed in line of battle both on my right and my left. Some of my regiments I placed in line of battle, and some in close column by divisions, to be ready to repel an attack of cavalry which might be made down the road, as I supposed the enemy's cavalry would come first in advance of the infantry. Soon after making this disposition, I found that some of my regiments had been moved from the position I had placed them in, and deployed into line; among others, the third Michigan. I inquired the reason of it, and Colonel Stevens, of the third Michigan—lieutenant colonel of that regiment—came to me about that time and inquired of me particularly why his regiment had been deployed from the position of close column by divisions into line of battle. He said that Colonel Miles had directed the movement. He said he wished to know which to obey, whether to obey Colonel Miles or me. I told him he had no business to move that regiment without the order came through me. He said he did not know what to do. Says I, "What is the matter?" Says he, "Colonel Miles comes here continually and interferes; and," said he, "we have no confidence in Colonel Miles." Said I, "Why?" "Because," says he, "he is drunk." Soon after this conversation, Captain Alexander—now Colonel Alexander of the general staff and corps of engineers—came up to me and said that General McDowell intrusted the whole disposition of the troops around that point to me. I told him I could do nothing as long as I was continually interfered with by a drunken man. I told him that Colonel Miles was drunk, and that he was continually changing everything that I did. He said that General McDowell knew that Colonel Miles was drunk, and that that would soon be attended to, and to go on and make my disposition of the troops. Several batteries of artillery had been placed in position on the hills, but I think the line of battle did not reach from one road to the other; it was too long a distance between them. That is to say, we were too far in advance. But there were also some hills behind us which were a little higher than the ground we stood on. Colonel Alexander said that the present line of battle was not a good one, and he would propose throwing back the right and left so that they could reach from one road to the other, and have the right flank rest on some woods on one road, and the left flank rest on some woods on the other road, and thus be secured against cavalry. I told him that I would make that disposition as fast as I could, as I believed it was better than the first one. The first disposition had been directed by Colonel Miles. I had the batteries of artillery with Major Barry, who was the chief of artillery at that time, massed in the centre and placed on these commanding hills; and I had the line of battle formed in front of the guns in a hollow, the batteries being high enough to play over the men's heads. The men were in the ravine in front, covered from the enemy's fire if they should come up. I considered that they were completely covered, and could not be hurt until the enemy came into close action, while, at the same time, our batteries could not be carried at all until the enemy came within sixty yards of our muskets. Of course our artillery had full sweep in the commanding position it had, which I considered the best position I could place our line in. I considered it a better line than the first because it was shorter, and at the same time our men were better protected.

By the chairman:

Question. We do not care so much about the particulars.

Answer. I want to show why the second line was better than the first, because it has been brought in evidence to show that the first line was better than the second. At the same time not all the infantry were placed in this position. Battalions in column closed in mass were placed behind the intervals of the battalions in front for support, so that we actually had two lines of battle instead of one, having more force to it than the first line that was formed.

Question. What happened to this line?

Answer. While I was going on with this General McDowell rode up to me. Said he, "Great God, Colonel Richardson, why didn't you hold on to the position at Blackburn's Ford?" I replied, "Colonel Miles ordered me to retreat to Centreville, and I obeyed the order." General McDowell said nothing more, except to take the general command of the troops. I said to him, "Colonel Miles is continually interfering with me, and he is drunk, and is not fit to command." I understood him to say that he had already relieved him from command, and desired me to go on with the preparations; that I had charge of all the troops at that point. I told him I would go on with the preparations as fast as I could. About half an hour before sunset when the lines were complete, the head of the enemy's cavalry made its appearance through the woods on the road towards Blackburn's Ford. I believe I was the first officer that saw that cavalry. I was standing by the side of a battery of 10-pounders, with a young lieutenant of artillery—Lieutenant Benjamin—I think he commanded the battery. Says I, "There is the head of the enemy's cavalry; you open on them with your two guns immediately and as fast as you can." He had his guns fired—I think it was twice each—on the head of the enemy's cavalry, and they fell back and we saw nothing more of them. The shells appeared to take effect, for they retreated immediately. Just before this Colonel Miles came up to where I was. Said he, "Colonel Richardson, I don't understand this." I was marching the 3d Michigan regiment over to the right at that time to fill up a space between them and the next regiment. Says he, "You should march that regiment more to the left." Says I, "Colonel Miles, I will do as I please; I am in command of these troops." Says he, "I don't understand this, Colonel Richardson." Says I, "Colonel Miles, you are drunk," and I turned away to lead off my men. Says he, "I will put you in arrest." Says I, "Colonel Miles, you can try that on if you have a mind to." I led the regiment on and placed them in position. He watched me, but said nothing more. At that time he could hardly sit on his horse. I could see from his reeling in the saddle, from his incoherent language, and from his general appearance, that he was drunk. I had been acquainted with Colonel Miles long before.

By Mr. Chandler:

Question. He had command of those three brigades through the day?

Answer. Yes, sir; the reserve.

Question. Why were they not ordered, or one brigade of them ordered, in front instead of being kept in the rear?

Answer. I have always thought that if Blenker's brigade, which was at Centreville, had been brought up to support me at my right—Davies's brigade was already on my left and had just repelled the enemy—we could have held that position until morning, when Runnion's reserve of 10,000 men at Fairfax Station could have come up. Some of his reserve had already arrived that night, and the rest of the reserve—among others the 37th New York, which is in my brigade now—was at Fairfax. They could have moved up against the morning, and then we should have been 24,000 strong, with the 35 guns which we had saved on the field already. They certainly could have held the position which I had held for three days alone.

By the chairman:

Question. Do you know any reason why that disposition was not given to the troops?

Answer. I cannot say why it was not made. But I have always thought that if a battery of artillery and some cavalry had been placed in the road at Centreville, so as to have opened on the fugitives, they could have been rallied at that place. I knew of something having been done once before like that. I know that at Buena Vista—although I was not there—some troops ran from Buena Vista as far as Saltillo, and Major Webster, who had command of two 24-pounder howitzers at Saltillo, loaded his guns and threatened to fire on them if they went any further; and they stopped at that place.

Question. Then you consider that Colonel Miles's order to you to retreat from the position you had fortified, while Davies had repulsed the enemy ——

Answer. I think if Blenker's brigade had been brought up on our right we could have held our position until morning, when a further reserve could have re-enforced us. And then, by cutting the timber in that direction, in two or three hours we could have made a position that we could have held. At the same time there is another thing I would like to say. From what we have learned since, the enemy handled every reserve they had, whereas our reserves were not handled at all. The three brigades of reserves—Blenker's, Davies's, and mine—that were on the field that day, and Runnion's reserve, which was at Fairfax Station, six miles off, I believe, and not handled at all, make 24,000 men who were useless, whereas the enemy handled all their reserves. This is nothing new. I said the same thing that night.

By Mr. Chandler:

Question. Runnion's reserve was only six miles off, you say?
Answer. At Fairfax Station.
Question. How many men?
Answer. Ten thousand.
Question. So that in reality there came under fire in that battle about 16,000 of our troops?
Answer. O! more than that. We marched 50,000 men and 49 pieces of artillery, of which we saved 35 pieces.
Question. So that about 26,000 were actually under fire?
Answer. I do not like to state about that.

WASHINGTON, D. C., *December* 24, 1861.
General SAMUEL P. HEINTZELMAN sworn and examined.

By the chairman:

Question. One item of the inquiry which we are commissioned to make is in regard to the occasion of the disaster at Bull Run, as near as we can ferret it out, by questioning military gentlemen who know. You will therefore please state in your own way, without much questioning, what you know about it; the time of starting, where you went, what you did, and what observations you made. State it in general, for we do not wish to descend to particulars at all. Just state your opinion of the causes of the disasters at Bull Run.
Answer. I cannot recollect when the other divisions started. My division marched on the morning of the 16th of July, which was Tuesday.
Question. You can give us a very rapid and general narrative, if you please, of what happened from the marching of your division. You need not be minute or particular in your statements.
Answer. The first brigade of my division started at 10 o'clock in the morning, and in the course of the day the whole division marched. We went as far as the Pohick the first night.
Question. How many men were in your division?
Answer. About 9,500. The last of the division did not get into camp until about one hour before daylight. We started the next morning soon after daylight, and found the road somewhat obstructed. When we got to Elzey's, I sent Wilcox's brigade on to Fairfax Station, and Franklin's brigade towards Sangster's, while I remained with ours at Elzey's. Just before we got to Elzey's we met some of the enemy's pickets, and received information that they had batteries at Fairfax Station, as well as between us and Sangster's. In about a half an hour I got word from Wilcox that the enemy were retreating from Fairfax Station. I immediately sent that information to General Franklin and followed on with the other brigade. I got to Sangster's with my two brigades late in the afternoon, and sent out reconnoitring parties, but could hear nothing of the enemy, further than they had retreated, some two hours before

we got to Sangster's, along the railroad, and had burned the bridges. We saw the smoke of the burning bridges when we got there. We stayed there all the next day. General McDowell came there about 12 o'clock, and we had a conversation there. The intention was, when we started, to go by the left flank to Wolf Run Shoals, or to Brentsville, and endeavor to cut the railroad in rear of Manassas. But from information received at Sangster's it was not considered feasible to follow up that plan. So he gave me orders to be at Centreville with my division between that time and daylight, and to get some provisions. Our three days' rations were out that day.

By Mr. Chandler:

Question. That was on Thursday.

Answer. Yes, sir. We started on Tuesday and got to Pohick. On Wednesday we got to Sangster's, and we stayed there until late in the afternoon of Thursday. About 5 o'clock, I think it must have been, I started. I had sent out to get beef, but could get nothing but an old cow; and we then went on without any provisions. We got to Centreville about dark, and found the rest of the army encamped about the place.

Question. That was Thursday night.

Answer. Yes, sir. We remained there until Sunday morning, when I advanced with the rest of the army.

By the chairman:

Question. What induced you to fight that battle on Sunday, and at that time, without knowing more particularly what Johnston and Patterson were about?

Answer. On Saturday we saw re-enforcements to the enemy arriving by the railroad, which we supposed were Johnston's. And every day's delay we knew was fatal to our success.

By Mr. Chandler:

Question. Can you tell us why you laid over at Centreville from Thursday until Sunday?

Answer. The day after we left Alexandria the provision train was to start. The wagons had not yet been collected, as I understood, and the consequence was that they did not start the next day, but the day after. On Thursday the provisions I had gave out. In fact, some of the men had got rid of their provisions the very first day; like volunteers, they did not take care of them, and as they got heavy they threw them away. I sent two or three times in the course of the morning, and finally I sent an officer to follow up until he found them. He went clear into Alexandria, and there he learned that the train had started the second day after we left, instead of the first, and had taken the road to Occoquan. As soon as I learned that, I pushed on towards Centreville, to try to get there before dark. At Centreville we the next day got some provisions. There was a reconnoissance made on Friday, or one attempted; but they met some of the enemy's pickets, and had to come back. There was another attempt made the next day, but I do not think they learned much then. But the supposition was that the enemy was in force at the Stone Bridge; that they had a battery there, and an abatis, and that the bridge was ruined; and that they had a force further up Bull Run at another ford, probably about half-way between Centreville and Sudley's Church. You asked me about the delay. The delay at Centreville, I suppose, was principally waiting for provisions, and for information of the position of the enemy.

Question. And during that delay Johnston's army came down?

Answer. Yes, sir.

Question. And likewise re-enforcements from Richmond?

Answer. Yes, sir; I suppose from every quarter whence they could send them.

By the chairman:

Question. Your first idea was the best one to cut off that railroad, was it not?

Answer. Yes, sir; we supposed the creek was not fordable but at few places; but at Sangster's we got information that satisfied us that there were very slight obstructions, and it would make that operation a very dangerous one, and it was given up.

By Mr. Chandler:

Question. Will you give us, as succintly as possible, the operations of your division on Sunday?

Answer. I perhaps had better state what occurred Saturday night.

Question. Very well.

Answer. Saturday night all the division commanders were directed to appear at General McDowell's headquarters to receive instructions what to do the next day. The order had been given to march, first, at 6 o'clock the afternoon of Saturday; but afterwards it was put off till 2 o'clock the next morning. We went there and got our instructions. General Tyler's division was to start first; then Hunter's, and then mine. I asked a few questions about what I was to do, and had some little change made about the hour of starting, and went back to my tent. The next morning, precisely at the hour fixed, I left. The head of the column got to Centreville, and found the road obstructed with troops. General Tyler's division had not passed yet. I waited there three hours for Tyler's and Hunter's division to pass. After crossing Cub Run a little ways we took the right-hand road. Major Wright, of the engineers, went with Hunter's column. He was to stop with the guide, where the road turned off to this second ford I spoke of. He could not find the road, and of course we kept on and reached Sudley's Church, or Bull Run, near the church, about 11 o'clock on the morning of Sunday. In the meantime we heard the firing on our left, across Bull Run, and could see the smoke, and could see two heavy clouds of dust, evidently caused by troops approaching from Manassas. A few minutes before we got to Bull Run General McDowell and his staff passed us, going on ahead. When we got to the run the last brigade of Hunter's division had not yet crossed. I ordered the first brigade of my division to fill their canteens, while I went on to see with my glass what was going on. About this time the firing in front of Hunter's division commenced. And in about a half an hour two of General McDowell's staff rode up and asked me to send forward two regiments, that the enemy were outflanking him. I ordered forward two regiments. The Minnesota regiment was one, but I have forgotten the other. I followed on and left orders for the rest of the division to follow as soon as the road was clear. Major Wright led the Minnesota off to the left, and I followed the upper road on the right until we came on the field. I stopped and made inquiries as to what was going on. I saw General McDowell, and the batteries which were on this ground. Two of them were ordered forward; one of them flanking my division. I followed them for a little while, sending orders for the zouaves and first regiment to follow and support them. I went up, after the zouaves arrived, on the right of the batteries with them. As I rose to cross the ridge, I saw beyond a line of the enemy drawn up at a shoulder-arms, dressed in citizen's clothes. It did not strike me at first who they were. But I just checked my horse and looked at them. I saw in an instant that they were a party of the enemy's troops, and I turned to the zouaves and ordered them to charge them. They moved forward some 20 paces and they fired, and both parties broke and run. Just at this moment some 30 or 40 of the enemy's cavalry came out through an old field and charged the rear of the zouaves. The zouaves turned upon them and emptied some five or six saddles, and the cavalry broke and run. Captain Colburn's company of cavalry, belonging to the regular army, was close by and got a shot at them with their carbines, and emptied some more saddles. That was the last I saw of them. And that was the famous black horse cavalry who made the charge.

Question. Only thirty or forty of them?

Answer. That was all. I did not see that many, but I was told there were thirty or forty of them. There was not a black horse among them that I saw. And there was one solitary man killed of that regiment by that fire. There was also a man fell out of the leading company. One of them disappeared, and I supposed he crawled off.

By the chairman:

Question. How far apart were they when that firing took place?

Answer. Thirty or forty yards.

Question. And they all fired over each other's heads?

Answer. The enemy were in the woods. As I was on horseback of course I saw them first. I stopped and ordered the zouaves to charge. By coming forward a few paces they could see over the ridge, and as soon as they saw each other they fired and then they both broke and run.

By Mr. Chandler:

Question. Did the zouaves rally after that during the day?

Answer. Not as a regiment. Many of the officers and men joined other regiments, or fought on their own hook.

By the chairman:

Question. What, in your opinion, really led to the disasters of that day?

Answer. It is hard to tell. There were a number of causes. In the first place, the delay of Friday and Saturday at Centreville was one efficient cause. Another cause was the three hours lost at Centreville on Sunday morning.

Question. Did their troops outnumber ours, do you suppose?

Answer. O! yes, sir, largely. I have no definite information as to the number of men they had. General Tyler's division went first, then General Hunter's, then mine. Hunter had furthest to go; the distance I had to go was the next furthest, and the distance Tyler had to go was the least. I think if we had reversed it—let Hunter start first, then let me follow him, and then Tyler follow me—that delay at Centreville would not have occurred.

By Mr. Chandler:

Question. Suppose the battery at Blackburn's Ford had been captured on Thursday night by Tyler's division, and an advance had been ordered on Friday morning, do you think there would have been much of a battle any way?

Answer. That is a difficult question to answer; I do not know what force the enemy had there. I doubt whether Tyler could have captured that battery. From what I have learned, I do not think he had sufficient force to do it. And he had no authority to make such a strong demonstration as he did.

By the chairman:

Question. Why was not the reserve brought up to that field?

Answer. The reserve at Centreville?

Question. Yes, sir.

Answer. I suppose the only reason was that Centreville was such an important point. If the enemy should get possession of it we should be cut-off entirely. I think that when we found on Saturday that re-enforcements were coming in so strongly, the reserve at Alexandria, here on the Potomac, should have been brought forward. That would have left the reserve that remained at Centreville in a position to be used.

Question. There were a great many troops at Fortress Monroe that might have been brought up, I should think. What prevented that?

Answer. I do not think there were many at Fortress Monroe. I do not recollect. I think there were troops enough around Washington, if they had been pushed forward on Saturday.

By Mr. Chandler:

Question. And, probably, if the battle had been made on Thursday or Friday, before their re-enforcements came up, you had force enough?

Answer. Yes, sir. I believe we should have been successful, at least, in getting possession of and holding Bull Run, if we could have advanced Friday morning. I was perfectly confident, when I went there on Thursday night, that we should advance on Friday morning, and the consequence was that I camped my division in very close order.

By the chairman:

Question. It always seemed singular to me that you went into battle on Sunday morning, when you found Johnston had re-enforced them. I should have supposed that you would have remained at Centreville until you had got your re-enforcements up to meet the new state of things.

Answer. I did not think, when we started on Sunday morning, that there would be a general engagement. I supposed, from what we were informed at head-quarters, that the enemy had a strong force at the Stone Bridge, as the rebels called it, and a small force at the ford I was to go to. I had orders not to cross until Hunter had crossed at Sudley's Church and come down opposite to me on the other side of Bull Run. Then I was to cross, and we were to follow on down opposite the Stone Bridge, and turn that. Tyler had orders, I believe, not to attack with his infantry at all, but merely to make a demonstration with his artillery at the Stone Bridge, and to wait until we came down. But when we crossed over there, we soon got engaged with a heavy force of the enemy.

Question. There was really no necessity for fighting on Sunday rather than on any other day. You chose your own time, I suppose?

Answer. It is reported that they had given their orders to attack us on Sunday morning at eight o'clock.

Question. Then I would have remained on the heights at Centreville and let them attack us there, and then they would have lost the benefit of their batteries.

Answer. The principal difficulty was the want of provisions in kind. I think that was one grand cause of the disaster. And the troops were not brigaded in time. And then we had a great many three months men.

By Mr. Chandler:

Question. You have been in command of the extreme left wing of this army for some time, I believe?

Answer. Yes, sir; between two and three months. I was on the left all last summer; but the day, or two days, before the battle my position was changed. I was to follow out on the Little River turnpike; and then they changed me further to the left, to go up the Fairfax road.

WASHINGTON, D. C., *December* 26, 1861.

General WILLIAM B. FRANKLIN sworn and examined.

By Mr. Chandler:

Question. You were in the battle of Bull Run, were you not?

Answer. Yes, sir.

Question. In command of a brigade?

Answer. Yes, sir.

Question. Were you in a council of war that decided upon delivering that battle of Bull Run?

Answer. I was not.

Question. Do you remember the time at which you started, with your brigade, for Bull Run?

Answer. We started the Tuesday before the battle; the battle was fought on Sunday.

Question. Will you state, briefly as possible, the daily marches of your brigade—the daily operations of your brigade—from that Tuesday until Sunday morning following?

Answer. On Tuesday we marched from our camp, near Alexandria, to Pohick creek, a distance of about fourteen miles, and there encamped. The next morning we marched to Sangster's Station; that was on Wednesday. Then on Thursday afternoon we marched from Sangster's to Centreville, and there encamped. There we laid until Sunday morning, at 2½ o'clock, when we marched to Bull Run.

Question. Can you tell why the army was delayed at Centreville from Thursday evening until Sunday morning? why a forward movement was not made at once?

Answer. I can only do that from inference; I have no direct information from headquarters. My impression is that it was on account of the non-arrival of the supplies for the army until some time on Saturday.

Question. The non-arrival of provisions?

Answer. Yes, sir.

Question. Which division of the army was your brigade connected with on that Saturday morning?

Answer. I belonged to General Heintzelman's division.

Question. Will you very briefly give us the particulars of your march on Sunday?

Answer. We left camp at 2½ o'clock in the morning, and marched about three-fourths of a mile, until the road that my brigade was on intersected the Warrenton turnpike. There we waited until nearly 6 o'clock for the passage of General Hunter's division. As soon as that had passed we started forward and turned off from the Warrenton turnpike just beyond Cub Run, and reached Bull Run, at Sudley's Stream, between 11 and 12 o'clock. At that time the engagement commenced. I was directed to send forward Ricketts's battery, which I did, and posted it where I was ordered to do so; and I immediately sent forward the 1st Minnesota regiment to a position indicated by Captain Wright, of the engineers. I then sent forward the 5th Massachusetts regiment to support Ricketts's battery, and immediately afterwards the 11th Massachusetts, the remaining regiment of my brigade, was brought up and took position alongside of the 5th Massachusetts, to be available for the fight wherever it might be needed. Ricketts's battery commenced firing and was doing excellent execution. I saw it presently move off from the position where I had stationed it without any orders from me. As I saw it move off I moved the 5th and 11th Massachusetts up to be in a position to support, in case it should get into difficulty. But it was taken before I could get through these arrangements.

Question. By whose order was that battery moved?

Answer. I have heard since that it was by order of General McDowell, but I do not know from my own knowledge. I went forward with the 5th and 11th Massachusetts, and did my best to get the battery back, and did get it back, either two or three times, I do not remember which. But every time when the time came to draw off the guns, the men could not be brought up to the scratch. They would come forward with their guns loaded and deliver their volley very well, and would then, instead of taking hold of the guns and drawing them off, fall back to a secure place and load. We must have remained in this position, with these two regiments going up, delivering their fire and falling back, until about three o'clock in the afternoon. At that time a large force of the rebels appeared in the woods on our right, when the men fled, and could not be brought up by any means I could use. And those two regiments were not collected again during the day. The Minnesota regiment was the only other regiment of my brigade. They did good work at the same point where these other regiments were, and did not break during the day : they went off the field in good order. The battery was taken, and that accounts for the whole of my brigade, as the 4th Pennsylvania left early in the morning.

Question. Had there been no delay, and had the battle commenced early in the morning, as was intended, what, in your opinion, would have been the result of that battle ?

Answer. I think the result would probably have been different, as far as I can judge now. I think we would have whipped them if we had begun the fight early in the morning.

Question. If the reserves had been brought up at any time, say from 12 to 3 o'clock in the afternoon, and brought into the fight, what, in your opinion, would then have been the result ?

Answer. My opinion after 2 o'clock was that nothing could save the day, I did not care how many troops came up.

Question. Your knowledge of the battle is confined to the action of your own brigade ?

Answer. Entirely to the action of my own brigade.

Question. Had your provisions been at Centreville when you reached there, and had you marched on Friday morning forward to Bull Run before the arrival of Johnson's reserves, and those from Richmond, what, in your opinion, would then have been the result ?

Answer. The result would have been in our favor. But mind, I do not know when those reserves of Johnson's and Smith's came up, and the reserves from Richmond. I do not know whether they were not there on Thursday.

Question. Did you, or did you not, hear the whistles of the locomotives and the running of the cars ?

Answer. I remember hearing the whistles all one night, and took it for granted that re-enforcements were being brought in.

Question. When was that?

Answer. On Friday night.

Question. You therefore inferred that reserves were brought there on Friday night ?

Answer. Yes, sir.

Question. And it is your opinion that, had the battle been delivered before those reserves came up, the result would have been different ?

Answer. Yes, sir.

By the chairman :

Question. On the Saturday before that battle was it known to officers that Johnson would probably be down there to join Beauregard ?

Answer. No, sir ; it was not, although, from hearing the whistles, we presumed he had come.

Question. You presumed that he had come ?

Answer. Yes, sir ; but we had no positive information that he had.

Question. I have always wondered that the battle was fought there when it was, after it was understood in the army that Johnson had come down, contrary to the expectation which was entertained that Patterson would hold him in check.

Answer. I will tell you what suggested itself to me when I got to Bull Run, and that is that we ought to have encamped on the fine hills there and waited there over night, and then got up early the next morning, when we would have whipped them.

The chairman: It has always seemed to me that when you knew that Johnson had come down you should have got 25,000 men from here, and as many more, perhaps, from Fortress Monroe, and then you would have had the thing sure. I have always wondered why that was not done when Patterson had not held Johnson in check, as it was understood he would do.

The witness: Patterson's officers give a very good account of him. He knew nothing about what the army was to do. He supposed the battle had come off on Tuesday, and knew nothing about what was really doing.

The chairman: It strikes me that it was a great fault that so important a circumstance was not understood before the battle was begun.

The witness: I think if we had stopped there at Sudley's Stream they would have fought us that morning, but we would have fought them on our own ground, and would have whipped them.

The chairman: They would then have lost the benefit of all their batteries? I have always wondered at your going into that fight then, when you should really have got re-enforcements of 20,000 to 30,000 more men.

The witness: I think it would have been an advisable plan to have stopped there at Bull Run. We would probably have had to fight about the same time, but then we should have fought on our own ground, and should have had a better position than they could have got. We could have had a beautiful position there.

Question. They would have had no batteries to protect them?

Answer. No, sir.

Question. I suppose if Patterson had come down and turned their rear about the same time they attacked you, you would have succeeded beyond a doubt?

Answer. Yes, sir.

By Mr. Chandler:

Question. Five thousand men making an attack in their rear at any time, I suppose, would have settled the battle?

Answer. Yes, sir.

By the chairman:

Question. Could not some of our men have been sent around to tear up the railroad?

Answer. No, sir; we were making for the railroad as fast as we could. That was our object. But they stopped us, and whipped us.

Question. You were too far to the left, were you not?

Answer. I think we should have gone further to the right.

WASHINGTON, D. C., *December 26, 1861.*

General IRVIN McDOWELL sworn and examined.

By Mr. Chandler:

Question. We were instructed to make some inquiry in regard to the battle of last July. In the first place, was that battle of Bull Run decided upon in a council of war?

Answer. No, sir. I will give you in a few words the way that was done. There is much that precedes the battle that would be interesting to you gentlemen to know. Not to be too long, I will say that the general-in-chief, General Scott, called upon me verbally to submit a plan of operations to go against Manassas, and to estimate the force necessary to carry out that plan. I cannot tell the day when this was done. I could give you a copy of the plan I submitted, but unfortunately the copy I kept has not, I think, the date to it. The one I sent to him has, I think. I sent the plan to General Scott, and he read it and approved of it. I was then summoned before the cabinet. There were some general officers there : General Sandford, General Tyler, General Mansfield, and General Meigs were there. I think those were all but I am not certain. I was then called upon to read my plan of operations, and I read it. No persons had any suggestions to make in reference to it except General Mansfield. He made some remarks, but said he had not thought about the matter, and did not know anything about it, and was not prepared to say anything in relation to it. As the plan was all approved of, without any alteration, and, I think, without any suggestion, except a slight one from General Mansfield, I then called the engineers to assist me, and gave the paper to them to discuss. They discussed it, and made no alterations, and had no suggestions to make except one. Captain Woodbury, now Major Woodbury, suggested that I should go by the right instead of by the left. I told him the reasons why I preferred to go by the left; that to go by the left was a conclusive movement, and to go by the right might not be.

Question. That is, to cut off the railroad?

Answer. Yes, sir. It was to go down by our left on their right and cut the railroad there. Your first question was as to whether there was any council of war on the plan. In reply, I said the plan was one that I submitted in compliance with verbal instructions from General Scott, and which plan received no modification either from the cabinet or from General Scott, except a mere verbal correction, changing "communications" to "communication." Nor did any of the engineers make any suggestion, except the one I have mentioned, to go by the right instead of the left. I told him why I did not want to go in that direction, but said I was the last man in the world pledged to my own views, and if any one could tell me anything better than I could myself, I would accept it, and give him the full credit of it. Now, in regard to my plan, I had, in the first place, to assume what the enemy had in front of me. I next assumed that there would be no secret of my preparing to go against them. They would know it, and as a consequence of that they would bring up whatever disposable force they had. Therefore, it was not so much what they had here, but what they would bring here, that I was to go against. I assumed that if General Butler would keep them engaged below, and General Patterson would keep Johnson engaged above, I would then have so much to go against. To do that I asked for a certain force. They agreed to it, and gave me the force, but very late in the day. But they did not fulfil the condition with me so far as General Johnson was concerned. I had a part to play in the matter. It was but a part in a whole; it was a large part, still only a part. I had no control over the whole; that was controlled by General Scott. On several occasions I mentioned to the general that I felt tender on the subject of General Patterson and General Johnson. In reply to some suggestion once made about bringing Patterson over to Leesburg, I said if he went there Johnson might escape and join Beauregard, and I was not in a condition to meet all their forces combined. I said that I went over there with everything green. That was admitted; but they said that the other side was equally green. I said that the chances of accident were much more with green troops than with veterans, and I could not undertake to meet all their forces together. General Scott assured me—I use his own words—"if Johnson joins Beauregard he shall have Patterson on his heels." He gave me this assurance, that there should be no question in regard to keeping Johnson's troops engaged in the valley of Virginia. I estimated to go from Vienna with the largest force, and get in behind Fairfax Court-House; go with one force down the Little River turnpike upon Fairfax Court-House; go with one force by way of Anandale, and then go off to the south by the old Braddock road, as it is called, and then have the fourth column go south of the railroad. The railroad was then blocked up and obstructed. They had broken down the bridges and torn up the track where they could, filled in the deep cuts with earth and trees, and obstructed the road as effectually as they could. I could not at first use that railroad, though I threw the largest part of the force called reserve upon the railroad to make the communications good. The largest part of the 30,000 men were in front. I moved down Tuesday evening. When General Scott was called upon, or when the question was asked in the cabinet, when he would be ready to carry out this plan, General Scott fixed for me that day week. Up to that time General Scott never wished anything done on the other side of the river further than to merely fortify Arlington Heights. General Scott was exceedingly displeased that I should go over there. He had other plans in view, and personal plans, so far as I was concerned. And he was piqued and irritated that I was sent over there, and the more so that General Sandford was here in somewhat an equivocal position. He was here for three months, a major general of troops in New York. General Scott did not wish to give him the command here in Washington; at least I infer so because he did not put him in command, and he put him in command on the other side of the river. But General Scott was told that he must put either General Mansfield or myself over there. He wished to keep General Mansfield here, and he put me over there. The general had opposed my somewhat rapid promotion, because he thought it was doing a hurt to General Mansfield, and when I was promoted he insisted that General Mansfield should also be promoted, and date back a week before my own promotion. When I was ordered to the other side General Scott sent me two messages by his aide-de-camp and military secretary, to make a personal request of the Secretary of War not to be sent on the other side. I said I could not do that. Just appointed a general officer, it was not for me to make a personal request not to take the command which I had been ordered upon. I could not stand upon it. I had no reputation, as he had, and I refused to make any such application. So I went on the other side, and the general was cool for a great while. He did not like that I did not comply with his suggestion and ask not to be sent there. I was on the other side a long while without anything. No additions were made to the force at all. With difficulty could I get any officers. I had begged of the Secretary of War and the Secretary of the Treasury, who at that time was connected with the Secretary of War in many of the plans and organizations going forward, that I should not be obliged to organize and discipline and march and fight all at the same time. I said that it was too much for any person to do. But they could not help it, or did not help it, and the thing went on until this project was broached. General Scott at the same time took occasion to say to the cabinet that he was never in favor of going over into Virginia. He did not believe in a little war by piecemeal. But he believed in a war of large bodies. He was in favor of moving down the Mississippi river with 80,000 men, of which I was to command the advance. We were to go down, fight all the battles that were necessary, take all the positions we could find, and garrison them, fight a battle at New Orleans and win it, and thus end the war. I did not think well of that plan, and was obliged to speak against it in the cabinet. I felt that it was beyond everything a hazardous thing for our paper steamboats, as you might term them, to try to go down the river on such an expedition. They have some considerable difficulty to get down safely in the most peaceable times and with all the precautions possible, and it would be exceedingly hazardous for them to undertake to go down there with a large army, with all their machinery above water and exposed, and obliged to attack works opposed to them all the way down. Here is the case of the Potomac now blockaded; we do not venture to land and attack the batteries here, though this is a wide river with a broad channel, one well known and which does not change. We attempt nothing of the sort here, and yet we were expected to go down the Mississippi a thousand miles, supply our force all the way down, attack the batteries, and be diminishing our force all the while by leaving garrisons in all the places we should deem of sufficient importance to retain. I thought the plan was full of most serious and vital objections. I would rather go to New Orleans the way that Packenham attempted to go there. I went over the river, as I have told you. General Mansfield felt hurt, I have no doubt, in seeing the command he had divided in two and a portion sent over there. I got everything with great difficulty. Some of my regiments came over very late; some of them not till the very day I was to move the army. I had difficulty in getting transportation. In fact, I started out with no baggage train, with nothing at all for the tents, simply transportation for the sick and wounded and the munitions. The supplies were to go on afterwards. I expected the men to carry supplies for three days in their haversacks. If I went to General Mansfield for troops, he said: "I have no transportation." I went to General Meigs and he said he had transportation, but General Mansfield did not want any to be given until the troops should move. I said: "I agree to that, but between you two I get nothing." The quartermaster begged of me not to move, because he was not ready. I said: "We must move on Tuesday;" which was one week after the time General Scott had fixed. All my force had not come over by the time he fixed. A large part came over on Sunday, and some on the very Tuesday I moved. I told the general·I was not ready to go. Said I to him: "So far as transportation is concerned, I must look to you behind me to send it forward." I had no opportunity to test my machinery; to move it around and see whether it would work smoothly or not. In fact, such was the feeling, that when I had one body of eight regiments of troops reviewed together, the general censured me for it, as if I was trying to make some show. I did not think so. There was not a man there who had ever manœuvred troops in large bodies. There was not one in the army; I did not believe there was one in the whole country; at least, I knew there was no one there who had ever handled 30,000 troops. I had seen them handled abroad in reviews and marches, but I had never handled that number, and no one here had. I wanted very much a little time; all of us wanted it. We did not have a bit of it. The answer was: "You are green, it is true; but they are green, also; you are all green alike." We went on in that way. But there is one thing clear beyond any doubt. If the movements which had been ordered had been carried out, we should have had no difficulty at all. My plan was simply this: It was to move out this force upon these four lines. I had to move them on four lines that had no communication with each other from the very nature of the country. But I thought I made each column strong enough to hold its own. If it could not penetrate it could stand still, and if attacked it could hold its own, while the other columns were pressing forward and trying to get behind the enemy. The roads from Alexandria radiate. One goes out to Vienna, one goes to Fairfax Court-House, one to Fairfax Station, and one further south to Pohick church. My orders were, that those on the right should go the first day—Tuesday—out to Vienna. I had taken the precaution before to send General Richardson, who commanded a brigade I had organized at Chain Bridge, out to examine the road he afterwards moved over. Generals Keyes, Schenck, Richardson, and Sherman, in all four brigades, were to be at Vienna that night. General Hunter, who commanded what I intended to be a sort of reserve, composed of General Burnside's command and General Porter's command, were to go on the Little River turnpike to Anandale. General Miles was to go to Anandale a little before and turn down on the Braddock road. General Heintzelman was to go out also from Alexandria on the railroad, and send up some force to Vienna to hold that point after our troops left it. The next morning General Tyler was to march from Vienna and go down upon the road towards Fairfax Court-House. General Hunter was to go forward to Fairfax Court-House direct. General Miles was to come down on the Braddock road to another road that crossed it, going from Fairfax Court-House to Fairfax Station, while Heintzelman went down below. They were to be there early in the morning, I think at 8 o'clock. At Fairfax Court-House was the South Carolina brigade. And I do not suppose anything would have had a greater cheering effect upon the troops, and perhaps upon the country, than the capture of that brigade. And if General Tyler could have got down there any time in the forenoon instead of in the afternoon the capture of that brigade was beyond question. It was but 5,000 or 6,000 men, and Tyler had 12,000, at the same time that we were pressing on in front. He did not get down there until in the afternoon; none of us got forward in time. That was due to two things, perhaps. The affair of Big Bethel and Vienna had created a great outcry against rushing into places that people did not know anything about. I think the idea of everyone was that we were to go into no such things as that; that we were to feel our way. That, perhaps, caused the march to be very slow; because, from Vienna across the march was not more than five or six miles, and if they started by 4 o'clock in the morning they should get there by 8 o'clock. They did not get there until 3 o'clock, and the South Carolina brigade marched at 11 o'clock, so that it slipped through our hands. Then, too, the men were not used to marching; they stopped every moment to pick blackberries or to get water. They would not keep in the ranks, order as much as you pleased. When they came where water was fresh they would pour the old water out of their canteens and fill them with fresh water; they were not used to denying themselves much. They were not used to journeys on foot; the men of the north no more than the men of the south were used to going on foot much. While the men of the south were accustomed to riding horseback, those of the north rode in wagons for the shortest journeys, and they were pretty well broken down with this short march; therefore, when I wanted them to push on to Centreville, they were so broken down that they could not get more than half way there. The subsistence was to come on the next morning. Thursday morning I went off to see about making this march off to the left. That day General Tyler got involved at Blackburn's Ford, which made it necessary to move the whole of the troops forward that day, instead of keeping them behind to draw their rations. The attack at Blackburn's Ford had a bad effect upon our men. They were all in high spirits before that, but had not succeeded in their first attack. That attack made all wish to know what we were going to do, and where we were going to go, so that the next two days were employed by General Barnard and those under him in trying to discover where we could penetrate this line. They went out and were unsuccessful. They went out again at night, and were again unsuccessful. On Saturday about noon they reported that they had found a place. I at once gave orders to march at 6 o'clock that night, going part of the distance and stopping, and then move on early in the morning; but General Burnside, who was the furthest off, said that it would be much less fatiguing for his men to make one march instead of two, and that if we started early enough in the morning we could reach there in time. I yielded to it at once, as it was only on account of the men that I wanted to stop. I started in the morning. We got around late, it is true; there were delays about getting into the road. General Tyler was late, and General Hunter was slow in getting around; still, we substantially carried out the plan. We got over there and met the enemy; and there I found that, in addition to General Beauregard, I had General Johnston—how much of him I did not know. I learned afterwards that some 7,000 or 8,000, the bulk of his force, had arrived. Still, we were successful against both until about 3 o'clock in the afternoon, when the remainder of his force came upon us upon our right when our men were tired and exhausted, and that caused the day to turn against us.

I have learned since, in relation to that movement of General Johnston, which was the fatal thing in the whole of this battle, and which General Scott assured me should not take place, or if it did General Patterson should be driving him in, that General Patterson was before General Johnston on Wednesday, and on Thursday morning, at 4 o'clock, he ordered his troops to march. I learned from General Morell—now in General Fitz-John Porter's division, but who was then on the staff of General Sandford, who commanded under General Patterson—that they all expected that they were going right down to Winchester on Thursday, and that all the men were in the highest possible spirits at the idea of going there, and that General Sandford believed they were superior to Johnston's force. But instead of going down to Winchester, after they got down to a place called Bunker Hill, they turned off to the left and went off towards Harper's Ferry. Then the men became so dissatisfied that they demanded their discharge. Up to that time there had been no indications of turbulence. General Johnston, on on that same day—Thursday—when he found out that Patterson had gone away, left in the afternoon between 2 and 3 o'clock, and pushed down in a masterly manner as hard as he could to join Beauregard. General Patterson in the meantime was, I am told, under the greatest possible alarm, and telegraphed all the time, and sent an officer down, who arrived on Sunday, to General Scott for re-enforcements against General Johnston, General Johnston at that very time being before me here; and General Scott was so impressed with this, that a large part of the force in Washington was ordered to go up there to join General Patterson. So completely was General Patterson outwitted that he thought General Johnston had 40,000 men there. One who was on his staff, and his adjutant general, told me that they had got records, reports, and returns to the effect that Johnston had something like 40,000 men. All I can say is, that if he had 40,000 men, I had the whole of them on me.

By Mr. Chandler:

Question. Do you believe he had 10,000?

Answer. I think he had from 12,000 to 15,000, and General Patterson had in the vicinity of 20,000. If he had 40,000, then I had them all. But I assume that he joined Beauregard in the first place with 8,000, and that his last re-enforcement was about 4,000.

By the chairman:

Question. When did you first learn that Johnston was released from Patterson and down here?

Answer. I first learned it in a way beyond all doubt on the field of battle. About 11 o'clock in the day I made some prisoners.

Question. Did no one tell you before?

Answer. A man came to me before. But, great God! I heard every rumor in the world, and I put them all aside unless a man spoke of his own personal knowledge. Some person came to me; I did not know who he was. I had people coming to me all the time, each one with something different. All that I paid no attention to. This person came to me and said, I think, "The news is that Johnston has joined Beauregard." He might have said that somebody else had joined Beauregard. He did not know it himself; had heard it from others. Some one said: "We heard the cars coming in last night." Well, I expected that. I expected they would bring into Manassas every available man they could find. All I did expect was that General Butler would keep them engaged at Fortress Monroe, and Patterson would keep them engaged in the valley of Virginia. That was the condition they accepted from me to go out and do this work. I hold that I more than fulfilled my part of the compact, because I was victorious against Beauregard and 8,000 of Johnston's troops also. Up to 3 o'clock in the afternoon I had done all and more than all that I had promised or agreed to do; and it was this last straw that broke the camel's back—if you can call 4,000 men a straw, who came upon me from behind fresh from the cars.

By Mr. Chandler:

Question. Has it not been a fact, all through this war, that our generals in front of the enemy—as was General Patterson in front of General Johnston—have been deceived as to the force of the enemy? General Patterson says that he had positive information that General Johnston had over 35,000 men, while he had only 20,000. Has this not been a bragging, lying force that they have been exhibiting along our lines all the time?

Answer. There is one thing: In war the object is to deceive the enemy as to your force and make him believe that you are stronger than you really are. I have taken the evidence of negro men and found it very good myself. But that is a matter of judgment; you may get yourself overreached.

WASHINGTON, *January* 23, 1862.

General IRVIN MCDOWELL recalled and examined.

By Mr. Chandler:

Question. There are one or two points in relation to the battle of Bull Run upon which the committee desire you to make some further explanation. You state in your official report, under date of August 4, 1861, that there was delay in the first division in getting on the road on the morning of the battle, and that this was a great misfortune. Will you please state more fully in relation to that delay?

Answer. In my general order, No. 22, of July 20, 1861, providing for the movement of the several divisions to attack the enemy, it was arranged that General Tyler's division should move at half past two a. m., precisely, on the Warrenton turnpike to threaten the possession of the bridge. General Tyler's division consisted of four brigades, three only of which moved at this time, as directed in the order referred to. Schenck's and Sherman's brigades were one mile from Centreville on the road from Centreville to the Stone Bridge—on the right and left of the road; Keyes's brigade was about a half a mile to the east of Centreville, on the right of the same road going west; the second division—Hunter's—was about two miles from Centreville, and to the east of it. This division was ordered to move at two o'clock a. m. precisely. Heintzelman's division was two miles distant from Centreville, and east of it, on what is called the old Braddock road. This division was to move at half past two a. m. precisely. Heintzelman's division consisted of the brigades of Wilcox, Franklin, and Howard. Hunter's division consisted of the brigades of Burnside and General Andrew Porter. All these divisions had the road in common, from the encampment of Sherman's and Schenck's brigades to the point where the road to Sudley's Springs turned off to to the right—at a blacksmith's shop—a little over a mile. Tyler was to move at half past two a. m., and Hunter was to move half an hour earlier, so that he might close up on Tyler's division. Heintzelman was to move at half past two a. m., so as to fall in the rear of Hunter's division. Tyler was expected to get over the ground, between the encampment of his advanced brigade and where the road turned off to the right at the blacksmith shop, in time to offer no obstructions to the road, which was to be used in common by all the divisions. I was sick during the night and morning, and did not leave my headquarters—a little over a mile, perhaps a mile and a quarter, east of Centreville—until I thought all the divisions were fully in motion, so as to give myself as much rest as possible. When I had got beyond Centreville about a mile, I passed the troops lying down and sitting down on the wayside. Upon asking why they did not move forward, the reply came to me that the road was blocked up. I saw some men coming from the left of the road through a cornfield into the road. When I asked to what regiment they belonged, they said the 2d New York, which formed a part of Schenck's brigade. I went forward, urging the troops to move on, until I got to the blacksmith's shop, where the road turned off to Sudley's Springs. I was making every effort, personally and by my aides, to have the road cleared, in order that Hunter's and Heintzelman's divisions might take up their march to the right by way of Sudley's Springs, to carry out the plan of battle.

By Mr. Odell:

Question. Whose division blocked up the road?
Answer. The first division, General Tyler's division. Major, now General, Barnard, who was the chief of engineers on my staff, in his report to me, dated July 29, 1861, says as follows: "You are aware of the unexpected delay. The two leading brigades of Tyler's did not clear the road for Hunter to this point (blacksmith shop, where the road turned to the right) until half past five." That was three hours after the time fixed to start.

By Mr. Chandler:

Question. What was the distance from the encampment of Tyler's leading brigades to the blacksmith shop?
Answer. About a mile. I directed one of my staff to notice when General Tyler commenced firing. It was six o'clock. Colonel, now General Heintzelman, in his report to me of July 31, states as follows:
"At Centreville we found the road filled with the troops, and were detained three hours to allow the divisions of Generals Tyler and Hunter to pass. I followed them with my division immediately in rear of the latter."
I will mention that General Tyler in moving forward as the troops were then moving forward—some 18,000 men—was so supported that it was felt that he might move with confidence and promptness upon the road. I have been thus particular in making this explanation because General Tyler has written me a letter, complaining that my report does him injustice, and asking me to set him right in reference to this matter of delay. Under the circumstances I did not feel that I could make any change. He also stated that he received no orders from me during the day.

By Mr. Chandler:

Question. I notice in your report that you state that you sent an aide-de-camp to General Tyler to direct him to press forward his attack, as large bodies of the enemy were passing in front of him to attack the division which had crossed over. Will you state what this order was, and by whom it was sent?
Answer. I sent an order to General Tyler to press forward the attack from a point near where this road that turns off at the blacksmith shop crosses Bull Run, near Sudley's Springs. I sent Lieutenant Kingsbury, my aide-de-camp, to General Tyler to press forward his attack, because I saw columns of dust, indicating large bodies of troops, moving up in front of General Tyler's division, and as but a small part of Hunter's division had, at that time, crossed Bull Run, I was afraid he would be crushed before we could get a sufficient body of troops forward to support him. Lieutenant Kingsbury reported to me that he had gone to General Tyler, and found General Tyler, with his aide-de-camp, near a tree, in the branches of which he had some men observing the troops of the enemy coming up on the opposite side. Lieutenant Kingsbury reported to me that he had told General Tyler it was my order he should press forward his

attack, and General Tyler replied, "What does he mean? Does he mean that I shall cross the stream?" Lieutenant Kingsbury said: "I give you the message exactly as it was given to me;" to which General Tyler returned answer, "I have a great mind to send some" regiment, or brigade, or something, "across the stream" Lieutenant Kingsbury made me a written report of this, which is mislaid. And while I was waiting at the blacksmith shop to see which direction the battle was to take I also sent an order to General Tyler by my then aide-de-camp, Major Wadsworth, now General Wadsworth.

By Mr. Gooch:

Question. When was Keyes's brigade ordered to move?

Answer. General Tyler states, in his report, that it was ordered to move at two o'clock in the morning. I did not give any orders to General Keyes, but to Tyler. General Tyler was ordered to move at 2½ a. m. He must have given the order to bring up his rear brigade at two o'clock. General Keyes says: "In compliance with the orders of Brigadier General Tyler, I have the honor to report my operations, leaving my camp at Centreville at two o'clock a. m."

Question. You were aware, when you gave the order to General Tyler, that Keyes's brigade was encamped at Centreville?

Answer. Yes, sir.

Question. Was there anything between Keyes's brigade and the remainder of General Tyler's division?

Answer. Nothing.

Question. Was there anything to prevent Keyes's brigade from moving up and joining the rest of the division?

Answer. There ought to have been nothing. There was, because I believe Hunter's division got into the road before him.

Question. Then if he was interrupted or obstructed in moving up and joining the remainder of Tyler's division, whose fault was it?

Answer. It must either have been his fault in getting off so late, if he was ordered to move at 2 o'clock by General Tyler, or the fault of some of Hunter's division in going too soon.

Question. The intention was that the whole of General Tyler's division should move from the point where Sherman and Schenck were encamped, and on the Warrenton turnpike, at 2½ o'clock?

Answer. Yes, sir. This brigade of Keyes's had, in consequence of previous movements, become dislocated from the other two, but that, practically, had no effect upon the march of Sunday morning. What I wished to do was to post this force of Tyler's at or near the Stone Bridge, and under the cover of his force make this flank movement to the right.

Question. Can you state whether or not Schenck's and Sherman's brigades had moved forward past the point where the road turns off at the blacksmith shop in time to give the road to the other divisions as they came up?

Answer. They had not; that is just the point.

Question. Then the other divisions of the army were held back, not only by Keyes's brigade, but by the other brigades of Tyler's division?

Answer. Keyes did not hold them back; he went into the field and they came up.

Question. Then they were held back by Schenck's and Sherman's brigades?

Answer. Yes, sir; by the slow movement of that part of the force.

Question. It has been said that General Tyler ordered Keyes's brigade up to join him prior to the day of the battle, and that order was countermanded by you, and the brigade remained back where it was.

Answer. That may have been, but it is a matter of no sort of consequence whatever. I do not know whether that was so or not. But it was of no consequence, because General Tyler and the whole of his forces were ahead; the others were behind.

Question. Would there have been any advantage in stationing the several divisions differently; that is, having some divisions which had further to march stationed where Tyler's was?

Answer. No, sir; Tyler got his position there logically from the way the force marched to Centreville. Tyler was to throw himself between Fairfax Court-House and Centreville. Hunter started from Anandale, and behind Tyler; Miles was below, and Heintzelman further below still. When Tyler moved forward to Centreville and commenced the fight at Blackburn's Ford the other divisions were behind. Now to have changed them around would simply have made an unnecessary inversion; there would have been no particular object in it. I should have ordered forward first whichever division might have occupied Tyler's position, so that, under cover of that, I might have made my flank movement to the right with the other divisions.

Question. It was desirable, then, that a force should be at Stone Bridge before any force passed up toward Sudley's Springs?

Answer. I think so. I wanted a strength there, and then, under cover of that, I could move my other divisions up. Had that not been done, there was danger that the other divisions going up to Sudley's church, having the longest distance to go, might be attacked and cut off.

Question. It was necessary that that division of the army which was to move to Stone Bridge should have the road, and reach and pass the point where the blacksmith shop stands, before the remaining portion of the army should turn off towards Sudley's Springs?

Answer. That was part of my well determined plan. I thought that was the better way. I do not think any other would have been a safe movement.

Question. I wish to ask you whether the force you left at Centreville was regarded by you as a reserve, or whether they were stationed as they were posted at the different points that day because it was necessary to have troops there to protect the rear of your army?

Answer. More the latter than the former, though partly both; to act as a reserve and, at the same time, to guard against an attack on our left or right. I remained at the turn-off by the blacksmith shop for nearly an hour, in doubt whether there would be an attack above at all. I was inclined to look for it at the left. And I have learned since that General Beauregard intended to attack me at eight o'clock, at Blackburn's Ford; and when General Tyler commenced firing at Stone Bridge and received no response, I was in doubt. In my order for the battle I say: "The enemy has planted a battery on the Warrenton turnpike to defend the approach to Bull Run, has mined the Stone Bridge," &c. I wanted to commence the attack on that point, which I was afraid I could not turn, and under cover of that attack to throw a large force up to the right. We expected the Stone Bridge to be a strong point, with batteries in position, regular works, &c. We expected the bridge would be blown up so that we could not use it, and I had made preparations so that the engineer should have another bridge to be used there. We were to make our move to the right and attack them under cover of this attack at the bridge.

Question. If it had not been for the disposition of the forces of Miles's division which you made on the day of the battle, would not your whole army have been exposed and liable to be cut off?

Answer. Yes, sir; by a movement of the enemy on my left.

Question. That is, by a movement from the enemy's right on your left?

Answer. Yes, sir; I can show you how I felt on that subject by referring you to my general order No. 22, in which I say: "The fifth division (Miles's) will take position at the Centreville Heights; Richardson's brigade will, for the time, become part of his (Miles's) division, and will continue in its present position. One brigade will be in the village, and one near the present station of Richardson's brigade. This division will threaten Blackburn's Ford, and remain in reserve at Centreville. The commander will open fire with artillery only, and will bear in mind that it is a demonstration only that he is to make. He will cause such defensive works, abattis, earthworks, &c., to be thrown up as will strengthen his position. Lieutenant Prime, of the engineers, will be charged with this duty." I will also further, in relation to this same matter, give an extract from my report: "I had also felt anxious about the road from Manassas by Blackburn's Ford to Centreville, along the ridge, fearing that while we should be in force to the front, endeavoring to turn the enemy's position, we ourselves should be turned by him by this road; for if he should once obtain possession of this ridge, which overlooks all the country to the west to the foot of the spurs of the Blue Ridge, we should have been irretrievably cut off and destroyed. I had, therefore, directed this point to be held in force, and sent an engineer to extemporise some field-works to strengthen their position."

Question. And you say now that you understand it was the intention of Beauregard to attack you at that point?

Answer. I have understood since that General Beauregard intended in the first place to attack me at 8 o'clock on the morning of the battle, and to attack me on my left, at this Blackburn's Ford, or in its vicinity; and I have also understood that during the battle he did order a heavy attack to be made in that direction. An attack was made there, but not in the force he intended. It failed on account of an order which he gave one of the commanders having miscarried.

Question. Would it, in your opinion, have been judicious, at any time prior to the rout of our army, to have ordered the force, or any portion of it, stationed at Centreville on to the field of action?

Answer. I do not think it would have been judicious to have sent them one moment earlier than they were sent for. A reference to the reports of Colonel Davies, Colonel Richardson, and Hunt, of the artillery, I think, will show this. They were there having a heavy attack on the left, which would have been heavier but for the failure I have referred to. General Barnard, in his report of July 29, says:

"It will be seen from the above that the combination, though thwarted by different circumstances, was actually successful in uniting three entire brigades, (excepting the brigade of Schenck, which had just opened its way to fall on the enemy's right at the moment when our lines finally gave way in front,) upon the decisive point.

"A fault, perhaps, it was that it did not provide earlier for bringing the two brigades of Miles (in reserve at Centreville) into action. One of his brigades (Richardson's) actually did participate, though not on the battle-field; and in its affair on Blackburn's Ford probably did neutralize the attack of the enemy."

General Barnard did not then know the extent of that affair on the left. He thought that only Richardson was engaged in it. A reference to the reports of Colonel Davies, commanding a brigade under Colonel Miles, Colonel Hunt, commanding a battery of artillery, and of Colonel Miles, will show why only one brigade from Centreville was sent forward to the front. And it will show that the affair on the left was a matter of much greater importance than General Barnard seems at that time to have supposed it to be. Davies's brigade was actually engaged, as was also that of Richardson, in repelling the attack of the enemy on the left. Colonel Miles, in his report, says that he received an order to put two brigades on the Warrenton turnpike at the bridge, and a staff officer was sent to order forward Davies's brigade; that whilst this staff officer was executing his instructions, Davies sent word that he wanted the reserve forward where he was, as he was attacked by 3,000 of the enemy; that the staff officer, therefore, properly suspended the giving of the order, and reported immediately to Colonel Miles, and this caused him to advance with only one brigade, Blenker's, to the position on the Warrenton turnpike.

Question. The shortest road from Manassas to Centreville was by Blackburn's Ford?

Answer. Yes, sir.

Question. When the retreat of our army took place, had the way by Blackburn's Ford not have been obstructed by the force you had placed there or near there, could not the enemy have moved forward immediately upon Centreville and cut off the retreat of your whole army?

Answer. Yes, sir; and I refer again to my report in answer to that question.

"At the time of our retreat, seeing great activity in this direction, (Blackburn's Ford,) also firing and columns of dust, I became anxious for this place, fearing if it were turned or forced the whole stream of our retreating mass would be captured or destroyed. After providing for the protection of the retreat by Porter's or Blenker's brigade, I repaired to Richardson, and found the whole force ordered to be stationed for the holding of the road from Manassas by Blackburn's Ford to Centreville on the march for Centreville under orders from the division commanders. I immediately halted it and ordered it to take up the best line of defence across the ridge that their position admitted of, and subsequently taking in person the command of this part of the army. I caused such disposition of the force as would best serve to check the enemy."

By Mr. Odell:

Question. Was the attack on Blackburn's Ford on Thursday, the 18th of July, made by your order?

Answer. No, sir, it was not. On July the 18th I was between Germantown and Centreville, General Tyler's division being between my then position and Centreville. I wrote him the following note, which was carried to him by General, then Colonel, Wadsworth, my aide-de-camp:

"BETWEEN GERMANTOWN AND CENTREVILLE,
"*July* 18, 1861—8.15 *a. m.*

"BRIGADIER GENERAL TYLER—*General :* I have information which leads me to believe you will find no force at Centreville, and will meet with no resistance in getting there. Observe well the roads to Bull Run and to Warrenton. Do not bring on any engagement, but keep up the impression that we are moving on Manassas. I go to Heintzelman to arrange about the plan we have talked over."

The plan was for the army to go around and attack the enemy's right.

I will give an extract from General Tyler's report of July 27 as bearing on this question:

HEADQUARTERS FIRST DIVISION DEPARTMENT NE. VIRGINIA,
Washington City, July 27, 1861.

"General McDOWELL, *Commanding Department :*

"SIR: On the 18th instant you ordered me to take my division, with the two 20-pounder rifled guns, and move against Centreville, to carry that position. My division moved from its encampment at 7 a. m. At 9 a. m. Richardson's brigade reached Centreville, and found that the enemy had retreated the night before; one division on the Warrenton turnpike, in the direction of Gainesville, and the other, and by far the largest division, towards Blackburn's Ford, on Bull Run."

This order of mine that I have referred to was given to him in person by then Major Wadsworth, who also cautioned him verbally from me not to do too much in the way of keeping up the impression that we were moving on Manassas.

I will now read from General Barnard's report of July 29. He was the chief of engineers on my staff:

"It should be borne in mind that the plan of campaign had been to turn the position and turn Manassas by the left; that is to say, that from Fairfax Court-House and Centreville we were to make a flank movement toward Sangster's and Fairfax Station, and thence to Wolf Run Shoals, or in that direction.

"In my interview with the commanding general he said nothing to indicate any change of plan; but, on the contrary, his remarks carried the impression that he was more than ever confirmed in his plan, and spoke of the advance on Centreville as a 'demonstration.'

"In proposing therefore to reconnoitre the enemy's position at Blackburn's Ford, it was not with the slightest idea that this point would be attacked; but a reconnoissance would be the carrying out of a 'demonstration.'

"Whilst I was awaiting Captain Alexander, I encountered Matthew C. Mitchell, who was secured as a guide. Representing himself as a Union man and a resident of that vicinity, I was engaged questioning him, when intelligence was received that General Tyler had sent back for artillery and infantry, and that the enemy was in sight before him. Riding to the front, I joined General Tyler and Colonel Richardson. Proceeding with them a short distance further, we emerged from the woods, and found ourselves at a point at which the road commences its descent to Blackburn's Ford. The run makes here a curve or bow towards us, which the road bisects. The slopes from us towards it were gentle and mostly open. On the other side the banks of the run rise more abruptly, and are wooded down to the very edge of the run. Higher up a clear spot could be seen here and there; and still higher, higher than our own point of view, and only visible from its gently sloping towards us, an elevated plateau, comparatively open, in which Manassas Junction is situated.

"Although, owing to the thickness of the wood, little could be seen along the edge of the run, it was quite evident from such glimpses as we could obtain that the enemy was in force behind us. I represented to General Tyler that this point was the enemy's strong position, on the direct road to Manassas Junction; that it was no part of the plan to assail it. I did not, however, object to a "demonstration," believing that it would favor what I supposed still to be the commanding general's plan of campaign.

"The two 20-pounders, of Parrott's, had been ordered up. They were opened upon the enemy's position, firing in various directions, without our being able to perceive the degree of effect they produced. They had fired perhaps a dozen rounds, when they were answered by a rapid discharge from a battery apparently close down to the run and at the crossing of the road. The 20-pounders continued their fire, directing at this battery, and Ayre's battery was brought up and stationed on the left. The enemy's batteries soon ceased answering. After ours had continued playing for about a half an hour, I felt it a useless expenditure of ammunition, and so stated to you, (Captain Fry, who arrived on the spot shortly before this,) and presumed General Tyler concurred in this opinion, as the firing soon ceased.

"I supposed this would be an end of the affair. But perceiving troops filing down towards the run, I thought it necessary to impress General Tyler with the fact that it was no part of the plan of the commanding general to bring on a serious engagement. I directed Captain Alexander (engineers) to state this fact to him, which he did in writing, having stated the same verbally before."

My own order was not to bring on an engagement, and here was the chief of my engineers, and my adjutant general besides, urging the same thing on General Tyler.

WASHINGTON, D. C., *December* 26, 1861.

General JAMES S. WADSWORTH sworn and examined.

By Mr. Chandler:

Question. You were an aid to General Mansfield at the battle of Bull Run, were you not?

Answer. Yes, sir.

Question. Did you consider the victory won from one to two o'clock in the afternoon of that day?

Answer. Yes, sir; and the reason we thought so was that we had driven the enemy from a large open battle-field some mile and a half back.

By the chairman:

Question. Suppose that Johnston had not come down, but had been kept back, what would have been the result?

Answer. Take out the whole of Johnston's command, and the victory would have been very easily won. But take out the portion of his command that came down under General Elger about three o'clock in the afternoon, and I still think the battle would have been won by us, but we could not say exactly. But we were holding our own, and had other troops to bring up. It is not certain that we should have won the battle, but General McDowell thought we should. I was where that re-enforcement arrived. I happened to be where the first discharge of musketry from that re-enforcement came in. It was very severe, and then they followed it up immediately with a very bold charge right on the field. They came through a piece of woods on to the battle-field. We had driven the enemy entirely out of the battle-field, which covered an area of 400 or 500 acres, and they were in the woods offering a very sturdy resistance, and it is impossible to say that we should certainly have overcome that resistance. Their last re-enforcement came up on their extreme left, and on our extreme right, so that they pretty nearly outflanked us. Their first discharge was upon some cavalry which had been withdrawn back to a point of comparative safety, as they were not of much importance to us. That killed several of them, and then they retired immediately, or rather stampeded in a very disorderly manner.

Question. At what time was it known among the officers that Patterson had failed to keep Johnston in check?

Answer. It was not known generally until the time of the action. I did not know it. I think it had been a matter of conversation before. I think General McDowell the day before expressed some apprehensions that Patterson had not kept Johnston occupied. I understand that General Cameron, who was out there on Saturday, reported something which led them to believe that Johnston might be there. What the extent of that information was, however, I have no means of knowing.

Question. What is your opinion as to the result of that battle had the provisions and transportation been brought up on Thursday, and the battle fought on Friday morning, instead of Sunday?

Answer. On Friday morning it would have been with no portion of Johnston's command there. I think there would have been no battle at all then; that we would have walked over the field. Johnston is regarded by our officers as much superior to Beauregard; as much the ablest officer in their army. All the reports show that he had a great deal to do with the disposition of the enemy on that day.

WASHINGTON, *December* 30, 1861.

Colonel STEPHEN G. CHAMPLIN sworn and examined.

By Mr. Chandler:

Question. You were in the fight at Blackburn's Ford on the Thursday before Bull Run, were you not?

Answer. Yes, sir.

Question. What was your opinion in regard to the capture of that battery, if you had been supported?

Answer. I think with one brigade in addition to prevent them from out-flanking us we could have taken it.

Question. Without heavy loss?

Answer. Yes, sir; we could have taken it at the point of the bayonet easy enough if we had had another brigade there. That was the way to have taken it.

Question. Then would you have had a severe battle on Friday morning, do you think?

Answer. My opinion is that that was the key of the position at that time.

Question. Would that have ended the matter?

Answer. Yes, sir; I think so. There would have been no battle at Stone Bridge, for we would have been in a position to have out-flanked them at Manassas. Every body of troops they threw up to the Stone Bridge would have been too far on their left.

By Mr. Gooch.

Question. You think those batteries should have been taken before pressing further on?

Answer. I think so. If we attacked the batteries at all at Blackburn's Ford we should have taken them and held them, for that was their centre at that time. They never could then have fought the battle at Stone Bridge, for we could have marched over the bridge and captured every man there. I think that on Thursday their forces in those batteries were light compared with what they were on Sunday. They saw there were demonstrations made at it, and they were apparently prepared to meet them.

By Mr. Odell:

Question. Were you in the Bull Run fight?

Answer. No, sir; we remained at the hill overlooking Blackburn's Ford to hold those batteries. If we had not held them they would have crossed over there and cut General McDowell's army all to pieces.

WASHINGTON, D. C., *December* 28, 1861.

General GEORGE W. MORELL sworn and examined.

By Mr. Chandler:

Question. You were on General Patterson's staff, were you not?

Answer. I was on General Sanford's staff, and with General Patterson a short time.

Question. You were with General Patterson from on or about the 16th to the 25th of July?

Answer. Yes, sir; that is, during the march from Martinsburg towards Winchester.

Part ii——4

Question. What was General Patterson's force at that time?

Answer. We estimated it at from 18,000 to 20,000 men.

Question. Mostly three months' men?

Answer. They were all three months' men except a small portion of regulars— a very small portion.

Question. General Johnston's force was at Winchester?

Answer. Yes, sir.

Question. General Patterson's force of from 18,000 to 20,000 men was at Martinsburg?

Answer. Yes, sir.

Question. Can you tell on what day of the month General Patterson's division advanced from Martinsburg towards Winchester?

Answer. Yes, sir; we left Martinsburg on the 15th of July, on Monday morning.

Question. Advancing towards Winchester?

Answer. Yes, sir; we went that day to Bunker Hill, a little over half way. We remained there until the 16th of July.

Question. What day of the week was that?

Answer. The 16th was Tuesday.

Question. That was within how many miles of Winchester?

Answer. I think it was eight or ten miles.

Question. Proceed.

Answer. I think we left the next morning, the 17th, at 3 o'clock.

Question. What direction did you then take and where did you go?

Answer. We first received orders in the evening to be ready to march in the morning, without the line of march being indicated to us. And just before we moved we received orders to go to Smithfield, or Midway, as it is called, which is on the main turnpike road from Harper's Ferry to Winchester.

Question. How far did you go?

Answer. We went to Smithfield; and then, instead of going to Winchester, we made a retrograde movement to Charlestown. Then we knew we were going to Harper's Ferry.

Question. While you were at Smithfield you were threatening Winchester?

Answer. Yes, sir.

Question. And had you remained at Smithfield you still threatened Winchester, and would have held Johnston in check by that threatening position?

Answer. I think we should.

Question. But the moment you turned down towards Charlestown you ceased to threaten Winchester?

Answer. Entirely so. That developed the whole movement.

Question. That left Johnston to start off where he pleased?

Answer. Yes, sir; and he did start that same day.

Question. Can you tell why that march towards Charlestown was made?

Answer. No, sir; I cannot.

Question. This place of Bunker Hill, or this of Midway, was threatening Winchester?

Answer. Yes, sir; within a few hours' march of Winchester.

Question. According to the best information you could get, what was the force of Johnston in front of you at Winchester at that time?

Answer. I suppose he had a little over 20,000 men; anywhere from 20,000 to 25,000.

Question. You suppose your force was sufficient at any rate to hold him in check?

Answer. I have no doubt of that. And even if we had fought him and been beaten he would have been in no condition to have come down here.

Question. Did the officers on the staff understand, when you made that forward movement, that it was to threaten and hold Johnston in that position?

Answer. He supposed we were going to fight him immediately.

Question. Was the spirit of the troops such as to lead you to expect a favorable result?

Answer. Yes, sir; though I saw but little of them, except our own division. Four New York regiments went up under General Sanford to re-enforce General Patterson. I was then on General Sanford's staff. Two of those regiments, the 5th and 12th, were excellent regiments. The other two were volunteers, and one of them was an excellent regiment. The New York troops were in excellent spirits until after we made that retrograde movement towards Charlestown. They then got a little shaky and dissatisfied.

By Mr. Odell.

Question. Did not General Sanford join these four regiments with four or six other New York regiments there?

Answer. He had more than four regiments there. I think he had about 5,000 men. These four regiments I speak of went up with him from here.

Question. Did not General Sanford then, with these four regiments, with another portion of New York troops, some who had been under him, but were then with Patterson, and which were assigned to General Sanford on his coming there?

Answer. Yes, sir; I think so. There were some troops previously with Patterson which were assigned to General Sanford's command.

Question. Are you cognizant of the fact that General Sanford offered to fight Johnston with these New York troops alone, if General Patterson would support him?

Answer. No, sir. General Sanford has made such a remark to me. I do not know that he made the offer to General Patterson. I do not know what occurred between General Sanford and General Patterson.

Question. My recollection is that General Sanford said to me that he offered to fight Johnston, in whatever force he might be, with the New York regiments he had, if Patterson would support him.

Answer. General Sanford was anxious to go forward, I know.

By Mr. Chandler.

Question. You understood perfectly well when you turned off to Charlestown that you relieved Johnston's army?

Answer. Yes, sir.

By the chairman.

Question. Do you know that any reason was given for that movement?

Answer. No, sir. I never heard any explanation of it. We joined General Patterson on Wednesday morning, I think, and moved the following Monday.

By Mr. Chandler.

Question. Were you cognizant of the fact that General Patterson sent to the War Department for still further re-enforcements on or about the 20th or 21st of July, about the time of the battle of Bull Run?

Answer. No, sir; I do not know anything of General Patterson's intercourse with the department, or what his orders were.

Question. You were not absolutely upon his staff?

Answer. Not at all.

Question. You were upon General Sanford's staff?

Answer. Yes, sir.

Question. With the army under Patterson?

Answer. Yes, sir.

By Mr. Johnson:

Question. Was it understood by the officers of the division there that this battle of Bull Run was to be fought on any particular day, or at any particular time?

Answer. We supposed it was to be fought about that time, but did not know any particular day for it. We knew that it was threatening, and supposed that General Patterson's movement upon Johnston would be at the same time, and with the view of holding him in check. And when we turned off towards Charlestown I was under the impression, without knowing anything about it, that our object was attained, and that we had held him in check as long as it was necessary.

By the chairman:

Question. What prevented your destroying the railroad Johnston came down on?

Answer. It was below Winchester. We would have had first to have beaten him.

By Mr. Chandler:

Question. If you had beaten him, then you could have done it?

Answer. Yes, sir; we could then have come down on the very road he did. Even if we had fought him and been whipped, which I very much doubt, he could not have come down here. We would have given him such a fight that he would not have been in a condition to have come down to Manassas.

By Mr. Odell:

Question. When you arrived at Charlestown the soldiers were very much infuriated against Patterson, were they not?

Answer. Some of them expressed themselves very strongly against the movement. It did not grow into any difficulty that I am aware of.

Question. Did he not have to leave?

Answer. O! no, sir. Among some of the regiments—among those three New York regiments I spoke of, and some of the others—there was a strong feeling against him expressed; but it did not rise to anything like difficulty. One of the regiments, the eleventh Indiana, under Colonel Wallace, tendered their services ten days after their time had expired, so I was told at Charlestown. The first troops that wanted to go home were Pennsylvania troops.

By Mr. Chandler:

Answer. But as long as you were going forward towards the enemy nobody wanted to go home?

Answer. Not that I know of.

Question. All the dissatisfaction among the troops occurred after you turned back?

Answer. The first I heard was at Charlestown.

By Mr. Julian:

Question. What reason was given for turning down towards Charlestown?

Answer. I never heard of any. The commanding officer gives his orders, and never assigns any reasons.

By Mr. Chandler:

Question. And when the order was given to march at three o'clock in the morning you supposed you were to march on the enemy?

Answer. Yes, sir; I supposed so. I know that on the day I was at Bunker Hill I was out with a large party, clearing out a side-road leading towards Winchester.

General HENRY W. SLOCUM sworn and examined.

By Mr. Chandler:

Question. Were you in the battle of Bull Run?

Answer. Yes, sir.

Question. In what command?

Answer. I had a regiment there.

Question. What regiment?

Answer. The 27th New York regiment.

Question. To which division of the army were you attached?

Answer. To General Hunter's.

Question. Then you occupied the extreme right?

Answer. Yes, sir.

Question. The final attack made by Johnston's reserves was made upon your division, was it not?

Answer. Yes, sir; it was.

Question. Will you, very briefly, and as concisely as possible, describe the position of your force at that time, and for an hour and a half before the arrival of Johnston's reserves?

Answer. I was wounded at two o'clock, and taken off the field, about the time Johnston's forces came on it.

Question. Then you were not a witness to that attack?

Answer. No, sir; I was not a witness to the final rout of our army.

Question. When you were wounded and taken off the field was it your opinion that you had the advantage of the enemy?

Answer. Yes, sir.

Question. And you have not learned anything since to change your opinion of that?

Answer. No, sir. I supposed, when they took me to the hospital, that the day was ours.

By Mr. Johnson:

Question. What did you understand to be the amount of that last re-enforcement of Johnston's?

Answer. I have been informed that it was about 4,000 men.

By Mr. Chandler:

Question. Can you tell me how far Schenck's brigade was from your troops at that time?

Answer. No, sir; I cannot tell where it was.

Question. All you know about was the action of Hunter's division?

Answer. Yes, sir.

By Mr. Odell:

Question. You were in Hunter's division and rested at Centreville, did you not?

Answer. Yes, sir.

Question. Do you remember why it was you rested there an hour, or an hour and a half, on Sunday morning?

Answer. I never understood that. I understood that there was some confusion among the troops ahead of us. Somebody was in their way, I understood. It was a very unfortunate resting spell.

By Mr. Chandler :

Question. But for that you would have won the day ?
Answer. Yes, sir; I think so.

By Mr. Odell:

Question. It changed the position of the enemy entirely, did it not?
Answer. It gave them this time to bring up their re-enforcements and rout us. If we had been there an hour sooner we should have carried the day. I was wounded on their strongest position. The place where I was wounded was where they had their best batteries at the time we came on the field ; they had retired from that position, and left it entirely, and were probably a mile from us.

By Mr. Chandler :

Question. At the time you were wounded?
Answer. Yes, sir.
Question. And were in rout—retreating ?
Answer. Yes, sir.

By Mr. Odell :

Question. Your regiment was camped in this city, in the open square back of Willard's Hotel, for some time, was it not ?
Answer. Yes, sir.
Question. And you started from there the morning of the advance ?
Answer. Yes, sir.
Question. You crossed the Long Bridge ?
Answer. Yes, sir; and went down to join McDowell's column just below the Long Bridge, going out by Bailey's Cross Roads.
Question. You rested there once one night?
Answer. We rested the first night at Anandale.
Question. And proceeded the next morning ?
Answer. Yes, sir

WASHINGTON, *December* 31, 1861.

General CHARLES W. SANFORD sworn and examined.

By Mr. Odell :

Question. We want to know especially your relation to the Bull Run battle ; that was the object of the committee in sending for you ; you were here, were you not ?
Answer. I made a movement into Virginia on the 24th of May. I left, under the orders of General Scott, directed to me, at 2 o'clock in the morning, with about 11,000 men, and took possession of Arlington Heights and the whole of that region, down to Alexandria, inclusive.
Question. What position did you then hold ?
Answer. I was called into service as a major general of the State of New York immediately after the news of the attack on Fort Sumter, at the request of General Scott, and with the sanction of the governor of my own State. I sent off as rapidly as possible all the troops I could for the relief of Washington. I sent off in the first week from the city of New York about 8,000 men, commencing on the 19th of April; and I then continued engaged in the organization of other troops there until General Scott sent for me, and I came from New York here on the 20th of May, having, in the meantime, sent off from my own division in the city of New York about 10,000 men. When I arrived here

General Scott issued an order placing me in command of all the troops from the State of New York. My own division proper comprises only the troops in the city and county of New York and the county of Richmond, having command of about 10,000 uniformed troops, and enrolling about 90,000 ununiformed troops in the whole district. When I arrived here, there being no general officer from my State, and I being the senior major general in the State of New York, General Scott issued an order placing all the troops from the State of New York, as fast as they arrived, under my command; and I continued in that command until I was sent into Virginia. I crossed over the morning of the 24th of May, and took command of the troops ordered into Virginia. That morning I proceeded up to the railroad beyond Ball's Crossing, and cut the railroad in two places, capturing some persons who came down on the railroad, to prevent their carrying information; and from there I examined the whole country all the way down to Alexandria. I remained there getting additional troops over, forming such plans as I thought necessary for the fortification and occupation of that region, and getting ready to move, as I proposed to do, further down into Virginia, until the morning of the 28th of May, when the cabinet appointed General McDowell to take command of a new department, organized as the department of Virginia; and General McDowell being a junior officer to me, being appointed to that department, of course superseded my command over there. I returned to Washington and resumed my command of the New York troops there; they continued to increase so, that on the 4th of July, independent of all I had sent over to Virginia, I had still 23 regiments of New York troops in the city of Washington, which I forwarded that day.

On the 29th of June a council of war was held at the White House by the President and his cabinet, and all the senior officers on service here, to consider the propriety of an attack on the enemy's lines at Manassas. I made some objections to the plan of that battle, and among other things—I only mention this because it comes in with what I did afterwards—I objected that no movement of that kind should be made until it was ascertained that General Patterson was in such a position as to prevent the junction between General Johnston's army and the troops at Manassas; that that ought to precede any advance against the enemy at Manassas, if it was made at all.

On the 6th of July I was sent for by Governor Seward, who informed me that, although a great deal of dissatisfaction had existed respecting the movements of General Patterson, the cabinet had decided not to remove him; but General Scott suggested—to use Governor Seward's words—that although General Patterson did not seem to be disposed to fight, he was satisfied that I was otherwise disposed; and that he had recommended that if I would go up and waive rank to General Patterson, I being a senior major general to him, General Patterson would be glad to give me an opportunity to fight a battle and have the credit of a victory if I succeeded. Governor Seward said that General Scott was desirous I should waive rank to Patterson, and go there and take a command under him for the purpose of pushing forward the army, and doing what I suggested was a necessary step prior to the battle of Manassas. I told Governor Seward that I would do anything, if it was to serve as a volunteer in the ranks, to aid the cause. He wrote a letter to General Scott stating what was the result of the interview between us, and I delivered it to the general, and received his orders to go with such troops as I deemed necessary to aid General Patterson, and to assume a command under him.

I sent off that night the 19th and 28th New York regiments, and followed the next day with two more regiments, the two best I had here, the 5th and 12th New York city regiments. I went around by way of Harrisburg and Hagerstown, which was the only way then open. I left Hagerstown a little before sundown, marching all the night of the 9th of July with those two regiments from

Hagerstown to Williamsport, and was there by daylight the next morning. The other two regiments arrived there the day before.

I reported to General Patterson, and arranged with him to take command of a division, consisting of about 8,000 men, the most of them New York troops. I delivered orders from General Scott to General Patterson, and urged a forward movement as rapidly as possible. With the troops that I took on were some others that I had detailed to General Stone, who arrived immediately after my arrival at Hagerstown. General Patterson's army was increased to 22,000 men, of which I had under my own command 8,000, with two batteries.

We had some delay at Martinsburg, notwithstanding the urgency of our matter; but we left there on the 15th of July, and went in the direction of Winchester. General Patterson, with two of his divisions, went down on the Winchester turnpike in a straight line from Martinsburg towards Winchester, while I took the side roads, more easterly, so as to get into a direction to enable me to flank Johnston, keeping constantly in communication with Patterson through the intervening country. I moved down, in fact, in advance of his force until I arrived a little to the eastward of Bunker Hill, General Patterson holding Bunker Hill, which was a little village in the lower part of Berkley county.

We halted there on the afternoon of the 15th of July. On that same afternoon General Patterson came around with his staff to where I was engaged in locating my camp, sending out pickets, &c. I had a conversation with him on the subject of our moving forward. I was anxious, of course, to progress as rapidly as possible, for fear this movement of Johnston might take place before we arrived at his camp. I was then within about nine miles of Johnston's fortified camp at Winchester. Patterson was complimenting me upon the manner in which my regiments were located, and inquiring about my pickets, which I had informed him I had sent down about three miles to a stream below. I had driven out the enemy's skirmishers ahead of us. They had some cavalry there. In answer to his compliments about the comfortable location I had made, I said, "Very comfortable, general, when shall we move on?" This was in presence of part of my staff; Colonel Morell, now General Morell, was one, and Patterson's own staff. They were mounted and we were on foot. He hesitated a moment or two, and then said: "I don't know yet when we shall move. And if I did I would not tell my own father." I thought that was rather a queer sort of speech to make to me under the circumstances. But I smiled and said, "General, I am only anxious that we shall get forward, that the enemy shall not escape us." He replied, "There is no danger of that. I will have a reconnoissance to-morrow, and we will arrange about moving at a very early period." He then took his leave. The next day there was a reconnoissance on the Winchester turnpike, about four or five miles below the general's camp. He sent forward a section of artillery and some cavalry, and they found a post and leg fence across the Winchester turnpike, and some of the enemy's cavalry on the other side of it. They gave them a round of grape. The cavalry scattered off, and the reconnoissance returned. That was the only reconnoissance I heard of while we were there. My own pickets went further than that. But it was understood the next afternoon that we were to march forward at daylight. I sent down Colonel Morell with 40 men to open a road down to the Opequan creek, within five miles of the camp at Winchester, on the side roads I was upon, which would enable me in the course of three hours to get between Johnston and the Shenandoah river, and effectually bar his way to Manassas. I had my ammunition all distributed, and ordered my men to have 24 hours' rations in their haversacks, independent of their breakfast. We were to march at four o'clock the next morning. I had this road to the Opequan completed that night. I had then with me, in addition to my eight regiments, amounting to about 8,000 men and a few cavalry, Doubleday's heavy United States battery of 20 and 30 pounders, and a very good Rhode Island battery.

And I was willing to take the risk, whether General Patterson followed me up or not, of placing myself between Johnston and the Shenandoah river, rather than Johnston escape. And at four o'clock I should have moved over that road for that purpose, if I had had no further orders. But a little after 12 o'clock at night I received a long order of three pages from General Patterson, instructing me to move on to Charlestown, which is nearly at right angles to the road I was going to move on, and 22 miles from Winchester. This was after I had given my orders for the other movement.

By Mr. Chandler:

Question. What day was that?

Answer. It was at 12 o'clock on the night of the 16th of July. I received that order—which was the first intimation I had of any kind or sort that we were not going to move on to Winchester—with a peremptory order to move at three o'clock in the morning to Charlestown, which was nearly at right angles to the position I was then occupying in my route towards Winchester, and twenty-two miles from Winchester.

By the chairman:

Question. And that left Johnston free?

Answer. Yes, sir; left him free to make his escape, which he did. (Pointing to the map.) Here is Martinsburg. After crossing the Potomac we came down to Martinsburg and then moved from Martinsburg down to Bunker Hill. This Winchester turnpike, passing down here, brought General Patterson down in a straight line from Martinsburg to Bunker Hill. I pursued the side roads for the purpose of flanking Johnston, who was at Winchester, just below. This is the road (pointing to it on the map) leading down from Bunker Hill to Winchester. It is nearly a straight line from Martinsburg right down to Winchester. I was there; my camp lay right in here, (pointing to the place;) and the general was with his two divisions at the little village of Bunker Hill. I pursued those cross roads and had sent down and opened this road, (pointing to it,) which was an old and almost discontinued road, to a bridge which was here on the Opequan creek. The distance from my position to the bridge was about three and one half miles. I advanced a strong picket of some two hundred or three hundred men to keep the enemy from burning the bridge, and made the road fit for the artillery to travel over. I was then directed, by this order I have referred to, instead of moving in this direction, which would have enabled me to get between Johnston and the Shenandoah river, to move on this road (pointing it out) until I got upon the road which leads from Winchester to Charlestown. The distance between Charlestown and Winchester was twenty-two miles, while the distance from Bunker Hill was only nine miles.

Question. In what direction would Johnston have had to move to get by you?

Answer. Right out to the Shenandoah river, which he forded. He found out from his cavalry, who were watching us, that we were actually leaving, and he started at one o'clock that same day with eight thousand men, forded the Shenandoah where it was so deep that he ordered his men to put their cartridge boxes on their bayonets, got out on the Leesburg road, and went down to Manassas.

By Mr. Odell:

Question. Now, about your orders?

Answer. I was here, (referring to the map,) a little southeast of Bunker Hill, and General Patterson was at Bunker Hill. Originally my arrangement was to go down this way, (pointing.) That was my own arrangement with Patterson's consent. That was part of the understanding with which we started from Martinsburg. And I still supposed, up to 12 o'clock on the night of the 16th of July, that I was to go down this way or continue where I was, and he was to sustain me if I got into a fight. I had not the slightest idea that we were going to retrograde.

Question. Had you given out your orders?

Answer. My orders were out for the men to have all the ammunition distributed, and to have one day's provisions, exclusive of breakfast, in their haversacks, and to march at 4 o'clock in the morning. And Patterson knew that I had 400 men out at this bridge, on the road I had opened, yet I was ordered to move at 3 o'clock in another direction, which operated to let Johnston escape. I have never made these facts public at all. I have spoken among my very personal friends about it; and I reported immediately, as soon as I got back here, to General Scott, who was extremely indignant about the whole matter. I did not speak of it as freely as I have done, until this very strange publication of General Patterson the other day, which appeared to put the burden of the whole matter upon General Scott, when, in fact, it was all his own act.

By the chairman:

Question. Did he assign any reason for that movement?

Answer. I was, of course, very indignant about it, and so were all my officers and men, so much so that when subsequently, at Harper's Ferry, Patterson came by my camp there was a universal groan—against all discipline, of course, and we suppressed it as soon as possible. The excuse given by General Patterson was this: that he had received intelligence that he could rely upon, that General Johnston had been re-enforced by 20,000 men from Manassas, and was going to make an attack upon him; and in the order which I received that night—a long order of three pages—I was ordered to occupy all the communicating roads, turning off a regiment here, and two or three regiments there, and a battery at another place, to occupy all the roads from Winchester to the neighborhood of Charlestown, and all the cross-roads, and hold them all that day, until General Patterson's whole army went by me to Charlestown; and I sat seven hours in the saddle near a place called Smithfield, while Patterson, with his whole army, went by me on their way to Charlestown, he being apprehensive, as he said, of an attack from Johnston's forces.

By Mr. Odell:

Question. You covered his movement?

Answer. Yes, sir. Now the statement that he made, which came to me through Colonel Abercrombie, who was Patterson's brother-in-law, and commanded one division in that army was, that Johnston had been re-enforced, and General Fitz-John Porter reported the same thing to my officers. General Porter was then the chief of Patterson's staff, and was a very excellent officer, and an accomplished soldier. They all had got this story, which was without the slightest shadow of foundation; for there had not a single man arrived at the camp since we had got full information that their whole force consisted of 20,000 men, of whom 1,800 were sick with the measles. The story was, however, that they had ascertained by reliable information of this re-enforcement. Where they got their information I do not know. None such reached me, and I picked up deserters and other persons to get all the information I could; and we since have learned, as a matter of certainty, that Johnston's force never did exceed 20,000 men there. But the excuse Patterson gave was that Johnston had been re-enforced with 20,000 men from Manassas, and was going to attack him. That was the reason he gave then for this movement. But in this paper he has lately published he hints at another reason—another excuse, which was that it was by order of General Scott. Now, I know that the peremptory order of General Scott to General Patterson, repeated over and over again, was this— I was present on several occasions when telegraphic despatches went from General Scott to General Patterson: General Scott's orders to General Patterson were that, if he were strong enough he was to attack and beat Johnston. But if not, then he was to place himself in such a position as to keep Johnston employed and prevent him from making a junction with Beauregard at Manassas. That was the repeated direction of General Scott to General Patterson; and it was because of Patterson's hesitancy, and his hanging back, and keeping so far beyond the reach of Johnston's camp, that I was ordered to go up there and reenforce him, and assist him in any operations necessary to effect that object. The excuse of General Patterson now is that he had orders from General Scott to move to Charlestown. Now, that is not so. But this state of things existed: Before the movement was made from Martinsburg, General Patterson suggested to General Scott that Charlestown would be a better base of operations than Martinsburg, and suggested that he had better move on Charlestown, and from thence make his approaches to Winchester; that it would be better to do that than to move directly to Winchester from Martinsburg; and General Scott wrote back to say that if he found that movement a better one, he was at liberty to make it. But General Patterson had already commenced his movement on Winchester direct from Martinsburg, and had got as far as Bunker Hill; so that the movement, which he had formerly suggested, to Charlestown, was suppressed by his own act. But that is the pretence now given in his published speech for making the movement from Bunker Hill to Charlestown, which was a retreat, instead of the advance which the movement to Charlestown, he first proposed to General Scott was intended to be.

By Mr. Gooch:

Question. He was to go to Charlestown in order to get to Winchester; and he had already gone where he was nearer to Winchester and in a better position to reach it?

Answer. Yes, sir. In the first place he was within ten miles of Winchester, and on a direct line of turnpike from Martinsburg to Winchester; and I was in a position, on a side road, which enabled me to flank Johnston. Charlestown is twenty-two miles from Winchester.

By the chairman:

Question. Was not that change of direction and movement to Charlestown a total abandonment of the object which you were pursuing?

Answer. Entirely an abandonment of the main principles of the orders he was acting under.

Question. And, of course, an abandonment of the purpose for which you were there?

Answer. Yes, sir.

By Mr. Odell:

Question. Was it not your understanding in leaving here, and was it not the understanding, also, of General Scott, that your purpose in going there was to check Johnson with direct reference to the movement here?

Answer. Undoubtedly. It was in consequence of the suggestion made by me at the council at the President's house. And the cabinet had under discussion whether to remove Patterson or not, because General Scott was dissatisfied at his tardy movements, he not having got down to within anything like striking distance of Johnston's camp. But the Secretary of State explained to me that they had decided that it was not expedient, at that time, to remove General Patterson. And upon the suggestion of General Scott they wanted me to go up there and assist Patterson in this movement against Johnston, so as to carry out the point I had suggested of first checkmating Johnston before the movement against Manassas was made here.

By the chairman:

Question. You and Johnston had about the same forces there, had you not?

Answer. Patterson and myself had twenty-two thousand men, while Johnston had twenty thousand, with eighteen hundred of them sick.

Question. Would there have been any difficulty in preventing Johnston from going to Manassas?

Answer. None whatever.

By Mr. Chandler:

Question. Has there been any court-martial on this subject?

Answer. No, sir.

Question. Can you tell me the reason why there has not been?

Answer. I do not know, except this: General Patterson's term of service—being called out with the three months' men—expired on the 27th of July. In the meantime I was compelled to remain there, and these facts were not reported at Washington with the minuteness that I have stated them here now. The result of these operations were, of course, well known at Washington—the movement of Patterson to Charlestown, the escape of Johnston, and all that. An order came, just before the 27th of July, dismissing General Patterson and the other three months, men whose terms then expired. Among others, General Patterson was mentioned as being honorably discharged from the service. That was a few days after this movement, which took place on the morning of the 17th of July, and Patterson's term of service expired on the 27th of July. An order came from the adjutant general's office, the date of which I do not now recollect, discharging Patterson honorably from the service. That superseded the idea of a court-martial.

By the chairman:

Question. I have heard it suggested that he undertook to excuse this movement on the ground that the time of many of his troops had expired, and they refused to accompany him.

Answer. That, to my knowledge, is untrue. The time of none of them had expired when this movement was made. All the troops that were there were in the highest condition for the service. These three months' men, it may be well to state to you, who are not military men, were superior to any other volunteer troops that we had in point of discipline. They were the disciplined troops of the country. The three months' men were generally the organized troops of the different States—New York, Pennsylvania, &c. We had, for instance, from Patterson's own city, Philadelphia, one of the finest regiments in the service, which was turned over to me, at their own request; and the most of my regiments were disciplined and organized troops. They were all in a fine condition, anxious, zealous, and earnest for a fight. They thought they were going to attack Johnston's camp at Winchester. Although I had suggested to General Patterson that there was no necessity for that, the camp being admirably fortified with many of their heavy guns from Norfolk, I proposed to him to place ourselves between Johnston and the Shenandoah, which would have compelled him to fight us there or to remain in his camp, either of which would have effected General Scott's object. If I had got into a fight it was very easy over this road I had just been opening for Patterson to have re-enforced me and come up to the fight in time. The proposition was to place ourselves between Johnston's fortified camp and the Shenandoah, where his fortified camp would have been of no use to him.

Question. Even if you had received a check there, it would have prevented his junction with the forces at Manassas?

Answer. Yes, sir. I would have risked a battle with my own division rather than Johnston should have escaped. If he had attacked me I could have taken a position where I could have held it, while Patterson could have fallen upon him and repulsed him.

By Mr. Odell:

Question. Had you any such understanding with Patterson?

Answer. I told him I would move down on this side road in advance, leaving General Patterson to sustain me if I got into a fight. So, on the other hand, if he should attack Patterson, I was near enough to fall upon Johnston's flank and support Patterson. By using this communication of mine to pass Opequan creek—where I had informed Patterson I had already pushed forward my pickets, 200 men in the day and 400 at night, to prevent the enemy from burning the bridge—it would have enabled me to get between Johnston and the Shenandoah river. On the morning of our march to Charlestown, Stuart's cavalry, which figured so vigorously at Bull Run, was upon my flank all day. They were apparently about 800 strong. I saw them constantly on my flank for a number of miles. I could distinguish them with my glass with great ease. Finally, they came within about a mile of the line of march I was pursuing, and I sent a battery around to head them off, and the 12th regiment across the fields in double-quick time to take them in the rear. I thought I had got them hemmed in. But they broke down the fences, and went across the country to Winchester, and I saw nothing more of them. They were then about 8 miles from Winchester, and must have got there in the course of a couple of hours. That day at 1 o'clock—as was ascertained from those who saw him crossing the Shenandoah—Johnston started from Winchester with 8,000 men, forded the Shenandoah river, and got to Manassas on Friday night; and his second in command started the next day with all the rest of the available troops—something like 9,000 men, leaving only the sick, and a few to guard them in the camp at Winchester—and they arrived at the battle-field in the midst of the fight, got out of the cars, rushed on the battle-field, and turned the scale. I have no doubt that if we had intercepted Johnston, as we ought to have done, the battle of Bull Run would have been a victory for us instead of a defeat. Johnston was undoubtedly the ablest general they had in their army.

Question. I think I read in the speech that Patterson made in Philadelphia that he excused himself in part by saying that he telegraphed to General Scott for orders to move, and he did not get them?

Answer. That is not so. General Scott was anxious, and night after night kept telegraphing to Patterson to move forward. And night after night they were receiving despatches from Patterson excusing himself, that he had not transportation enough, or he had not troops enough, or something of that kind. And I was sent up with re-enforcements that he might be sure to have enough; with peremptory orders from General Scott if he was strong enough to fight Johnston, or if not to hold him in check. It was the intention to delay the battle here until after it was known that Johnston was checkmated.

Question. Did he receive any orders to move back?

Answer. He certainly did not. I had a conversation with General Scott in New York, and he was very much surprised to find on his return from Europe that Patterson should make such statements in his speech. Patterson's speech was made after General Scott left the country, and I suppose after Patterson thought General Scott had left it forever. Since General Scott's return I have had two conversations with him; one since I received this summons from you. I supposed it might have some reference to this matter, and I went on Sunday afternoon to see him, and had a conversation with him, and told him that I had been summoned here to Washington, and it probably had some reference to this affair of Patterson. General Scott was as much surprised as I was at Patterson's pretending that this movement was made by his order; General Scott having at all times pressed upon him simply these two things: to attack and defeat Johnston if he was strong enough, or, if not, so to move as to prevent Johnston getting to Manassas.

By Mr. Chandler:

Question. You spoke of a council of war being held late in June. What was the decision of that council as to the propriety of delivering a battle?

Answer. That council of war was to decide the question of an attack upon Manassas. At that council General McDowell presented his plan for an attack upon Manassas; and the question submitted to the President and his cabinet and the general officers present was as to the propriety of that movement. I was a little peculiarly situated in regard to the matter, because I had been superseded by General McDowell, a much younger officer than myself. And yet I deemed it my duty to say that I did not approve of the movement from my knowledge of the country and the state of things. But, if the movement was to be made, I objected to two points in the movement. The one was the marching 14 miles to win a battle, which I considered almost equivalent to a defeat itself; and secondly, that no such movement should be made until it was ascertained that Patterson was between Johnston and Manassas. On a subsequent day they had a meeting of the cabinet to decide upon the subject of Patterson's removal, which resulted in this request to me, to go up there and waive rank to him.

Question. And in that subsequent council of war it was decided to deliver the battle.

Answer. In the council of war on the 27th of June, General McDowell was authorized to make his arrangements for this battle, if he found every other thing concurred in making the movement. It was an unfortunate movement, in my opinion, in every point of view. In the first place, no such attack should have been made upon Manassas at all, because other means of dislodging them might have been attempted. In the second place, it was an unfortunate commencement of a battle to march 14 miles to begin it. It was a very exhausting march over such a country as I knew that to be, and it turned out to be a very great drawback to the troops.

Question. But had Patterson not marched you down to Charlestown, and you had held Johnston in check, have you any doubt of the favorable result of that battle?

Answer. No, sir; none at all. In the first place, it was not only the acquisition of those 8,000 troops that Johnston took down himself, but those that came in fresh on Sunday. And then they had the ablest man in the confederate army to manage that fight, and it was done with great adroitness and ability. I have no doubt at all that that battle was fought chiefly by Johnston, for he is a superior strategist to Beauregard.

Question. Your conclusion, then, is, as I understand you, that the battle was properly planned by General McDowell, and would have been a success had you attacked and whipped Johnston; that McDowell would have whipped Beauregard.

Answer. I have no doubt McDowell would have whipped Beauregard had Johnston been kept out of the field; although I do not believe in the plan of the battle.

By Mr. Odell:

Question. Did not General McDowell suffer a great deal from the character of the officers under him? Did not a great many incompetent ones resign immediately after that battle?

Answer. Yes, sir; but some good officers resigned as well as incompetent ones

Question. But the most of the resignations were of incompetent officers?

Answer. Yes, sir.

By Mr. Gooch:

Question. After the movement from Bunker Hill to Charlestown, did you have any conversation with General Patterson in relation to the matter; and if so, what explanation did he give of it at the time?

Answer. I had no conversation with him personally; I had with Colonel Abercrombie, his brother-in-law and one of his leading advisers. I was very much annoyed to see that the whole object of my going there was frustrated, and I sought no interview with General Patterson. But Colonel Abercrombie, understanding how much I was dissatisfied, came to me on purpose to explain the reason of this movement.

Question. Probably sent by Patterson?

Answer. Probably sent by Patterson. The explanation he made was that they had reliable information that Johnston was re-enforced with 20,000 men from Manassas, and was going to attack and destroy Patterson's army. Now, in the first place, he could not have done it if he had had the 20,000 men, because the country there was such that we could have resisted him. But I knew it to be untrue, and I think General Patterson knew it to be untrue. There had been a company of 120 men from the vicinity of Martinsburg pressed into the service of the rebels. I say this, because I saw the orders. They were brought to me by one of my pickets. The orders had been issued to the commanding officers to force these men out. They were forced out and went to Harper's Ferry, and were there at the time of its occupation by the rebels. Of these men, all but forty deserted on the march from Harper's Ferry to Winchester, or while at Winchester. We had a great many of them in and about Winchester while we were there. And all the information from those men, as well as from others coming in from time to time to our camp, satisfied General Patterson and satisfied me perfectly that Johnston's whole numbers could not exceed 20,000 men; and after we got to Bunker Hill, still some of these Martinsburg deserters came in repeating the same information. This was down to the very night before we moved that these men repeated the story that the numbers in the whole camp at Winchester did not exceed 20,000, and they generally estimated them from 18,000 to 19,000, and up to the evening of the day, when we marched the next morning at three o'clock, all the information concurred in that same statement, and we know now that it was so, and that Johnston did not receive any re-enforcements.

Question. Then at that time General Patterson relied for his vindication of his conduct in not going forward upon the fact that he had heard, or pretended that he had heard, that Johnston was re-enforced by 20,000 men, and was to attack him?

Answer. Yes, sir; that was the vindication set up for him by his brother-in-law, Colonel Abercrombie, and, as I understood, by Colonel Porter, the chief of his staff.

Question. Did General Patterson know at that time that it was the intention of General McDowell to attack Manassas?

Answer. Certainly he did. I carried him that information.

Question. On what day did you suppose that attack was to be made?

Answer. I supposed that, in pursuance to the suggestion I had made, they were waiting to hear from us that we were in position to prevent Johnston from joining Beauregard, and that that was the only cause of delay in making the attack. I expected that attack to be made the instant we satisfied them that we were in position. I did not believe, from the communication made to me by Governor Seward, and the reason for sending me up there, I did not suppose that General McDowell would make a movement until we had got into position to prevent Johnston from joining Beauregard. I went up there with the opinion that the attack would be made upon Manassas the moment it was ascertained that we were in a position to keep Johnston occupied.

Question. And when you communicated that fact to the authorities at Washington, then General McDowell would make the attack and not until then, and Patterson knew that?

Answer. He was so informed by me, and was so informed by a written communication from General Scott.

Question. Did you know that the army here was making a forward movement?

Answer. Yes, sir; we knew they were prepared to make that movement the instant it was certain that Johnston could not move on them. So that when this movement on Charlestown was made I thought it a direct dereliction of duty. Our movement was made on the morning of the 17th, and that same day at one o'clock Johnston crossed the Shenandoah river where I expected to have intercepted him.

Question. Our troops moved forward from the Potomac here on the 16th of July, I believe?

Answer. Yes, sir; the day before we commenced the march to Charlestown.

Question. How soon was General Scott or the authorities here at Washington advised of the movement on Charlestown? Do you know when that knowledge reached them?

Answer. I do not know. There was a communication constantly between General Patterson and General Scott, but they had to send some distance in order to reach the telegraph.

Question. In how short a time could General Patterson have communicated to General Scott the fact that he had moved on to Charlestown?

Answer. He could have communicated in twenty-four hours, by sending an express to the telegraph station on the other side of the Potomac.

Question. And that fact could have been known here three days before the battle?

Answer. Yes, sir. There is a gentleman here in Washington—Colonel Townsend, now, I believe, in the adjutant general's office—who was the chief of General Scott's staff at that time, and who knows all about the orders at that time. He has possession of all the communications that passed, so General Scott told me on Sunday last—all that passed between General Scott and General Patterson in relation to this matter; and I am authorized to say to him, and I shall make it my business to-day to say to him from General Scott, that the general is anxious that they should be known. General Scott, being now aware of General Patterson's statements, is willing that these facts should be known. I state this myself in vindication of General Scott, because I was present night after night when these communications were going on between General Scott and General Patterson, urging Patterson forward before I went up there to join him.

By Mr. Odell:

Question. Do you know of your own knowledge that it was a subject of discussion in the cabinet councils—the inefficiency of General Patterson and the propriety of his removal?

Answer. I do not know that his inefficiency was the subject of discussion; but the great delays he made in his movements in that part of Virginia were the subject of discussion.

By Mr. Gooch:

Question. That was something they could not understand?

Answer. Something that they could not understand the reason for. At one time he wanted more artillery; another time he wanted more means of transportation; and his movements were altogether so slow that it created a great deal of uneasiness here. Of course, being second in command, I made no com munication to the department here in relation to our movements up there until my return to this city. I had no right to do so before I came back here; and I must say that it appeared very strange to me that so important a change in our movements there should have been made without my being consulted at all upon the subject. But General Patterson chose to consult only his own staff, but none of the officers under his command.

By the chairman:

Question. You are an officer who has reflected a great deal on the condition of things here, and know the ground and the condition of affairs well. Now, we would like to have your opinion as to whether it would be proper for the army at this time of the year, and under all the circumstances, to make an advance or not, or whether it shall act on the defensive until the spring opens.

Answer. Perhaps I am not qualified at this moment to judge of that, because I am not informed as to the strength and position of the enemy at the present time on the other side of the Potomac. But no matter what their strength is, I would make certain movements which would materially affect the condition of the enemy, and perhaps lead to more serious operations. In the first place I have been very much annoyed and chagrined at the retreat of that part of our army that was occupying that portion of upper Virginia. They should never have left Harper's Ferry. It was one of the causes of my asking to be recalled to Washington. When Patterson was superseded, and General Banks came there, I sent a communication requesting to be recalled to Washington. I was not willing to serve under a general so much my junior as General Banks was, who was, at that time, entirely without any military knowledge at all, and because General Banks's first operations were to retreat out of Virginia, which I thought he ought not to do. The whole of the enemy at that time there was some thousand cavalry marauding around the country, while we had 12,000 men. But General Banks retreated out of Virginia, though I knew that General Scott could and would send forward re-enforcements there to enable us to move forward; and I think we should now undertake movements to occupy that part of Virginia, and effectually clear the route of the Baltimore and Ohio road. One consequence of our abandoning that part of Virginia, was their re-occupying the whole line of the Baltimore and Ohio railroad through that country, and the removal of a large quantity of iron to enable them to make good their connexions between Winchester and Manassas. That would have been all avoided if we had continued to occupy it. But, unfortunately, though a very excellent statesman and a man of talent, General Banks came there entirely a new man in his military duties, instead of there being some man of military experience sent there; and that part of the service has, consequently, been paralyzed.

Question. You would occupy Winchester and take possession of that railroad?

Answer. I would send troops, now, to occupy the whole of that upper part of Virginia, and Leesburg and Winchester, take possession of that turnpike, and effectually clear the whole of that part of Virginia through which the Baltimore and Ohio railroad runs.

Question. Would not that bring on a general battle?

Answer. If it did we would beat them effectually, because, to make a movement for a battle there, they would weaken their strength so much at Manassas as to make it impossible to maintain their lines before our large force opposite them here. In making such a movement as that which I should contemplate from the vicinity of Harper's Ferry and Point of Rocks, unquestionably we would be upon the *qui vive* here to see what movements were made by the enemy to meet our movements there. And that part of Virginia should be occupied, at all hazards, for another reason. There is a very large body of Union men in that part of Virginia. I discovered that while I was there, and if we

Part ii——5

had continued in possession of that part of Virginia, the whole of that part of the State would have been loyal this day, although there were a great many secessionists there. I was there within pistol-shot of the residence of Faulkner, and such men as he—leading secessionists. But a large portion of the inhabitants—pretty much all the people that remained at Martinsburg—were loyal, and when we went there they hailed us with acclamations and were glad to see us. I had invitations from all the leading people to come and dine and sup with them. They were well disposed towards us, and indignant at the immense injury done by the enemy to their property throughout all that part of the country.

Question. What, in your judgment, would be the effect of our taking possession of Winchester and that valley?

Answer. To cut off, effectually, all the supplies they now get from the valley of the Shenandoah.

Question. Where would they get their supplies then?

Answer. They undoubtedly are receiving some supplies from the neighborhood of Richmond, and I understand that cattle are sent up to them all the way from Louisiana, even; but they derive a very large portion of their supplies from the upper part of Virginia—from that valley, which is a rich one. I think the whole valley of the Shenandoah is as rich as the Genesee valley.

Question. Then, if we move a very strong force up towards Winchester, you think they would not come out and give us a general battle, with all their force, here?

Answer. Yes, sir; and we must make that movement so strong as to drive all their present force there before us, and watch their movements in this quarter, so as to be able to checkmate them if they undertake to make any important movement from here. General Banks's division could be increased so as to sweep that country with the utmost ease.

By Mr. Gooch:

Question. You mean that our whole right wing should be thrown across the river?

Answer. Yes, sir.

Question. Did you infer from what has transpired in relation to the movement at Ball's Bluff that such was the intention at that time?

Answer. I supposed at that time—not from any knowledge upon the subject, but from watching the operations that were going on—that when our folks crossed at Ball's Bluff the residue of General Banks's army was going down to Leesburg from the other direction, and that General Stone was ordered to cross there to support that movement. I could not see any other explanation of that movement. I am judging now only from what I see in the papers. I supposed that that movement was only a portion of just such a movement as I am now suggesting—that is, for General Banks to move across at Point of Rocks and so on down to Leesburg, and General Stone to meet General Banks at Leesburg. Where the fault is I do not know. General Stone I know to be a good soldier and a capital officer. He was under me for some length of time, and I urged, when I left for New York, that he should be put in command of our force along the Potomac; and I cannot imagine that General Stone made that movement unless he expected to be sustained by finding General Banks at Leesburg when he got there. Whether General Banks had such orders or not, of course I do not know.

WASHINGTON, *January* 3, 1862.

Major ABNER DOUBLEDAY called and examined.

By the chairman:

Question. What is your position in the army, your rank, &c.?

Answer. I am a major of the 17th infantry, one of the new regiments that has not yet been raised. I was promoted from the 1st artillery.

Question. Were you in Fort Sumter with the then Major Anderson?

Answer. Yes, sir.

Question. I wish to direct your attention to the time that you joined General Patterson. Will you please state how long you were with him, and what took place there? State it in your own way.

Answer. I started from New York harbor, and went to Chambersburg shortly after General Patterson went there. I suppose we were there a week or ten days.

By Mr. Odell:

Question. What force did you take with you?

Answer. I took two companies of artillery without their guns, armed only as infantry.

By the chairman:

Question. And joined General Patterson at Chambersburg?

Answer. Yes, sir; and he placed me in command of two more companies. Captain Dodge's company of regulars were ordered to join me, and McMullin's company of Philadelphia detectives were placed under my command also. We marched from Chambersburg to Hagerstown, and from there to Williamsport. We remained at Williamsport, I think, from two to three weeks. I was, during that time, ordered back to Washington with my command. I should state, first, that they sent for some heavy guns for me. They concluded they would send siege artillery to break down some of the intrenchments of the enemy, and they directed me to send an officer to New York for a heavy battery; and just before the battery joined me—when it was on its way, say at Harrisburg—I was ordered to proceed without delay to Washington with my command. I got as far as Little York, near Baltimore, when I received a despatch directing me to return with all possible haste and to mount the guns for action. This was while the army of General Patterson was lying at Hagerstown. I hired special trains and returned and resumed my encampment. When I got again to Hagerstown, I found that it was a false alarm. Shortly afterwards we marched to Williamsport, where our heavy guns were put in position on a high hill to command the ford. In the meantime, while I was absent, the troops had crossed into Virginia, had proceeded a few miles, and then been ordered precipitately to return to Williamsport. We entered Virginia a second time, by order of General Scott, I think, and marched to Martinsburg. Our advance encountered the enemy at a place called Falling Waters, or Hoge's Run. A smart little action took place there, resulting in the success of our troops.

By Mr. Odell:

Question. Just there. How did our troops behave themselves in that action?

Answer. They behaved very well, so far as I could see. I heard no charges made against them of misbehavior at that place.

The enemy retreated before us and encamped outside of Martinsburg, and we followed and took possession of Martinsburg. We remained there, it seems to me, some ten days. During this time it was reported that the enemy were in line of battle, seven miles from us, with a force nearly equal to our own. It was reported to us that they had 2,000 less than we had.

Question. At what point were they?

Answer. Seven miles from us on the road to Winchester; I think it was in front of Dorcasville. They remained there, I think, three or four days—it was so reported to me; referred to by our staff officers, &c. I think it had then been determined to make a depot at Martinsburg, and the orders had been given to that effect; but the orders were countermanded, and the army ordered to advance, some six days after the enemy had fallen back towards Winchester. In the interim I was ordered to send two guns back to Williamsport to guard the ford there in case of retreat or disaster. But the guns were ordered to return again, after they had been about an hour in position. When we advanced it was determined not to have a depot at Martinsburg, but to break it up and send the stores back to Williamsport, and around by the canal to Harper's Ferry. We advanced to a place called Bunker Hill, about half-way to Winchester, I think. We stayed there for a day—perhaps two days, I have forgotten which—and then we retrograded to Charlestown, some seven miles, I think, from Harper's Ferry.

By the chairman:

Question. What number of troops had you, and what number had the enemy while you were at Bunker Hill, before you went to Charlestown?

Answer. Well, I thought we had about 20,000. They did not give their numbers to me; the information all goes to the general, and the exact number of troops we have is not always known. But I heard them estimated at 20,000.

Question. What was the condition of the troops at that time?

Answer. They seemed as eager for action as men could be; excited in the highest degree at the idea of getting a fight.

Question. Where were the enemy at the time you were at Bunker Hill?

Answer. It was reported that they had fallen back to a place called Stevenson's Station, on the railroad, four miles from Winchester, and that they had fortified Winchester.

Question. How far was this Bunker Hill from Winchester?

Answer. I think it is about fifteen miles; from twelve to fifteen miles.

Question. Have you any knowledge of the force of the enemy; what were their numbers and strength?

Answer. We had various reports of them. The enemy were reported to have had some irregular levies in Winchester; to have sent and obtained some raw militia, badly armed, and almost all new men; so I understood. Most of our men were full of enthusiasm when we turned back to Charlestown, for they thought all the time that we were marching, that we were going to Winchester.

Question. Were you with General Sanford?

Answer. I was not under his command, but I saw a great deal of him. He was with us.

Question. He commanded the left of your army at that time, did he not?

Answer. Yes, sir; I think he did. But I do not know certain about that.

Question. Did he cut a road from this Bunker Hill, or near there, down some three or four miles to a creek?

Answer. I do not remember of his doing that. There was an old road there. We marched along an old road.

Question. He repaired it?

Answer. Yes, sir; he repaired it, I imagine.

Question. Was this before the battle of Bull Run, as it is called?

Answer. Yes, sir.

Question. How long before, as near as you can recollect?

Answer. But two or three days before. I think the enemy was said to have left Winchester the moment their scouts told them we had retrograded.

Question. General Johnston was commanding the army before you?

Answer. Yes, sir.

Question. What was the purpose of General Patterson there? What were the orders to him, or do you know?

Answer. I did not know what his object was. At one time, I suppose, it was to defend the Baltimore and Ohio railroad.

Question. Did you know at the time that he was acting in concert with General McDowell; he to prevent Johnston's going down to Manassas while McDowell was to encounter the enemy there?

Answer. I did not know it at the time. But I was satisfied, on hearing that the enemy had gone in that direction, that they were going to Manassas. When we were going to Charlestown it seemed to be the impression of our generals that the enemy was coming in our rear.

Question. Can you tell any object General Patterson had, or intended to accomplish, by going to Charlestown at that time?

Answer. Well, I do not know. I was not called into his council of war. I do not know what his object was.

Question. I will ask you if he, in your judgment, had the power, while at Bunker Hill, to pursue, encounter, and prevent Johnston from getting down to Manassas on that railroad, judging from the position that each occupied there?

Answer. I should think that his light troops could have engaged him. But I believe there was a difference of some twelve miles between them; and if Johnston had made a rush quickly, General Patterson might not have been able to stop him.

By Mr. Odell:

Question. To have overtaken him?

Answer. Yes, sir.

Question. Do you mean that if General Johnston had started off for Manassas quickly, General Patterson might not have been able to overtake him?

Answer. Yes, sir; that was what I meant. There were twelve miles between them.

Question. He might have reached Manassas?

Answer. Yes, sir.

By the chairman:

Question. Do you recollect the orders of General Patterson while waiting at Bunker Hill that night?

Answer. No, sir; but I thought that if we had had the time that we waited at Williamsport and Martinsburg we might have done very well.

Question. I will put a hypothetical case: Had General Patterson received orders to engage Johnston, and prevent his going down on that road, could he have accomplished it if he had directed his energies to accomplishing that purpose?

Answer. [Looking at the map.] I think I have got the distance between the two armies too far. I think he could have done that. I think if there had been a desire to do it, it could have been done.

Question. In turning off from Bunker Hill to Charlestown he must have abandoned the idea of intercepting Johnston?

Answer. Of course.

Question. And left him a free passage to go down to Manassas?

Answer. Yes, sir.

Question. That must have been known to the commanding general, of course?

Answer. Of course.

Question. Did you hear any reason given why that was not done; such as that the time of the troops were out, and they would not consent to remain and encounter Johnston?

Answer. I heard that their time was out, and that he could not induce them to stay unless he could assure them that he would attack the enemy.

By Mr. Odell:

Question. They would stay for a fight?

Answer. They would stay if he would guarantee them a fight.

By the chairman:

Question. They did not object that their time was out to prevent a fight?

Answer. He wanted them to stay, whether or no. But they were indignant about it, and did not feel like remaining there without a fight.

Question. Were there complaints among the troops that General Patterson had turned off, so as not to engage the enemy?

Answer. There was a great deal of surprise. But I was so busy with my own command that I did notice that much. It had been supposed that Harper's Ferry was a much better base of operations than Williamsport. It is nearer to Winchester, and nearer to our forces. It would have been a better point in every respect for us to occupy and move from. But in occupying it we found one objection, that it is almost impossible to retreat from it. There is but a little pathway along the canal, and one wagon could block an army.

By Mr. Gooch:

Question. You say that Johnston might perhaps have moved down towards Manassas so rapidly that Patterson would not have overtaken him. Suppose that he had done so, and Patterson had followed him down to Manassas, what would have been the effect upon the enemy?

Answer. Johnston would have gone by rail. General Patterson might have come up with him at the cars before they got their men and the munitions of war with him all on board.

Question. Were you not sufficiently near him to have intercepted him and engage him before he could have sent off his forces by rail?

Answer. I should think that by a forced march we could have done it.

Question. What is the distance from Winchester to Manassas?

Answer. I do not know. They marched by the Millwood road, and got on the cars at Oak Hill. That would seem to be about twenty-four miles from Winchester. Our movements indicated that we did not seem to know what Johnston had gone for. We were taking precautions to prevent him attacking us at Charlestown, where we had retrograded. It was supposed he was going in behind the mountain chain, and get in behind us there. I think an officer, one of the general's engineers, remarked that—gave that impression to me; indicating by our measures of self-defence against Johnston that the general did not know what his object was in going to the railroad.

By the chairman:

Question. Was it believed in the army that Johnston's forces were superior to those of Patterson?

Answer. Up to the time he occupied Winchester it was thought they were inferior. At that time it was said he had rallied some militia.

Question. That would not tend to strengthen him much, would it?

Answer. No, sir; I think not. It was represented that they were nearly all Union men. Berkley county gave some eight hundred majority for Union, even under secession bayonets.

By Mr. Odell:

Question. Did you hear anything about the condition of Johnston's army?

Answer Spies came in occasionally. It was stated that he had fortified Winchester.

By the chairman:

Question. If Patterson had received orders to encounter Johnston, and prevent him going to Manassas on the day of the battle there, could he, in your judgment, have prevented his going down there?

Answer. Well, I think it is a little doubtful. The enemy had a larger force of cavalry than we had. We could only have overtaken him with cavalry, with the start he had. If he had twelve miles the start he could have kept that much in advance. The only way to have compromised that was to have encountered him with our light troops and kept him engaged until the rest of our forces came up.

By Mr. Odell:

Question. You have corrected that statement, have you not, about the twelve miles distance?

Answer. Yes, sir; he was nearer than twelve miles if he was at Stevenson's Station. He was about eight miles from us. I think the main body was about eight miles from us. The main bodies of the two armies were about eight miles apart, as near as I can judge.

Question. And the advance was nearer?

Answer. The advance might have been nearer.

Question. Within about how near do you suppose the advance was, that is, Sanford's column?

Answer. I do not know that he was far in advance of the army at that time. His advance party might have been nearer. Under those orders, if those were the orders, a battle ought to have been attempted certainly.

By Mr. Gooch:

Question. Johnston was fortified at Winchester?

Answer. Yes, sir; it was said he was fortified there.

Question. Do you know whether or not he made any forward movement from Winchester until after you had made a retrograde movement towards Charlestown?

Answer. I only heard at the time from deserters that the moment he found that we had retrograded—that his light cavalry sent him word to that effect—he immediately left in all haste for Millwood.

Question. Was it not your opinion as a military man, from all you learned, that Johnston intended to remain at Winchester within his fortifications until after your army had moved towards Charlestown?

Answer. Well, I do not know what his intentions were. He was at Stevenson's Station.

Question. From what was done, what do you infer he intended to do?

Answer. I understood he had orders to prevent us at all hazards from joining McDowell. That is what I heard from some deserter, or a report of what some deserter had stated.

By Mr. Chandler:

Question. That is, you were both engaged in the same business, each to prevent the other from joining the main army?

Answer. Yes, sir. If necessary for that purpose he would take up a station until he was certain he could get on the railroad. He could afford to leave us rambling around through Virginia there, if in that brief period he could have gained the battle here. He could afford to let us make an inroad into the country for a brief period if he could have gained that.

Question. If you could have got in advance of Johnston, between his position and the railroad, could he have reached Manassas?

Answer. No, sir; I think we could have prevented it. I think that General

Stone, while at Point of Rocks, wanted to make a dash at the railroad and destroy it.

By the chairman:

Question. What was the difficulty in the way of breaking up that road?

Answer. Where we were, we were some distance from it. General Stone had been in command of a force at Point of Rocks. He told me he could very easily have made a forced march and destroyed the bridges, and he wanted to do it, but he received the most pressing orders to join Patterson at once. The Point of Rocks is where the railroad comes down to the Potomac. That is about half-way between Washington and Williamsport. By making a secret march half-way with his infantry, and then making a dash with his cavalry. General Stone told me he was very desirous of breaking up that road, and could have done it; but he received the most peremptory orders to join General Patterson without a moment's delay—a most urgent demand.

By Mr. Gooch:

Question. From whom did he receive those orders?

Answer. From General Patterson.

Question. Did you remain in the army after General Banks took command of that division of the army?

Answer. Yes, sir.

Question. Where were you when General Banks took the command?

Answer. At Harper's Ferry.

Question. Why did you retire from Harper's Ferry? Why did you leave it?

Answer. The reason given was that while there we were in a *cul-de-sac*. In case of an attack and a disaster the force could not retreat from Harper'sFerry; it would have had to stay there; there was no way to leave. And it was thought better to go on the other side and occupy Maryland Heights, which commanded Harper's Ferry, so that we could have crossed any time we chose. It was still an occupation of Harper's Ferry, but a change of position and of encampment.

Question. In your judgment, as a military man, was that a judicious movement—a wise movement?

Answer. I thought it was a discouraging movement; but I did not see any better way of occupying and holding Harper's Ferry than that—holding it from the Maryland side, rather than on the other side.

Question. So that you do approve the movement?

Answer. Yes, sir; I thought we could hold it from the Maryland side, and have all the advantages of it.

Question. How long did you remain at Charlestown before going to Harper's Ferry?

Answer. Some four or five days, I think.

Question. The army moved to Harper's Ferry under General Patterson?

Answer. Yes, sir.

Question. What was the number of that division at the time General Banks took command?

Answer. I think about 15,000. However, I do not know as to that. I think the number was greatly reduced by many being sent off. I think the loss of those two or three weeks at Williamsport, and eight or ten days at Martinsburg, had a very decided effect upon us. We should have marched on Winchester, I think. We would have had three weeks longer time with these three-months' men.

By Mr. Odell:

Question. Was your force there a well-appointed one?

Answer. I think we had all the necessaries. They complained of a deficiency of transportation from Williamsport, I think.

By Mr. Gooch:

Question. Was there such a deficiency as to prevent a movement of the army?

Answer. I do not know how much the deficiency was, or how far it extended. But I heard complaints that there was not a sufficient number of wagons. The whole country seemed to be full of them, if we had the power of purchasing, or of pressing them into service.

WASHINGTON, *January* 5, 1862.

General CHARLES P. STONE sworn and examined.

By Mr. Chandler:

Question. Were you present with General Patterson's army, or near it, on or about the 20th of July last?

Answer. I was.

Question. Were you with him on his march from Martinsburg?

Answer. Yes, sir.

Question. In what capacity?

Answer. I commanded a brigade in that column for a part of the month of July.

Question. And you were with that column when it marched towards Johnston's army?

Answer. Yes, sir.

Question. Will you explain to the committee the march and position of that column until it reached Bunker Hill? Explain it concisely, if you please.

Answer. Bunker Hill is on the road to Winchester. General Patterson's column was concentrated at Martinsburg.

Question. And Johnston was at Winchester?

Answer. Supposed to be at Winchester.

Question. Give the date on which you started, and how far you went; explain the action of that column, not in detail, but in general.

Answer. So much has happened between that time and this that it is difficult for me to remember all the dates. We arrived at Harper's Ferry on the 21st of July, the day of the battle of Bull Run.

Question. That is, on your retreat.

Answer. On our return.

Question. Assume that it was Tuesday or Wednesday when you left Bunker Hill.

Answer. Without giving the date of leaving Martinsburg, we made a march in one day as far as Mill Creek, or, as I believe it is now called, Bunker Hill. We remained there, I think, over one day. I remember being one day there. Then we moved in one day's march from Bunker Hill, through Middleway, otherwise called Smithfield, to Charlestown. I think we arrived at Charlestown on Wednesday afternoon, and then remained there until the following Sunday, when we marched to Bolivar Heights.

Question. When you were at Martinsburg you were threatening Johnston's force at Winchester, were you not?

Answer. I should think so.

Question. And when you reached Bunker Hill you threatened it still more?

Answer. I think so.

Question. Had you intrenched and remained at Bunker Hill, would not your close proximity have prevented Johnston from weakening his force at Winchester?

Answer. I do not think it would; I think it was so important a move for him to come down to Manassas that he would have abandoned every house and woman and child in Winchester for the sake of joining the other column.

Question. Could you not then have pursued him—you were within seven or eight miles—and compelled him to give battle before he struck the railroad?

Answer. I think so.

Question. Or, if General Patterson had thrown his force down between Johnston and the railroad, he would then have had to come out and give you battle, or else remain where he was?

Answer. If that had been done, yes, sir.

Question. Did you consider his force so strong that it was unsafe to retain your position at Bunker Hill, or take up that position between him and the railroad?

Answer. I certainly did not conceive that his force was so strong as to make it unsafe for us to intrench at Bunker Hill?

By the chairman:

Question. Do you know the reason why Patterson turned off from Bunker Hill to Charlestown?

Answer. At the time I supposed the object was to get on Johnston's right flank.

By Mr. Chandler:

Question. But he actually went twenty odd miles from his right or left flank?

Answer. Yes, sir.

Question. Leaving the road perfectly open to go where he saw fit?

Answer. Yes, sir; I think so.

Question. Was it in contemplation by you at one time to have gone out and cut that railroad?

The witness: From the place below, before I came under General Patterson's command?

Mr. Chandler: Yes, sir.

Answer. I wanted to do it.

Question. And had you done it, it would have been impossible for Johnston to have got his forces down here, would it not?

Answer. Yes, sir.

Question. Did you receive peremptory orders from General Patterson to join him at once?

Answer. I did.

Question. Do you know when, or if at all, General Patterson sent a request to Washington to have re-enforcements sent up to him?

Answer. I do not know.

By the chairman:

Question. I wish to know of you, as a military man, whether, if it had been the object and purpose of Patterson to encounter Johnston and prevent him from going down to Manassas on that road, you think he could have employed him so as to have had a battle with him? Was the position such that he could have forced him to an engagement?

Answer. I think he could have forced him to give battle.

Question. I mean if he had been ordered to prevent Johnston from going to Manassas. He was in a position to have done that by an engagement, was he not? You know the position of the two armies when you approached the nearest, when you turned off to Charlestown.

Answer. I think he was in a position at one time when he might either have brought Johnston to battle, or have joined General McDowell about as soon as Johnston could have joined the other side.

Question. What position was that when you suppose it was in his power to have effected that?

Answer. At Martinsburg.

By Mr. Chandler:

Question. Was he not in the same position at Bunker Hill?

Answer. I think he might have made a move there; but that is only a military opinion.

By the chairman:

Question. That is all we want.

Answer. I think he might have moved then, so as to have taken possession of the gaps of the Blue Ridge at least.

By Mr. Chandler:

Question. And had he taken possession of the gaps of the Blue Ridge, it would have been very difficult for Johnston to have dislodged him, would it not?

Answer. I think so; I thought so then.

By Mr. Odell:

Question. Did you understand, while you were there, that the object of Patterson's division was to hold Johnston in check, and prevent him from joining Beauregard? We know from testimony that we have here that that was the object. I want to know if it was known to you while there?

Answer. Let me get your question exactly.

Question. The question is this: Was it your understanding that Patterson's division of the army was to hold Johnston there, while General McDowell was engaged with Beauregard here?

Answer. I certainly thought that was the intention.

By Mr. Chandler·

Question. What was your estimate of the relative strength of Patterson's and Johnston's forces?

Answer. The best information I got of Johnston's forces was that he had about 14,000 in the neighborhood of Harper's Ferry. That was when I was on the river below.

Question. I mean when you were at Martinsburg and he was at Winchester?

Answer. I had lost there my independent means of getting information of him. The information I received there was through the reconnoissances ordered by General Patterson. That was very varied, indeed. Sometimes you would hear that he had 15,000, sometimes 22,000, sometimes 30,000.

Question. What was your own estimate, if you had any, of their force?

Answer. I imagined that he had not far from 20,000 men, including his militia.

Question. And your force was about 22,000. Was it not?

Answer. I do not know what General Patterson's force was. I heard various estimates of that.

WASHINGTON, *January* 6, 1862.

General LOUIS BLENKER sworn and examined.

By the chairman:

Question. Were you at the Bull Run fight?

Answer. Not a great fighter, but I did what I could. I was present from the first until the last hour.

Question. To what do you attribute the defeat of that day particularly?

Answer. My idea is that the general-in-chief, General McDowell—an honorable officer, a very well-educated officer—at that time had not prepared enough his staff officers, and all the other plans were spoiled by the baggage wagons which he had ordered to be there not coming as he ordered. The whole trouble was in going in so risky a way that any general—even the greatest in the world—would be beaten that day, if the enemy was strongest. But the ememy were losing a great deal more than we. They were retreating. But still I do not think it is a blame for anybody to lose that battle. It was a panic, all at once. There was a panic which nobody can explain. The colonels there, a great many of them, never have a command. They look around and say: What shall we do? That is strange music—the bullet—and strange feeling to be killed. But what to do is the question. They are running. Some begin to retreat, and it is not possible to give orders to keep them together. If one regiment runs, the others go too. That has been the case in every army—French army, Austrian army, and every good army in the world. I would not blame any officer for that. The regiment I had three times ordered, was ordered to retreat; and then I see I can do a little more if I stay. And then I think I advance two miles further against the enemy. I see the spirit was good in my troops. I see a great deal there that I shall never forget in my life. It is the most interesting matter for me, indeed, in my military experience—that battle. I never had a chance to study a great deal. I am only a brigade officer, but if the moment comes I know what to do. The enemy only risk a little attack of cavalry, and if that was a good attack they would go further. But General McDowell, he was so much hurt that I feel the greatest sympathy for him to-day. I would not allow anybody to blame him to-day. He was not assisted enough. I was, in the evening, at the council where the plan was discussed. Of course Colonel Miles was in the best spirits with him, and he said: "We have but little anxiety to be in the reserve." But the general said: "Colonel, you can be sure there is great danger if we do not have that reserve there, and so we make our preparations." The next day they fight; and the orderly came with the message that the battle is lost. There were a great many around me, and it would have curious effect. They asked: "What is the matter?" I said, we are victorious. And they hurra. At once I make my preparation for an advance. After one mile we pass the troops retreating. My troops said: "What the devil is that?" I said, it is a mistake; go on. Not even my adjutant understand what I want. So I went to the front, and we make a good effect, because the enemy could see us. That was all I wanted at that time. I never expected to see anything else. I do not speak good enough English to express myself. But if the time comes I hope I may make good the honor conferred upon me.

Question. You understood, I suppose, at that time, the position of Patterson and Johnston to be about Winchester?

Answer. Yes, sir.

Question. Was it understood by you on the field that Patterson was to engage Johnston, or to prevent his going down to that battle?

Answer. I am very much informed now, because I had a conversation with General Sanford, who was with General Patterson's division.

Question. What did you understand about the matter on that day?

Answer. I knew it just the same as General Sanford told me from what I have seen in the papers.

Question. What I mean is, not what General Sanford or the papers have said, but what was the understanding on the battle-field when you had the council?

Answer. The understanding was that Johnston was to be kept back there; there is no doubt that is so, and every one who knows anything about the operations would know that Johnston should never have had the chance to come to Manassas.

Question. Had Patterson held Johnston back, what would have been the result at Manassas?

Answer. There is no doubt we should have taken Manassas, because they were so much knocked down that they were just ready in a moment to retreat; both parties retreated. And because we are not a despotic educated army, we are here a peaceful nation, and we could not do better at first; but we will repair that the next time.

By Mr. Gooch:

Question. Your division was stationed at Centreville?

Answer. My brigade was, under the division of Colonel Miles.

Question. Was that a reserve stationed at Centreville, because it was necessary that that point should be protected?

Answer. It was both. It was stationed there as a reserve for the army engaged in the battle, and at the same time we made our position stronger, so that we should not be flanked by the right wing of the enemy. First, we were to be in reserve ready, for if we were not there they would come straight down to Alexandria and Washington.

Question. You would not have considered it a good plan for the commander-in-chief not to have left any force at Centreville on that day?

Answer. No commander-in-chief would do that.

Question. That was a point it was necessary to protect?

Answer. Necessary for all eventualities, and for all circumstances; that was the point.

Question. That force was only to be moved forward from that point in case it should be absolutely necessary to support the army already on the field?

Answer. Exactly; it was a reserve to be ready if they were called on, or be careful that no enemy should flank us; that is a disposition which must be taken under such circumstances.

By the chairman:

Question. We have had some testimony in relation to the condition of Colonel Miles that day, and I deem it but justice to him, as you were there and must know his condition, to ask you what was the condition of Colonel Miles that day, whether he was intoxicated at all, or partially so, or not?

Answer. I will tell you as a man of honor. Every word I say is truth and fact. I was with him the whole day till about two or three o'clock. There was nothing like intoxication. He took, once in awhile, a drop. Never mind, that is nothing. I never saw him intoxicated. From that time he was out observing. When I received that message that the battle was lost, I was the first man who sent an officer of the general staff to report to Washington, and I told him I would go right away with my brigade. He took my hand and said: "Go and die on the ground." I go then. The whole question about his intoxication was in the evening about five or six or seven o'clock. I did not see him then; but if I had seen him I would just as soon say he was drunk as to say he was not.

Question. Then I understand you to say that you saw him during the day down to three o'clock?

Answer. Yes, sir; and then he was in a fit condition to give every order as an officer, when I saw him last.

Question. What time was that?

Answer. Between three and four o'clock, or a little earlier, perhaps.

WASHINGTON, *January* 6, 1862.

General ROBERT PATTERSON sworn and examined.

By the chairman :

Question. Please state in as brief a manner as you can conveniently the connexion that you have had with the present war. State it in your own way without questioning at first. Give us a narrative as brief as you can properly and conveniently make it.

Answer. If any testimony has been given that affects the management of my column, I would like to have it read before I begin. I believe it is customary to have that done.

Question. We are not impeaching the conduct of any man. We are merely endeavoring to get all the light we can upon the conduct of the war. We take every man's narrative of it, which we endeavor to keep secret, and which we request the witness to keep secret, for the present at least.

Answer. My only object is to answer anything that has been said.

Question. That would be best answered by a plain statement of the facts of the case. I will state that our purpose is not to impeach any man in any connexion he may have had with the war. What Congress expects of us, their committee, is to obtain such facts as we suppose will be useful in throwing light upon the military operations of the army, in order to apply any remedy that may be necessary. I perceive, by the documents that you have before you, that you are about entering upon what is probably a very minute narration; that might be necessary if you were accused—it might then be very proper. But we have no such object in view.

Answer. It is scarcely possible for me to give you in fewer words than I have got here the operations of the army under my command.

After some conversation in relation to the order of proceeding, on motion of Mr. Johnson the witness was allowed to pursue his own way of replying to the interrogatory of the chairman.

The witness accordingly proceeded as follows :

By general orders No. 3, from the headquarters of the army, dated 19th April, 1861, [App. No. 1,] I was appointed to the command of the department of Washington, consisting of the States of Pennsylvania, Delaware, Maryland, and the District of Columbia. Until the early part of June I was actively engaged in organizing, equipping, and forwarding regiments to Washington, Annapolis, and Baltimore, and in opening, occupying, and defending the lines of communication with the capital. I was then permitted to turn my attention to the organization of the column destined to retake Harper's Ferry. The impression has been permitted to go forth from this city, and has been most extensively circulated elsewhere, that I had not obeyed orders. I have with me, and will place in your possession, documents to prove that I did all that I was ordered to do, and more than any one had a right to expect, under the circumstances in which I and my command were placed. And I defy any man, high or low, to put his finger on an order disobeyed, or even a practicable suggestion that was not carried out. My column was well conducted; there was not a false step made, nor a blunder committed. The skirmishers were always in front, and our flanks were well protected ; we were caught in no trap, and fell in no ambush. My command repeatedly offered the enemy battle, and when they accepted it in the open field we beat them ; there was no defeat and no retreat with my column.

The facts in the case would have been made known immediately after I was relieved at Harper's Ferry in July, but the publication of the documents at that time would have been most detrimental to the public interest. Some two months ago I supposed an investigation could be made without injury; and on the 1st of November I complained to the War Department of the injustice done me, and asked for a court of inquiry, or permission to publish the correspondence between the general-in-chief and myself, and of his orders to me. On the 3d of November the Assistant Secretary of War, Hon. T. A. Scott, acknowledged the receipt of my application. On the 26th of November I respectfully asked the attention of the Hon. Secretary of War to my letter; and on the 30th the Secretary replied, declining, for reasons assigned in his letter, to appoint a court of inquiry.—(Appendix No. 2.) I then requested Hon. John Sherman, senator of the United States from Ohio, who had done me the honor to serve on my staff as aide-de-camp, to offer a resolution, calling for all the correspondence and the orders. The distinguished senator did so; it passed unanimously. The Secretary of War has declined to publish the papers, as it would be incompatible with the public interests. I furnish herewith a copy of the resolution offered at my request by Senator Sherman, and the reply of the Hon. Secretary.—(Appendix No. 3.) On the 3d of June I took command at Chambersburg. On the 4th of June I was informed by the general-in-chief that he considered the addition to my force of a battery of artillery and some regular infantry indispensable. In this opinion I cordially concurred.—(Appendix No. 4.) On the 8th of June the general-in-chief sent my letter of general instructions.—(Appendix No. 5.) In this I am told, "there must be no reverse. But this is not enough. A check or a drawn battle would be a victory to the enemy, filling his heart with joy, his ranks with men, and his magazines with voluntary contributions. Take your measures, therefore, circumspectly; make a good use of your engineers and other experienced staff officers and generals, and attempt nothing without a clear prospect of success." This was good instruction and most sensible advice; good or bad I was to obey, and I did so.

On the 13th of June the general-in-chief sent me two communications.—(Appendix Nos. 6 and 7.) In one I was informed "that Ben McCullough had two regiments of sharpshooters coming from Texas, and that he was now on the spot preparing to meet my column, and then to fall back to Harper's Ferry." In the other I was told "that, on the supposition I would cross the river Monday or Tuesday next, Brigadier General McDowell would be instructed to make a demonstration from Alexandria in the direction of Manassas Junction one or two days before."

I know not what induced this supposition. On the seventh I had written to General Scott, (Appendix No. 8,) "that I desired in a few days to occupy the roads beyond Hagerstown and to establish my headquarters in that town, and to intrench my left flank on the Boonsboro' road, placing there the force with which I can threaten the Maryland Heights, and, should a favorable occasion offer, storm them."

I was therefore surprised at the suggestion, as I had said nothing about crossing the river, and had neither men nor guns sufficient for the purpose. But knowing and appreciating the great experience, skill, and sagacity of my commander, I promptly adopted measures to carry it out.

On the fifteenth I reached Hagerstown, and on the 16th two-thirds of my forces had crossed the Potomac. The promised demonstration by General McDowell in the direction of Manassas Junction was not made. On the same day, only three days after I had been told I was expected to cross, and when a large portion of my command had crossed, I received three telegrams from the general-in-chief.—(Appendix Nos. 9, 10, and 11.) The first says: "Send to me at once all the regular troops, horse and foot, with you, and the Rhode Island regiment." The second says: "You are strong enough without the regulars with you—are most needed here; send them and the Rhode Island regiment as fast as disengaged. Keep within the above limits until you can satisfy me you ought to go beyond them." The third is as follows: "You tell me you arrived last night at Hagerstown, and McClellan writes you are checked at Harper's Ferry. Where are you?" On the twelfth I had informed the general (Appendix No 12) that "I regretted my command was not in condition and sufficiently strong in facing a powerful foe to detach at present a force towards Cumberland," and "respectfully suggested that two regiments at least, if they could be devoted to that purpose, be designated to protect the road in the rear and permit Colonel Wallace to approach."

In a letter dated 16th June (Appendix, No. 13) I informed the general that "to-day and to-morrow about 9,000 men cross to Virginia," and submitted my desire, "first, to transfer to Harper's Ferry my base of operations, depots, headquarters, &c.; second, to open and maintain free communication, east and west, along the Baltimore and Ohio Railroad; third, to hold at Harper's Ferry, Martinsburg, and Charlestown a strong force, gradually and securely advancing as they are prepared, portions towards Winchester, &c.; fourth, to re-enforce Cumberland and move north to Romney, Morehead, &c., and operate with the column in the third proposition towards Woodstock, and cut off all communications with the west. We will thus force the enemy to retire, and recover, without a struggle, a conquered country," &c. I also added that, "if I am permitted to carry out this plan, the Baltimore and Ohio railroad and the canal will be in operation in a week, and a free line of communication to St. Louis be established."

On the 17th the general-in-chief telegraphed me, (Appendix No. 14:) "We are pressed here; send the troops that I have twice called for without delay." This was imperative, and the troops were sent, leaving me without a single piece of artillery, the enemy having over twenty guns, and for the time but a single troop of cavalry, not in service over a month—the enemy with a full regiment of cavalry—and with not 10,000 infantry, all raw, the enemy having 15,000 trained infantry. It was a gloomy day and night. But I succeeded in getting my forces over the river again with the loss of only one man.

I refrain from making any comments on these extraordinary orders, except to say that I was mortified and humiliated at having to recross the river without striking a blow. I knew that my reputation would be seriously damaged by it; the country could not understand or comprehend the meaning of the crossing and recrossing, the marching and countermarching, and that I would be censured without stint for such apparent vacillation and want of purpose. But I loved and honored my commander; I had served under him before, and had never suffered a personal feeling or interest to interfere with my loyalty and duty to him and my country. I knew that he trusted me, and I trusted him, confident that in his own time and in his own way he would put me right before the army and country. Meanwhile I would bear the odium unjustly cast upon me, and not throw it on others.

On the 20th of June the general-in-chief asked me, (Appendix No. 15,) "without delay to propose to him a plan of operations." On the 21st I gave him one, (Appendix No. 16,) proposing, "first, to occupy the Maryland Heights with a brigade, (2,100 men,) fortify and arm with Doubleday's artillery, provision for twenty days, to secure against investment; second, to move all supplies to Frederick, and immediately thereafter abandon this line of operations, threatening with a force to open a route through Harper's Ferry, this force to be the sustaining one for the command on Maryland Heights; third, to send everything else available, horse, foot, and artillery, to cross the Potomac near the Point of Rocks, and unite with Colonel Stone at Leesburg; from that point I can operate as circumstances demand and your orders require."

Had this plan been adopted, the army of General McDowell and my own would have been precisely where they ought to have been. I would have been in a position to have aided General McDowell; to have taken and torn up, if I could not have held, a portion of "the railroad leading from Manassas to the valley of Virginia." This would not only have destroyed "the communications between the forces under Beauregard and those under Johnston," but it would have prevented either from throwing large re-enforcements to the other when assailed. And if I could not prevent Johnston from joining Beauregard, which I certainly could not do while stationed anywhere between Williamsport and Winchester, I could have joined McDowell in the attack on Manassas, and assailed and turned the enemy's left. Had my suggestions been adopted, the battle of Bull Run might have been a victory instead of a defeat.

On the 23d of June I informed the general-in-chief (App. No. 17) that deserters "were coming in daily, and all agreed in saying that the whole of the force originally at Harper's Ferry, said to be 25,000 men, is still between Williamsport and Winchester;" that the advance of the enemy was approaching Falling Waters, the remainder in a semicircle, all within four hours of the advance. I added, "that this force might soon annoy me; if so, I would not avoid the contest they may invite."

On the 25th I was directed (App. No. 18) to "remain in front of the enemy while he continued in force between Winchester and the Potomac; if his superior or equal in force, I might cross and offer him battle." On the 27th General Scott informed me (App. No. 19) that "he had expected I was crossing the river that day in pursuit of the enemy." What could have induced this expectation it would have been difficult to imagine. On the 4th of June the general-in-chief had told me that "a battery of artillery and some regular infantry to be added to my force was indispensable," and both had been taken away. On the 8th of June he had told me I must "attempt nothing without a clear prospect of success." And on the 16th he had told me to "keep within the above limits until I could satisfy the general-in-chief that I ought to go beyond them." It is true Major Doubleday had three siege guns, movable only in favorable ground, and that Captain Perkins had six field guns, not rifled; but they could not be moved, as he had no harness, and did not get any until the 29th. Both had asked for rifled guns, and had been informed in letter of the 27th of June (App. No. 20) that "the ordinary guns which have been furnished the battery are considered as sufficiently effective by the general-in-chief." On the 28th of June I informed the general-in-chief (App. No. 21) that "Captain Newton, of the engineers, a most intelligent and reliable officer, had returned, after two days' absence, and reported General Johnston to have 15,000 men and twenty to twenty four guns and a large cavalry force, and thinks General Negley, whose brigade is on my left near Sharpsburg, will be attacked, the river being fordable at almost every point." And I might have added that on the 20th General Cadwalader had reported the enemy as having twenty guns; "they were counted as they passed." To meet this force of 16,000 men and twenty-two guns, I had but 10,000 volunteer infantry, 650 cavalry and artillery, and six guns; the artillery being nearly all recruits, the horses untrained, and still without harness for the battery. In the same letter I informed General Scott that I had "repeatedly asked for batteries, and ought to have had one for each brigade; that I had neither cavalry nor artillery enough to defend the fords of the river, and that I would not, on my own responsibility, cross the river and attack without artillery a force so much superior in every respect to my own, but would do so cheerfully and promptly if the general-in-chief would give me explicit orders to that effect." In the same letter I asked for the troops that had "been taken from me, and a number of field guns equal to those of the insurgents," that I might be enabled "to choose my point of attack and offer battle to the enemy;" adding that if "the general-in-chief would give me a regiment of regulars and an adequate force of artillery I would cross the river and attack the enemy, unless his force was ascertained to be more than two to one." No regulars were sent me, and but one field battery of artillery, leaving me greatly inferior in that important arm. The number of my troops has always been overestimated. There were twelve regiments ordered to join me—say, one Delaware and three New Jersey on the 24th of May, two New York regiments on the 30th of May, two Ohio and two northern regiments on the 4th of June, and two Pennsylvania regiments on the 10th of June—but they did not do so. I crossed the Potomac on the 2d of July with less than 11,000 men and six guns, the enemy having 16,000 men, mostly confederate troops, (not State troops,) and twenty to twenty-four guns. My largest force was accumulated at Martinsburg, and they did not exceed 19,000 men. My own estimate of their number was 18,200. When I marched from there I had to leave two regiments, taking about 16,800 men with me; and, deducting from them the sick, the rear and wagon guards, I could not have gone into action at Martinsburg with more than 15,000 men, or at any time after that with more than 13,000; and at the time Johnston marched from Winchester I could not have gone into action with 8,000 men.

On the 26th of June, anxious for the safety of Maryland and the frontiers of Pennsylvania, I had written to Major General McCall as follows:

"HEADQUARTERS DEPARTMENT OF PENNSYLVANIA,
          "*Hagerstown*, June 26, 1861.

"MY DEAR GENERAL : If I can get permission to go over into Virginia I intend to cross the river and offer battle to the insurgents. As the regulars and Rhode Island regiment and the battery have been taken from me, I will require all the force now here, and must leave the Pennsylvania line unguarded. Please inform me how many men you could throw forward, and how soon.

          "Very repectfully and truly yours."

I will read Major General McCall's reply:

          "HARRISBURG, *Sunday*, June 30, 1861.

"MY DEAR GENERAL: On my return from Pittsburg, this morning, I find your note of the 26th instant, informing me of your purpose to cross the river and offer battle to the insurgents, and asking what force I can throw forward upon the Pennsylvania line.

"In reply, I have to say that the only force (one regiment rifles, and one infantry, with a section of artillery) of my command as yet armed and equipped has been pushed forward to the support of Colonel Wallace at Cumberland, and for the protection of our border setlers in that direction; the other regiments are without clothing, arms, or equipments still, notwithstanding my efforts to fit them for the field. You will, therefore perceive how impossible it will be for me, although I much regret it, to comply with your request.

"With great regard, very truly yours,
                    "GEORGE A. McCALL."

It will be seen from the letter of General McCall that with all his efforts he had but two regiments fit for the field, and those two regiments, under

Colonels Biddle and Simmons, were then beyond Bedford, "for the support of Colonel Wallace at Cumberland, and for the protection of our border settlers in that direction." I was thus made responsible for our entire frontier from Cumberland to Edwards's Ferry, while I had not cavalry or artillery enough to guard the fords between Hancock and Harper's Ferry.

On the 28th of June I had used, in writing to General Scott, (App. No. 21,) the following emphatic, if not prophetic, language: "I beg to remind the general-in-chief that the period of service of nearly all the troops here will expire within a month, and that if we do not meet the enemy with them we will be in no condition to do so for three months to come. The new regiments will not be fit for service before September, if then; meanwhile the whole frontier will be exposed." Why did General Scott delay the attack on Manassas until the 21st of July?

On the 29th of June the harness for Perkins's battery arrived, and on the 30th orders were issued (App. No. 22) for a reconnoissance in force to be made early next morning. The whole army, except camp guards, were to march with two days' provisions, leaving tents and baggage, and to cross in two columns at Dam No. 4 and Williamsport, hoping thus to get the column crossing at Dam No. 4 in rear of the enemy encamped at Falling Waters, and to capture them; failing in that, to attack and defeat them. The troops were to commence crossing at midnight, but the ford was found impracticable, and after hours of labor and exposure to a severe rain the attempt was abandoned. The troops were then all concentrated at Williamsport, and on the next day, the 2d of July, crossed into Virginia and advanced in two columns. Just beyond Falling Waters the advance brigade of the enemy, 3,500 infantry, with artillery and a large cavalry force, all under General Jackson, were encountered, and after a sharp contest, principally with Colonel Abercrombie's brigade, was forced back and driven before our troops for several miles, the relative loss of the enemy being very heavy.

On the 3d of July the army under my command entered and took possession of Martinsburg. There I was compelled to halt and send back for supplies, and to wait for Colonel Stone's command, ordered on the 30th of June to join me—which he did do on the 8th of July—and for more means of transportation, without which it was impossible to advance, having wagons and teams for baggage only, and none for a supply train. The re-enforcements being without wagons only added to my difficulties.

In General McDowell's report of the battle of Bull Run, he states that "the sending of re-enforcements to General Patterson, by drawing off the wagons, was a further and unavoidable delay." There is no doubt that the gallant general believed that what he said was true. But it may be as well to inform the committee that the re-enforcements sent from Washington to me amounted to three regiments, under General Sanford; that they came without wagons, and that General Scott informed me I would have "to furnish transportation for them." Not one wagon, horse, mule, or set of harness was sent from Washington to me. All the transportation I had was furnished under my own orders by the energetic efforts of my efficient deputy quartermaster general, Colonel Crosman.

On the 4th of July I informed the general-in-chief (App. No. 23) that I had halted to bring up supplies; that my transportation was entirely inadequate; that "the terms of the three months volunteers was about to expire, and that they would not, in any number, renew their service, though I thought the offer should be made" to them. I also informed the general-in-chief that General Johnston, with from 15,000 to 18,000 foot, 22 guns, and 650 artillery, were within seven miles of me, my own force consisting of 10,000 foot, 6 guns, and 650 cavalry, in a hostile country, a river in the rear, and not over two days' supplies.

On the 5th, the general-in-chief informed me (App. No. 24) that he had ordered certain regiments to join me, adding "you will have to provide transportation for them." These troops were greatly needed, but they increased the difficulty as regarded transportation, which, as the general-in-chief had been informed, was not over half sufficient for the troops then at Martinsburg. On the same day I informed General Scott that large re-enforcements had come in to General Johnston from Manassas, and being much inferior to the enemy in men and guns, I ordered Colonel Stone (App. No. 25) to join my column at the earliest moment.

On the 7th, General Scott informed me (App. No. 26) that he could "not yet say on what day he would attack the enemy in the direction of Manassas Junction; he hoped, however, to be ready before the end of the week."

On the 8th of July Colonel Stone's command arrived, and the following orders to advance were immediately issued. The object being to attack the enemy at Winchester:

> " HEADQUARTERS DEPARTMENT OF PENNSYLVANIA,
> "*Martinsburg, Va., July* 8, 1861.

" General Order—Circular.]

"The troops will move to-morrow morning in the following order:

"The 1st (Thomas's) brigade, with the Rhode Island battery temporarily attached thereto, will advance by the Winchester turnpike, accompanied by one squadron of cavalry.

"The 7th (Stone's) brigade, with Perkins's battery attached thereto, will take the main street of the town, by the court-house, and will continue on the road parallel and east of the Winchester turnpike. One company of cavalry will be attached to this command.

"The 1st (Cadwalader's) division will follow the march of Thomas's brigade; Doubleday's battery will advance with this division; one regiment of which will be detailed for its guard, to accompany wherever it may be ordered.

"The 2d (Keim's) division will pursue both routes, General Negley's brigade following the march of Colonel Stone, and Colonel Abercrombie's and Colonel Wynkoop's that of General Cadwalader.

"The 28th and 19th New York regiments will be temporarily attached to General Keim's division.

" General Keim will detail a strong rear guard of his division for the wagon train. The rear guard will march on the flanks and rear of the train, and will be re-enforced by a squadron of cavalry. General Keim will detail a competent field officer to command the rear guard.

"The wagons will advance in one train in the rear of the troops, and will be required to keep closed.

"The troops of the several divisions and brigades will keep closed.

"By order, &c."

About midnight the order was countermanded, as some of the troops that had arrived under Colonel Stone that day were reported so weary and footsore as to be quite unable to endure the fatigue of a further march and be in a condition to fight.

On the next morning, the 9th of July, finding from conversation with some of my officers that the opposition to my plan of advancing upon Winchester, made known by the circular, appeared to be very strong and decided, I was induced, before renewing the order, to call a council of all the division and brigade commanders, the engineer officers, and chiefs of the departments of supply. I submitted to the council my instructions, orders, and the following statement:

"This force was collected originally to retake Harper's Ferry. That evacuated, it was directed to remain as long as Johnston remained in force in this vicinity. Threatening, as he was, either to move to the aid of the force attacking Washington, or annoying the frontier of Maryland, this army was permitted to cross the Potomac and offer battle. If accepted, so soon as Johnston was defeated, to return and approach Washington.

"The enemy retires, for what? Is it weakness, or a trap? Can we continue to advance and pursue if he retires? If so, how far? When shall we retire? Our volunteer force will soon dwindle before us, and we may be left without aid. If our men go home without a regular battle, a good field-fight, they will go home discontented, will not re-enlist, and will sour the minds of others. We have a long line to defend, liable at any moment to be cut off from our base and depot, and to a blow on our flank. Our forces must not be defeated, not checked in battle, or meet with reverses. It would be fatal to our cause.

"A force threatens Washington. If we abandon our present position Johnston will be available to aid. The command has been largely re-enforced to enable us to sustain our position, to clear the valley to Winchester, to defeat the enemy if he accepts battle, and to be in position to aid General McDowell, or to move upon Washington, Richmond or elsewhere, as the general-in-chief may direct. General Sanford, with two rifled guns and three regiments, will be up to-morrow. Our force will then be as large as it ever will be, under the prospect of losing a large portion of our force in a few days by expiration of service. What shall be done?"

The result of the deliberation is given in the following minutes, taken at the time by Major Craig Biddle, of the staff:

"*Minutes of council of war, held July 9, 1861, at Martinsburg, Va.*

"Colonel Crosman, quartermaster, thought 900 wagons would be sufficient to furnish subsistence, and to transport ammunition to our present force. The calculation for the original column was 700 wagons, of which 500 were on hand, and 200 expected. The great difficulty will be to obtain forage for the animals, the present consumption being twenty-six tons daily.

"Captain Beckwith, commissary. The question of subsistence is here a question of transportation. Thus far no reliance has been placed on the adjacent country. A day's march ahead would compel a resort to it. As far as known those supplies would be quite inadequate.

"Captain Simpson, topographical engineers. The difficulty of our present position arises from the great facility the enemy has to concentrate troops at Winchester from Manassas Junction. By the railroad 12, 000 men could be sent there in a day, and again sent back to Manassas. Our forces should combine with the forces at Washington.

"Captain Newton, engineers. Our present position is a very exposed one. General Johnston can keep us where we are as long as he pleases, and at any time make a demonstration on our rear. Our whole line is a false one. We have no business here, except for the purpose of making a demonstration. He threatens *us* now. We should be in a position to threaten him. We should go to Charlestown, Harper's Ferry, Shepherdstown, and flank him.

"Colonel Stone. It is mainly a question for the staff. Our enemy has great facility of movement, and to extend our line would be accompanied with great danger. Johnston should be threatened from some other point. We might leave two regiments here, two guns at Shepherdstown, and proceed to Charlestown, and threaten from that point.

" General Negley, ditto to Captain Newton.

" Colonel Thomas approves of a flank movement to Charlestown.

" Colonel Abercrombie the same.

"General Keim the same.

"General Cadwalader opposed to a forward movement."

On the day the council was held I wrote to the general-in-chief (App. No. 27) that I was deficient in supply trains; that my difficulties would increase as I advanced. This was the great want of my army; and on the 7th, 12th, 16th, and 21st of June, and the 4th and 5th of July, I had written to General Scott very fully on this subject. I refer to it here to show why I could not move when and where I wished. Colonel Crosman, the efficient quartermaster of my army, had done all that could be done, and more than I had supposed could be accomplished; but the troops sent from Washington and elsewhere, with the exception of the Rhode Island regiment, had brought no transportation with them. The enemy, though far superior in number of men and guns, had retired in succession from one position to another. I wrote that "his design evidently was to draw our force on as far as possible from the base, and then to cut our line or to attack with large re-enforcements from Manassas." In view of all these difficulties, I presented to the general-in-chief a plan by which I "proposed to move my force to Charlestown, establish my depot at Harper's Ferry, and connect with the Maryland shore by a bridge of boats," which I had caused to be gathered in a safe place. I also desired to know when the general-in-chief "wished me to approach Winchester, and on what day the attack would be made on Manassas;" and I requested that the general-in-chief would indicate the day, by telegraph thus: "Let me hear from you on ———."

On the 11th of July I received from the general-in-chief the following telegram:

"WAR DEPARTMENT,
"Washington, July 11, 1861.

"Major General PATTERSON,
"Martinsburg, Virginia.

"The author of the following is known, and he believes it authentic :

"WASHINGTON, July 9, 1861.

"The plan of operations of the secession army in Virginia contemplate the reverse of the proceedings and movements announced in the express of yesterday and Saturday. A schedule that has come to light meditates a stand and an engagement by Johnston, when he shall have drawn Patterson sufficiently far back from the river to render impossible his retreat across it on being vanquished, and an advance then by Johnston and Wise conjointly upon McClellan, and after the conquest of him, a march in this direction to unite, in one attack upon the federal forces across the Potomac, with the army under Beauregard at Manassas Junction, and the wing of that army, the South Carolina regiments chiefly, now nine (9) miles from Alexandria. Success in each of these three several movements is anticipated, and thereby not only the possession of the capital is thought to be assured, but an advance of the federal troops upon Richmond prevented.

The plan supposes that this success will give the confederate cause such prestige, and inspire in it such faith, as will insure the recognition of its government abroad, and at the same time so impair confidence in the federal government as to render it impossible for it to procure loans abroad, and very difficult for it to raise means at home. Real retreats, which have been anticipated, it will be seen, are by this plan altogether ignored. According to it, fighting and conquest are the orders"

This paper speaks for itself—comment is needless. Yet one cannot avoid raising the question, how the general-in-chief could ask or expect me to attack General Johnston's large force of men and guns in their intrenched camp at Winchester in less than a week after he had officially informed me that

" a schedule that had come to light meditates a stand and an engagement by Johnston, when he shall have drawn Patterson sufficiently far back from the river to render impossible his retreat across it, after being vanquished." That this was the plan agreed upon by the confederate generals there is no doubt; and it was a judicious one. Information of a similar kind had come in from various quarters. My most experienced officers of the regular service, with whom I fully and freely consulted—Colonels George H. Thomas, Abercrombie, and Crosman, Major Fitz-John Porter, Captains Newton, Beckwith, and many others, men of long service, merit, and great experience—all concurred in the opinion that I was too far advanced at Martinsburg; that Johnston had fallen back for no other purpose than to lure me on; that Johnston had a trap set somewhere, and that, if not very cautious, I would fall into it. Each of the above-named distinguished officers not only approved warmly of the management of my command, but opposed, both in and out of council, a further advance from Martinsburg. With their opposition to an advance well known, five of the number have since been made brigadier generals.

On the 12th of July, not hearing from the general-in-chief, the substance of my letter of the 9th was repeated by telegraph. The general-in-chief was also informed that I considered " a regiment of regulars, and more if possible, essential to give steadiness to my column, and to carry on active operations against a determined opposition." The necessity of this will be manifest when it is known that nearly all of Johnston's army were confederate troops, well disciplined and well commanded. I also stated that "many of my men were barefooted, and could not be employed on active service." Colonel Menier had reported the 3d Pennsylvania as unable to march for want of shoes.

On the same day, the 12th of July, General Scott telegraphed me, (App. No. 28 :) " Go where you propose in your letter of the 9th instant. Let me hear from you on Tuesday." That is, " go to Charlestown ; we shall attack Manassas on Tuesday ; I wish you to approach Winchester on that day." That was our translation of the whole matter.

On Saturday, the 13th of July, General Scott telegraphed me, (App. No. 29 :) " I telegraphed you on yesterday. If not strong enough to beat the enemy early next week, make demonstrations to detain him in the valley of Winchester ; but if he retreats in force towards Manassas, and it would be hazardous to follow him, then consider the route *via* Keyes's Ferry, Hillsboro', and Leesburg." On the same day I informed General Scott that " Johnston is in position beyond Winchester to be re-enforced, and his strength doubled just as I could reach him ;" and that I " would rather lose the chance of accomplishing something brilliant than by hazarding my column to destroy the fruits of the whole campaign to the country by defeat. If wrong, let me be instructed."—(App. No. 30.)

This correspondence is very plain. It can hardly be misunderstood by the most obtuse intellect. Any one who can read plain English can comprehend it I proposed to my superior to go to Charlestown. I am ordered to do so. In my letter of instructions I am told "there must be no reverse, no check, no drawn battle." I am told "take your measures circumspectly, and attempt nothing without a clear prospect of success." These instructions had not been rescinded or modified, and I was bound to obey them. Had I disobeyed and been defeated, as I most certainly would have been— and in this opinion I am sustained by every officer of the regular army serving with me, and, so far as I am informed, by all or nearly all the officers of volunteers—I would have deserved the severe censure which has so unjustly been cast upon me. I preferred the performance of my plain duty to a distinction which could have been gained only by the sacrifice of my men, and with great detriment to the cause in which I was engaged. I informed my commander of the difficulties and dangers of my position, the strength and great advantages of my antagonist, and that I would not, on my own responsibility, hazard my column and the interests of the country by a defeat—asking "if wrong, let me be instructed." If my superior thought differently, and that an attack should be made, why did he not assume the responsibility of his station and give the order? There was not one person in that column, from myself down to the youngest drum-boy, who would not most cheerfully have gone into battle, knowing that every individual would be killed, if they believed the interest and honor of the country required the sacrifice, or if General Scott had ordered it. Although I asked to be instructed, no instructions were given. I therefore inferred, as my opinions were not overruled, that I was right, especially as I was actually ordered to go to Charlestown.

On the 14th I informed General Scott (App. No. 31) that on the morrow I would advance to Bunker Hill preparatory to the other movement—that is, preparatory to going to Charlestown. "If an opportunity offers, I will attack, but unless I can rout I will be careful." General Scott was therefore thoroughly informed of what I was doing and intended to do one week before the battle of Manassas.

On Monday, the 15th, leaving two regiments—one being unable to march for want of shoes—to guard Martinsburg, I marched with the remainder of my army to Bunker Hill, forcing the enemy's cavalry before me, killing one and taking some prisoners.

On Tuesday, the 16th, the day General Scott said he was going to attack Manassas, and desired a demonstration, a reconnoissance in force was made, driving the enemy's pickets into Winchester. This, with a loss on the part of the enemy of several killed and wounded, was reported the same day to the general-in-chief, who was informed (App. No. 32) that the reconnoissance found the road from Bunker Hill to Winchester "blocked by fallen trees and fences placed across it." And "a sketch of the works of defence, prepared by Captain Simpson," a very reliable officer, was sent him. This sketch showed that the works erected and the guns mounted were of the most formidable character. The general-in-chief was also informed on the same day that on "to-morrow we would move to Charlestown;" that preparations had already "been commenced to occupy and hold Harper's Ferry; that the time of a large number of the men would expire that week, and they would not remain;" and "that after securing Harper's Ferry I would, if the general-in-chief desired, advance with the remainder of my troops *via* Leesburg, and desired to be informed if this proposition met with the approval of the general-in-chief." From this it will be seen that I did all that I was ordered to do, and at least as much, if not a great deal more, than any one had a right to expect.

On Tuesday, the 16th, according to General Scott's promise, Manassas was to be attacked. I expected, and had a right to expect, that as I had performed my part in delaying Johnston in Winchester, General Scott would have performed his, and assail Manassas. If anything had occurred to render the attack on Manassas inexpedient on that day, then General Scott should have informed me and directed me to continue my demonstrations, which could have been done just as easily from Charlestown as from Martinsburg; or he should have given me the order to march at once with all my force to Leesburg, as suggested by me, and delayed the attack on Manassas until I had arrived and been joined in the battle. The neglect or omission to do either is inexplicable. I kept General Scott well informed of all my movements. It was due to me, and necessary for the success of our armies, that I should have been equally well informed of the movements of corps with which it was expected I should co-operate.

On the 17th of July I again informed General Scott (App. No. 33) that the "term of 18 of my 26 regiments would expire within seven days, commencing to-morrow;" that "I could rely on none of them renewing their service;" and "that I must be at once provided with efficient three years men, or withdraw entirely to Harper's Ferry." Here was direct information that I could not hold Johnston, and that unless troops were sent me to take the place of those whose time was up, I could not even remain at Charlestown, but would have to fall back to Harper's Ferry. If troops could not be spared to re-enforce me, why was I not then ordered with my entire command to march to Leesburg and unite with McDowell in the assault on Manassas?

[At the request of the witness, the further examination was postponed until to-morrow.]

WASHINGTON, *January* 7, 1862.

General R. PATTERSON resumed as follows:

I omitted yesterday to read a letter from the general-in-chief, dated July 5, 1861. It is as follows:

"HEADQUARTERS OF THE ARMY,
"*Washington July* 5, 1861—11 *p. m.*

"Major General PATTERSON, *Hagerstown Md.:*

"Your letter of the 4th is received. Orders were sent this morning to Madison for the 3d and 4th regiments from Wisconsin to repair to Williamsport *via* Chambersburg and report to you.

"The 19th and 28th New York regiments leave here for Hagerstown to-morrow at half past 2 p. m. You will have to provide transportation for them thence to the post you may order them to.

"If any three months men will re-engage for the long term, designate a regular officer of your command to muster them, provided a sufficient number can be obtained to form a regiment.

"Having defeated the enemy, if you can continue the pursuit without too great a hazard, advance *via* Leesburg or Strasburg towards Alexandria, but consider the dangerous defiles, especially *via* Strasburg, and move with great caution, especially *via* Strasburg, halting at Winchester, and threatening a movement by Strasburg or the passage of the Potomac twice, and coming down by Leesburg may be the more advantageous movement."

On the 6th of July I sent to the general-in-chief an official report of the battle of Falling Waters.—(Appendix No. 34.) It is due to the officers who distinguished themselves that it should be made known. It has been made public, and never yet, for some reason or other, allowed to go out of the Adjutant General's office. I also sent a circular, accompanying the report.—(Appendix No. 35.) In a telegram, of date July 6, I informed the general-in-chief that "the insurgents have unquestionably received large re-enforcements, and are said to have 26,000 men, with 24 guns, many rifled, and some of very large calibre." I then expected to have by the night of the 8th 18,000 men and 16 guns, and intended to march on the 9th and attack them. On the 8th of July an order was issued (Appendix No. 36) reducing the number of tents to four common and one wall tent to each company, and also an order to march the next morning.—(Appendix No. 37.) On the 11th of July I issued a circular (Appendix No. 38) requiring division, brigade, and regimental commanders and quartermasters to have their commands ready to march at a moment's warning. On the 19th of July I telegraphed the general-in-chief that "the 2d and 3d Pennsylvania volunteers demand discharge, and I send them home to-morrow." On the 20th General Cadwalader sent in a report (Appendix No. 39) of the dates of expiration of term of service of the different regiments composing his division, in which he states "his fear that the men of two of his regiments would give us trouble," and "that there was a strong feeling in one regiment on the subject of returning to-morrow." On the 19th of July I reported to the adjutant general of the army (Appendix No. 40) "that almost all the three months volunteers refuse to serve one hour after their time, except three regiments."

I closed my narrative yesterday with a reference to my report of July 17 to the general-in-chief, in which I stated that the term of service of 18 of my 26 regiments would expire within seven days. It should be remembered that this report of mine was from Charlestown where I had gone on the 17th, having on the day appointed made the demonstration ordered by General Scott on the 13th, and performed my part perfectly. No information was sent to me on either the 14th, 15th, or 16th, the last being the day on which General Scott said Manassas would be attacked. If any change took place, and the attack was not to be made on the 16th, then it was the imperative duty of the general-in-chief to have informed me, that I might have arranged my movements in accordance, and have made my demonstrations against Winchester at the proper time. Confident that Manassas Junction would be attacked on Tuesday, I moved from Martinsburg on Monday, and drove Johnston's pickets in on Tuesday. If I had known the assault on the Junction would not have been made until Sunday, I would not have moved until Saturday. I am not therefore responsible for the appearance of General Johnston at Manassas on Sunday, the 21st. The same neglect or inattention kept me from being at Manassas to meet Johnston. No information of any kind was given me by General Scott from the 13th to the 17th.

On the 17th he telegraphed me, (Appendix No. 41,) "McDowell's first day's work has driven the enemy beyond Fairfax Court-House; the Junction will probably be carried to-morrow." This anticipation was unfortunately not realized.

Let me recapitulate the essence of General Scott's last three despatches. On the 12th, "Go to Charlestown; I will attack Manassas on Tuesday." On the 13th, "If not strong enough to meet the enemy early next week, make demonstrations, so as to detain him in the valley of Winchester." On the 17th, "McDowell's first day's work has driven the enemy beyond Fairfax Court-House; the Junction will probably be carried to-morrow." With this despatch of the 17th in possession, I and the officers under me were relieved from great anxiety, indeed were very exultant. With Fairfax Court-House in possession of our troops, and the Junction to be taken the next day, all I had to do was to be ready to meet and repel the attack which all expected.

On the 18th of July General Scott telegraphed me (Appendix No. 42) as follows: "I have certainly been expecting you to beat the enemy; if not, to hear that you had felt him strongly, or at least have occupied him by threats and demonstrations. You have been at least his equal, and I suppose superior in numbers. Has he not stolen a march and sent re-enforcements towards Manassas Junction? A week is enough to win a victory. The time of volunteers counts from the day of muster into the service of the United States. You must not retreat across the Potomac. If necessary, when abandoned by the short-term volunteers, intrench somewhere, and wait for re-enforcements." I had no doubt that the opinion of the general-in-chief was correct, that "a week was enough to win a victory." My own army had gained a decided victory in less than four hours on the day I crossed the Potomac, and it was the opinion of myself and all the officers under my command that we would have gained many victories several days earlier if the general-in-chief had not emasculated my army by ordering from me my regulars, (infantry, artillery, and cavalry,) with the Rhode Island regiment and battery, just at the moment when they were most needed. But the want of artillery and transportation compelled me to wait at Martinsburg until the enemy, previously my superior in men and guns, had time to be re-enforced heavily with both, and to intrench themselves at Winchester having nearly 50 field guns, and more siege guns, of the heaviest calibre and of longer range, than I had of all kinds.

Were I disposed to indulge in recrimination I might retort with some severity upon the lieutenant general the expression so unjustly used towards myself. For full three months after the remark General Scott has been obliged to retire from the command of an army in which are concentrated all the choice troops of the country without that victory with which he was so anxious to close his brilliant career. In fact, the whole country, who looked for the most brilliant results from the rawest of all troops, now apprehend, as well, perhaps, as the lieutenant general himself, that one who attempts to precipitate a victory will run the risk of finding also that "a week is long enough for a defeat."

On the same day, the 18th, I sent three telegrams and one letter (Appendix Nos. 43, 44, 45, and 46) to the general-in-chief, informing him of the condition of my command; that many of my men "were without shoes;" the men had received no pay, and neither officers nor soldiers had money to purchase with ; that under the circumstances I could not ask or expect the three months men to stay longer than one week; that I had "that day appealed almost in vain to the regiments to stand by the country for a week or ten days; the men were longing for their homes, and nothing could detain them;" that "Captain Newton had been sent that day to Harper's Ferry to arrange for defence, and re-establish communication with Maryland;" that the general's order had been obeyed "to threaten and make demonstrations to detain Johnston at Winchester;" that Johnston had been largely re-enforced, and that even if I could "take Winchester it would be only to withdraw my men, and be forced to retreat, thus losing the fruits of victory." At 1.30 a. m. that morning I telegraped General Scott that "telegraph of date received. Mine of to-night gives the condition of my command. Some regiments of my command have given warning not to serve an hour over their time. To attack under such circumstances the greatly superior force at Winchester is most hazardous. My letter of the 16th gives you further information."

I will read here my letters of the 14th and 16th to the general-in-chief:

"MARTINSBURG, *Virginia, July* 14, 1861.

"I have thus far succeeded in keeping in this vicinity the command under General Johnston, who is now pretending to be engaged in fortifying at Winchester, but prepared to retire beyond striking distance if I should advance far. To-morrow I advance to Bunker Hill, preparatory to the other movement. If an opportunity offers I shall attack, but, unless I can rout, shall be careful not to set him in full retreat upon Strasburg. I have arranged for the occupation of Harper's Ferry, opposite which point I have directed provisions to be sent. Many of the three months volunteers are very restless at the prospect of being retained over their time. This fact will soon cause you to hear of me in the direction of Charlestown. Want of ample transportation for supplies and baggage has prevented my moving earlier in the direction I desired."

In my letter of the 16th, from Bunker Hill, I wrote:

"I have the honor to report, for the information of the general-in-chief, my advance and arrival at this place yesterday, opposed only by a body of six hundred cavalry, of which one was killed and five taken prisoners. To-morrow I move upon Charlestown. A reconnoissance shows the Winchester road blocked by fallen trees and fences placed across it, indicating no confidence in the large force now said to be in Winchester. I send you a sketch, prepared by Captain Simpson, of the works said to have been erected in the vicinity of Winchester. Preparations have already been commenced to occupy and hold Harper's Ferry with the three years troops. If the general-in-chief desires to retain that place, (and I advise it never to be evacuated,) I desire to be at once informed by telegraph. I have to report that the time of service of a very large portion of this force will expire in a few days. From an undercurrent expression of feeling I am confident that many will be inclined to lay down their arms the day their time expires. With such a feeling existing, any active operations towards Winchester cannot be thought of until they are replaced by three years men. Those whose term expires this week, and will not remain, I shall arrange to send off by Harper's Ferry; those for Philadelphia *via* Baltimore; those for Harrisburg *via* Hagerstown. If Harper's Ferry is to be held, after securing that, I shall, if the general-in-chief desires, advance with the remainder of the troops *via* Leesburg, provided the force under Johnston does not remain at Winchester, after the success which I anticipate from General McDowell. I wish to be advised if these preparations meet with the approval of the general-in-chief. The Wisconsin regiments are without arms and accoutrements, which I have directed the commander of Frankfort arsenal to provide."

On the 17th I wrote from Charlestown:

"The term of service of the Pennsylvania troops (eighteen regiments) expires within seven days, commencing to-morrow. I can rely on none of them renewing service. I must be at once provided with efficient three years men, or withdraw to Harper's Ferry. Shall I occupy permanently Harper's Ferry, or withdraw entirely? I wrote yesterday on this subject, and now wish to be informed of the intentions of the general-in-chief. My march to-day was without opposition or incidents of importance. The country has been drained of men. This place has been a depot for supplies for force at Winchester, and the presence of the army is not welcome."

I telegraphed the general-in-chief from Charlestown, at 1.30 a. m., on the 18th: "Telegram of date received. Mine of to-night gives the condition of my command. Some regiments have given warning not to serve an hour over time. To attack under such circumstances, against the greatly superior force at Winchester, is most hazardous. My letter of the 16th gives you further information. Shall I attack?"

On the same day, at 1 p. m., I telegraphed the general-in-chief: "I have succeeded, in accordance with the wishes of the general-in-chief, in keeping General Johnston's force at Winchester. A reconnoissance in force on Tuesday caused him to be largely re-enforced from Strasburg. With the existing feeling and determination of the three months men to return home, it would be ruinous to advance or even to stay here without immediate increase of force to replace them. They will not remain. I have ordered the brigades to assemble this afternoon, and shall make a personal appeal to the troops to stay a few days, until I can be re-enforced. Many of the regiments are without shoes; the government refuses to furnish them. The men have received no pay, and neither officers nor soldiers have money to purchase with. Under these circumstances I cannot ask or expect the three months volunteers to stay longer than one week. Two companies of Pennsylvania volunteers were discharged to-day and ordered home. I to-day place additional force at Harper's Ferry and re-establish communication with Maryland. I send Captain Newton to prepare for its defence."

On the same day I telegraphed again to the general-in-chief: "Telegram of to-day received. The enemy has stolen no march upon me. I have kept him actively employed, and, by threats and reconnoissance in force, caused him to be re-enforced. I have accomplished, in this respect, more than the general-in-chief asked, or could be expected, in face of an enemy far superior in numbers, with no line of communication to protect."

On the 18th I wrote from Charlestown as follows: "I arrived at this place on the 17th instant; nothing of importance occurred on the march. The principal inhabitants left some ten days since, anticipating its occupation by the federal troops. It was till our arrival the location of a band of secession militia, engaged in pressing into the service the young men of the country.

"I have to acknowledge the receipt of two telegrams from the general-in-chief, of the 17th and 18th instant, both looking to a movement and attack upon Winchester. A state of affairs existed which the general-in-chief is not aware of, though, in some respects, anticipated by his instructions, that if I found the enemy too strong to attack, to threaten and make demonstrations to detain him at Winchester. I more than carried out the wishes of the general-in-chief in this respect. Before I left Martinsburg I was informed of a large increase of Johnston's command, and of the visit to Winchester of the leading members of the confederate army. Just before General McDowell was to strike I advanced to Bunker Hill, causing surprise, and, I have since learned, an additional increase of force. On Tuesday I sent out a reconnoitring party towards Winchester; it drove in the enemy's pickets, and caused the army to be formed in line of battle, anticipating an attack from my main force. This party found the road barricaded and blocked by fallen trees. The following day I left for this place.

"Before marching from Martinsburg I heard of the mutterings of many of the volunteer regiments, and their expressed determination not to serve one hour after their term of service should expire. I anticipated a better expression of opinion as we approached the enemy, and hoped to hear of a willingness to remain a week or ten days. I was disappointed, and when I was prepared for a movement to the front, by an order for the men to carry two days' provisions in their haversacks, I was assailed by earnest remonstrances against being detained over their term of service; complaints from officers of want of shoes and other clothing, all throwing obstacles in the way of active operations. Indeed, I found I should, if I took Winchester, be without men, and be forced to retreat, thus losing the fruits of victory. Under the circumstances neither I nor those on whom I could rely could advance with any confidence.

"I am therefore now here with a force which will be dwindling away very rapidly. I to-day appealed almost in vain to the regiments to stand by the country for a week or ten days. The men are longing for their homes, and nothing will detain them. I send Captain Newton to-day to Harper's Ferry to arrange for defence and re-establish communication with Maryland and the Massachusetts regiments. The 3d Wisconsin will soon be there. Lieutenant Babcock has been at Sandy Hook several days trying to get the canal in operation, prepare the entrance to the ford, putting in operation a ferry, and reconstructing the bridge. Depots for all supplies will soon be established, and there I shall cause to be turned in the camp equipage, &c., of the regiments. And to that place I shall withdraw if I find my force so small as to render my present position unsafe. I cannot intrench sufficiently to defend this place against a large force. I shall direct the regiments to be sent to Harrisburg and Philadelphia, to be mustered out by Captain Hastings and Major Ruff and Captain Wharton.

On the 19th I wrote to the adjutant general of the army:

"Almost all the three months volunteers refused to serve an hour over their time, except three regiments, which will stay ten days; the most of them are without shoes and without pants. I am compelled to send them home, many of them at once. Some go to Harrisburg, some to Philadelphia, one to Indiana, and, if not otherwise directed by telegraph, I shall send them to the place of muster, to which I request rolls may be sent, and Captain Hastings, Major Ruff, and Captain Wharton ordered to muster them out. They cannot march, and unless a paymaster goes to them they will be indecently clad and have just cause to complain."

I will state here that the troops I appealed to to remain were those from Pennsylvania. I did not appeal to the Indiana regiment, but the next day they marched up to my headquarters and offered to remain. I was very much delighted I assure you.

As I have before stated, at 1.30 a. m. of the 18th of July I telegraphed General Scott that "some regiments of my command have given warning not to serve an hour over their time. To attack under such circumstances the greatly superior force at Winchester is most hazardous. My letter of the 16th gives you further information," and closed by asking, "Shall I attack?" Let it be borne in mind that this was despatched at half past one in the morning; and to be ready for the order to attack, if it came, the following order, addressed to commanders of divisions and brigades, was issued: "Have cooked provisions provided immediately for your men in haversacks, and be ready to march whenever called upon." General Scott might have left it to my discretion to act as circumstances required, or have ordered me to attack Johnston, or have ordered me to march with all speed to Leesburg and join with McDowell in the attack on Manassas. If left to myself, I would, as the correspondence proves, have done the latter; and if I had, it is probable that with my little army in the action, Bull Run would not have been a drawn battle. I had carefully and correctly kept General Scott advised of all my movements, and of the great superiority of the enemy; and when goaded by the taunt, "a week is enough to win a victory," I asked "shall I attack," the responsibility of an answer, negative or affirmative, is evaded.

General Scott begins his despatch of the 18th with, "I have certainly been expecting you to meet the enemy," and closes by saying, "You must not recross the Potomac. If necessary, when abandoned by the short-time volunteers, intrench somewhere and wait for re-enforcements." These passages do not fit well together in the same despatch, and come with a bad grace after having ordered me to go to Charlestown and "make demonstrations to detain Johnston in the valley of Winchester." I knew, and so repeatedly informed General Scott, that Johnston was far superior in men and artillery. After the council of July 9 was held, reliable information was received by me that General Johnston was so largely re-enforced with men and guns as to render an assault upon his intrenchments utterly hopeless. The immense superiority of the enemy at Winchester in men and guns, as well as in position, was well known. The information was obtained from Union men who had been there, from prisoners, from deserters, and from various sources, all agreeing on an average of forty thousand men and over sixty guns. A captain named Morrill, or Wellmore, belonging to a Maryland regiment, and taken prisoner at Charlestown by a party from Harper's Ferry, gave forty thousand. A gentleman of Berkeley county, of high respectability, serving under Johnston as an unwilling Virginia volunteer in Jackson's brigade at the battle of Falling Waters, subsequently gave the following statement, taken down by General Negley, and by him given to me:

" General Jackson retreated with his brigade, consisting then of four regiments and four pieces of artillery, (Captain Pendleton,) to Big Spring, three and a half miles south of Martinsburg. General Johnston arrived at Darkesville the same night with about fourteen thousand men. He was then re-enforced by one regiment and one battery (four guns) flying artillery. General Jackson retreated to that point. The army made a stand there for four days ; they then retreated to Winchester. When we arrived there, we found fortifications commenced by the militia. All the army then assisted, and in two days the city was fortified all around, within two miles of the suburbs, with intrenchments. Re-enforcements commenced pouring in. Ten forty-two pounders were placed, masked, around the fortifications ; also artificial thickets planted for riflemen. The force consisted of forty-two thousand, including four thousand militia. General Johnston then received a despatch, as read to the men, that General Patterson was out of the way; that he had gone to get in Beauregard's rear; and that Jeff. Davis had ordered him to cut off General P. in order to save the country; that Gen. B. had been attacked by an overwhelming force. General Johnston's army moved at 1 o'clock p. m. Thursday, consisting of nine brigades, with fifty-two pieces of flying artillery, including three ten-inch columbiads, represented to me as such. Amongst the artillery was a detachment of the Washington Artillery, consisting of eight guns, four of which were rifled cannon. General J. took with him thirty-five thousand men, leaving the militia and volunteers, to the number of seven thousand, in Winchester."

Another gentleman gave the following statement, taken by General Cadwalader, and by him given to me. Mr. ——— says:

" General Johnston's force at Winchester was forty-two thousand men, infantry, artillery, and cavalry, of which eight hundred Virginia cavalry, under Colonel Stuart, and three hundred from southern States. Forty regiments, thirty-five thousand men, left Winchester at 1 o'clock p. m. on Thursday, by order of General Beauregard; took the road to Berry's Ford, on the Shenandoah, thirteen and a half miles over the Blue Ridge to Piedmont Station, on the Manassas Gap railroad, fifteen miles, making twenty-eight and a half miles, requiring two days' march. Freight and passenger cars had been hauled over the road, on their own wheels, to Strasburg last week, and on them Johnston's forces were expected to be transported on the Manassas railroad from Piedmont to Manasas Junction, thirty-eight to forty miles. There remained at Winchester 7,000 troops until Saturday afternoon, when they left for Strasburg on their way to Manassas, except about 2,500 of the militia of the neighboring counties, disbanded and sent home. A large quantity of arms in boxes was sent to Strasburg. The Virginia cavalry remained, (under Colonel Stuart,) and went to Berrysville to observe the movements of General Patterson's column. The rest of the cavalry went with General Johnston. They had at Winchester sixty-two pieces of artillery in position in the fortifications; about ten 42-pounders (some they thought were columbiads) were left. The remainder were taken by General Johnston. A detachment of the Washington Artillery, from New Orleans, had eight heavy guns, of which four were 32-pounders. These were hauled by twenty-eight horses each, the rest (smaller guns) by six and four horses each. Part, if not all of them, were brass rifled guns. The fortifications surrounded Winchester, except to the southward, upon the high ground; very heavy earthworks made with bags and barrels filled with earth, &c. In front of the breastworks deep trenches were dug communicating below with inside of the works. The guns were all masked with artificial thickets of evergreens, which were intended in some cases to be used as ambuscades for riflemen and sharpshooters. Among the regiments was one of Kentucky riflemen armed with heavy bowie-knives. They refused to take more than one round of cartridges. They proposed to place themselves in the bushes for assault. All the fences had been levelled for miles in front of Winchester. The fortifications extended two and a half miles. The trees had been felled between Bunker Hill and Winchester to impede our advance. Fifteen hundred sick at Winchester confined with measles, dysentery, and typhoid fever. Prisoners taken from our column were sent to Richmond. Wise has been recalled, it is said, with his troops from Western Virginia. Beauregard and Davis had done it in opposition to General Lee's advice."

On the 23d of July General Scott, a witness who cannot be suspected of a desire to overrate the enemy's force in men and guns, telegraphed to General Banks, at Harper's Ferry, (App. No. 47,) "there are nine 32-pounders, four 44-pounders, two 6-pounders, and a very large amount of powder, balls, and shell at Winchester." Add to these siege guns the twenty field guns reported by General Cadwalader and Captain Newton on the 20th June, and you have from two of our own officers of the highest rank in the service, Scott and Cadwalader, official information that the enemy at Winchester had double the number of guns I had. But it is well-known that Johnston carried over fifty guns, some of the largest calibre, with him.

On the same day he telegraphed to General Banks, (App. No. 48,) "I deem it useful, perhaps highly important, to hold Harper's Ferry. It will probably soon be attacked, but not, I hope, before I shall have sent you adequate re-enforcements. A Connecticut regiment may soon be expected by you. Others shall to-morrow be ordered to follow." This despatch speaks for itself. If my army was stronger than Johnston's, why, I again ask, send re-enforcements to General Banks? A most reliable and respectable gentleman furnished my engineer with a detailed statement (App. No. 49) giving the regiments from each State—say, two from Kentucky, two from Tennessee, five from Alabama, five from Georgia, one from North Carolina, five from Mississippi, two from Maryland, &c.—making a total force of over 35,000 confederate troops at Winchester. These statements, which I have seen and examined, with the names of the gentlemen who furnished them, with many others taken by different officers from different persons at different times and places, agree very much in the main facts. From these and other documents, and from information obtained in various ways, there is no doubt of the fact that General Johnston had not only the advantage of extensive intrenchments in his own country, with abundant supplies, and a railroad which could bring him re-enforcements at the rate of 12,000 men a day, and I could get none, but that he had at least three men and four guns to my one, and that nothing but the good order of my column saved it from annihilation and capture by Johnston. Why should I have made an attack with such awful odds against me? I had done all I was asked to do, and all that was necessary, if General Scott's plan of attack on Manassas had been carried out in season. I was informed that, on the 16th, the assault on Manassas would be made; and had no information to the contrary until the receipt of General Scott's telegram of the 17th, saying it would probably be taken on the 18th. I then supposed it would be taken on the 18th, and had no information of the repulse of General McDowell's column until I heard through the newspapers of the unfortunate affair of the 21st. It is just within the bounds of possibility that, with a frightful slaughter of my men, I might have taken Winchester. But why hazard the safety of the army, possibly of the country, upon such a contingency? If General Scott had taken the Junction, I was in position, my army intact, ready for anything required of me. If our army had been repulsed at Manassas, I was in position to do what I did do—prevent the army from crossing the Potomac to assail Washington, Baltimore, and Philadelphia, and desolating

Maryland and Pennsylvania. If I could with heavy loss have taken Winchester, it would have been a bloody and a barren victory. I had but twenty-six regiments under my command; of these the terms of service of eighteen from Pennsylvania and one from Indiana expired within ten days. I could not have held Winchester if I had taken it. The general-in-chief knew when the term of service of the regiments in my army, and at Washington, expired. If General McDowell's army could not be got ready to fight on the 16th, no battle ought to have been fought then. I knew that General Johnston was too good a soldier to retreat with an army of over 18,000 men and twenty-two guns before an army of 10,000 men and six guns, for that was about the relative strength the day my army entered Martinsburg. He would not retreat except for a purpose. It was the opinion of the officers of the old army, and of most of the new, that Johnston had a trap set for me, and many feared I would fall into it. But fortunately I had full and reliable information which convinced me, and every officer of my staff, that Johnston's object in falling back as I advanced was to lure me on to an attack on the entrenched camp at Winchester. If the bait had taken defeat was inevitable, and a large portion of my army would probably have been destroyed, and the residue been made prisoners of war. The affair would have been more disastrous than that of Bull Run, for my force had no intrenchments to fall back upon. The Potomac was behind me, and the retreat would have been a disgraceful rout. The enemy, flushed with two victories instead of one, and no army intact to check them, would have been in possession of Washington, Baltimore, and possibly Philadelphia within five days. If General Scott really "supposed" me "superior in numbers," why the necessity of ordering me "not to retreat across the Potomac, but to intrench somewhere and wait for re-enforcements." Why send re-enforcements if I was stronger than the enemy? Did I retreat, or attempt to retreat, across the Potomac? Certainly not. I held Harper's Ferry until I was relieved on the 25th of July, and would, under the order of the 18th, have held it until the crack of doom, unless relieved or ordered away. On the 20th of July I telegraphed General Scott as follows: "With a portion of his force Johnston left Winchester, by the road to Millwood, on the afternoon of the 18th—his whole force 35,200." That is, he marched with that number of confederate troops—leaving 7,000 volunteers and militia in Winchester. With this information in the hands of the general-in-chief what excuse can be given for fighting on the 21st, when it is apparent to the eye of any one who reads the reports of General McDowell, and of his division and brigade commanders, that our army was in no degree fitted for the encounter? The frank, manly, and soldier-like report of General McDowell proves this. If General Scott chooses to fight, or force others to fight when not ready, I am not responsible for the unfortunate result. My case is in a nut-shell. Johnston's force was always much stronger than mine in men and guns. I was not to fight unless I was equal or superior to him, but to threaten in order to keep him at Winchester until Manassas was attacked, which, by instructions, was to be on Tuesday, the 16th. Johnston was kept until the Thursday following, and the attack on Manassas was not made till Sunday, the 21st, and then not in the morning. Had others discharged their duty, mine having been accomplished, the contest would have been different in its results. Had the enemy been beaten at Manassas all praise would have been bestowed on my command for having manœuvred to keep Johnston so long at Winchester. I have gone over my papers, in detail, to enable the committee to understand the operations and conduct of my column. I have asked for a court of inquiry, and it has been refused. I have asked, through the Senate of the United States, for all the correspondence between General Scott and myself, and all the orders of that distinguished soldier to me. This, also, has been refused, and for the same reason, that it would be incompatible with the public interests. I do not question the propriety of 'the refusal. The knowledge of the fact that it would be injurious, and very injurious, has caused me to submit to all manner of misrepresentations for the last six months. The youngest soldier in the army is entitled to fair play. I have been a major general for nearly forty years, and hope it will not be denied to me. I was honorably discharged on the 19th of July—two days before the battle of Bull Run. On that day I was pleading with the troops to stand by the government. I am not here to make a defence—there is no official charge against me. My record is perfect. I seek controversy with no man. But if there is any man of sufficient rank and character, or of rank without character, or character without rank, to entitle him to consideration, who has any charge to make against my military conduct, I not only will invite but will thank him to make it, and bring it before a court-martial or of inquiry, and I will meet it. All I ask is justice, strict justice for service rendered. It is the duty of the government to protect the character of officers who have performed their duty, been honorably discharged, and are unjustly assailed. I am confident this committee will see fair play.

[At the request of the witness the committee will consider the question of attaching his farewell order to his testimony.]

Adjourned till to-morrow.

WASHINGTON, *January* 8, 1862.

General R. PATTERSON resumed as follows:

In my testimony before the committee as regards the expiration of the terms of service of the volunteers, I omitted to state that an order or circular from the War Department, dated somewhere about the 12th or 13th of July, directed that the regiments should be sent to the places of muster in their respective States in time to reach there on the day their terms of service expired. A strict obedience to this order would have reduced my command to a very small number on the 18th of July. I also omitted to state that, although the general-in-chief had on the 17th of July informed me that "the Junction will probably be carried to-morrow," he had neglected to inform me that it was not carried on the 18th, or on the 19th, or on the 20th. It was certainly due to me, and to the great interests at stake, that if the general did not do what he said he would do I should have been informed of it. If on the evening or night of the 17th, or on the morning of the 18th, he found he could not make an assault on the Junction, why did he not telegraph me of the fact, and direct me to make an attack or a demonstration? I was all ready; my men had three days' rations in their haversacks, and I had that morning, at half-past one, put the question to him direct—"Shall I attack?" I could have made a demonstration on Winchester just as easy from Charlestown as from Bunker Hill, and I could have made an attack much easier from Charlestown than from Bunker Hill, as the road from Bunker Hill was blocked and barricaded, and the road from Charlestown was not, and with the great additional advantage of being so much nearer my base and depots. I do not charge the neglect or inattention to which I have referred as intentional, but to physical inability to perform the immense labor of his official station in the present state of the country. I desire to speak of the general-in-chief as I feel, with all kindness, courtesy, and respect, and with all honor for his loyalty and great services.

By Mr. Gooch:

Question. Can you designate each of the regiments of your command, and the time when their terms of service expired?

Answer. I hand in a report from Brevet Major General Cadwalader, giving in detail the names and numbers of the regiments belonging to his division, and the time at which their terms of service expired.—(App. No. 39.) I have made out, with the aid of General Cadwalader's report, and from memory, a memorandum of all the regiments composing my column, and the time fixed or supposed as near as I could approximate to the expiration of their terms of service:

1st regiment Pennsylvania volunteers, Colonel Yohl, July 18 ; 2d regiment Pennsylvania volunteers, Colonel Menier, July 19 or 20; 3d regiment Pennsylvania volunteers, Colonel Stambaugh, July 19 or 20; 6th regiment Pennsylvania volunteers, Colonel Negley, July 22; 7th regiment Pennsylvania volunteers, Colonel Irwin, July 22; 8th regiment Pennsylvania volunteers, Colonel Emlee, July 22; 9th regiment Pennsylvania volunteers, Colonel Longnecker, July 22, 23 and 24; 10th regiment Pennsylvania volunteers, Colonel Meridith, July 25; 13th regiment Pennsylvania volunteers, Colonel Rowley, July 23; 14th regiment Pennsylvania volunteers, Colonel Johnston, supposed July 23; 15th regiment Pennsylvania volunteers, Colonel Oakford, supposed July 23; 16th regiment Pennsylvania volunteers, July 20, 21, 25, 26, 27 and 30; 17th regiment Pennsylvania volunteers, Colonel Patterson, supposed July 21; 20th regiment Pennsylvania volunteers, Colonel Grey, July 30; 21st regiment Pennsylvania volunteers, Colonel Ballier, July 29; 23d regiment Pennsylvania volunteers, Colonel Dare, July 21; 24th regiment Pennsylvania volunteers, Colonel Owen, supposed July 30; one-half (five companies,) 25th regiment Pennsylvania volunteers, July 18; Wisconsin regiment, Colonel Starkweath, early in August; Indiana regiment, Colonel Wallace, about July 20; Massachusetts regiment, Colonel Gordon, three year's men; 1 New Hampshire; 1 New York, under Colonel Stone, last of July; 4 New York, under General Sanford, last of July and early in August; 2d and 3d regiments left at Martinsburg.

Pennsylvania regiments, seventeen and one-half; New York and other regiments, nine; making a total of twenty-six and one-half regiments, averaging, present and fit for service, six hundred and fifty men, equal to seventeen thousand two hundred and twenty-five; to which add cavalry, artillery, and one company of rangers, in all one thousand, making a total of eighteen thousand two hundred and twenty-five.

Question. When you fix the time at which their term of service expires, do you reckon from the time when they were mustered into the service of the United States?

Answer. Yes, sir; not from the time when they were enrolled, but from the day they were mustered into service, that being the decision of the War Department, and so communicated to me by the general-in-chief.

Question. And the term of service, as you have stated it, is fixed on that basis?

Answer. Yes, sir. Most of those regiments, however, were enrolled and on duty a week or ten days before. My son's was the first that turned out, on the 16th, by my own order.

Question. I suppose you found out, from the movements of your army, that it is impossible to say, a week or ten days beforehand, that you will be at a given point on a certain day.

Answer. Yes, sir; I could not tell a week beforehand where I would be.

Question. Is not that a difficulty which is incident to the moving of all large bodies of men?

Answer. Yes, sir.

Question. It is impossible for a commander to tell, even a week beforehand, what he will be doing, or where he will be a week hence?

Answer. Yes, sir.

Question. You moved from Martinsburg to Bunker Hill on the 15th July?

Answer. Yes, sir.

Question. And remained at Bunker Hill over the 16th?

Answer. A part of my army did. A large force was sent forward to reconnoitre and drive in the pickets of Johnston's army.

Question. On the morning of the 17th you moved to Charlestown?

Answer. Yes, sir.

Question. When you were at Bunker Hill how near were you to Winchester?

Answer. About 12 miles.

Question. How near at Charlestown were you to Winchester?

Answer. From 15 to 17 miles, I think.

Question. Is it not further than that?

Answer. I think not.

Question. We have had it stated at 22 miles.

Answer. I cannot answer certainly, because I do not know. That is a matter that General Newton could answer better than I can.

Question. We have had the distance given as 22 miles. You say you are uncertain as to the distance?

Answer. I am uncertain as to the distance.

Question. Did you know the force of General Johnston when you moved from Martinsburg?

Answer. Our estimate then was that it was over 30,000 men.

Question. When you moved from Martinsburg?

Answer. Yes, sir; we took several prisoners, and got additional information at Bunker Hill, making his force from 35,000 to 40,000. In my statement to General Scott on the 6th of July I reported that he had 25,000 men.

Question. As you moved from Martinsburg to Bunker Hill I think you stated that General Sanford was in command of one division, and moved down on the road to the left, and the other divisions of your army moved to the right of him?

Answer. Yes, sir.

Question. Did you propose, on Tuesday the 16th, to advance towards Winchester from Bunker Hill?

Answer. No, sir.

Question. You made a reconnoissance that day?

Answer. Yes, sir; I made a reconnoissance in force to see the condition of the country, &c. The object was to learn the enemy's strength and his preparations, so as to know whether we ought or ought not to go forward.

Question. What did you learn from that reconnoissance?

Answer. The report was decided against a forward movement.

Question. I did not ask what the report was, but what the facts were.

Answer. We learned that the roads were barricaded, fences were built across it, trees cut down, and all manner of impediments thrown in the way; that in front of the town of Winchester everything was levelled, fences and everything, trees cut down, and in some cases houses pulled down, so that their guns should have a clear and complete sweep; and that there were fortifications extending two miles and a half, with heavy guns.

Question. Then you issued no orders for an advance from Bunker Hill towards Winchester?

Answer. I did, but countermanded it.

Question. At what time was that order countermanded?

Answer. On the return of the reconnoissance, or some time afterwards—some time in the afternoon or evening. My own desire was to go ahead, but I was opposed by all around me.

Question. General Sanford was in command of a division?

Answer. Yes, sir.

Question. You say that you yielded to the opinions of others. Was General Sanford's opinion taken in relation to that?

Answer. No, sir; General Sanford's opinion was not taken at any time. General Sanford joined—I forget now the exact time—perhaps the 10th, or may be the 11th of July, at Martinsburg. There was no council held at Bunker Hill. General Sanford was not in time to join the council of the 9th, and there was no council held after that. The opinions taken by me at Bunker Hill were the opinions of the gentlemen of my own staff, and the old officers of the regular army, who had great experience—those with whom I had been in the habit of counselling from the time I had taken command. There was no council; but any person of the class referred to who came into headquarters was consulted. But no council was held there on that day.

Question. Why did you move from Bunker Hill to Charlestown, instead of remaining at Bunker Hill?

Answer. Because there I was in a most dangerous position. I should have considered it an act of utter insanity to have remained there with so long a line behind me, my force not nearly half the number, not more than one third the number of the enemy. I was under constant expectation of an attack, and being cut off from my base; and I had the warning of the general-in-chief, dated the 11th of July, that that would be done. And also because all my officers told me that Johnston was luring me on, and that I would be caught. The desire of my officers was that I should move direct from Martinsburg to Charlestown. My objection to that movement was this : that I was passing a long distance directly across the enemy's front, and he could have sent out parties to kill all my teamsters, cut up my wagon guards, shoot the animals and make a regular stampede, and I could not by any possibility get into a position to fight him. Going to Bunker Hill, I was to a certain extent going towards Winchester, and as soon as I got to Smithfield I then diverged to the left. We there expected to be attacked, and I had arranged my command with the left in front, to be ready for an attack, should it be made while on our march. Everybody expected that we should be assailed there. All my wagons were in the front, out of the way. I could not have left Martinsburg and marched half the way without the enemy knowing it. But I could leave Bunker Hill and march to Charlestown, because they would not know where we were going.

Question. If it had been the intention of Johnston to attack you were you not more exposed to his attack in your movement from Bunker Hill to Charlestown than to remain at Bunker Hill?

Answer. If I remained at Bunker Hill I was just as liable to be attacked as on the road to Charlestown, and just as liable to be attacked on the road as there. But I could not remain at Bunker Hill forever. My remaining there was very perilous. To return to Martinsburg was not very soldier-like; and I was ordered to go to Charlestown, and I obeyed my orders.

Question. Then, do you say you went to Charlestown because you were ordered to go there?

Answer. Yes, sir; and because I considered it judicious to go there, and was advised to do so by my council. And I went there because I was ordered there, whether right or wrong.

Question. During all this time you considered it your especial business to take care of Johnston, did you not?

Answer. Yes, sir.

Question. That was the object and purpose of your army?

Answer. My especial object—yes, sir.

Question. And you were to take care of him until after the attack had been made by McDowell upon Manassas, and keep him so occupied as to prevent his being present to take part there in the battle, if you could possibly do so?

Answer. Yes, sir; if I could.

Question. On the 9th of July you made a communication to General Scott, in which you stated to him your plans of operations for the future?

Answer. Yes, sir.

Question. And under that head you wrote as follows:

"Under these circumstances, I respectfully present to the general-in-chief the following plan, which, with my present views, I desire to carry into operation so soon as I can do so with safety, and the necessity for following Johnston ceases. I propose to move this force to Charlestown, from which point I can more easily strike Winchester; march to Leesburg; when necessary, open communication to a depot to be established at Harper's Ferry, and occupy the main avenue of supply to the enemy. My base will then be some seven miles nearer, more easily reached by road, and my line of communication rendered more secure than at present. I can establish communication with the Maryland shore by a bridge of boats. In this way I can more easily approach you; and the movement I think will tend to relieve Leesburg and vicinity of some of its oppressors. My present location is a very bad one in a military point of view, and from it I cannot move a portion of the force without exposing that of what remains to be cut off."

Then, in the last part of that communication, you say:

"When you make your attack I expect to advance and offer battle. If the enemy retires, shall not pursue. I am very desirous to know when the general-in-chief wishes me to approach Winchester. If the notice does not come in any other way, I wish you would indicate the day by telegraph, thus: ' *Let me hear from you on* ———.' "

In reply to that you received the following telegraph:

"Go where you propose in your letter of the 9th instant. Should that movement cause the enemy to retreat upon Manassas *via* Strasburg, to follow him at this distance would seem hazardous; whereas the route from Charlestown *via* Keyes's Ferry, Hillsboro', and Leesburg, towards Alexandria, with the use of the canal on the other side of the river for heavy transportation, may be practicable. Consider this suggestion well; and except in an extreme case do not recross the Potomac with more than a sufficient detachment for your supplies on the canal. Let me hear of you on Tuesday. Write often when *en route*."

That was a telegraphic despatch which you received in reply to your communication of the 9th?

Answer. Yes, sir; and your reading of that has reminded me of the strongest reason for not remaining at Bunker Hill. We had but supplies for two days, and could not remain there.

Question. Then you received on the next day this telegraphic despatch?

"I telegraphed you yesterday if not strong enough to meet the enemy early next week, make demonstrations so as to detain him in the valley of Winchester. But if he retreats in force towards Manassas, and it be hazardous to follow him, then consider the route *via* Keyes's Ferry, Leesburg," &c. Now, did you not understand from these communications from General Scott that you were either to detain Johnston in the valley of Winchester until after you had heard of the result of the attack on Manassas, or, in case of his retreating, to follow him directly, or come down by the other route which General Scott had indicated, *via* Keyes's Ferry, Leesburg, &c., so as to be present and participate in the action at Manassas?

Answer. Unquestionably, if I could detain him. I was undoubtedly to detain him if I could, but I was not to follow him down there, or to move on the other route, unless circumstances required it. In my letter of the 20th or 21st I stated ———

Question. I would rather you would confine your answer to this question.

Answer. Unquestionably I was to detain him and to remain there as long as he remained there. Will you repeat the question?

Question. [The question was repeated.]

Answer. Yes, sir. The reason I did not follow him is stated in my letter of July 21st to the general-in-chief. On the 20th I telegraphed thus : " With a portion of his force, Johnston left Winchester by the road to Mill-wood on the afternoon of the 18th, his whole force about 35,200." I believed then, and so did the officers of my command, that it was very likely that Johnston had information, and we had not, of the battle of Manassas, and that he had gone down on the right bank of the Shenandoh to cut me off ; and on the night of the 20th, at midnight, I had ordered General Cadwalader to send a strong brigade down to Keyes's Ferry, and hold it, as I expected Johnston to attempt to come in my rear. On the 21st I reported to General Scott thus : "I came here (Harper's Ferry) to-day. Yesterday Winchester and this country was abandoned by all armed parties. Johnston left for Millwood to operate on McDowell's right, and to turn through Loudon upon me. I could not follow." I had no men to follow on the 20th or the 21st. I had made every effort on the 18th, but the men would not stay.

Question. You were still apprehending an attack from Johnston on the 20th.

Answer. I was expecting an attack from Johnston any hour from the 18th until I went into Harper's Ferry.

Question. When did you first know that Johnston had left?

Answer. On the 20th, and the instant I received that information I sent a telegram announcing the fact to the general-in-chief, with orders to go with all speed, and that despatch was received in this city that night.

Question. Did you not know that your position at Charlestown offered no obstacle to General Johnston joining the forces of Beauregard at Manassas?

Answer. It offered no more obstacles than at any other point, except that I was nearer to him than at Martinsburg. I could not stay at Bunker Hill, for I had no supplies.

Question. You were not threatening Johnston at Charlestown so as to prevent him joining Beauregard at Manassas?

Answer. No, sir ; I remained there because I was ordered to remain in front of him until he left.

Question. You knew at that time that you were not offering any obstacle to his going down to Manassas?

Answer. Perfectly. I knew I had not the means to do it.

Question. Why did you not communicate that fact to General Scott immediately?

Answer. I did communicate my condition and where I was.

Question. When?

Answer. On the 16th. I wrote him in detail from Bunker Hill; on the 17th I wrote again; and on the 18th I gave him all the information necessary. And it was his business to order me, not my business to make any further suggestions to him.

Question. Did you communicate to him by telegraph?

Answer. Certainly. I sent three telegrams to him on the same day.

Question. On what day?

Answer. On the 18th. At half-past one in the morning I telegraphed him my condition, and asked him if I should attack. To have sent further information to him would have been rather impertinent, and he would have so considered it.

Question. On the 17th he telegraphs you thus: "I have nothing official from you since Sunday, but am glad to learn through Philadelphia papers that you have advanced. Do not let the enemy amuse and delay you with a small force in front, whilst he re-enforce the Junction with his main body."

Answer. Yes, sir, I received that.

Question. And on the 18th you telegraphed to General Scott: "Telegram of date received. Mine of to-night gives the condition of my command. Some regiments have given warning not to serve an hour over time. To attack under such circumstances against the generally superior force at Winchester is most hazardous. My letter of the 16th gives you further information. Shall I attack?" Did you send him any other telegram on the 18th?

Answer. Certainly ; two others.

Question. I find this one on the 18th : "Telegram of to-day received. The enemy has stolen no march upon me. I have kept him actively employed, and by threats and reconnoissance in force caused him to be re-enforced. I have accomplished in this respect more than the general-in-chief asked, or could well be expected in face of an enemy far superior in numbers, with no line of communication to protect."

Answer. I beg to state that in that telegram of the 17th is one of those things that I take exception to as bad treatment. I had written to the general-in-chief, as I stated in my examination in chief, every day ; and yet I am told that he has nothing official from me since Sunday—no information except through the papers. Now, I telegraphed him on the 12th, on the 13th, and on the 14th. I did not telegraph him on the 15th, because I was marching that day. But I telegraphed him three times afterwards, and wrote him on the 18th.

Question. In your telegraph of the 18th you told him distinctly that the enemy had stolen no march upon you, that you had kept him actively employed, and by threats and reconnoissance in force caused him to be re-enforced.

Answer. Yes, sir.

Question. And you intended that General Scott should understand at that time that Johnston had not made any movement towards Manassas ?

Answer. Yes, sir; and he had not at that time.

Question. On what day did he leave ?

Answer. He left on that day, but had not left then. But I did not know it for two days afterwards.

Question. My question is, why did you not inform General Scott that you were then not in a condition to offer any obstacle to Johnston's joining Beauregard ?

Answer. I should have considered it rather a reflection on him to have told him so. He knew my condition.

Question. You told him in your telegraph that you had kept Johnston actively employed.

Answer. And I had.

Question. But you did not give the general any information that you were not then doing it, or that you were not still able to do it ?

Answer. I had all along been remaining there according to his orders, but in no condition to do it. I was perilling my army, but was willing to do it, because it was my orders. If he had ordered me to go anywhere, I should have gone. He knew my force, my condition, and my aide-de-camp was also sent down to inform him. He knew my condition perfectly well. He could order me.

Question. On the 18th he telegraphs you thus:

" I have certainly been expecting you to beat the enemy; if not, to hear that you had felt him strongly, or, at least, occupied him by threats and demonstrations. You have been at least his equal, and, I suppose, superior in number. Has he not stolen a march and sent re-enforcements towards Manassas Junction? A week is enough to win a victory. The time of volunteers counts from the day mustered into the service of the United States. You must not retreat across the Potomac. If necessary, when abandoned by the short term volunteers, intrench somewhere and wait for re-enforcements."

That was on the 18th of July?

Answer. Yes, sir.

Question. During all this time you knew that General Scott expected of you that you should either engage and beat Johnston, or detain him in the valley of Winchester; or, in the event that he should come down by a route where you could not follow him, that you should follow down *via* Keyes's Ferry and Leesburg?

Answer. Yes, sir.

Question. And yet when you were at Charlestown you found yourself not in a condition to do either; now my question is, why did you not communicate that fact to General Scott?

Answer. There was no occasion for it, in my judgment. He knew my condition, and to have added to the information he already had would have been a waste of time and paper. I had informed him of my condition, and it was his business to order me what to do. I had asked him, " Shall I attack?" It was not my business to say anything beyond that Johnston was there.

Question. But you say yourself that you were not in a condition to attack at that time?

Answer. In saying that, I did not mean that the men I had were not in a condition to fight, but that I had not force enough to fight. My men, I believe, were in about as good a condition, if not better, than any other column in the field. They had been drilled from eight to ten hours a day, and I have no doubt a good portion of them would have cheerfully gone up with me. I was in as good a condition then to fight as I would be at any time after that; and if I had got the order, I would have gone up with all who would have gone with me. I do not mean to say that my men would not fight, or that they would not have obeyed an order to attack, but that I was not numerically strong enough to hold him anywhere, or to justify an attack, unless it was indispensable to save some other army, or to carry out a part of some great scheme. If General Scott had wanted me to sacrifice 1,000, or 5,000, or 10,000, or the whole, for the purpose of settling the question as to Johnston going down to Manassas, and had he given me the order I had asked, I should have done it.

Question. General Scott wanted you to do one of three things: either to attack Johnston and beat him, or to detain him, or, if he left, to follow him?

Answer. Yes, sir.

Question. You have just said that if it were necessary, in order to save or protect any other division of the army, or to secure any great object, you would have felt it your duty to have run some hazard or make an attack. Now did you not know that such was the fact, that General McDowell was just about to make an attack upon Manassas, and that it was of the first importance that Johnston should not be allowed to join Beauregard?

Answer. On what day?

Question. About this time.

Answer. I did suppose that on the 18th he had done it.

Question. Did you suppose it was an absolute certainty that the attack was made on the 18th?

Answer. With the preparations that were going on, I had no more doubt of it than I had of my own existence.

Question. Did you not, as a military man, know that it was impossible to fix beforehand, even for a week, when a battle should come off; that it depends as much upon one side as upon the other, especially where large bodies of men are to be moved?

Answer. I know that it is very uncertain. But I know that if you are moved up within fighting distance, you certainly ought to fight within a day of the time you say; and if you do not it is the duty of the man who does not fight to inform the other. I know it is uncertain; but I never saw anything yet to keep men from Tuesday until Sunday.

Question. On the 17th you had a telegraph showing that the fight had not taken place that day?

Answer. The despatch of the 17th showed that he had begun the day he fixed. He said the first day's work was done.

Question. That day was Wednesday?

Answer. Yes, sir.

Question. Then in case the attack had been begun there was no certainty that it would be finally concluded on the day of the attack?

Answer. No, sir.

Question. The battle might last one day, or two days, or three days, and Johnston was in a position to join Beauregard in a very short time?

Answer. No, sir, he could not do it in a very short time; not under three days, and I knew the general could reach me by telegraph in an hour or an hour and a half. There was no answer to any of my three despatches, or to my letter of the 18th.

Question. Do you deem that you, as a military man, had the right to assume, with the knowledge you had that it was merely proposed to fight the battle of Manassas on a certain day—do you deem that you had the right to assume that the battle had been fought and concluded on that day, and therefore leave Johnston at liberty to move forward on Manassas?

Answer. I assumed as a military man that if the general-in-chief told me that he would fight on Tuesday, the 16th, and on the 17th had told me that he had driven the enemy beyond a certain point and would probably complete the operation on the next day—I assumed it was his duty to inform me if he had not done it; otherwise I had a right to infer that he had done it.

Question. On the 18th you got still another despatch, saying, "I have certainly expected you to beat the enemy," still showing you that General Scott deemed it of the first importance that you should detain Johnston there; and certainly you might presume from that telegraph that the battle of Manassas had not been fought.

Answer. I at that time supposed so, certainly. And yet it would have been perfectly convenient for the general to have said so. I looked upon that telegraph, and so did every gentleman on my staff, as nothing more nor less than an exhibition of bad temper.

Question. Why did you suppose the general-in-chief was in bad temper?

Answer. I could not tell. He states that he supposes I am Johnston's superior, after having repeatedly been informed by me that I was not equal in number to him.

Question. Did you feel justified in regarding that telegraph as an exhibition of bad temper, and paying no attention to it?

Answer. Certainly not—most assuredly not—because I would pay regard to anything, to the slightest wish that General Scott ever put out—to anything.

Question. And yet you did not do anything to prevent Johnston going to Manassas, notwithstanding that you on the 18th were notified by General Scott—or you inferred from his telegraph—that the battle of Manassas had not been fought?

Answer. It strikes me as very singular, indeed, after my statements of my efforts to keep my troops—the whole of the 18th was occupied in making speeches—I appealed to nearly every regiment in my command—it strikes me as very singular that I could by any possibility have thought of doing anything without an order from General Scott. An order from him would have helped me.

Question. And you have stated this morning that you could have attacked on the 18th if you had been ordered to do so?

Answer. I would have done it, because I would not have gone to making speeches. Up to the 20th, late in the day, I believed Johnston still to be there; and I would at once, if the order had come, have gone and attacked, if I had taken with me but 5,000 men. I suppose I could have carried 8,000 of them; they could have detained him if the whole of them had been killed; but I would have done it.

Question. You say you could have attacked on the 18th if ordered to do so. You knew the necessity of detaining Johnston, and you must have inferred from the telegraph of General Scott that he expected or required of you that you should do something in that direction. Why did you not do all that you could to detain him without an order?

Answer. Because I could not go up then without fighting, as I could not fall back again. I had no reason to believe that that telegraph was not written in the morning in reply to mine of that morning. There was no reason why General Scott did not fight that day; and there was no more occasion for my going up and perilling my men without an order than of doing anything entirely uncalled for—not the slightest occasion for it. I had every reason to believe Johnston was at Winchester. I knew he could not get down to Manassas under three days, for I knew that the day before I had driven him in. If General Scott did not fight, and saw the necessity for my acting, I repeat, it was his business to give the order.

Question. Did not Johnston come down in less than three days?

Answer. No, sir; he left Winchester on Thursday, and got in on Sunday afternoon.

Question. Did not a portion get in on Sunday, and another portion get there before Sunday?

Answer. No, sir. And I will state here that a gentleman showed me the Philadelphia Press of this morning, which contained a speech of General Beauregard at some dinner party, in which he stated that the first appearance of any part of Johnston's force on the battle-field was from three to four o'clock in the afternoon of Sunday, and he at first thought it was my column, and gave up the day.

Question. Could you not on the 18th, without making an actual attack on Johnston, have made such demonstrations towards him as would probably have prevented, or tended to have prevented, his moving his force down to Manassas?

Answer. I could have gone up; but if I had I must have gone up to fight. I could undoubtedly have made a demonstration. But while he was there, and I under the belief that the general-in-chief was fighting that day, it was uncalled for and unnecessary, and no soldier in my army would have thought of such a thing. General Scott knew where I was, and whether he was fighting or not. We waited for him to indicate what was to be done. It was not for us to do so. Having made a demonstration the day before, it would have been unpardonable for me to have thrust all my men into action without cause. I had made a demonstration on the day he had indicated that the battle would be fought. I knew that Johnston was there, and could not get down under three days, and I knew that the general ought to inform me if he did not fight. He fixed the day, and it was his business to fight on that day, or inform all the commanders of corps depending on his movements that he had not fought. If he did not fight on the 18th, or the 19th, or the 20th, it was his business to inform me every day until he did fight.

By the chairman:

Question. The all important fact was to detain Johnston until that battle was fought, let that be when it might?

Answer. Yes, sir.

Question. Now when you ascertained that you could not detain Johnston, the very moment you came to that conclusion was it not of the utmost importance that that should be known to General Scott and to General McDowell?

Answer. I was ordered not to go beyond Harper's Ferry, but to keep that place. If I had marched down without General Scott's orders, I left the whole Pennsylvania border unprotected.

Question. That is not the question I put.

Answer. What is the question?

Question. Why did you not, the moment you found you could not detain Johnston, inform General Scott of that fact?

Answer. I had informed him time and time again that I was not strong enough to hold him. I was in that condition a month before. I never was able to hold him.

Question. Why, in reply to his telegram, ordering you to detain him in the valley of Winchester—why did you not tell him that you had not the force, and could not detain him?

Answer. The impression upon the minds of all of us was that by remaining in the neighborhood of Johnston he would not leave Winchester; that although we were not strong enough to attack him, he would not abandon the valley of Winchester to us. My order was to detain him in the valley of Winchester. Consequently, as long as I staid there I carried out that order to the best of my ability.

Question. But if I have understood you, there was a time when you found that from various reasons you had not the force to detain him. The knowledge of that important fact would undoubtedly have governed the action of the army at Manassas, our army under General McDowell, and they would have made their calculations and arrangements for the battle in accordance with that important fact. Had they been informed that you were unable to keep Johnston off, they might have delayed the attack until you could follow Johnston down with what force you could?

Answer. As long as we were in the neighborhood, at one place or the other, it was impossible for Johnston to know what force was in my army. Just so long as we remained there, there was a corps that would have been exceedingly troublesome to him. We inferred—I did and so did all the gentlemen around me—that because my request to go down, time and time again, was not complied with, General Scott wanted us to stay there without reference to our strength. I had informed the general-in-chief, over and over again, that I was not able to hold Johnston there. I had sent Mr. Sherman, and my staff, one after the other, to get leave to go below.

Question. There was a time when you supposed Johnston was re-enforced?

Answer. Yes, sir.

Question. What time was that; just before you turned off to Charlestown?

Answer. No, sir; I think I reported on the 6th of July; I reported that Johnston had unquestionably received large re-enforcements and had then 25,000 men.

By Mr. Gooch:

Question. In your telegram of the 18th you say to General Scott:

"Telegram of to-day received. The enemy has stolen no march upon me. I have kept him actively employed, and by threats and reconnoissance in force caused him to be re-enforced. I have accomplished in this respect more than the general-in-chief asked, or could well be expected in face of an enemy far superior in numbers, with no line of communication to protect."

Would the general-in-chief understand from that that General Johnston was then in a position where there was no obstacle in the way of his going to Manassas?

Answer. I expected him to understand that Johnston was in Winchester, as he was.

By the chairman:

Question. This is exceedingly important, in a military point of view. Was it not a most important fact for General Scott and General McDowell to know when Johnston started to go down to Manassas?

Answer. Undoubtedly it was; and the instant I got the information it was communicated to him.

Question. As soon as he started you communicated the information?

Answer. Not as soon as he started, but as soon as I knew it, without a moment's delay.

Question. What day was that?

Answer. That was on the 20th, on Saturday.

Question. That was the first you discovered he was gone?

Answer. Yes, sir; the first intimation I had of it.

Question. How was that information communicated?

Answer. By telegram, immediately, not by post; horses from Charlestown to Harper's Ferry, and telegraphed from thence here; and the despatch was known all over this town on Saturday evening.

Question. Did that telegram reach General Scott?

Answer. I do not know; I cannot say as to that.

Question. I understood you to say that you found yourself, in view of his re-enforcements and of your own condition, too weak to detain Johnston?

Answer. What I meant to say was this: it would have accomplished nothing if I had taken Winchester; I could not have kept him up there; and I supposed that General Scott was perfectly safe then, because on the 18th Johnston was still there, and could not under three days get to Manassas.

Question. I know you say you supposed the battle at Manassas had been fought; yet you might have been mistaken about that.

Answer. I was mistaken, no doubt, about that; I was mistaken.

Question. But this is what I am trying to get at: The moment you found you had not a force sufficient to resist the purpose of Johnston to go down to Manassas, it was a fact all important for General Scott and General McDowell to know.

Answer. As far as General McDowell was concerned, I could have no communication with him.

Question. I know that.

Answer. And I had the order of General Scott to remain in front of Johnston as long as he remained in the valley of Winchester; and I had no right to move. If I had had the order on the 18th to come down here, I could have got down in time; on the 20th I could not.

Question. What I mean is this: you found yourself, in your own estimation, too weak to resist Johnston's moving down to Manassas. Now, when that fact was known to you, ought you not to have communicated it to General Scott at once, and said to him: "I am not able to detain Johnston here?"

Answer. I communicated to General Scott every circumstance connected with my command. On the 9th I communicated the fact that I was in a false position, and asked to go to Charlestown. On the 12th he acknowledged the receipt of that, ordered me to go Charlestown, and told me he would attack on Tuesday. On the 13th he directed me to make a demonstration to hold Johnston. On Tuesday I made the demonstration and occupied his time. On the next day I moved to Charlestown, where General Scott had ordered me to go, and where I had asked leave to go; and then I was in a condition to come down here, and was in no condition to restrain Johnston.

Question. When you found you was in no condition to detain Johnston, was it not all important that that fact should have been communicated to General Scott—not the fact that you could not fight Johnston, but that you could not detain him, that your strength was insufficient to do that, and he could not rely upon his being kept back?

Answer. I never supposed for a moment that General Scott believed for the fifty-fifth part of a second that I could hold him.

Question. It is evident that his orders all along presuppose that you could detain him.

Answer. Could occupy him. If you will look back to the testimony in relation to the 13th and 16th of June, you will find that he then reproved me for trying to disturb him. What was the use of trying to drive him down to Strasburg? The impression upon my mind, and upon the minds of all around me, was that General Scott did not wish him to be disturbed at Winchester.

Question. General Scott wanted him to be prevented from forming a junction with Beauregard?

Answer. Yes, sir; not to drive him out of Winchester upon Manassas.

Question. And he made his arrangements for the battle in view of that all-important fact?

Answer. Yes, sir.

Question. Now if it occurred to you that it could not be done, was it not all-important that he should have been advised of it?

Answer. Yes, sir; but my belief all the time was that so long as I remained there he would have stayed; and it is clear he would have stayed if he had not been ordered down.

Question. He would obey orders. But you knew he had an all-prevailing motive to make such a junction, and of course you had just as strong a one to prevent it?

Answer. Precisely.

Question. And it was just as important that General Scott should know the first moment it could be ascertained that you could not prevent Johnston forming that junction; because he could then make his arrangements, in view of that most decisive fact.

Answer. Yes, sir.

Question. So that I say it occurs to me that the moment you found you could not detain Johnston, for any reason, you should have informed General Scott that you could not do it.

Answer. I had not found I could not do it, for I believed that by remaining there I could do it.

By Mr. Gooch:

Question. You say you would have fought General Johnston in an open field?

Answer. I certainly should not have avoided it.

Question. Did he make any demonstration towards coming out into the open field to fight you?

Answer. No, sir.

Question. He kept behind his batteries at Winchester?

Answer. Yes, sir.

Question. Then as you were in your position at Bunker Hill, and he was behind his batteries at Winchester, and had placed obstructions in your way to prevent your reaching him—did you not infer from that that he did not desire to meet you in the open field?

Answer. My impression was that he meant to induce us to believe he was weak; that by putting up these obstacles it was adding to the lure, that it was a decoy, and that he desired us to come up; that these things were not put there really to prevent us from coming up, but actually to coax us up.

Question. Was not Johnston obliged to cross the Shenandoah river when he left his position at Winchester to go towards Manassas?

Answer. Yes, sir.

Question. Might you not have taken some position on that river, or in the vicinity of that river, where you could have rendered his crossing it exceedingly difficult and hazardous?

Answer. I could not have got there without the liability of being entirely cut off. That would have placed me between him and Beauregard, have put him in my rear. I went to Charlestown, near the river; but I could not have got to any point above that without getting between him and Beauregard. I would have put myself in what soldiers call a false position. I could have put myself where I could have harassed him exceedingly; but I would have put myself where the chances were ninety-nine to one I would have been captured. At Bunker Hill I had no supplies; and if I had gone to the other place indicated I could not have got a mouthful without fighting for it.

Question. Would it not have been possible, if you had put yourself below Johnston, and he had pressed you, for you to have come down and formed a junction with General McDowell, leaving Johnston in your rear by tearing up the railroad bridges as you came down?

Answer. I could not have got down by railroad. The road goes from Winchester to Strasburg, and if I had attempted to go to the railroad, I would have had further to march than he had.

Question. Some eight or ten miles further?

Answer. Yes, sir. Besides that, I was in the enemy's country without any supplies, and with a railroad at his and Beauregard's command, by which he could have sent up 12,000 men a day.

Question. That was one of the matters discussed in your councils, was it?

Answer. Not in the council at Martinsburg, but among my staff at Bunker Hill, and afterwards at Charlestown.

Question. That was a thing proposed?

Answer. Yes, sir; and discussed fully. That was a matter we talked of at Bunker Hill, going to a place called Smithfield or Middleway, and then striking off in that direction. But the opinion was universal that we should get ourselves in a false position, and unquestionably be all captured.

Question. You were just stating that the general-in-chief, having fixed a day on which he would fight, should have notified you that he had not fought on that day, and so on, from day to day, until the battle actually took place.

Answer. Yes, sir. The ground I placed that upon was this: I was the subordinate of the general-in-chief; bound to obey his orders. As I had nothing to do with the day he was to fight on, he ought not to have informed me until he was ready to fight. But having informed me that he would fight on a certain day, if he did not fight on that day, it was his province to have informed me that he did not fight on that day, and to have informed me, from day to day, until he did fight.

Question. And yet you knew, as a military man, that it was exceedingly difficult, or that it was altogether impossible, to fix some days beforehand a day certain on which a battle would be fought; and did you not consider it your duty to continue to act in reference to Johnston precisely the same as though the battle at Manassas had not been fought, until you had been told that it was fought?

Answer. Not if I had been told it would be fought on a certain day. If I had not been told that, then it would have been my duty to have gone on with my demonstrations. When he informed me that it would be fought on a certain day, then that consideration ceased to have weight.

Question. Did you suppose that you were justified in not doing anything to detain Johnston? Did you suppose that under the circumstances you were justified in failing to do anything that you would have done had you not been told when it was intended the battle of Manassas should be fought?

Answer. I did not fail to do anything I would have done. I did exactly all that could have been done, unless I had been ordered down.

Question. During all the time that General Sanford was with you, in command of a division, going up, as he did, from the city of Washington, having knowledge, as he might be presumed to have, in relation to the contemplated movements here, especially those of General McDowell, did you have any consultation with him in relation to the movements of your army and the best course to pursue?

Answer. None whatever.

By Mr. Odell:

Question. Did you receive any information from General Sanford in reference to the intended movements of the army here?

Answer. None whatever.

By Mr. Gooch:

Question. He made no communication to you in regard to that?

Answer. None whatever. General Sanford brought me a note from General Scott, but made no communication of any kind. Our intercourse was very pleasant as gentlemen. He did me the favor to call upon me, and I returned his call; but he brought me no information from the general-in-chief, and I had no consultation with him whatever.

By Mr. Odell:

Question. You stated, I think, in answer to a question here, that you had given orders for a forward movement on the 16th or the 17th?

Answer. On the 16th, while at Bunker Hill. The orders had not been put out. I had given them to the staff officers, but they had not been published.

Question. You had issued such an order to the proper staff officers?

Answer. Yes, sir.

Question. At what time did you recall that order?

Answer. I suppose it was somewhere between 3 and 4 o'clock in the afternoon; I cannot exactly fix the time now. It was in the afternoon; late in the afternoon.

Question. What time on the 17th did you move from Bunker Hill?

Answer. Very early in the morning.

Question. What do you mean by "very early?"

Answer. The order was to move at three or four o'clock in the morning, but we did not get off at that time. I started about sunrise; a part of my command was, of course, before me.

Question. While you were at Bunker Hill you held Johnston?

Answer. No, sir; I was just in a straight line from him the other way. In other words, he was directly between me and Manassas Junction. He could leave when he pleased.

Question. The effect of your being at Bunker Hill was to hold Johnston in his position?

Answer. Yes, sir; as well as at any other place.

Question. Do you know now at what time Johnston left his position in front of you?

Answer. He left in the afternoon of the following day.

Question. Of the 17th?

Answer. No, sir; of the 18th.

Question. The effect of your going to Charlestown was to untie Johnston and his forces?

Answer. Yes, sir; I could not hold him at Martinsburg.

Question. I am not speaking of any other position than Charlestown. When you went to Charlestown you untied Johnston and enabled him to go forward?

Answer. Yes, sir; but I could not remain at Bunker Hill, because I had no supplies there, and was crippled in my movements.

Question. Now, in reference to the dissatisfaction of the troops, did not that manifest itself more after you had gone to Charlestown from the enemy than it did while you were at Bunker Hill?

Answer. I do not think there was any more dissatisfaction at the one place than at the other. The men had talked about going home until they had determined on it. I speak now of the Pennsylvania troops. I saw very little of the others. I speak of the Pennsylvania troops, including those that joined me late. And the others, I think, were the same. I do not think the going to Charlestown made any difference with them at all. They had talked about it, made up their minds about it, and they were determined to go. With the majority of them their time was up, and their hearts were bent upon going.

By Mr. Julian:

Question. Were not all willing to stay, without regard to the expiration of their time, if you would lead them against the enemy?

Answer. No such expression was manifested to me; no such communication was made to me. There has been a statement that Colonel Butterfield begged, time and again, to do that. But no such application was made to me. No regiment, or colonel, or general, or officer, under my command, ever asked to be led to the front—not one. I am satisfied there was a great desire, on the part of all, to have a fight. There is no doubt about that. But we were not allowed to go towards the enemy at Winchester until a certain day. I have here my general order of July 20, of which I read paragraph 3, as follows: "The detachment of about 250 of the 1st Pennsylvania regiment, claiming their immediate discharge at expiration of term of service, will be sent *via* Baltimore to Harrisburg, Pennsylvania, to be mustered out of service. A muster-roll of the detachment will be sent with the party." These 250 men were so discharged on that day. They refused to serve longer, although appealed to by me, appealed to by their gallant colonel, and, I believe, by other officers. But they went off without their officers, with their muster-rolls, to be discharged. The remainder of the regiment agreed to stay six days longer. I have a document here which I desire to put upon record. It is a letter dated the 13th of July, and signed by nine captains of one regiment refusing to stay beyond the time when

their term of service expired.   I think it had better go upon the record.—
(Appendix No. 50.)

The witness stated that he would like to have some officers who served
there under him, and who are entirely familiar with the whole campaign,
appear before the committee and testify.

The chairman stated that the witness could furnish a list of names of
such persons as he might desire to be called, and the committee would take
the matter into consideration.

Subsequently, having read over his testimony as written out by the re-
porter, the witness returned it with the following statement:

In reference to the question by Mr. Odell:

"Question. The effect of your going to Charlestown was to untie Johnston and his force ?"

I could not have understood that question, or I should not have made
such an answer.   Johnston was never tied, and I could not hold him at
Martinsburg, Bunker Hill, or anywhere else.   He was before me at Falling
Waters, at Martinsburg, at Big Spring, at Darkesville, at Bunker Hill, and
at Winchester.   I could hold him at neither place; he retired as I approached.

APPENDIX TO THE TESTIMONY OF GENERAL ROBERT PATTERSON.

No. 1.

[Extract.]

HEADQUARTERS OF THE ARMY,
Washington, April 19, 1861.

General Orders No. 3.]

The military department of Washington is extended so as to include, in addition to the District of Columbia and Maryland, the States of Delaware and
Pennsylvania, and will be commanded by Major General Patterson, belonging
to the volunteers of the latter State.

*   *   *   *   *   *   *   *   *

WINFIELD SCOTT.

By command.

E. D. TOWNSEND, *A. A. G.*

A true extract.

ROBERT E. PATTERSON,
Lieutenant Colonel and Division Inspector.

No. 2.

PHILADELPHIA, *Pennsylvania, November* 1, 1861.

SIR : Believing to the present moment that, on account of other persons, a
public examination into the manner in which the affairs of the department of
Pennsylvania, while 'under my command, were conducted, and that the publication of the correspondence with and orders to me of the general-in-chief,
especially connected with the late campaign in Maryland and Virginia, might be

detrimental to the interests of the service, I have refrained from asking for an investigation or permission to publish the orders by which I was controlled.

The same reason has caused me studiously to avoid verbal statements on the subject, in reply to numerous inquiries.

Charges have been publicly made through the press, and the impression created, that the design of the campaign was not carried out by me, but rather deranged by my neglect or violation of orders.

Intimations against my loyalty have been insidiously circulated.

From the silence of my immediate commander, I infer he does not design to relieve me from the odium attached to these reports and rumors.

While I am willing, if the general good demand it, to suffer personally, and am desirous that no course on my part shall prove injurious to public interests, yet I believe the time has arrived when the question as to the manner in which I executed the duties intrusted to me may be fully investigated with safety, so that the failure to accomplish certain results, never anticipated of my command by the general-in-chief until he saw his defeat, may be ascribed to the real cause.

Further silence on my part would confirm the impression that I plead guilty to the charges against my honor, my loyalty, and my military capacity. I have a right at least to be relieved from the position in which my long silence, caused solely by an earnest desire for the success of our cause, has left me.

In presenting this my application for a court of inquiry, a permission to publish my correspondence with the general-in-chief, I claim and am now ready to substantiate it—

1st. That if the general-in-chief ever designed my command to enter upon the soil of Virginia with prospect of success, he destroyed my power when greatest, and when that of the enemy was weakest, by recalling to Washington, after they had crossed the Potomac, all my regular troops, with the Rhode Island regiment and battery, leaving me but a single company of cavalry, which had not then been one month in service, and entirely destitute of artillery.

2d. The general-in-chief forbade my advance and compelled me to recall to Maryland all the troops which, confident of success, had crossed the Potomac into Virginia, in execution of a plan which had been submitted to him and had received his cordial approbation.

3d. That for a long time the general-in-chief kept my command in a crippled condition, and demanded my advance after he had withdrawn from me all my available artillery, and only after the enemy had had time to become vastly my superior in artillery, infantry, and cavalry, and was intrenched. In answer to my earnest appeals he re-enforced me, only after the occasion for employing re-enforcements had passed away.

4th. That if the general-in-chief designed me to do more than threaten the enemy at Winchester, he did not divulge his wish.

5th. That if the general-in-chief expected me to follow to Manassas "close upon the heels of Johnston," he expected a physical impossibility; the enemy moving part of the way by rail, from an intermediate point, and an army on foot, entering an enemy's country, and guarding a heavy train, and a depot retained by him in an improper place.

6th. The general-in-chief forbade pursuit of the enemy, in the event that he should retire towards Manassas, fearing to press him on Washington.

7th. That I was informed by the general-in-chief the attack on Manassas would be made on Tuesday, the 16th July, instead of Sunday, the 21st, at which time he directed me to make such a demonstration upon Winchester as to keep the enemy at that place. I claim that the demonstration was made on that day, and that he did not avail himself of the fruits of that movement, as he had expected to do. All that was demanded of me, and more, was effected.

8th. That if the army I commanded had attacked Winchester on Tuesday, the 16th July, as it has since been claimed I was ordered to do, two armies instead of one would have been demoralized, and the enemy would have turned with all the flush of victory to a triumph in front of Washington.

9th. That I have suffered additional injustice at the hands of the general-in-chief who sanctioned and fixed the impression that the enemy at Winchester was inferior to me in force in every arm of service, and yet has not corrected that report, although he knew, two days after the battle of Bull Run, that siege artillery, three times as numerous, and heavier than mine, had been left by the enemy at Winchester, while a greater number of guns had been carried away.

Very respectfully, your obedient servant,

R. PATTERSON, *Major General.*

WAR DEPARTMENT,
Washington, November 3, 1861.

DEAR SIR: I have the honor to acknowledge the receipt of your letter, bearing date November 1. The Secretary of War is absent on a visit north. I will forward to him by this day's mail, and ask for instructions.

Very respectfully,

THOMAS A. SCOTT, *Ass't Secretary of War.*

General R. PATTERSON, *Philadelphia.*

PHILADELPHIA, *November 26, 1861.*

SIR: I respectfully request that you will do me the justice to refer to my letter of the 1st instant, and give it your early attention. I cannot refrain from intimating a confident hope that my application for a court of inquiry will meet with your favorable consideration, and that an order for the detail will be made at the earliest moment consistent with the interests of the service.

I have the honor to be, with great respect, your obedient servant,

R. PATTERSON, *Major General.*

Hon. SIMON CAMERON, *Secretary of War.*

WAR DEPARTMENT, *November 30, 1861.*

GENERAL: I have to acknowledge the receipt of your letter of the 26th instant, calling my attention to your communication of the 1st of November, which contains a request for an inquiry into the late campaign in Virginia, in which you commanded a part of the United States forces.

Your letter did not reach me until my return to this city, and subsequent to the departure of Lieutenant General Scott for Europe.

There appears to have been no precedent in our service for an investigation or trial of an officer's conduct after he has received an honorable discharge. The inquiry you desire to have instituted would equally concern the late general-in-chief, and, as it appears to me, in justice to him, should not be made in his absence.

The respect I have always entertained for you, as well as the friendly relations which have long existed between us, would claim for any personal request from you the most prompt and favorable attention; but in my public capacity, in the present condition of affairs, I cannot convince myself that my duty to the government and to the country would justify me in acceding to your request. I must, therefore, reluctantly decline the appointment of a court of inquiry at this time.

With much respect, your obedient servant,

SIMON CAMERON, *Secretary of War.*

General R. PATTERSON, *Philadelphia, Penn.*

No. 3.

SENATE OF THE UNITED STATES, *December* 17, 1861.

On motion of Mr. Sherman,

Resolved, That the Secretary of War be requested, if not incompatible with the public interest, to furnish the Senate with copies of the correspondence between Lieutenant General Scott and Major General Patterson, with all orders from the former to the latter from the 16th day of April, 1861, to the 25th day of July, inclusive.

WAR DEPARTMENT, *December* 24, 1861.

SIR: In answer to a resolution of the Senate of the 17th instant, I have the honor to transmit herewith a report of the adjutant general, from which it will be perceived that it is not deemed compatible with the public interest at this time to furnish the correspondence between Generals Scott and Patterson, as called for.

Very respectfully, your obedient servant,

SIMON CAMERON, *Secretary of War.*

Hon. H. HAMLIN, *President of the Senate.*

HEADQUARTERS OF THE ARMY,
Adjutant General's Office, Washington, December 23, 1861.

SIR: In compliance with your instructions, I have the honor to report that, after due consideration, the general-in-chief is of the opinion it would be "incompatible with the public interest to furnish the Senate with copies of the correspondence between Lieutenant General Scott and Major General Patterson, and with all orders from the former to the latter from the 16th day of April, 1861, to the 25th day of July, inclusive," as called for in the Senate resolution of December 17, 1861.

I am, sir, very respectfully, your obedient servant,

L. THOMAS, *Adjutant General.*

Hon. SECRETARY OF WAR.

No. 4.

HEADQUARTERS OF THE ARMY,
Washington, June 4, 1861.

General Scott says do not make a move forward until you are joined by a battery of the fourth artillery and a battalion of five companies of 3d United States infantry, to leave here the 6th instant for Carlisle. Company F, fourth artillery, is the one to be mounted. Orders have been given to purchase horses and collect the guns, equipments, &c., as soon as possible at Carlisle.

It will require some days, but the general considers this addition to your force indispensable. If two Ohio regiments come to you retain them; also halt the first two regiments that may pass through Harrisburg from the north to this city and add them to your force. You will receive a letter from the general before you move.

E. D. TOWNSEND, *A. A. G.*

Major General R. PATTERSON,
Chambersburg, Pennsylvania.

No. 5.

HEADQUARTERS OF THE ARMY,
Washington, June 8, 1861.

SIR : I think your expedition against Harper's Ferry well projected, and that success in it would be an important step in the war. But there must be no reverse. Hence I have given you the best re-enforcements within my reach, and have just ordered Colonel Burnside's fine Rhode Island regiment of infantry, with its battery, (about 1,200 strong,) to proceed to Carlisle and there receive your orders.

A company of the fourth artillery, (to receive its horses and battery at Carlisle,) with the battalion of the third infantry, took the same route, and with the same instruction, yesterday. This battery may not be ready for you in time. These heavy rains must swell the Potomac and delay your passage some days.

I am organizing, to aid you, a small secondary expedition under Colonel Stone. He will have about 2,500 men, including two troops of cavalry and a section (two pieces) of artillery. The movements by road and canal will commence the 10th instant, and passing up the country, (touching at Rockville,) be directed upon the ferry opposite Leesburg. This may be but a diversion in your favor, but possibly it may be turned into an effective co-operation. Colonel Stone will be instructed to open a communication with you, if practicable, and you will make a corresponding effort on your part.

I do not distinctly foresee that we shall be able to make any diversion in your behalf on the other side of the Potomac, beyond repairing the lower part of the railroad leading from Alexandria towards the Manassas Gap.

I have said that we must sustain no reverse—but this is not enough ; a check or a drawn battle would be a victory to the enemy, filling his heart with joy, his ranks with men, and his magazines with voluntary contributions. Take your measures, therefore, circumspectly ; make a good use of you engineers and other experienced staff-officers and generals, and attempt nothing without a clear prospect of success, as you will find the enemy strongly posted and not inferior to you in numbers.

With entire confidence in your valor and judgment, I remain your brother soldier,

WINFIELD SCOTT.

Major General PATTERSON,
United States Forces.

No. 6.

HEADQUARTERS OF THE ARMY,
Washington, June 13, 1861.

GENERAL : Information has been given the general-in-chief that Ben McCulloch has two regiments of sharpshooters coming from Texas, and that he is now on the spot preparing to meet your column, and then to fall back on Harper's Ferry. Indications received from this side confirm the impression you seem to have that a desperate stand will be made at Harper's Ferry by the rebels. The general suggests that sharpshooters be met by sharpshooters.

This will be handed to you by Lieutenant Babcock, corps of engineers, ordered to report to you.

I am, sir, very respectfully, your obedient servant,

E. D. TOWNSEND, *A. A. G.*

Major General PATTERSON,
Chambersburg, Pennsylvania.

No. 7.

HEADQUARTERS OF THE ARMY,
Washington, June 13, 1861.

The general-in-chief directs me to say that, on the supposition you will cross the river on Monday or Tuesday next, Brigadier General McDowell will be instructed to make a demonstration from Alexandria in the direction of Manassas Junction one or two days before. The general does not wish you to hasten, but to keep him informed, so that General McDowell may properly time his movement.

Colonel Stone is advancing on Edwards's Ferry and towards Leesburg, to intercept supplies and be governed by circumstances. If he finds means to communicate with you, and it is expedient to effect a junction with you, he has instructions to do so.

The general has sent a Mr. William Johnston to endeavor to pass through Harper's Ferry, and then to join you and give you useful information. It is hoped the facilities he seemed to possess will make his mission successful.

I have the honor to be, sir, very respectfully, your obedient servant,
E. D. TOWNSEND, *A. A. G.*

Major General PATTERSON,
Chambersburg, Pennsylvania.

No. 8.

HEADQUARTERS DEPARTMENT OF PENNSYLVANIA,
Chambersburg, Pennsylvania, June 7, 1861.

SIR: The enclosed telegrams will inform the general-in-chief how the Elmira regiments succeeded in passing out of this department, and what companies of the second infantry have been to Pittsburg. From private information I have reason to believe company "C," second infantry, will soon be in from Fort Ripley. Am I authorized to take it and others of the regiments passing east?

I desire in a few days to occupy the roads beyond Hagerstown, and to establish my headquarters in that town, but do not, in the face of the order of the general-in-chief not to make a forward movement, like to advance beyond Green Castle, to which point Colonel Thomas's brigade moved to-day. I can, in a few days hence, throw with wagons over 8,000 men beyond that point, and by rail, at the same time, 2,000 more.

While the river is high, from recent rains, I wish to establish my depots and to intrench my left flank on the Boonsborough road, placing there the force with which I can threaten the "Maryland Heights" and, should a favorable occasion offer, storm them. This force will be that which I will not be able to provide with sufficient transportation at present.

The approaches to Harper's Ferry are so well guarded, and the sympathizers with the rebels in the immediate vicinity so numerous, that no spy can approach their works. The little information I can gain assures me they are fortifying west of Harper's Ferry as well as at the "Maryland Heights," and design, on this field, to make a desperate struggle for supremacy.

Independent of the regular force with Colonel Thomas, I have now, in this vicinity, seventeen regiments, all the force which is to join me, except the New York and Ohio regiments, of which I know nothing.

I am, sir, very respectfully, your obedient servant,
R. PATTERSON,
Major General Commanding.

Lieutenant Colonel E. D. TOWNSEND,
Assistant Adjutant General, U. S. A., Washington.

No. 9.

WASHINGTON, *June* 16, 1861.

What movement, if any, in pursuit of the enemy, do you' propose to make,
consequent on the evacuation of Harper's Ferry; if no pursuit, and I recom-
mend none specifically, send to me, at once, all the regular troops, horse and
foot, with you, and the Rhode Island regiment.

WINFIELD SCOTT.

Major General PATTERSON.

No. 10.

WASHINGTON, *June* 16, 1861.

Why a detachment upon Winchester? If strong enough, the detachment
would drive the enemy from Winchester, Strasburg, and Manassas Junction; or,
perhaps, from Winchester, *via* Staunton, towards Richmond. What would be
the gain by driving the enemy on either of these places? And if your detachment be not strong it would be lost. Hence the detachment, if not bad, would
be useless. The enemy is concentrating upon Arlington and Alexandria, and
this is the line to be looked to. Is Wallace, at Cumberland, threatened from below; if so, the threatening detachment is cut off by your passage of the Potomac. McClellan has been told, to-day, to send nothing across the mountains
to support you since the evacuation of Harper's Ferry. You are strong enough
without. The regulars with you are most needed here; send them and the
Rhode Island as fast as disengaged. Keep within the above limits until you
can satisfy me you ought to go beyond them Report frequently.

WINFIELD SCOTT.

Major General PATTERSON, *Commanding*.

No. 11.

WASHINGTON, *June* 16, 1861.

You tell me you arrived last night at Hagerstown, and McClellan writes you
are checked at Harper's Ferry—where are you.

WINFIELD SCOTT.

Major General PATTERSON, *Commanding*.

No. 12.

HEADQUARTERS DEPARTMENT OF PENNSYLVANIA,
Chambersburg, Pennsylvania, June 12, 1861.

SIR: I yesterday notified you of the occupation of Cumberland by the
Indiana regiment, under Colonel Wallace, and the fact of secession militia being
in his neighborhood, upon whom he designed to call. I now enclose, for the information of the general-in-chief, the satisfactory report of his journey through
Virginia.

I have reasons to believe that, with a few exceptions, the people of Maryland
are loyal, and wherever federal forces will appear disloyalty will hide its head,
and the government receive powerful auxiliaries. The Unionists now present
a bold front and call for aid, which, as I cannot now give aid properly sustained,
would invite attack and probably cause defeat.

In the counties bordering the Potomac are many Union-loving people, but the secessionists are so powerful and violent and well armed that our friends dare not express open sympathies, and are often forced to array themselves against us. For this reason, and to sustain the command at Cumberland, which can gradually work its way east repairing bridges, I would respectfully suggest that two regiments at least, if they can be devoted to that purpose, be designated to protect the road in the rear and permit Colonel Wallace to approach. Supplies must also be sent by rail from Wheeling, and require protection.

I regret my command is not in condition and sufficiently strong, in facing a powerful foe, to detach at present a force towards Cumberland. I am resolved to conquer, and will risk nothing. On Saturday my depot will be established in Hagerstown, and immediately thereafter my headquarters will be transferred to that place. The amount of wagons and the difficulty of procuring teams rapidly enough has troubled me and does so yet, but on Saturday night I shall have in front of Hagerstown 10,000 men strongly posted, with depot there established; the different commands will be filled with expedition and pushed toward the river. The 4th artillery battery will not receive horses before Saturday. The heavy battery will arrive in Hagerstown after me. Before being prepared to advance to that point the troops will be well drilled and disciplined. A marked improvement is daily manifested in their military exercises, and the regiments lately arrived are in excellent condition and drill. Their success ere long will, I hope, prove we have gained by delay.

I am, sir, &c., &c.,

R. PATTERSON,
Major General Commanding.

Colonel E. D. TOWNSEND,
Assistant Adjutant General U. S. A., Washington City.

No. 13.

HEADQUARTERS DEPARTMENT OF PENNSYLVANIA,
Hagerstown, Maryland, June 16, 1861.

COLONEL: I have the honor to report, for the information of the general-in-chief, my arrival last evening in this place. From time to time I have notified you of the condition of the command to move, and of my intention soon to advance to this place with a force that could maintain any position it might take. With our own transportation, aided by every wagon and team that could be hired contiguous to our camps in Pennsylvania and in this place, I advanced yesterday, (the earliest moment,) General Cadwalader's division, and sent the largest portion of General Kejm's. The remainder with supplies are rapidly coming in.

General Cadwalader camped last evening near Williamsport; to-day, under my instructions, he will cross the river and occupy the ford to Falling Waters, and will be prepared to push on to Martinsburg, to which place he sends an exploring force. He will be sustained by Generals Wynkoop and Negley, whose brigades are posted for this purpose.

Early yesterday morning I received, simultaneously, reliable information of the evacuation of Harper's Ferry, and a threatened attack upon Colonel Wallace, at Cumberland, with a call for aid, which General Morris, in rear, has refused. I directed Colonel Wallace to hire transportation, maintain a bold front to the last moment, and if hard pressed to move toward Hancock, in which direction horse, foot, and artillery would be sent with orders to push on to him, or at his discretion to fall back upon Bedford, communicating the fact to the column this side. With the spirit of a true soldier, he has prudently determined to stand, and retire contesting the ground unless he will have to sacrifice his men.

Confident the enemy had retired and was in rapid retreat from Harper's Ferry, I ordered a force to be detached to Cumberland. Owing, as will be seen by the accompanying letters, to the want of means of transportation, and the fagged condition of the command, the march being long and the day oppressively hot, the command could not be put in motion.

Major Porter, at midnight, visited General Cadwalader, at Williamsport, and arranged to send to-day a section of artillery, a squadron of cavalry, and the Rhode Island regiment, Colonel Burnside, a gallant soldier and a gallant command, to support the noble Indiana regiment similarly commanded.

The transportation for that command exhausted all available wagons and checked, had I been able and it prudent, further advance to push on a flying enemy.

On the approach suddenly on their rear of this well organized force, and the steadily advancing column under Colonel Stone, the enemy appear to have hastily decided to evacuate the position they had openly declared should be held at all hazards. They have fled in confusion. Their retreat is as demoralizing as a defeat, and, as the leaders will never be caught, more beneficial to our cause.

Harper's Ferry has been retaken without firing a gun. The moral force of a just cause, sustained by a strong and equitable government, has conquered.

I am prevented advancing rapidly by want of transportation. The interests of the government are too momentous to risk a defeat, or even a check, and hence I send out no inferior force. To-day and to-morrow about nine thousand men cross to Virginia, there to await transportation and to be sent forward in detachments, well sustained. In the mean time I propose and submit for the consideration of the general-in-chief—

1st. To transfer to Harper's Ferry my base of operations. depots, headquarters, &c. &c.

2d. To open and maintain free communication east and west along the Baltimore and Ohio railroad.

3d. To hold at Harper's Ferry, Martinsburg, and Charlestown, a strong force, gradually and securely advancing, as they are prepared, portions towards Winchester, Strasburg, &c.

4th. To re-enforce Cumberland and move south to Romney, Morehead, &c., and operate with the column in the 3d proposition toward Woodstock and cut off communication with the west. We will thus force the enemy to retire, and recover without a struggle a conquered country. To carry out this plan time is required, and that, with a strong, firm hand, will restore peace and unity to our distracted country.

To effect what I propose requires the co-operation of General McClellan, and force from him to be under my control at Cumberland, both to secure the road as far as Grafton and to advance to Romney, &c. With Harper's Ferry in possession, Baltimore falls. Maryland will be a quiet spectator, awaiting the result of the campaign, with her interests developing a feeling in favor of a permanent federal government.

If this proposition be adopted I shall continue my present operations, which have been directed to this end, and shall, as soon as I am prepared, occupy Harper's Ferry, Martinsburg, secure the railroad and canal to Cumberland, using the railroad hence to Harrisburg as accessory only.

In connexion with this subject I respectfully request—presuming Baltimore to be so far peaceable that the safety of the railroads can be relied upon—permission to take from the Philadelphia and Baltimore road, and the Northern Central railroad, the regiments now guarding them. The latter I should at once transfer to the Baltimore and Ohio railroad, the former to the line of operations.

If I am permitted to carry out this plan, the Baltimore and Ohio railroad and the canal will be in operation in a week, and a free line of communication to St. Louis be established.

I shall continue to carry out these views until checked ; but if my course be approved, I wish to be informed. I am advancing into another department ; but so essential is it that, for the instant, I do not consider the sanction of the general-in-chief requisite. The telegram of the general-in-chief recalling regulars is at hand. My reply is the substance of this communication, with the request that the regulars be permitted to remain for the present. Until Harper's Ferry is occupied and fortified, I should fear the return of the rebels. This force is a good one ; but the general-in-chief has, by the regular troops and commanders he has given me, made it a reliable one, and caused Harper's Ferry to fall.

I am, sir, very respectfully, your obedient servant,

R. PATTERSON, *Maj. Gen. Commanding.*

Colonel E. D. TOWNSEND,
 Assistant Adjutant General U. S. A., Washington City.

No. 14.

HEADQUARTERS OF THE ARMY,
Washington, June 17, 1861.

To General PATTERSON :

We are pressed here. Send the troops that I have twice called for, without delay.

WINFIELD SCOTT.

No. 15.

Telegraph to General R. Patterson, U. S. Army, Hagerstown.

HEADQUARTERS OF THE ARMY,
Washington, June 20, 1861.

I desire you to cause to be examined the Maryland Heights overlooking Harper's Ferry, with a view to a battery sufficient to hold the same ; and also without delay to propose to me a plan of operations with a portion of your forces to sweep the enemy from Leesburg towards Alexandria, in co-operation with a strong column from this end of the same road. Of course it is designed that you should absorb the column of Colonel Stone, now covering the fords and ferries on the Potomac below Leesburg. The remainder of your troops (how many?) to be left to cover the detachment on the Maryland Heights. Reply promptly.

WINFIELD SCOTT.

Copy signed.

E. D. TOWNSEND, *A. A. G.*

No. 16.

HEADQUARTERS DEPARTMENT OF PENNSYLVANIA,
Hagerstown, Maryland, June 21, 1861.

COLONEL: I have the honor to acknowledge the receipt of the telegram of the general-in-chief, calling for a plan of operations with a portion of my force to sweep the enemy from Leesburg, &c.

Enclosed is a copy of my telegraphic reply. The following is my plan :

To carry out the views of the general-in-chief, I propose—

1st. To occupy the Maryland Heights with a brigade (2,100 men;) fortify and arm with Doubleday's artillery; provision for 20 days to secure against investment.

2d. To move all supplies to Frederick, and immediately thereafter abandon this line of operations, threatening with a force to open a route through Harper's Ferry, this force to be the sustaining one for the command on Maryland Heights.

3d. To send everything else available, horse, foot, and artillery, to cross the Potomac near Point of Rocks, and unite with Colonel Stone at Leesburg. From that point I can operate as circumstances shall demand and your orders require.

If no blow is to be struck here I think this change of position important to keep alive the ardor of our men, as well as to force an enemy. The reasons for this change of depot will be so apparent to the general-in-chief that I need not refer to them. By the employment of the local transportation of the country I can soon make the necessary changes, and will hasten to carry out your orders.

I have many reports in regard to the movements of the force opposite us in Virginia, and have reason to believe that when the regulars were withdrawn General Johnston, with 13,000 men and 22 pieces of artillery, was marching to the attack, that night posted his forces, expecting an attack the following morning. I regret we did not meet the enemy, so confident am I that, with this well-appointed force, the result would have been favorable to us, and that this portion of Virginia would now be peaceably occupied. Reports of the enemy having returned to Harper's Ferry and driven the occupants to this shore reached me yesterday. I immediately despatched a strong force to take the position in the vicinity of Sharpsburg and protect all parties on this side of the river, and drive back any force which may attempt to cross.

I am, colonel, very respectfully, your obedient servant,

R. PATTERSON,
Major General Commanding.

Colonel E. D. TOWNSEND,
Assistant Adjutant General U. S. Army, Washington, D. C.

No. 17.

HEADQUARTERS DEPARTMENT OF PENNSYLVANIA,
Hagerstown, Maryland, June 23, 1861.

COLONEL: Up to the present instant I have received from Captain J. Newton, engineer corps, only a report of a part of his reconnoissance of the Maryland Heights and the ground adjacent, made in compliance with the injunctions of the general-in-chief. I hasten to give the result thus far, expecting to-morrow evening to present the whole.

Captain Newton approached the heights from this side, ascending over rough and steep roads, difficult for artillery. The summit he found capable of defence, of ample character, by about 500 men. The main difficulty to be overcome is the supply of water, the springs, which a week since afforded an ample supply, having become dry. He found no water within a half mile of the position selected on the heights for an intrenched camp. In Pleasant Valley, on the east, near the base of the mountain, springs are reported to abound; their character will be ascertained to morrow. Water would have to be hauled from this valley, and he reports the ascent very difficult. In this valley I propose to place the force sustaining that on the heights. The whole command, if the location prove favorable, need not exceed 2,500 men. That force would render the position safe; anything less would invite attack.

The following is what I have to report in relation to the enemy. Deserters from their ranks, some one or more of whom come in daily, all agree in saying that the whole of the force originally at Harper's Ferry (said to have been

25,000 men) is still between Williamsport and Winchester, about 8,000 coming this way arrived on Friday at Martinsburg. The remainder are distributed in a semicircle, and on the route to Winchester, within four hours' march of the advance. The advance is approaching Falling Waters, under the command of General Jackson, who now commands the whole.

The force under Jackson controls the people of Berkeley county, whom, I believe, are sorely oppressed, and would welcome our approach. That force has become some little encouraged from our not advancing, and may soon annoy us. If so, I shall not avoid the contest they may invite; indeed, if it meets the approval of the general-in-chief I would march my whole force, as soon as the batteries receive harness, upon the enemy and drive him step by step to Winchester. I believe this force can in ten days rid the adjoining portion of Virginia of its oppressors. I may be forced to this course. My fear is that I may interfere with the general plan of the general-in-chief, and drive the enemy to the aid of the main body. They would, however, go as fugitives to aid in its demoralization. My means of transportation are coming in rapidly.

I am, sir, very respectfully, your obedient servant,

R. PATTERSON, *Major General Commanding*.

Colonel E. D. TOWNSEND,
   A. A. General U. S. Army, Washington, City.

No. 18.

[Telegram]

HEADQUARTERS OF THE ARMY,
Washington, June 25, 1861.

I write by mail in substance. Remain in front of the enemy while he continues in force between Winchester and the Potomac. If you are in superior or equal force you may cross and offer him battle. If the enemy should retire upon his resources at Winchester, it is not enjoined that you should pursue him to that distance from your base of operations without a well-grounded confidence in your continued superiority.

Your attention is invited to a secondary object, a combined operation on Leesburg between a portion of your troops and the column of Colonel Stone at, and probably above, the Point of Rocks, to hold that village. The enemy has re-enforced Leesburg to sixteen hundred (1,600) men, and may increase the numbers. Inquire.

WINFIELD SCOTT.

Major General PATTERSON.

No. 19.

WASHINGTON, *June 27, 1861.*

I have your telegram of this date about a prisoner, but no acknowledgment of mine of the 25th, and letter of the same date. Under the latter I had expected you crossing the river to-day in pursuit of the enemy. You needed no special authority for sending prisoners to Fort McHenry.

WINFIELD SCOTT, *General-in-Chief.*

General PATTERSON, *U. S. A.*

No. 20.

HEADQUARTERS OF THE ARMY,
Washington, June 27, 1861.

SIR: The letter of Captain Doubleday, suggesting that the guns composing his heavy battery be sent one by one to be rifled, has been referred to the colonel of ordnance. The measure proposed is not now practicable, but a rifled 30-pounder gun has been ordered to be sent from Washington arsenal. The rifled guns required for Captain Perkins's battery have been issued, and there are none on hand. The ordinary guns which have been furnished the battery are considered as sufficiently effective by the general-in-chief.

I am, sir, very respectfully, your obedient servant,

E. D. TOWNSEND, *A. A. G.*

Major General PATTERSON, U. S. A.,
　　Commanding, &c., Hagerstown, Maryland.

No. 21.

HEADQUARTERS DEPARTMENT OF PENNSYLVANIA,
Hagerstown, Maryland, June 28, 1861.

COLONEL: I have the honor to acknowledge the receipt of a telegram from the general-in-chief, dated 27th instant, saying: "I had expected you crossing the river to-day in pursuit of the enemy." I infer from this that orders have been sent me to cross and attack the enemy. If so, I have not received them.

Captain Newton, of the engineers, returned at midnight, after two days' absence in the direction of Sharpsburg and Dam No. 4, and reports, on information he considers reliable, 5,000 men from Falling Waters to Dam No. 4, 4,500 men in the vicinity of Shepherdstown under General Jackson, and a reserve of 5,500 men under General Johnston, near Bunker Hill. He also reports twenty to twenty-four guns and a large cavalry force with General Jackson, and thinks General Negley, whose brigade is on my left, near Sharpsburg, will be attacked, the river being fordable at almost every point.

To meet this force of 15,000 men, with 22 guns and nearly 1,000 cavalry, I have about 10,000 volunteer infantry, and 650 cavalry and artillery, the latter being nearly all recruits. The horses are untrained, and we are still without harness for the battery.

I have repeatedly asked for batteries, and ought to have one for each brigade, but have none. The only one fit for service sent me was the Rhode Island battery, and that the general-in-chief was compelled, by the necessities of his own position, to take from me when most wanted, and within a week after it joined me. I have neither cavalry nor artillery sufficient to defend the fords of the river between Harper's Ferry and Hancock, but I would much rather attack than defend, and would have far more confidence in the result. While I will not, on my own responsibility, attack without artillery and superior force, I will do so cheerfully and promptly if the general-in-chief will give me an explicit order to that effect.

To insure success, I respectfully but earnestly request that the troops taken from me when Washington was menaced be sent to me with all speed, with a number of field guns equal to those of the insurgents. I will then be enabled to choose my point of attack, offer battle to the enemy, and, I trust, drive them before me, clearing the valley in front, and taking such position as the general-in-chief may indicate.

I respectfully suggest that Colonel Stone's column be sent me, with other re-enforcements, and venture to add that the sooner I am re-enforced with reliable troops and abundant field artillery the better.

I am making arrangements for crossing the river, and will do so, without waiting for orders or re-enforcements, if I find that the strength of the enemy has been overrated.

I beg to remind the general-in-chief that the period of service of nearly all the troops here will expire within a month, and that if we do not meet the enemy with them we will be in no condition to do so for three months to come.

The new regiments will not be fit for service before September, if then, and meanwhile this whole frontier will be exposed.

I have got my command into as good condition as I could expect in so short a time. Officers and men are anxious to be led against the insurgents, and if the géneral-in-chief will give me a regiment of regulars and an adequate force of field artillery, I will cross the river and attack the enemy, unless their forces are ascertained to be more than two to one.

I beg you to assure the general-in-chief of my sincere desire to sustain him faithfully, and to promote, by all the means at my command, the success of his general plan of operations.

I am, sir, very respectfully, your obedient servant,

R. PATTERSON,
Major General Commanding.

Colonel E. D. TOWNSEND,
Assistant Adjutant General U. S. Army, Washington, D. C.

No. 22.

[Circular.]

HEADQUARTERS DEPARTMENT OF PENNSYLVANIA,
Hagerstown, Maryland, June 30, 1861.

A reconnoissance in force will be made to-morrow morning to the Virginia shore, for the purpose of ascertaining the strength of the enemy, as follows:

The 6th brigade, Colonel Abercrombie commanding, will, under the guidance of Captain John Newton, engineer corps, cross the river near Dam No. 4, and be sustained by the 1st brigade (Colonel Thomas) and four pieces of artillery.

The 2d and 5th brigades, (Generals Wynkoop and Negley,) the 5th in advance, will sustain these commands, Major General Keim commanding. The 3d and 4th brigades, Major General Cadwalader commanding, under the guidance of Captain Simpson, with one squadron of cavalry and one section of Perkins's battery, will cross the river at Williamsport.

The first column will advance its light troops sufficiently far to ascertain the proximity of the enemy, and if the latter be not strong in front and left will move to the right, towards Falling Waters, to drive the enemy from that position, and form a junction with the 2d. If heavy firing is heard, the 5th brigade will advance to the assistance of the 6th and 1st.

General Cadwalader will advance cautiously towards Falling Waters and ascertain the strength of the enemy; hold him in check, and, if he attempts to move towards the other column, will attack.

The troops will be in Downeysville at 12 to night, prepared to move as follows:

The 6th brigade opposite Dam No. 4, with one section of artillery.

The 1st brigade in rear of the 6th, one section of artillery and squadron of cavalry in rear.

The 5th brigade.

The 2d brigade.

The 2d column at Williamsport. The light troops will cross at 3 a. m. Camp guards will be left with each regiment. The quartermaster will send to-day ambulances to each brigade. These to follow the columns.

Each command will take two days' provisions in haversacks, and be prepared to be separated from their baggage one night. The men will take forty rounds of ammunition.

Regimental commanders and all officers will compel their men to keep in ranks, and at all halts to lie down on their arms, and give orders and see that no man fires his gun without orders.

The division and brigadier commanders will meet the commanding general in Colonel Thomas's camp to-day at 4 p. m.

By order of Major General Patterson.

No. 23.

HEADQUARTERS DEPARTMENT OF PENNSYLVANIA,
Martinsburg, Va., July 4, 1861.

SIR : I avail myself of a favorable opportunity hastily to inform you of my arrival at this place with no opposition of any character since the 2d instant, but with a warm welcome from the populace. The rebel cavalry retired from the town as the command entered, and scattered in several directions ; the infantry and artillery retired towards Winchester.

I have halted temporarily to bring up supplies, which will be here to-morrow, having to-day returned all my wagons for the purpose.

Provisions in this part of the country are limited, and, consequently, with my present transportation, I can advance but a short distance before I am compelled to halt.

As soon as provisions arrive I shall advance to Winchester to drive the enemy from that place, if any remain. I then design to move towards Charlestown, to which point I believe Colonel Stone is advancing ; and if I find it not hazardous to continue to Leesburg, I must do this or abandon the country by retiring the way I came in consequence of the term of the three months volunteers being about to expire ; they will not in any number renew their service, though I think the offer should be made.

The Union sentiment here is apparently very strong ; but many fear a reverse, and that this force will retire either voluntarily or forcibly. The people cannot be made use of to raise a force for self-defence unless supported by a strong force of United States troops.

I desire to be informed of the wish of the general-in-chief in regard to the continued occupation of this region. I have ordered up all the force in the rear, except the Connecticut regiment, five companies of which are stationed at each of the depots, Williamsport and Hagerstown. The Rhode Island battery and the 13th Pennsylvania volunteers join me to-night.

I am, sir, very respectfully, your obedient servant,

R. PATTERSON, *Major General Commanding.*

Colonel E. D. TOWNSEND,
Assistant Adjutant General, Washington, D. C.

No. 24.

HEADQUARTERS OF THE ARMY,
Washington, July 5, 1861—M p. m.

Your letter of the 4th is received. Orders now sent this morning to Madison for the 3d and 4th regiments from Wisconsin to repair to Williamsport, *via* Chambersburg, and report to you. The 19th and 28th New York regiments leave here for Hagerstown to-morrow at half past two p. m.; you will have to provide transportation for them thence to the post you may order them to. If any three months men will re-engage for the long term, designate a regular officer of your command to muster them, provided a sufficient number to form a regiment can be obtained.

Having defeated the enemy, if you can, continue the pursuit, without too great a hazard; advance, *via* Leesburg or Strasburg, towards Alexandria; but consider the dangerous defiles, especially *via* Strasburg, and move with great caution, especially *via* Strasburg, halting at Winchester, and threatening a movement by Strasburg, or the passage of the Potomac twice, and coming down by Leesburg, may be the most advantageous movement.

WINFIELD SCOTT.

Major General PATTERSON.

No. 25.

HEADQUARTERS DEPARTMENT OF PENNSYLVANIA,
Martinsburg, Va., July 5, 1861.

SIR: The commanding general directs you to join' the column at the earliest moment, indicating the crossing at Williamsport as insuring the greatest expedition and securing the rear.

If you are short of transportation, you are authorized to hire all necessary vehicles in the country, to press, with promises to pay, the teams of unwilling owners.

The general wishes to hear from you at the earliest moment.

I am, sir, very respectfully, your obedient servant,

F. J. PORTER, *Ass't Adjutant General.*

Colonel CHARLES P. STONE,
  Commanding expedition en route for this place.

No. 26.

HEADQUARTERS OF THE ARMY,
Washington, July 7, 1861.

SIR: Besides Colonel Wallace's regiments, and Colonel Stone's three regiments and a half, there are now *en route*, or under orders to join you as soon as practicable, two regiments from Madison, Wisconsin; one regiment (to start to-morrow) from Boston, and four New York regiments from this city. Two of the latter went by rail yesterday, and two go to-day. All these regiments are directed to Williamsport, that being the most convenient point in regard to transportation of supplies, &c.

General Sanford (a major general of twenty-five years standing) has, in the best possible spirit, volunteered with two of his most efficient regiments to assist you. The general-in-chief desires you to make up for him a suitable command, and to employ him, as he desires, for the good of the service. You will find him worthy of your best respect and atttention.

As you were informed by telegraph, this morning, Governor Curtin has been requested, with the sanction of the Secretary of War, to order the regiments of State troops to hold Cumberland for the present, which regiments are instructed to obey you, or (in an extreme case) any orders they may receive from General McClellan.

The general desires me to add that, waiting for horses, we cannot yet say on what day we shall be able to attack the enemy in the direction of Manassas Junction. We hope, however, to be ready before the end of this week.

I am, very respectfully, your obedient servant,

E. D. TOWNSEND, *Assistant Adjutant General.*

Major General R. PATTERSON,
  United States Army, Martinsburg, Virginia.
  Part ii——9

No. 27.

HEADQUARTERS DEPARTMENT OF PENNSYLVANIA,
Martinsburg, July 9, 1861.

COLONEL : I have received the telegrams of the general-in-chief notifying of the additional regiments sent to me. Colonel Stone and the nineteenth and twenty-eighth New York regiments arrived yesterday. General Sanford, with fifth and twelfth New York regiments, will join to-morrow.

Since I last addressed you I have made no movements, in fact have been prevented by the necessity of sending all my wagons to the rear, to obtain provisions for a few days in advance, and to bring up troops. The commissary has supplies (with those in hands of troops) for about two days. Though the quartermaster has spared no exertion, and his agents have been very active, he has not, as yet, been able to provide a supply train for the command. I am therefore much restricted in my movements, being compelled, after three days advance, to send back for provisions. The difficulty will increase as I advance ; indeed I am now almost at a stand. Instead of receiving aid from the inhabitants, I find myself in an enemy's country, where our opponents can procure supplies and we nothing, except by seizure. Even information studiously kept from us. Supplies, especially provisions, are very scarce, and not even one day's rations can be relied upon. The supply of grain also is very limited. Under these circumstances I respectfully present to the general-in-chief the following plan, which, with my present views, I desire to carry into operation so soon as I can do so with safety, and the necessity for following Johnston ceases : I propose to move this force to Charlestown, from which point I can more easily strike Winchester, march to Leesburg when necessary, open communication to a depot to be established at Harper's Ferry, and occupy the main avenue of supply to the enemy. My base will then be some seven miles nearer, more easily reached by road, and my line of communication rendered more secure than at present. I can establish communication with the Maryland shore by a bridge of boats. In this way I can more easily approach you ; and the movement, I think, will tend to relieve Leesburg and vicinity of some of its oppressors. My present location is a very bad one, in a military point of view, and from it I cannot move a portion of the force without exposing that of what remains to be cut off.

General Sanford informs me by letter that he has for me a letter from you. I hope it will inform me when you will put your column in motion against Manassas, and when you wish me to strike. The enemy retired in succession from Darkesville and Bunker Hill to Stevenson's Station, a few miles from Winchester. There he has halted and, report says, is intrenching. His design, evidently, is to draw this force on as far as possible from the base, and then to cut my line, or to attack with large re-enforcements from Manassas. As I have already stated, I cannot advance far, and if I could I think the movement very imprudent. When you make your attack I expect to advance and offer battle. If the enemy retires, shall not pursue. I am very desirous to know when the general-in-chief wishes me to approach Winchester. If the notice does not come in any other way, I wish you would indicate the day by telegraph thus : *" Let me hear from you on."*

I am, sir, very respectfully, your obedient servant,

R. PATTERSON, *Major General Commanding.*

Colonel E. D. TOWNSEND,
    Assistant Adjutant General U. S. Army, Washington, D. C.

No. 28.

WASHINGTON, *July* 12, 1861—1.30 *p. m.*

Go where you propose in your letter of the 9th instant. Should that movement cause the enemy to retreat upon Manassas *via* Strasburg, to follow him at this distance would seem hazardous; whereas the route from Charlestown *via* Keyes's Ferry, Hillsboro', and Leesburg towards Alexandria, with the use of the canal on the other side of the river for heavy transportation, may be practicable. Consider this suggestion well, and, except in an extreme case, do not recross the Potomac with more than a sufficient detachment for your supplies on the canal. Let me hear of you on Tuesday. Write often when *en route.*

WINFIELD SCOTT.

Major General R. PATTERSON,
 Martinsburg, Virginia.

No. 29.

WASHINGTON, *July* 13, 1861.

I telegraphed you yesterday if not strong enough to beat the enemy early next week make demonstrations so as to detain him in the valley of Winchester; but if he retreats in force towards Manassas, and it be hazardous to follow him, then consider the route *via* Keyes's Ferry, Leesburg, &c.

WINFIELD SCOTT.

General R. PATTERSON.

No. 30.

HEADQUARTERS DEPARTMENT OF PENNSYLVANIA,
 Martinsburg, Virginia, July 13, 1861.

Received the announcement of McClellan's victory with great gratification. His success, however, makes no change in my plans. This force is the "keystone" of the combined movement, and injury to it would counteract the good effects of all victories elsewhere. Johnston is in position beyond Winchester to be re-enforced, and his strength doubled just as I would reach him. My position is a trying one, but I must act cautiously while prepared to strike.

R. PATTERSON, *Major General Commanding.*

Colonel E. D. TOWNSEND,
 Ass't Adj't Gen'l United States Army, Washington, D. C.

HEADQUARTERS DEPARTMENT OF PENNSYLVANIA,
 Martinsburg, Virginia, July 13, 1861.

McClellan's victory received here with great joy. Received without comment from the general-in-chief. I have given and now give mine. My column must be preserved to insure to the country fruits of this and other victories which we hope will follow. My determination is not changed by this news. I would rather lose the chance of accomplishing something brilliant than, by hazarding this column, to destroy the fruits of the campaign to the country by defeat. If wrong let me be instructed.

R. PATTERSON, *Major General Commanding.*

Colonel E. D. TOWNSEND,
 Ass't Adj't Gen'l United States Army, Washington, D. C.

No. 31.

HEADQUARTERS DEPARTMENT OF PENNSYLVANIA,
Martinsburg, Virginia, July 14, 1861.

COLONEL: I have thus far succeeded in keeping in this vicinity the command under General Johnston, who is now pretending to be engaged in fortifying at Winchester, but prepared to retire beyond striking distance if I should advance far. To-morrow I advance to Bunker Hill, preparatory to the other movement. If an opportunity offers, I shall attack; but, unless I can route, shall be careful not to set him at full retreat upon Strasburg. I have arranged for the occupation of Harper's Ferry, opposite which point I have directed provisions to be sent.

Many of the three months volunteers are very restless at the prospect of being retained over their time. This fact will soon cause you to hear from me in the direction of Charlestown. Want of ample transportation for supplies and baggage has prevented my moving earlier in the direction I desired.

I am, sir, very respectfully, your obedient servant,

R. PATTERSON, *Major General Commanding.*

Colonel E. D. TOWNSEND,
Ass't Adj't Gen'l United States Army, Washington, D. C.

No. 32.

HEADQUARTERS DEPARTMENT OF PENNSYLVANIA,
Bunker Hill, Virginia, July 16, 1861.

COLONEL: I have the honor to report, for the information of the general-in-chief, my advance and arrival at this place yesterday, opposed only by a body of 600 cavalry, of which one was killed, and five taken prisoners. To-morrow I move upon Charlestown. A reconnoissance shows the Winchester road blockaded by fallen trees, and fences placed across it, indicating no confidence in the large force now said to be at Winchester. I send you a sketch, prepared by Captain Simpson, of the works said to have been erected in the vicinity of Winchester. Preparations have already been commenced to occupy and hold Harper's Ferry with the three years troops. If the general-in-chief desires to retain that place, (and I advise it never to be evacuated,) I desire to be at once informed by telegraph.

I have to report that the term of service of a very large portion of this force will expire in a few days. From an under current expression of feeling I am confident that many will be inclined to lay down their arms the day their time expires. With such a feeling existing any active operations towards Winchester cannot be thought of until they are replaced by three years men. Those whose terms expire this week, and will not remain, I shall arrange to send off by Harper's Ferry; those for Philadelphia *via* Baltimore; those for Harrisburg *via* Hagerstown.

If Harper's Ferry is to be held, after securing that I shall, if the general-in-chief desires, advance with the remainder of the troops *via* Leesburg, provided the force under Johnston does not remain at Winchester after the success which I anticipate from General McDowell.

I wish to be advised if these preparations meet with the approval of the general-in-chief.

The Wisconsin regiments are without arms and accoutrements, which I have directed the commander of Frankford arsenal to provide.

I am, sir, very respectfully, your obedient servant,

R. PATTERSON,
Major General Commanding.

Colonel E. D. TOWNSEND,
Assistant Adjutant General U. S. Army, Washington, D. C.

No. 33.

HEADQUARTERS DEPARTMENT OF PENNSYLVANIA,
Charlestown, Virginia, July 17, 1861.

The terms of service of the Pennsylvania troops (eighteen regiments) expire within seven days, commencing to-morrow. I can rely on none of them renewing service. I must be at once provided with efficient three years men, or withdraw to Harper's Ferry.

Shall I occupy permanently Harper's Ferry, or withdraw entirely? I wrote yesterday on this subject, and now wish to be informed of the intentions of the general-in-chief. My march to-day was without opposition or incident of importance. The country has been drained of men. This place has been a depot for supplies for force at Winchester, and the presence of the army is not welcome.

R. PATTERSON,
Major General Commanding.

Colonel E. D. TOWNSEND,
Assistant Adjutant General U. S. Army, Washington, D. C.

No. 34.

HEADQUARTERS DEPARTMENT OF PENNSYLVANIA,
Martinsburg, Virginia, July 6, 1861.

SIR: I telegraphed my intention to cross the Potomac on the 1st instant. I now have the honor to report my movements since that date.

I left Hagerstown on the afternoon of the 30th ultimo, the earliest day my command could take the field in a proper condition for active service, intending the following morning to enter Virginia with two columns, (at Dam No. 4 and at Williamsport,) to be united the same day at Hainesville, the location of the rebels. Owing to the danger and difficulty attending the fording at Dam No. 4, I placed all the force at Williamsport.

My order of march for the 2d instant is given in the accompanying circular. The advance crossed the Potomac at 4 a. m., all taking the main road to Martinsburg, with the exception of Negley's brigade, which, about one mile from the ford, diverged to the right to meet the enemy should he come from Hedgesville, to guard our right, and to rejoin at Hainesville.

About five miles from the ford the skirmishers in front and on the flank suddenly became engaged with the enemy posted in a clump of trees. At the same time their main body appeared in front, sheltered by fences, timber, and houses. Abercrombie immediately deployed his regiments (1st Wisconsin and 11th Pennsylvania) on each side of the road, placed Hudson's section, supported by the first troop Philadelphia city cavalry, in the road, and advanced to the attack against a warm fire before him. The enemy, being supported by artillery, resisted for twenty-five minutes with much determination. Lieutenant Hudson, after getting in position, soon silenced their guns.

In the meantime Thomas's brigade rapidly advanced and deployed to the left flank of the enemy. The enemy seeing this movement and being pressed by Abercrombie retired, hotly pursued for four miles by artillery and infantry The cavalry could not be employed on account of numerous fences and walls crossing the country. In the enemy's camp was found camp equipage, provisions, grain, &c.

This brush was highly creditable to our arms, winning, as we did, the day against a foe superior in number to those engaged on our side. They were well posted, sheltered by timber, and sustained by artillery and cavalry. Our men advanced over open ground against a warm fire of artillery and infantry. I present the report of the Colonels Abercrombie and Thomas and Lieutenants Perkins and Hudson, and take much pleasure in bearing testimony as an eye witness to the admirable manner in which their commands were handled and their commendations earned.

I also bear testimony to the efficient service in posting portions of the troops and conducting them to the front and into action rendered by the members of my staff present and on the field of battle, Colonel Porter, Captain John Newton, and Lieutenant Babcock, and Majors Price and Biddle, who were employed conveying orders, also Surgeon Tripler in attention to the wounded.

The loss of the enemy was over sixty in killed. The number of wounded cannot be ascertained, as a large number were carried off the field.

I am, sir, very respectfully, your obedient servant,

R. PATTERSON,
Major General Commanding.

Colonel E. D. TOWNSEND,
Assistant Adjutant General U. S. Army, Washington City.

No. 35.

[Circular.]

HEADQUARTERS DEPARTMENT OF PENNSYLVANIA,
Hagerstown, Maryland, June 30, 1861.

A reconnoissance in force will be made to-morrow morning to the Virginia shore for the purpose of ascertaining the strength of the enemy, as follows:

The sixth brigade, Colonel Abercrombie commanding, under the guidance of Captain John Newton, engineer corps, will cross the river near Dam No. 4, and be sustained by the first brigade, Colonel Thomas, and four pieces of artillery.

The second and fifth brigades, Major General Cadwalader commanding, under the guidance of Captain Simpson, with one squadron of cavalry and one section of Perkins's battery, will cross the river at Williamsport.

The first column will advance its light troops sufficiently far to ascertain the proximity of the enemy, and if the latter be not strong in front and left, will move to the right towards Falling Waters, to drive the enemy from that position, and form a junction with the second. If heavy firing is heard the fifth brigade will advance to the assistance of the sixth and first.

General Cadwalader will advance cautiously towards Falling Waters and ascertain the strength of the enemy, hold him in check, and if he attempts to move towards the other column will attack.

The troops will be in Downeysville at 12 to-night, prepared to move as follows:

The 6th brigade, opposite Dam No. 4, with one section of artillery.

The 1st brigade in rear of the 6th, and one section of artillery and squadron of cavalry in rear.

The 5th brigade.

The 2d brigade.

The second column at Williamsport. The light troops will cross at 3 a. m.

Camp guards will be left with each regiment. The quartermaster will send to-day ambulances to each brigade, these to follow the columns.

Each command will take two days' provisions in haversacks, and be prepared to be separated from their baggage one night. The men will take forty rounds of ammunition.

Regimental commanders, and all officers, will compel their men to keep in ranks, and at all halts to lie down on their arms, and give orders and see that no man fires his gun without orders.

The division and brigade commanders will meet the commanding general in Colonel Thomas's camp to-day at 4 p. m.

By order of Major General Patterson.

F. J. PORTER, *Ass't Adjutant General.*

No. 36.

HEADQUARTERS DEPARTMENT OF PENNSYLVANIA,
Martinsburg, July 8, 1861.

Special Orders No. 94.]

Division and brigade commanders will require those regiments which have not reduced their number of tents to four common and one wall tent for each company, and one wall tent for other officers, at once to pack the surplus, mark them, and turn them in to Captain Woods, acting assistant quartermaster, at the depot. The spare wagons which will thus be created must be used to carry provision. Every wagon which can be spared from transporting the regiments will at once be taken to Colonel Crosman, who is authorized to call for what he requires.

The commanding general calls upon every one to reduce their amount of transportation to enable him to move a larger force to the front, and to keep his army provisioned.

By order of Major General Patterson.

No. 37.

HEADQUARTERS DEPARTMENT OF PENNSYLVANIA,
Martinsburg, July 8, 1861.

General Orders—Circular.]

The troops will move to-morrow morning in the following order:

The first (Thomas's) brigade, with the Rhode Island battery temporarily attached thereto, will advance by the Winchester turnpike, accompanied by one squadron of cavalry.

The seventh (Stone's) brigade, with Perkins's battery attached thereto, will take the main street of the town, (by the court-house,) and will continue on the road parallel and east of the Winchester turnpike. One company of cavalry will be attached to this command.

The first (Cadwalader's) division will follow the march of Thomas's brigade. Doubleday's battery will advance with this division, one regiment of which will be detailed for its guard, to accompany wherever it may be ordered.

The second (Keim's) division will pursue both routes, General Negley's brigade following the march of Colonel Stone's and Colonel Abercrombie's, and General Wynkoop's that of General Cadwalader.

The 28th and the 19th New York regiments will be temporarily attached to General Keim's division. General Keim will detail a strong rear guard of his division for the wagon train. The rear guard will march on the flanks and rear of the train, and will be re-enforced by a squadson of cavalry. General Keim will detail a competent field officer to command the rear guard.

The wagons will advance in one train in the rear of the troops, and will be required to keep closed. The troops of the several divisions and brigades will keep closed.

By order of Major General Patterson.

No. 38.

Circular to Commanding Officers of Divisions and Brigades.

HEADQUARTERS DEPARTMENT OF PENNSYLVANIA,
Martinsburg, Virginia, July 11, 1861.

The commanding general wishes to have as much as possible of this command ready to move at a moment's notice, and now directs an immediate examination and report of the ability of each regiment to march with transportation and at least three days' provisions.

The commanding general relies upon each division, brigade, and regimental commander, and each quartermaster, to keep his command in marching order, and not, when a march is ordered, to be asking at the last moment for what he should have called for in proper time, and it is impossible to give.

If any wagons can be spared from the transportation of a regiment, the commanding general wishes them, as soon as it is known, turned over to Colonel Crosman.

To bring up a large portion of these troops transportation of other commands had to be taken, and the commanding general must now know what condition the commands are in to designate marching orders.

By order of Major General Patterson.

No. 39.

HEADQUARTERS FIRST DIVISION,
Charlestown, Virginia, July 20, 1861.

SIR: In reply to your communication of this date, requesting information in regard to the dates of expiration of term of service of different regiments composing this division, I have the honor to state that the first brigade, Colonel George H. Thomas commanding—

6th regiment Pennsylvania volunteers, Colonel Nagle commanding, was enrolled and mustered into service on the 22d day of April, 1861. 21st regiment Pennsylvania volunteers, Colonel Ballier commanding, was enrolled on the 21st April, and mustered into service on April 29, 1861. 23d regiment Pennsylvania volunteers, Colonel Dare commanding; date of enrolment, April 18, 1861; date of muster, April 21, 1861, of some of the companies, but of the date of the muster of the last company was the 26th April, 1861.

Third brigade, General Williams commanding.

7th regiment Pennsylvania volunteers, Colonel Irwin; term of service expired, July 22, 1861. 8th regiment Pennsylvania volunteers, Colonel Emlee; term of service expired, July 22, 1861. 10th regiment Pennsylvania volunteers, Colonel Meredith; term of service expired, July 25, 1861. 20th regiment Pennsylvania volunteers, Colonel Gray; term of service expired, July 30, 1861.

Fourth brigade, Colonel Longnecker commanding.

9th regiment Pennsylvania volunteers: Field and staff.—When mustered, April 24, 1861; expiration of term, July 24, 1861. Company A.—When mustered, April 22, 1861; expiration of term, July 22, 1861. Company B.—When mustered, April 23, 1861; expiration of term, July 23, 1861. Company C.— When mustered, April 23, 1861; expiration of term, July 23, 1861. Company

D.—When mustered, April 24, 1861; expiration of term, July 24, 1861. Company E.—When mustered, April 22, 1861; expiration of term, July 22, 1861. Company F.—When mustered, April 22, 1861; expiration of term, July 22, 1861. Company G.—When mustered, April 24, 1861; expiration of term, July 24, 1861. Company H.—When mustered, April 24, 1861; expiration of term, July 24, 1861. Company I.—When mustered, April 23, 1861; expiration of term, July 23, 1861. Company K.—When mustered, April 23, 1861; expiration of term, July 23, 1861.

13th regiment Pennsylvania volunteers, Colonel Rowley, was mustered into service on April 23, 1861; term expires July 23, 1861.

16th regiment was mustered into service as follows: Company A.—When mustered, April 20, 1861; expiration of term, July 20, 1861. Company B.—When mustered, April 30, 1861; expiration of term, July 30, 1861. Company C.—Mustered for the war, May 20, 1861. Company D.—When mustered, April 26, 1861; expiration of term, July 26, 1861. Company E.—When mustered, April 27, 1861; expiration of term, July 27, 1861. Company F.—When mustered, April 25, 1861; expiration of term, July 25, 1861. Company G.—When mustered, April 25, 1861; expiration of term, July 25, 1861. Company H.—When mustered, April 25, 1861; expiration of term, July 25, 1861. Company I.—When mustered, April 26, 1861; expiration of term, July 26, 1861. Company K.—When mustered, April 21, 1861; expiration of term, July 21, 1861.

From a conversation which I had with Colonel Dare, to-day, he informs me that there is a strong feeling in his regiment upon the subject of returning to-morrow.

Many of his men are without shoes, and some are so nearly worn out that it increases their anxiety to return to-morrow. I fear that the men of this regiment and of Colonel Irwin's (7th) will give us trouble.

It is possible that if there was an understanding with Colonel Dare's men that they would not be asked to remain longer than the 26th, (the day of the muster of the last company of the regiment,) that they would be satisfied to remain until that day. This, I think, it would be expedient to do at once to anticipate any action they may adopt for to-morrow. Should I be requested to do so, I will give it prompt attention on hearing from you.

I am, very respectfully, your obedient servant,

GEO. CADWALADER,
Brevet Major General Commanding.

Colonel F. J. PORTER,
Ass't Adjutant General, Headquarters Department of Pennsylvania.

No. 40.

HEADQUARTERS DEPARTMENT OF PENNSYLVANIA,
Charlestown, Va., July 19, 1861.

Almost all the three months volunteers refuse to serve an hour over their time, and, except three regiments which will stay ten days, the most of them are without shoes and without pants. I am compelled to send them home, many of them at once. Some go to Harrisburg; some to Philadelphia; one to Indiana; and, if not otherwise directed by telegraph, I shall send them to the place of muster, to which I request rolls may be sent, and Captain Hastings, Major Ruff, and Captain Wharton ordered to muster them out. They cannot march, and, unless a paymaster goes to them, they will be indecently clad, and have just cause of complaint.

R. PATTERSON,
Major General Commanding.

ADJUTANT GENERAL U. S. A.,
Washington, D. C.

No. 41.

HEADQUARTERS OF THE ARMY,
Washington, July 17, 1861.

I have nothing official from you since Sunday, but am glad to learn, through Philadelphia papers, that you have advanced. Do not let the enemy amuse and delay you with a small force in front whilst he re-enforces the Junction with his main body.

McDowell's first day's work has driven the enemy beyond Fairfax Court-House. The Junction will probably be carried to-morrow.

WINFIELD SCOTT.

General PATTERSON,
Commanding U. S. forces, Harper's Ferry.

No. 42.

HEADQUARTERS OF THE ARMY,
Washington, July 18, 1861.

I have certainly been expecting you to beat the enemy; if not, to hear that you had felt him strongly, or, at least, had occupied him by threats and demonstrations. You have been, at least, his equal, and, I suppose, superior in number. Has he not stolen a march and sent re-enforcements toward Manassas Junction? A week is enough to win a victory. The time of volunteers counts from the day mustered into the service of the United States. You must not retreat across the Potomac. If necessary, when abandoned by the short term volunteers, intrench somewhere and wait for re-enforcements.

WINFIELD SCOTT.

Major General PATTERSON,
Commanding U. S. forces, Charlestown, Va.

No. 43.

HEADQUARTERS DEPARTMENT OF PENNSYLVANIA,
Charlestown, Va., July 18, 1861—1.30 *a. m.*

Telegram of date received. Mine of to-night gives the condition of my command. Some regiments have given warning not to serve an hour over time. To attack, under such circumstances, against the greatly superior force at Winchester, is most hazardous. My letter of the 16th gives you further information. Shall I attack?

R. PATTERSON,
Major General Commanding.

Colonel E. D. TOWNSEND,
A. A. G. U. S. A., Washington, D. C.

No. 44.

[To same—1 p. m.]

I have succeeded, in accordance with the wishes of the general-in-chief, in keeping General Johnston's force at Winchester. A reconnoissance in force on Tuesday caused him to be largely re-enforced from Strasburg.

With the existing feeling and determination of the three months men to return home, it would be ruinous to advance, or even to stay here without immediate increase of force to replace them. They will not remain.

I have ordered the brigades to assemble this afternoon, and shall make a personal appeal to the troops to stay a few days until I can be re-enforced. Many of the regiments are without shoes; the government refuses to furnish them; the men have received no pay; and neither officers nor soldiers have money to purchase with. Under these circumstances I cannot ask or expect the three months volunteers to stay longer than one week. Two companies of Pennsylvania volunteers were discharged to-day and ordered home. I to-day place additional force at Harper's Ferry, and establish communication with Maryland. I send Captain Newton to prepare for its defence.

R. PATTERSON,
Major General Commanding.

No. 45.

HEADQUARTERS DEPARTMENT OF PENNSYLVANIA,
Charlestown, Virginia, July 18, 1861.

Telegram of to-day received. The enemy has stolen no march upon me; I have kept him actively employed, and by threats and reconnoissance in force caused him to be re-enforced. I have accomplished more in this respect than the general-in-chief asked, or could well be expected, in face of an enemy far superior in numbers, with no line of communication to protect.

In future, post office, Sandy Hook.

R. PATTERSON,
Major General Commanding.

Colonel E. D. TOWNSEND,
Assistant Adjutant General U. S. Army, Washington, D. C.

No. 46.

HEADQUARTERS DEPARTMENT OF PENNSYLVANIA,
Charlestown, Virginia, July 18, 1861.

COLONEL: I arrived at this place on the 17th instant. Nothing of importance occurred on the march. The principal inhabitants left some ten days since, anticipating its occupation by the federal troops. It was, till our arrival, the location of a band of secession militia, engaged in pressing into the service the young men of the country. I have to acknowledge the receipt of two telegrams from the general-in-chief, of the 17th and 18th instant, both looking to a movement and attack upon Winchester. A state of affairs existed which the general-in-chief is not aware of. Though in some respects anticipated by his instructions, that if I found the enemy too strong to attack, to threaten and make demonstrations to retain him at Winchester. I more than carried out the wishes of the general-in-chief in this respect. Before I left Martinsburg I was informed of a large increase to Johnston's command, and of the visit to Winchester of the leading members of the confederate army, just before General McDowell was to strike. I advanced to Bunker Hill, causing surprise, and, I have since learned, an additional increase of force. On Tuesday I sent out a reconnoitering party towards Winchester. It drove in the enemy's pickets, and caused the army to be formed in line of battle, anticipating an attack from my main force. This party found the road barricaded and blocked by fallen trees. The following day I left for this place.

Before marching from Martinsburg I heard of the mutterings of many of the volunteer regiments, and their expressed determination not to serve one hour after their term of service should expire. I anticipated a better expression of opinion as we approached the enemy, and hoped to hear of a willingness to remain a week or ten days. I was disappointed; and when I prepared for a movement to the front, by an order for the men to carry two days' provisions in their haversacks, I was assailed by earnest remonstrances against being detained over their term of service, complaints from officers of want of shoes, and other clothing, all throwing obstacles in the way of active operations. Indeed, I found I should, if I took Winchester, be without men, and be forced to retreat, thus losing the fruits of victory; under these circumstances, neither I nor those on whom I could rely could advance with any confidence. I am, therefore, now here with a force which will be dwindling away very rapidly. I to-day appealed almost in vain to the regiments to stand by the country for a week or ten days. The men are longing for their homes, and nothing can detain them. I sent Captain Newton to-day to Harper's Ferry to arrange for defence, and re-establish communication with Maryland and the Massachusetts regiments. The 3d Wisconsin will soon be there. Lieutenant Babcock has been at Sandy Hook several days, trying to get the canal in operation, prepare the entrance to the ford, putting in operation a ferry, and reconstructing the bridge. Depots for all supplies will soon be established, and there I shall caused to be turned in the camp equipage, &c., of the regiments, and to that place I shall withdraw if I find my force so small as to render my present position unsafe. I cannot intrench sufficiently to defend this place against a large force.

I shall direct the regiments to be sent to Harrisburg and Philadelphia to be mustered out by Captain Hastings, Major Ruff, and Captain Wharton.

I am, sir, very respectfully, your obédient servant,

R. PATTERSON,
Major General Commanding.

Colonel E. D. TOWNSEND,
Assistant Adjutant General U. S. Army, Washington, D. C.

No. 47.

WAR DEPARTMENT,
Washington, July 23, 1861—11.30 *p. m.*

The following information has just been received from A. N. Rankin, editor of Republican and Transcript: There are nine 32-pounders, four 44-pounders, and two 6-pounders, and one thousand stand of arms at Winchester, with but five hundred men, raw militia, to guard the same. There are also about one thousand tents, and a very large amount of powder, balls, and shell.

WINFIELD SCOTT.

Major General BANKS,
Headquarters Army, Harper's Ferry.

No. 48.

WAR DEPARTMENT,
Washington, July 23, 1861.

I deem it useful, perhaps highly important, to hold Harper's Ferry. It will, probably, soon be attacked, but not, I hope, before I shall have sent you adequate re-enforcements.

A Connecticut regiment may soon be expected by you; others shall, to-morrow, be ordered to follow.

WINFIELD SCOTT.

Major General BANKS, *Harper's Ferry.*

No. 49.

Mr. Lackland, brother of Colonel Lackland, residing a short distance from Charlestown and just returned from Winchester, says, July 20, 1861, that Johnston had at Winchester—

2 regiments from Kentucky, Duncan and Pope	1,300
2 regiments from Tennessee	1,800
5 regiments from Alabama, strong	4,500
5 regiments from Georgia, strong	4,600
1 regiment from North Carolina	1,000
5 regiments from Mississippi	4,500
2 regiments from Maryland	1,200
Several regiments from Virginia	10,000
Militia from Virginia	5,000
One regiment of cavalry	600
Several batteries	700
Total	35,200

On Wednesday, the 18th, at 2 p. m., he commenced his movement southeast. Number taken, 30,000 confederate troops; number left, 5,200 militia.

No. 50.

CAMP NEAR MARTINSBURG, VIRGINIA,
Saturday, July 13, 1861.

DEAR SIR: It has been intimated to us, commanding officers of companies in the 6th regiment of Pennsylvania volunteers, under your command, that the United States government would like to retain the regiment in its service for some short period beyond the 22d instant, when its term of enlistment ends. We wish, respectfully, to say to you, for ourselves and in behalf of the men in our respective companies, that we decline continuing in the service after that day. We would suggest, also, that it would be injudicious to prolong, or attempt to prolong, our stay, and that the regiment would better be in Harrisburg, where it was enlisted, as early, at least, as the 22d instant, to be then mustered out and paid off. There is a disposition among large numbers of the men, after being at home a couple of weeks, to re-enlist and return as part of a regiment for three years more. If they are promptly discharged now, this disposition will be encouraged, and their services secured; otherwise, not. We and the men will serve faithfully the three months engaged for, but we believe the government will lose and not gain by keeping the regiment in the field, remote from the place of mustering out, until the last day. We will add that we make these representations to you with deference, and both for your own consideration and with a view to have you make such use of them as you see fit with the superior officers who control our movements.

Very respectfully,

J. K. SIGFRIED, *Captain Company C.*
DANIEL NAGLE, *Captain Company D.*
I. SEITZINGER, *Captain Company E.*
H. J. HENDLER, *Captain Company F.*
HIRAM CHANCE, *Captain Company G.*
C. TOWER, *Captain Company H.*
JOHN CRAIG, *Captain Company I.*
THOMAS WILHELM, *Captain Company K.*
D. B. KAUFMAN, *Captain Company B.*

Colonel JAMES NAGLE.

HEADQUARTERS COMPANY A, 6TH REGIMENT PENN. VOL'S,
Charlestown, Virginia, July 17, 1861.

While lying at Martinsburg a petition was gotten up by the officers of the 6th regiment Pennsylvania volunteers, declining to serve longer than our present term of enlistment, (ninety days,) and at the presentation of it to you, you was surprised and displeased that the ten captains of a regiment would sign such a document.

Sir, you will, therefore, please excuse me in taking the liberty of this communication.

I command company A of said regiment, and did *not* sign the petition; I was called on to do so, but remonstrated, saying it was premature; that we had been mustered in for three months and that the supposition was that we would be discharged at the expiration of that time, unless our government stood in need of our services, in which event I believe it to be the duty of all of us to remain a few days beyond the term of our enlistment. I said, also, that the paper would have a bad effect on our regiment in case the government *did* find it necessary to keep us a few days over our time; and the result has shown that I was right in my predictions. Many of our men, and a few of the *officers*, openly declare that they will not remain one *hour* after their term of enlistment shall have expired.

Again, the two captains that hail from the same town as myself, (Mauch Chunk,) viz: Captains Craig and Wilhelm, I have *no doubt* signed the aforementioned petition under a misunderstanding of facts, as they have both since told me that they signed it hoping to prevent being kept at Martinsburg after their term of enlistment should be up.

I am as anxious to get home when our time is up as any one can be, for I want to help get up a regiment for the three years service. But I want it understood that I stand ready *now* and *ever* to do the bidding of my commanding officer, and will do so, by your order, in *any* capacity, and at any time.

As a captain of a company in the said 6th regiment, I have felt it to be a duty that I owe to myself and friends to address you as I have; and hoping that my course will meet your approbation, I am, with *much* respect,

> Your obedient servant,
>
> ELI T. CONNER,
> *Captain Company A, 6th Regiment Pennsylvania volunteers.*

Major General PATTERSON, *United States Army,*
Commanding Department of Pennsylvania.

WASHINGTON, *January* 7, 1862.

General WILLIAM F. BARRY sworn and examined.

By Mr. Gooch:

Question. Were you at the battle of Bull Run, as it is called?
Answer. Yes, sir.
Question. In what capacity?
Answer. As chief of artillery.
Question. Can you state to us what led to the rout of our army on the field that day?
Answer. There were a great many causes.
Question. We want to get at the causes, the most obvious causes?
Answer. I think the principal cause was the uninstructed state of our

troops. The troops were raw; many of the officers were indolent, and they did not all behave themselves as they should have done on that day. I think that was one cause. All troops are liable to panics. But the great fault I found with our men was that after they had fallen back some distance, and were out of the enemy's fire, they could not be rallied. I look upon that as a difficulty inseparable from green troops. And in rallying men we need the assistance of the regimental and company officers very much, and that assistance was not rendered in many cases.

Question. Can you tell us at what time of the day and at what point the panic first showed itself?

Answer. On the right of our line was the place that I thought the panic first took place.

Question. In whose division?

Answer. The troops were very much scattered. They had been moved from point to point. They had been successful on the left of us, and the enemy had been driven back pretty nearly a mile, and having nothing to do, several of the regiments had been brought up towards the right. I had been with the army but three days. I had just arrived from Fort Pickens with my battery of artillery, and found that I was promoted to be a major. I gave up my battery to my successor, and General McDowell appointed me chief of artillery. I joined them the second day of the march, and was not very familiar with the organization of the troops.

Question. Were you present near the place where Ricketts's and Griffin's batteries were when they were captured?

Answer. Yes, sir; I was there at that very spot.

Question. What led to the capture of those batteries by the enemy?

Answer. The infantry support abandoned them, and that enabled the enemy to advance and capture the guns, or a portion of them; they did not capture them all. Nearly all the horses were shot down, and it was nearly impossible for the moment to remove the guns.

Question. Were those batteries ordered forward immediately preceding their capture?

Answer. Yes, sir; I suppose a half an hour before.

Question. Did you convey the order?

Answer. I gave the order in person to Captain Perkins and Captain Griffin; and not only that, I superintended the movement.

Question. Were those batteries supported?

Answer. Yes, sir; two entire regiments were procured at my request; the 11th New York, commonly called the Fire Zouaves, and the 14th New York militia.

Question. This was about three o'clock, was it?

Answer. I did not look at my watch during the entire day. I should suppose it was about half past two o'clock, for I think we left the field about four o'clock.

Question. In what condition were the Fire Zouaves at that time?

Answer. In what order, do you mean?

Question. Were they then an efficient regiment?

Answer. I thought so. I knew very little of them, except by newspaper reports. I knew what New York firemen were, and I supposed there was fight and pluck in them. I was struck with the manner they marched forward, very handsomely in line of battle. I rode with the major of the regiment—now colonel of the regiment. They marched up very handsomely in line of battle, passed the various obstacles they met in the usual tactical manner. I thought they did very well, and was very much disappointed and surprised when they broke.

Question. How many men should you think there were in the regiment at that time?

Answer. It looked to me as though there were about seven hundred.

Question. They supported which battery?

Answer. Both. The two regiments went up together, one just after the other. They had to go down a declivity, cross a little stream, and then go up a sharp acclivity. The ground was a little heavy in one or two places, and the artillery moved up in column of pieces, and formed the battery after they got on the ground.

Question. Did they take position on the hill indicated for them?

Answer. Yes, sir; and commenced firing, and fired some time.

Question. Was there any objection made by the officers of those batteries to advancing when the order was given to them?

Answer. Not the slightest that I heard.

Question. Was there any complaint that they were not properly supported?

Answer. I never heard of such a thing.

Question. How many guns were there in Griffin's battery?

Answer. Six guns in Griffin's battery, and six in Ricketts's battery.

Question. Twelve guns in all?

Answer. Yes, sir. However, I am under an impression that just at that moment one, if not two, of Griffin's guns had been left behind. I think one of his guns had become choked by careless loading; the cartridge bag had become twisted, and it could not be got in or out. That gun, I think, was not brought forward; but I am not certain about that. I did not count the guns.

Question. How many infantry would be a proper support for the guns of those two batteries?

Answer. Two regiments, I suppose, would be amply sufficient. I think if those two regiments had stood firm and done their duty those guns would never have been captured.

Question. Is there not a rule, or an understanding, as to the number of infantry that should support a battery?

Answer. No, sir; that depends upon circumstances very much; upon the amount of force opposed. If they are opposed by a large force you must have a corresponding force. And in addition to these two regiments of infantry there was a squadron of cavalry sent up by General McDowell afterwards, but moving faster than the infantry they arrived almost at the same time.

Question. Were the enemy in position in front of those batteries?

Answer. We could not see them.

Question. When were they first seen?

Answer. After the firing commenced.

Question. How soon after the order to advance was given?

Answer. I should suppose twenty minutes or half an hour. It must have taken nearly fifteen minutes to get to the place, because after I had designated the place that had been designated to me by General McDowell, and had started the batteries there, I then went to this infantry support and moved up with it. While I was doing that both of the batteries mistook the place, came a little short of it. I went forward and corrected that mistake, which produced some little delay. So I suppose the batteries were fully fifteen minutes in getting in position where they finally opened fire, which was the position I first designated.

Question. When did you see the enemy first in front of these batteries?

Answer. I suppose it was fifteen or twenty minutes after the firing commenced. It is hard to mark the lapse of time under such circumstances. I had very much to do then, passing from one battery to another, and looking to the infantry regiments coming up.

Question. Was there any mistake as to the character of a regiment that appeared in front of these batteries ?

Answer. Yes, sir.

Question. What was that mistake ?

Answer. It was a mistake in reference to a regiment that came out of a piece cf woods into which one of the infantry regiments that supported the batteries had gone a few minutes before—this fourteenth regiment from Brooklyn.

Question. What was that mistake ?

Answer. This regiment came out in line of battle, and a few minutes after they came out they delivered their fire upon us.

Question. Was it supposed by any one that that was one of our regiments ?

Answer. I supposed it was. They had no colors. I supposed it was this same regiment that had gone into the woods, as they disappeared in that direction. Whether they went into the woods or not I do not know. The ground was somewhat rolling, and they would disappear from sight for a few moments.

Question. Did Captain Griffin suppose it was one of the regiments supporting him ?

Answer. I do not know what he supposed. He directed my attention to it.

Question. Did he propose to open fire on that regiment ?

Answer. Not that I remember. If he had chosen to do it, he was competent to do it.

Question. Did you give him orders ?

Answer. No, sir ; I gave no orders to either captain. They were both competent men.

Question. You say you have no knowledge that he did not receive orders not to fire upon that regiment ?

Answer. No, sir ; I gave no orders not to fire.

Question. That regiment opened fire directly upon these batteries ?

Answer. Yes, sir.

Question. They captured these batteries ?

Answer. No, sir ; after they had produced a great deal of havoc, the troops immediately in front advanced—not that regiment which was on one side. There was nothing left for it then, for the infantry support broke in confusion and scattered in all directions.

Question. Was not this the first indication of a panic manifested ?

Answer. No, sir ; because I had seen regiments in the first part of the day break and fall back, and we were afterwards very handsomely successful.

Question. Do you not consider that the capture of these two batteries had a very decided influence on the fate of the battle on that day ?

Answer. I think it had an influence, but I do not know whether it was a very decided influence. I think the circumstance that had the most decided influence was the arrival of those fresh troops on our right flank, after the men had become wearied. Our men had had a long march ; been moving back and forth, and became very tired.

Question. Were not those fresh troops those that appeared in front of these batteries ?

Answer. No, sir ; I think not, because after that there were troops that came up on our right flank, almost at right angles, and those were the troops that I always took to be the fresh ones. Those that advanced on the guns when they were no longer supported, I have always supposed were the enemy's left that we had driven back.

Question. You do not suppose those troops that took the batteries were Johnston's men that had just come ?

Answer. No, sir ; I do not think they were. I am sure they were not. I think they were the enemy's right, which we had driven back two or three times. I saw very plainly their batteries limber up and go off to the rear and take up a new position. I saw that twice. Finally they went back so far that Captain Ricketts and Captain Griffin could see nothing of the men to fire at. You could not see the horses even; only a puff of smoke.

Question. When was this?

Answer. Before the two batteries moved forward.

Question. I mean after the two batteries moved forward. Did not some regiments appear in front of and capture these batteries within ten or fifteen minutes after they opened fire at this last position?

Answer. No, sir. The infantry support broke and abandoned the batteries. Then they of course felt emboldened to advance, because there was no opposition to them. There were a great many men killed and wounded, and a large number of horses knocked over by that single discharge of that one regiment, which was to our front and right—not really in front. It came out of this piece of woods. There was a very tall Virginia fence, eight or nine rails high, and I could just see the tops of their bayonets—not the clothes of the men, at all, but perhaps ten inches of their bayonets. They had no colors.

Question. What did you suppose that regiment to be?

Answer. I supposed it to be one of our regiments. But if I had known it to be one of their regiments, it would have been no time to do anything before they delivered their fire; that is, after I saw them. It was almost instantaneous after I saw them. I did not see them until my attention was directed to them by Captain Griffin, who said, "See there!" or "Look there!" I was then looking at the direction the guns were firing, and I could see nothing in front, even then. I had been with Captain Ricketts's battery, and just as I came to Captain Griffin's battery he called my attention to this regiment. It was all the work of a moment. There was a high, tall fence, and looking at it obliquely, as we did, it made a very close fence to us where we were. If we had been looking at it in front, we could have seen more plainly. But I could see nothing except this line of bayonets, and they delivered their fire almost instantaneously after I first saw them.

Question. Was their fire delivered from behind the fence?

Answer. Yes, sir; right through the fence. It made but a small obstacle to them, because they were close to the fence and the rails were of the usual width apart in that kind of fence, so that they could very readily see through it and fire through it. But even if we had known they were the enemy there would have been no time to have turned the guns upon them before their fire was delivered. If the infantry support had stood, the force in front of us would not have advanced.

Question. Did you consider the batteries were properly supported at that time?

Answer. I did. I think two entire regiments were ample support, and this squadron of cavalry was with them.

Question. How many cavalry?

Answer. Two troops of cavalry. They were commanded by Captain Colburn, who is now a lieutenant colonel upon General McClellan's staff. There were two troops of cavalry, commonly called a squadron, perhaps 100 men.

By Mr. Odell:

Question. Did the cavalry stand?

Answer. Yes, sir; until General McDowell ordered them to fall back, for after the enemy advanced they were only too much exposed, as there was no opportunity for them to charge there. The enemy made a sort of charge down the road—30 or 40 men of them. The troops were very much exhausted, the fire zouaves called it the "black horse cavalry," and spoke of the wonders they performed. But there were no black horses there or black uniformed men. They were ordinary bay and sorrel horses with single-rein snaffle-bits. I examined them very closely, because I had lost my pistol and wanted to get one of theirs, and I examined three or four very closely for that purpose. The fire zouaves fired upon them as they passed, for the cavalry could not be held, but ran by almost pell-mell.

Question. We never recovered the possession of Griffins's battery, as I understand?

Answer. Yes, sir; the guns were retaken twice. The official report states that fully. They were taken the first time and the men tried to drag them off. But they were encumbered with dead horses, and there were no other horses to hitch to them. After dragging them some distance the enemy advanced in large force and drove us back. Then some other troops with those of the infantry support which could be rallied again came back once more, but there was a large force advancing, and they had nothing left but to fall back. The infantry fire had pretty much ceased towards the left. There were several regiments in the road and resting upon their arms, and they were ordered up. If those two regiments had held on a little while we would have had a strong force. It was impossible to rally the 11th regiment—the fire zouaves. I rode in among them and implored them to stand. I told them that the guns would never be captured if they would only stand. But they seemed to be paralyzed, standing with their eyes and mouths wide open, and did not seem to hear me. I then reminded them of all the oaths they had sworn at Alexandria, after the death of Ellsworth, and that that was the best chance they would ever have for vengeance. But they paid no attention to what I said at all.

Question. I suppose the mere fact that a panic had spread among the troops once should not create a distrust of those troops again?

Answer. O no, sir. General McDowell and myself took regimental flags which we saw and begged the troops to rally around them; and a few did, but not a sufficient number to warrant the hopes that we would have had with good troops.

Question. How many did you estimate the force in front, and this regiment on the right, together?

Answer. I could not tell. They covered themselves very well. That was a remarkable feature in that battle : they kept themselves remarkably well covered.

Question. The ground permitted them to do that?

Answer. Yes, sir; the ground they advanced over was not so level as that our troops went over. Our troops marched very handsomely in line of battle. One instance, I saw a whole brigade advance as handsomely as ever any troops did.

Question. So far as the whole fight was concerned, the enemy had infinitely the advantage of our troops in position?

Answer. Yes, sir; the ground was their own selection. I think if the battle had been fought at the hour it was expected to be fought at, 8¼ or 8½ o'clock in the morning, we would have won it. There was a loss of three hours there, which I think had a very important effect upon the success of the day. It enabled those fresh troops to get up: it prevented our turning their flank so completely as we would have done by surprise; for when our columns halted, the enemy discovered the direction we were going to take, and prepared for it. And worse than that, the halting, the standing still, fatigued the men as much if not more than by marching that time.

Question. So that our men were really very much exhausted when they went into the field?

Answer. Yes, sir.

Question. But if the battle had been fought three or four hours earlier, then Johnston's reserve would not have been up in time?

Answer. I think the fate of that day would have been decided before they got upon the ground. I look upon that delay as the most unfortunate thing that happened. The troops that ought to have been out of the way were in the way before we could get to the turning-off point of the road.

Question. You were to have marched at 6 o'clock on Saturday night under the first order?

Answer. No, sir; the only order I heard was to move at half-past 2 o'clock in the morning.

Question. Was not the first order to advance our troops on Saturday night at 6 o'clock, or a portion of them?

Answer. Not that I ever heard of.

Question. Was it not proposed—I do not know that the order was issued—that the troops should march at 6 o'clock on Saturday night?

Answer. Never that I heard of.

Question. Was not there some delay on account of rations—of provisions?

Answer. I never heard of any.

Question. I will ask you, as you were in General McDowell's staff, whether the battle was not fought a day or two later than was first proposed?

Answer. I think not. The intervening time, from our arrival at Centreville and the time of advancing, was occupied by the engineers in observation. The affair of the 18th showed that the enemy was in great force at that position. I presume General McDowell's next idea was to discover some place to cross Bull Run without this opposition and turn their flank. I know the time was taken up by reconnoitring by a party of engineers, and a great deal of it was occupied at night to escape the observation of the enemy.

Question. I think it has been stated that there was a delay of one or two days for want of provisions?

Answer. I do not know about that. I joined General McDowell only a day or two before. I arrived here at 8 o'clock in the evening, and had to take my battery down to the arsenal, fill up with ammunition, get fresh horses, &c. General McDowell had marched the day before, and I made two marches in one and overtook him at Fairfax Court-House, and the next day he had me relieved because I was promoted, and assigned me to a position on his staff. So that what his views and intentions were previously to that I do not know. Half past two in the morning was the hour appointed. When he had the assembly of all his division commanders, and explained to them the movements and everything, he was very particular in giving directions about General Tyler's division being out of the way, as his division was the first to take the road, so as not to stop up the road for the others.

By Mr. Odell:

Question. You spoke of the delay of two or three hours being in your judgment a very serious one upon the success of the day?

Answer. Yes, sir.

Question. What was the occasion of that delay?

Answer. I always heard that it was occasioned by General Tyler not getting his division out of the way of the troops that were to follow. He was to lead, and was to march down the road past the point where they were to turn off to go up to the place with the other divisions, and his division did not get past in time to prevent that delay.

Question. Were not the other divisions waiting for him to pass?

Answer. I always heard so; always supposed so. We had to take one common road at first, and after crossing the little stream called Cub Run, where so much baggage and guns were lost on the retreat by the bridge being broken down, after crossing the little run a short distance we came to this turning off point.

Question. Have you any knowledge of the occasion of his delay?

Answer. I have not. There was some little firing ahead; was firing slowly at long intervals. I went down to where he had a large Parrott gun in the middle of the road in position. I asked the officer what he was firing at. He said they saw some small parties of men. I told him not to waste the ammunition of a heavy gun like that in firing at little parties of men.

By Mr. Odell:

Question. Was there the same difficulty in rallying the 14th New York regiment as in rallying the 11th regiment?

Answer. No, sir. But they were under the disadvantage of having lost their colonel. But they were rallied to some extent afterwards by General Heintzelman.

WASHINGTON, *January* 8, 1862.

General E. D. KEYES sworn and examined.

By Mr. Gooch:

Question. Were you in the battle of Bull Run as brigadier general?

Answer. Yes, sir; I was acting brigadier; I was then a colonel.

Question. Will you tell us in what part of the field you were; and, in short, what you saw—what came under your own observation on that day?

Answer. I crossed Bull Run, directly following Sherman. I was in Tyler's division and followed Sherman, and came into action on the left of our line, and my line of operations was down Bull Run, across the Warrenton turnpike. I crossed about half a mile above Stone Bridge and came into action a little before 11 o'clock, and passed to the left, and moved down a little parallel to Bull Run; and when I received orders to retire, I was nearly a mile in advance of the position where I had commenced. When I started into the action I was close up with Sherman's brigade; but as I advanced forward, and got along a line of heights that overlooked Bull Run, Sherman's brigade diverged from me, and I found myself separated from them, so that I saw nothing up there, except at a distance, beyond what related to my own brigade. I continued to advance, and was continually under fire until about 4 o'clock, when I received orders that our troops were retiring. I came off in perfect order, and was in perfect order all the day.

Question. You were on the left?

Answer. Yes, sir; opposed to the right of the enemy.

Question. Then, so far as you saw in your immediate vicinity, there was no rout?

Answer. No, sir; there was no confusion. I retired in just the same order nearly as I went into the fight; but when the masses mingled together as they came to cross Bull Run, there was confusion.

Question. What proportion of our troops reached the run without rout?

Answer. I being on the extreme left, of course all our people who withdrew before the enemy had to go a much longer distance than I had to go to reach Bull Run, because I was near to it at the time I received orders to retire. I moved up almost perpendicularly to the line of retreat of the balance of the army. As I approached the line of men in retreat they were all walking; I saw nobody run or trot even until coming down to Bull Run. In coming down there a great many wounded men were carried along, and I was detained so that the whole of my brigade got past me. I saw the quartermaster when I crossed Bull Run, and asked him where the teams were, and he said they were ahead; he saved them all but one, and got them back to camp. I then inquired of some ten or twelve squads of men to find out if they belonged to my brigade, and I found but one that did. Shortly after that a staff officer of mine came up and told me that my brigade was all ahead. I increased my pace, and got back to Centreville a little after dark, and found nearly all my brigade there. I did not come to the Potomac until Tuesday evening. There was no confusion at all in the whole affair, so far as my brigade was concerned, except very slightly in the retreat from Bull Run to the camp at Centreville; that I considered a perfect rout.

Question. You were in Tyler's division, and you moved first on the field in the morning?

Answer. Our division started first; but I received orders to make way for Hunter's and Heintzelman's divisions to pass through, as they had to go further to the right. So that before I got into action it was nearly eleven o'clock.

Question. Do you know why your division was stopped for the other divisions to pass through?

Answer. I thought it very obvious. Hunter had to go furthest up Bull Run to cross; then Heintzelman had to go next; and the next lower down was Tyler's division. To enable the several divisions to arrive about simultaneous against the enemy, Hunter should go first and Heintzelman next. The reason we started first was, because our division was encamped ahead of the others mostly.

Question. How far from where you started did Hunter's and Heintzelman's divisions turn off?

Answer. Heintzelman's division passed through mine in the neighborhood of Cub Run.

Question. How far did they go on the same route you were going?

Answer. About a half or three-quarters of a mile beyond Cub Run, I think. I was not with them, but that is my impression.

Question. Do you know from whom the order proceeded for you to let the other divisions pass through your division?

Answer. My first order was from General Tyler, and then I received another order from General McDowell to remain where I was. When I sent word forward to know if I should go forward, General McDowell sent orders to remain where I was.

Question. Could you not have have passed on to the point where the other divisions turned off without bringing you in immediate contact with the enemy?

Answer. I think I could; yes, sir. But I did not know that at the time, and I do not know whether it was known to others or not.

By the chairman:

Question. To what did you attribute the disaster of that day?

Answer. To the want of 10,000 more troops—that is, I think if we had had 10,000 more troops than we had to go into action, say at eleven o'clock in the morning, we should certainly have beaten them. I followed along down the stream, and Sherman's battery diverged from me, so that it left a wide gap between us, and 10,000 more men could have come in between me and Sherman, which was the weak point in our line, and before Johnston's reserves came up it would have been won. I thought the day was won about two o'clock; but about half past three o'clock a sudden change in the firing took place, which, to my ear, was very ominous. I sent up my aide-de-camp to find out about the matter, but he did not come back.

Question. What time was it that you ascertained on the field of battle that Patterson had not detained Johnston's column, but that it would probably be down there? Was it before the fight commenced?

Answer. There were rumors about the camp, to which I attached no particular importance. I supposed that Patterson was engaged up the river there, and would hold Johnston in check or follow him up if he should retreat. That was my impression at the time.

Question. Was that so understood at the time the battle was planned?

Answer. We had a council of war the night before the battle, but it was a very short one. It was not a council of war exactly; it was a mere specification of the line in which we should all proceed the next day. The plans appeared to have been digested and matured before that meeting was called. Whether anything was said about Johnston and Patterson at that meeting, I am not sure. I think not. That subject was discussed about the camp; but I know my own impression was that Patterson was opposed to Johnston, and would certainly follow him up if he should attempt to come and molest us. I know I conversed with some persons about it; but I do not think a word was said about it at the meeting the night before the battle.

Question. Had it been known that Patterson had not detained Johnston, would it not have been imprudent to hazard a battle there any how?

Answer. If it had been known that the 30,000 to 40,000 men that Johnston was said to have had, would have been upon us, it would have been impolitic to have made the attack on Sunday.

Question. If Johnston had not come down to the aid of Beauregard's army, what, in your opinion, would have been the result of that battle?

Answer. My impression is that we should have won it. I know that the moment the shout went up from the other side, there appeared to be an instantaneous change in the whole sound of the battle, so much so that I sent my aid at the top of his speed to find out what was the matter. That, as far as I can learn, was the shout that went up from the enemy's line when they found out for certain that it was Johnston and not Patterson that had come.

Question. Even after the disaster, what prevented your making a stand at Centreville, and sending for re-enforcements and renewing the fight there?

Answer. I was not the commander-in-chief.

Question. I know that; I only ask your opinion of what might have been done there.

Answer. If we had had troops that were thoroughly disciplined it would have been the greatest military mistake in the world to have retreated further than Centreville. But as our troops were raw, and this capital appeared to be the point in issue, I think men of decided military ability might have been in doubt as to the policy of remaining there. There was a striking want of generalship on the other side for not following us. If they had followed us they might have come pell-mell into the capital.

Question. Was it not as likely that you could defend the capital on Centreville Heights as well as after the rout here?

Answer. I will simply tell you what I did myself. I came back to my old camp at Fall's Church, and remained there until five o'clock on the afternoon of Tuesday, with my whole command. Then I marched them in good order, and passed three or four miles before I saw any of our own people. My impression then was that I could rally them there better than here. I acted upon that impulse myself. I did not bring my troops into town, which was the worst place in the world to restore order, but kept them in my camp at Fall's Church.

Question. Was there not a strong brigade on Centreville Heights that had not been in the engagement at all on that day?

Answer. There was a division there—three brigades.

Question. Could not a stand have been made there; and if it had been made, would our troops have been so demoralized as they were by running further?

Answer. It was a complicated question, and required, in my opinion, a first-rate head to decide; and if you have not a first-rate head of course you must guess a little. In my opinion it is a question that involves many considerations; first, the want of absolute command of the troops. The troops then were not in a sufficient state of discipline to enable any man living to have had an absolute command of them. The next point was to balance all the probabilities in regard to this capital; that is, was it more probable that the capital would fall into the hands of the enemy by retreating than by remaining there? I confess it was a question so complicated that I cannot answer it very definitely.

Question. If you had had knowledge on the ground, before the battle, of the condition of things with Patterson and Johnston, it seems to me that battle should not have been fought that day at all.

Answer. I should not have done it myself, certainly, if I had had that knowledge.

By Mr. Gooch:

Question. I suppose there was no such absolute knowledge as that?
Answer. No, sir; I do not think there was.

By the chairman:

Question. Ought not military men to have been informed of that important and decisive fact before we made a movement?
Answer. It is certainly one of the axioms of the art of war to know what the columns are going to do, and where they are.

Question. Could not the railroad have been broken so as to prevent Johnston from coming down?
Answer. I suppose that Hunter's column intended to push forward and disable that railroad, but he found work enough to do before he could undertake that. And in the heat of the day, after marching some fifteen miles, and being called upon to fight, they could not very easily have torn up a bridge.

WASHINGTON, *January* 11, 1862.

General FITZ-JOHN PORTER recalled and examined.

By Mr. Gooch:

Question. Were you on General Patterson's staff?
Answer. Yes, sir; I was his assistant adjutant general, and with him from almost the commencement of his expedition. At all events, I was with him from about the 1st of May.

Question. Then you were with him when he moved from Martinsburg?
Answer. Yes, sir.

Question. Will you state concisely the movement from Martinsburg?
Answer. I do not recollect the dates.

Question. We understand that he moved from Martinsburg on the 15th of July.
Answer. We moved from Martinsburg direct upon Bunker Hill.

Question. What distance?
Answer. I think it was about twelve miles. We there remained one day. There was a heavy force towards Winchester, and the following morning we moved from Bunker Hill to Charlestown.

Question. Johnston was at that time intrenched at Winchester?
Answer. Yes, sir.

Question. When you were at Bunker Hill how far were you from Winchester?
Answer. I think about twelve miles.

Question. How far is it from Charlestown?
Answer. About the same distance.

Question. You sent forward a heavy force towards Winchester on Tuesday, the 16th?

Answer. Yes, sir.

Question. Did they meet any enemy?

Answer. The cavalry of the enemy came in contact with them, some 500 or 600 of them; that is the report we received; I do not know it myself. They met that force, and I think a few cannon shot and a few infantry shot passed.

Question. Did they find any obstruction?

Answer. The road, as I understood, had trees felled across; had a fence put across it; was barricaded.

Question. Did they go near enough to ascertain whether Johnston was intrenched at Winchester?

Answer. They did not.

Question. Did you know at that time whether he was or not intrenched at Winchester?

Answer. Yes, sir; we knew it six weeks before.

Question. And these barricades were thrown up to prevent your progress towards Winchester?

Answer. Yes, sir; I always presumed these barricades were put there with the design, if he retired, (as I supposed he was prepared to do,) that we should not be able to pursue him.

Question. To prevent your pursuit if he retired towards Manassas?

Answer. Yes, sir; to give us all the obstructions he could while he was at his ease.

Question. While at Bunker Hill you were threatening Johnston?

Answer. Yes, sir; and I always considered that to be the design unless our force was superior to Johnston.

Question. You considered that during that campaign you were to take care of Johnston's force, and particularly at this period of the campaign?

Answer. Yes, sir; it was to try and hold him at Winchester.

Question. It was deemed of the first importance that Johnston should be held in the valley of Winchester at that time, in order that he might not be present and participate with Beauregard at Manassas when General McDowell made his attack?

Answer. Yes, sir; and there was also a fear which was expressed by General Scott in one of his despatches in a direction to be careful not to drive Johnston on Manassas.

Question. But to threaten him.

Answer. Yes, sir.

Question. You being on the staff of course saw the despatches of the commander-in-chief to General Patterson?

Answer. Yes, sir; they were all filed away under my direction.

Question. Did you not understand, from the general character of these despatches, that General Scott especially desired that Johnston should be held by Patterson's force?

Answer. Yes, sir.

Question. That was the great point that General Scott required there.

Answer. Yes, sir; that was the desire. And he also expressed the desire that if Johnston retired from Winchester in force not to pursue him, but take into consideration the route *via* Leesburg, through Keyes's Ferry, or better still, cross the Potomac twice and go, *via* Leesburg, down this way.

Question. That is, in case Johnston went down by way of Strasburg, it was deemed hazardous to follow him in that direction.

Answer. Yes, sir.

Question. And in order that you might be up with him, you were to take the other road right down as rapidly as possible.

Answer. Yes, sir.

Question. So that, in case Johnston should get down and form a junction with Beauregard, you should be on hand to join McDowell?

Answer. That was the design.

Question. When you made the march from Bunker Hill towards Charlestown, you were then retreating from Johnston, going further from him?

Answer. That was regarded at that time as a necessity.

Question. The fact was, you were going from Johnston?

Answer. Yes, sir; we were retiring, or rather it was going further from Winchester.

Question. Of course you were threatening Johnston less at Charlestown than you were at Bunker Hill?

Answer. Yes, sir. But the design in going to Charlestown was to get near our depot where provisions could be provided. From that point the design was, and the directions were given, to move again upon Winchester.

Question. When did you first learn of the battle of Bull Run, of the engagement of McDowell with the rebels there?

Answer. The first information was a telegraph from General Scott stating that the first move of McDowell had caused the enemy to abandon Fairfax Court-House. But there was no intimation after that, I think, until the Thursday night afterwards.

Question. Thursday, the 18th of July.

Answer. Yes, sir.

Question. You got the news then that he had moved and driven the enemy from Fairfax?

Answer. Yes, sir.

Question. Then you say you do not know when you first got the news of the battle at Bull Run.

Answer. No, sir; I do not recollect?

Question. You were about to explain why the movement was made from Bunker Hill to Charlestown.

Answer. It was in part the carrying out a plan which had been submitted to General Scott to take Charlestown and make Harper's Ferry a depot. The communication, *via* Williamsport, up to Martinsburg was a long one, and continually threatened. From Charlestown down to Harper's Ferry was a short distance, and there was a railroad there available for use; and another thing, it was much easier to go down in this direction by immediately crossing to Leesburg and striking from there, if necessary, over to Manassas. The proposition had been submitted several days before this movement was made, but there was no reply made to it by General Scott until, I think, three or four days after its probable receipt by him. It was then too late for us to make the move which had been indicated, and go to Charlestown and there establish a depot and threaten Johnston on the Tuesday when it was designed to make the threat. We had a great many supplies, and transportation was not very abundant, and the movement of the supplies from Martinsburg to Charlestown had to be covered by an advance upon Bunker Hill; and in order to carry out General Scott's wish to threaten Johnston strongly on Tuesday, as that was the day he said he was going to make the attack on Manassas, the movement to Bunker Hill was made, and we there remained threatening him. We could not carry at any time more than three days' provisions. In the mean time the provisions were being changed, and all the supply train that could possibly be gathered from Hagerstown and Williamsport was brought up there, and the movement to Bunker Hill covered the movement of the train to Charlestown.

Question. The question submitted to General Scott whether our forces should be at Charlestown or Martinsburg for threatening Johnston?

Answer. Yes, sir.

Question. And as between Charlestown and Martinsburg General Scott approved of Charlestown?

Answer. Yes, sir.

Question. That brought you into a better position with reference to Johnston at Winchester than you were in at Martinsburg?

Answer. Just about the same relative position, but better for us if we had required a forward movement.

Question. You were not threatening Johnston at Charlestown so much as at Bunker Hill?

Answer. While we were at Bunker Hill all the train we could get together at Martinsburg was carrying all our supplies over to Charlestown, and it was covered by the movement of the army over to Charlestown by Bunker Hill. If we had been compelled to come down to the assistance of McDowell, we would have been compelled to abandon everything at Martinsburg if we had remained there, or even at Bunker Hill.

Question. That was not true at Charlestown?

Answer. No, sir; everything there could have been pushed at once to Harper's Ferry and secured.

Question. Johnston was at Winchester when you were at Bunker Hill?

Answer. Yes, sir; before and afterwards.

Question. And he remained there until the next day, when you moved to Charlestown?

Answer. Yes, sir.

Question. And on Thursday, the day following, he moved to Manassas?

Answer. He broke up, I think, at 2 o'clock on Thursday.

Question. Do you know how long it took him to make the passage from Winchester to Manassas?

Answer. I think he got to Manassas on the day of the battle, Sunday.

Question. So that if you had detained him one day longer at Winchester, he would have been too late for the battle?

Answer. Yes, sir; but I do not believe he could have been detained; that was my own impression.

Question. Was it your impression at the time you were at Bunker Hill that Johnston would move down to Manassas?

Answer. Yes, sir; when it was necessary for him to go to Manassas.

Question. You believed, then, that he would go?

Answer. Yes, sir.

Question. That that was his intention?

Answer. Yes, sir; and that it was an utter impossibility for us to hold him.

Question. You came to that conclusion when you were at Bunker Hill?

Answer. Yes, sir; and not only then, but long before. We came to that conclusion when we were at Hagerstown.

Question. Did General Patterson come to that conclusion?

Answer. I do not know.

Question. Was that question discussed in your councils at all?

Answer. In speaking of it—General Patterson, Captain Newton—we all were under the impression that if we went to Winchester the enemy, as we advanced, would quietly retire; that as we went along, they would also go along a little further back, and gradually draw us forward until the time came when they would suddenly strike us, and make a dash at Manassas.

Question. The prevailing opinion among General Patterson's staff was, that the enemy would, at an opportune moment, dash forward so as to be at Manassas?

Answer. Yes, sir; that is my impression of the existing opinion.

Question. Do you know whether any such impression as that was ever communicated to the general-in-chief?

Answer. I do not.

Question. You do not know whether any such communication was ever made to the general-in-chief?

Answer. No, sir; I have no recollection of anything of the kind.

Question. You say General Scott had indicated Tuesday as the day he would fight?

Answer. Yes, sir.

Question. Therefore you deemed it of prime importance to hold Johnston over Tuesday?

Answer. Yes, sir; of great importance to hold him over Tuesday. Even if the fight was delayed, or not decided for one or two days, Johnston could not reach there.

Question. Did you not also deem it of prime importance that you should, if possible, detain Johnston until you knew the result of the attack by General McDowell upon Manassas?

Answer. Yes, sir; and when we got to Charlestown preparations were made at once to advance upon Winchester and continue the same movement.

Question. Was there any demonstration ever made from Charlestown towards Winchester?

Answer. Yes, sir. Quite a heavy reconnoissance was sent from there under Colonel, now General, Thomas.

Question. The enemy must have inferred from your movement from Bunker Hill to Charlestown—must have come to the conclusion that you did not intend to commence an attack upon them?

Answer. They may have come to that conclusion. I presume their thought was that we were then making a move to get down to Leesburg, and so on down.

Question. They probably inferred that you intended to go down by way of Leesburg?

Answer. Yes, sir.

Question. And therefore they must hasten their forces forward and go down, so as to be equal with you?

Answer. Probably so.

Question. That would have been natural?

Answer. Yes, sir.

Question. If they had drawn that inference they would have done what they did do?

Answer. Yes, sir; and to prevent their drawing that conclusion this force was sent out the following morning.

Question. You felt it was necessary to do something to do away with that impression?

Answer. Yes, sir; and a force was thrown out for that purpose. I will say here that when we were at Bunker Hill there was a commencement—in fact, it commenced at Martinsburg—of demoralization among the troops, which tended to prevent an attack. Some of them positively refused. There was a petition from one of the regiments, signed by a number of the captains, which I think is, or ought to be, in General Patterson's possession. He always kept it. It never went on the files of the records of the office.

Question. Have you any doubt that your men would have gone forward from Bunker Hill if you had desired them to do so?

Answer. I think they would have gone, but with very great reluctance—with no confidence. I think the great confidence of that command was destroyed immediately after the withdrawal of the regular troops from the command, when it first crossed the Potomac.

Question. Did you communicate to General Scott, immediately upon your withdrawal to Charlestown, the fact that you were not in position then to hold Johnston?

Answer. I have no recollection of it.

Question Why did you not follow down by way of Leesburg, *via* Keyes's Ferry, as indicated by General Scott in his despatch to which you have referred ?

Answer. My impression about that is that General Patterson was ordered to remain there.

Question. And that was the reason he did not move immediately down ?

Answer. Yes, sir.

Question. Otherwise he would have moved immediately forward ?

Answer. That I do not know.

Question. You would suppose so ?

Answer. I do not know. I cannot say with reference to General Patterson's opinion at all.

Question. I do not ask you what General Patterson's opinion was.

Answer. I think the reason we did not move forward was the effort being made to retain Johnston at Winchester. That is my own impression; that was my own view at the time we were there; and, in order to retain Johnston, orders were given for the men to carry two days' provisions, and those provisions were being prepared for the purpose. The circular was sent around, and immediately after a number of officers came in. Some of them spoke to me, and begged, if I had any influence at all, I would prevent that movement. One came in and said his men were very much demoralized, and said they would not go.

Question. On what day was this ?

Answer. I think that was Thursday.

Question. Do you remember what officer that was who said his men would not go ?

Answer. I think it was Colonel Johnson, Colonel Meredith, or Colonel Minier; one of those three I think it was.

Question. When you were at Bunker Hill an order was given, was it not, to move forward on Wednesday towards Winchester ?

Answer. Not that I am certain of; I think not.

Question. Was not General Sanford's division ordered to move forward on Wednesday ?

Answer. Not towards Winchester that I know of.

Question. Do you know what time on Tuesday the order was issued to move on Charlestown on the next day, Wednesday ?

Answer. I do not think it got out until one o'clock that night.

Question. Then you were in doubt during the day of Tuesday about the movement on Charlestown ?

Answer. There was a design of remaining at Bunker Hill that day, but provisions would not permit them to remain there over Wednesday. We were obliged to meet the provisions at Charlestown, which were then in the train moving from Martinsburg. The regiments were ordered to leave Martinsburg with three days' provisions; but many of them did not take one day's provisions; some of them were very improvident. There were two regiments, and one was Colonel Johnson's, that had no provisions at all.

Question. Could you not have brought your provisions from Charlestown to Bunker Hill as well as have gone from Bunker Hill to the provisions at Charlestown ?

Answer. We could have got them up, but not in time to move forward and make an attack.

Question. They could have reached you at Bunker Hill ?

Answer. Yes, sir. I would like to say this much : that at the time this order was given for the movement from Charlestown the officers came in and requested that it should be delayed, and that an appeal should be made to the men. It was suspended until General Patterson went out and made his appeal. The intention then was to move upon Winchester.

Question. That was on Thursday?

Answer. Yes, sir; the day after we got to Charlestown. He went out and made this appeal, and a very earnest one; and from some of the regiments that he asked at first the cry immediately was for shoes and pants.

Question. Was the appeal that they should go on and attack Winchester?

Answer. I was not present at this appeal, but I was informed that they were told that this movement was to be made, or that they were wanted for a few days longer. Some of them said they would not march—they were unprepared.

By Mr. Covode:

Question. Did not some of the regiments say they would remain if they were led to battle?

Answer. Not a word said upon that.

By Mr. Gooch:

Question. Your men had got very tired of marching?

Answer. I think that was the case; I think they had not much confidence in each other. There were a great many of the men without shoes. There was one regiment which afterwards came forward, expressing its willingness to remain—Colonel Wallace's regiment from Indiana; and when General Patterson thanked them for it a number of the Pennsylvania regiments did the same thing—offered to remain; others refused. Colonel Wallace turned to me and said: "Those boys have come up to offer their services to remain or move forward; but if they were called upon to march, there would not be three hundred of them that could march for want of shoes." I think General Patterson's great desire was to hold Johnston at Winchester. I think he felt he could not do so; I am certain of it. I think the main portion of that command felt that if they made an attack upon Winchester there would be nothing left of them.

Question. You think it was the general feeling in General Patterson's staff that it was absolutely beyond your power to hold Johnston?

Answer. I think so.

Question. And you think that General Patterson shared that feeling with his staff officers?

Answer. Yes, sir.

By the chairman:

Question. At what time was that feeling?

Answer. I do not think it was in the mind of any of General Patterson's staff, or any of the brigade commanders, that Johnston would stay in Winchester to meet an attack unless he was very powerful; and if he was wanted down in this direction, he could move whenever he pleased, and we could not touch him. I think that was the prevailing opinion.

Question. Can you tell why General Patterson did not communicate to General Scott the fact that he could not hold Johnston, as soon as he was satisfied of that fact?

Answer. I cannot tell you why he did not. I am of the opinion that General Scott was of that opinion himself. I think he says so in his despatch, where he says if Johnston retires in force do not follow him.

By Mr. Gooch:

Question. That is, if he retire by Strasburg?

Answer. I do not think he said if he retire by Strasburg—but if he retire in force. I never expected that he would retire by Strasburg.

By the chairman:

Question. It was the design, in that case, for Patterson to follow down to Manassas.

Answer. He said, take into consideration the going by way of Leesburg.

Question. General Scott did at one time think that Patterson could detain Johnston in the valley of Winchester, did he not?

Answer. I do not think there is anything in his despatches to that effect. I think that General Scott, by sending more troops there, showed that he thought we had not enough.

Question. Your idea is that General Scott did not suppose that General Patterson would detain Johnston in the valley there?

Answer. I do not think he thought so.

Question. Of course, then, in your estimation, any such expectation could not have entered into his calculations in regard to the attack upon Manassas?

Answer. I think not. General Scott may have had the hope that we would detain Johnston.

Question. Why did General Patterson advance towards Winchester at all if he did not think he could detain Johnston?

Answer. The object in advancing towards Winchester was partly to cover the movement of his supplies from Martinsburg to Charlestown, and partly also to carry out what General Scott directed him to do on Tuesday, to make a demonstration with the hope of holding Johnston at Winchester. I believe General Patterson, if he had thought there was any chance at all of whipping Johnston at Winchester, would have gone there. I heard him often express the wish, and say, "we will move at such or such a time." And in some cases he gave orders to that effect. But I think General Patterson began to feel that his troops would not carry him out if he went to Winchester.

Question. He had no confidence in his troops?

Answer. I think not. Many of the officers had not, and came forward and so expressed themselves. I think he was influenced by that. I do not say he did not have confidence in his troops, but I think he was influenced in his movements by the opinions that the officers expressed.

By Mr. Covode:

Question. Did you ever know of Colonel Johnson refusing to go with General Patterson previous to the time that you came back to Charlestown; that is, was it before or after the time that you went from Bunker Hill to Charlestown that Colonel Johnson signified his unwillingness to remain?

Answer. I do not think that Colonel Johnson himself signified that, but a large portion of his regiment.

Question. Was it before or after you went to Charlestown?

Answer. It was while we were at Charlestown. I never heard it before. And I never heard Colonel Johnson refuse to remain; on the contrary, he wanted to remain there.

Question. Do you know of any other regiments that refused to remain in the service previous to the time you turned back to Charlestown?

Answer. Yes, sir; one regiment presented its petition at Martinsburg. And that written petition, I think, is in General Patterson's possession now.

Question. Do you recollect what regiment that was?

Answer. I think it was the 6th Pennsylvania regiment. I think it was a written statement that their regiment would not remain, but demanded to be sent home by the time their service expired. There was another thing occurred while we were at Martinsburg. Information came to the men—how it got there no one ever knew—that an order had been published by the Secretary of War directing all volunteers then in service to be returned to their homes in time to be mustered out at the expiration of their term of service. That information was brought up there at Martinsburg. I supposed at the time that it was brought up there by some person probably friendly to the enemy.

General JOHN G. BARNARD sworn and examined.

By the chairman:

Question. Were you at the battle of Bull Run?

Answer Yes, sir.

Question. In what capacity?

Answer I was the chief of the engineer corps of General McDowell's army.

Question. Without going minutely into the matter, will you state concisely to what you attribute the disaster to our army in that battle?

Answer. One of the influential causes was, I think, the loss of time in getting under way the morning of the fight. The fact that the repulse turned into a disastrous defeat I attribute to the fact that our troops were all raw. General McDowell had not even time to see all his troops. They were brigaded only for the march, and put under officers whom the troops had not time to know, and who had no time to know the troops; and they had not been under military training long enough to be thoroughly educated as to what they had to do. With every disposition to fight well, they had not acquired the knowledge and experience they should have had, and when they were driven back on the narrow roads, in small bodies, they became so mixed up that it was almost impossible to recognize them.

Question. You attribute the first bad phase of that battle to the fact that our troops did not get on the ground in time?

Answer. Yes, sir. I think an hour's difference would have gained the battle. We had almost gained it as it was.

Question. What caused that delay?

Answer There were two cause distinct from each other. One was that in the plan of attack General Tyler's division was to move first on the Warrenton turnpike to Stone Bridge, while the really attacking column which was to turn the enemy's left flank, and which consisted of Hunter's and Heintzelman's divisions, had to follow Tyler until they reached the road where they were to turn off to make this detour. The road into which they were to turn was not a beaten, travelled road, but a mere country path. And Tyler's division was not out of the way so that they could get up to that turn-off for an hour and a half later than was expected. So that, instead of getting at that point at four o'clock, the head of Hunter's column was not able to get there until, say about half-past five. That was the first cause.

Question. What delayed Tyler's division; did you ever know?

Answer. When General McDowell and his staff rode along after waiting for the columns to get in motion—this was at four or half past four o'clock—we found the columns standing in the road waiting for one of Tyler's brigades to get out of camp and under motion. Perhaps there was some fault in planning it, in overlooking the fact that Tyler's division was so large, including three brigades, and the want of experience that we all had in moving large bodies of men. But whether it was General Tyler's fault in not getting his troops under way in time, I am not competent enough to decide. I think that after we had waited for some time General McDowell had to stop the last brigade of Tyler's division until Hunter's division filed past.

I said there were two causes for that delay. The second was the much longer time it took for the column of Hunter's to get around to Sudley's Ford than we calculated for. In going over the ground as far as we could the day before, we fell upon the enemy's patrol, and, not liking to attract their attention that way, we did not explore the ground up to the ford. We found that the ground was perfectly free; that there was nothing to obstruct cavalry or artillery; and the guide took them by a detour, saying that we would be exposed to the enemy's batteries if we took the shorter road. So that we were three or four hours making that march through the woods. We did not get to the ford until half past nine or ten o'clock, and we ought to have been there at six o'clock. We succeeded in our operations. We deceived the enemy as to the point we were going to attack. We turned his left flank. He actually did not know the point of attack until twelve o'clock, when he commenced accumulating his forces at that point. If we had been earlier, we should have got on the Warrenton turnpike, in the rear of Stone Bridge, before he could have got there We should have concentrated three divisions there.

Question. There was a strong brigade on Centreville Heights after the retreat began?

Answer. Yes, sir.

Question. What would have been the effect of ordering up that force to support the retreating columns?

Answer. When I saw that there was danger of losing the battle—when I saw the first charge, the first repulse of the Zouave regiment, the first capture of Ricketts's battery—I began to fear that we would be beaten. I had felt confident of a victory up to that time, but then I began to see the possibility of a repulse. We supposed that the Stone Bridge was unguarded, and if we were beaten, and the enemy should cross there, we would be cut off. I had got separated from General McDowell, and I hunted up the adjutant, who was behind attending to some duty, and requested him to order up the brigade at Centreville to the Stone Bridge, in order to support us there, as we supposed the division of Tyler had entirely got across the bridge. General McDowell left that brigade at Centreville as a reserve at a central point, as he was afraid that while we were operating on the enemy's left, making this long detour to do so, the enemy would pass Blackburn's Ford and manœuvre up by Centreville on our left flank. I had rather overlooked that until I saw it in General McDowell's report And General Beauregard says that if we had not anticipated him, he would have attacked us. He actually did send an order to General Ewell to move up and attack our communication that way; and the reason it was not done was because the order miscarried in some way, so that that part of his plan failed. If they had attacked and carried that position at the same time that we were repulsed on our left, we would have been worse off than we were.

Question. But would not have been defeated, would you, if that strong division at Centreville had been at the fight? They would have gone right through them, would they not?

Answer. If our line had held out for a half an hour longer, we would have beaten the enemy as it was, because Schenck's brigade at the Stone Bridge was at that moment just ready to act. The enemy had made an abattis on the other side; cut down the woods for some two hundred yards back from the bridge. Two of Tyler's brigades had crossed over to join our left. Schenck's brigade had remained at the bridge, and Captain Alexander had cut through the abattis and was ready to move on the enemy's right just at the moment that they received news that our men were retreating. I believe if we had held out a half an hour, or even but a quarter of an hour, longer, we should have beaten them.

Question. If Patterson had held Johnston back, what would have been the effect?

Answer. We should have beaten them. That was the only thing that saved them.

Part ii——11

Question. At what time before the battle commenced was it understood that Patterson was not holding Johnston back?

Answer. All that I knew about it, and all, I believe, that was distinctly known in the army about it, was that we heard the railroad cars running all night long. We were near enough at Centreville to hear the locomotives at Manassas.

Question. Suppose that when Patterson turned off from Bunker Hill to Charlestown, the moment that he knew he was no longer able to hold Johnston back, he had given notice to General Scott, and that notice had come to you, what would have been the effect of it upon your councils, had you heard it the day before the battle?

Answer. I think we should have fought any way. We could not have delayed any longer; that would have done us no good. The time of the three months' volunteers was expiring. We had made that march to fight, and I think we would have fought.

Question. Suppose you had held your own there until Patterson had followed Johnston down?

Answer. If we had received something definite—a communication of that kind—I think it is likely the determination would have been altered.

Question. I mean if that communication had been given directly from Patterson to General Scott, and from General Scott had been sent immediately to you, I suppose the effect upon your council would have been at least to wait until Patterson had followed Johnston down?

Answer. If we had received the information in a distinct form, we might have acted differently. I know that, with what information we had, it was uncertain. The question was discussed, "Shall we defer the attack?" and it was concluded that we better fight as soon as we could. We heard the railroad cars running all night, and presumed that Johnston's forces were coming in. But the moral effect of a delay would have been bad, and that action at Blackburn's Ford had a bad effect on the army.

Answer. Could you not have brought up 10,000 or 15,000 more troops from Washington by a little delay?

Answer. By stripping Washington entirely of all its troops we might have done so, I suppose. I do not recollect what the whole force was here then.

Question. General Tyler was sent around to make a reconnoissance merely, as we have been told, not to make an attack, on the 18th?

Answer. He was not expected to go further than Centreville, I think. I think he was not expected to make any attack at all.

Question. Seeing that he did make an attack, he should have carried those batteries, should he not, if he could have done so? And if he had, would it not have cleared the way for the next battle, so that you could have turned their left?

Answer. He ought not to have made the attack at all without knowing that he could do something. He ought to have made the attack with the intention of carrying the position, or not have made it at all. I was on the spot, and warned him twice that it was not intended to fight a battle there; that it was on the straight road to Manassas, at one of the strongest crossings on Bull Run, and that it was evident the enemy was moving up his force to meet us there. And as he had no orders to fight, and as there was no plan to fight there, I did all I could to get him to desist. I had no objection to his opening his artillery fire, for that was a sort of reconnoissance, to make them show just what they were. But I had no idea that they were going to march down to the Run and fight as they did.

WASHINGTON, *January* 11, 1862.

Colonel DAVID B. BIRNEY sworn and examined.

By the chairman:

Question. What is your rank and position in the army?

Answer. I am colonel of the 23d regiment of Pennsylvania volunteers, from Philadelphia. I was the lieutenant colonel of the same regiment in the three months' service, under General Patterson.

Question. What number of troops, with which to operate against Johnston's army, had General Patterson while at Martinsburg?

Answer. I have only my own estimate from seeing the regiments. I have no official knowledge of it.

Question. Will you give your best estimate?

Answer. I thought there were about 25,000 men—from 20,000 to 25,000—merely from seeing the camps and troops; that is only my estimate of them.

Question. What number of troops had General Johnston under him at that time, according to the best estimate that you had about it?

Answer. There was a great variety of opinions about that. I thought, from information that I got from the people there, in the country, that he had from 15,000 to 20,000 men.

Question. Was his army thought to be superior in numbers to that of General Patterson?

Answer. I do not know as I could state that; there was such a variety of opinion about it. Our regiments were all very anxious to try that point —to meet them—but they had no chance. That was the great trouble with our regiments.

Question. How long did you remain at Martinsburg?

Answer. We remained at Martinsburg some ten days, I think.

Question. Where was Johnston understood to be during those ten days?

Answer. On the road between Martinsburg and Winchester, and intrenched at Winchester. We marched from Martinsburg to Bunker Hill.

Question. How far was that?

Answer. About seven miles.

Question. Can you give the date of your march from Martinsburg to Bunker Hill?

Answer. I know we spent the 4th of July at Martinsburg. It was a few days after the 4th of July, but I cannot tell exactly the date.

Question. When you got to Bunker Hill, how long did you stay there?

Answer. We got there in the evening and encamped. The next day I was sent by General Patterson, with a detachment of six companies of infantry, a squadron of cavalry, and two sections of artillery of the Rhode Island battery, with instructions to make a demonstration and persuade the enemy that the army was marching upon Winchester, and to approach within two or three miles of Winchester. I marched down the road until we came to Stuart's cavalry. We fired upon them and they retreated, and I continued my march as far as I thought was prudent. I found the road barricaded—trees across it, and fences built across it. My instructions were only to give the enemy the idea that the army was coming. When I thought I had done that, I halted and came back. I suppose I went to within about four miles of Winchester.

Question. How far is Bunker Hill from Winchester?

Answer. I think the sign-post shows it to be eight miles.

Question. While you were at Bunker Hill what direction would Johnston's army have to take to get down to Manassas? How near to where you were stationed would they have to pass?

Answer. As I understand the geography of the country, they would come no nearer to us.

Question. They would still keep about the same distance from you?

Answer. Yes, sir.

Question. They would have to pass within about eight miles of you?

Answer. Yes, sir.

Question. If you had remained at Bunker Hill, would there have been any difficulty in your encountering them on their way to Manassas, if you had sought to intercept them on their way? Would there have been any difficulty in having an encounter with them, supposing they had come out of Winchester to go down to Manassas?

Answer. They would have been going in a side direction—laterally. They would not have come any nearer to us.

Question. You could have moved so as to have prevented their going down without an engagement with you, could you not?

Answer. Yes, sir; that could have been done by a forced march.

Question. Do you know any reason why you turned off from there to Charlestown?

Answer. No, sir; I do not.

Question. That, however, opened the way to them—gave them a free way to Manassas, did it not?

Answer. Yes, sir. Well, we would not have obstructed them if we had remained where we were at Bunker Hill. But we were told when we left Bunker Hill on our march that morning, that we were to take a road about half-way between Bunker Hill and outflank them. We were told that, as the road from Bunker Hill to Winchester had been found to be barricaded, we were to march towards Charlestown, and take the road turning off to the right as we approached Charlestown, and thus outflank them and prevent their coming down to Manassas. We had no idea of marching to Charlestown.

Question. You had no such idea when you started?

Answer. No, sir. We understood from our brigade commanders, &c., that we were still going to march upon Winchester, but to take this side road, instead of the one that was barricaded, and thus intercept them and prevent their joining Beauregard down here?

Question. Do you know the real purpose that was expected to be effected by this army of Patterson? Was it to prevent Johnston from joining Beauregard? Was that understood to be the object of Patterson's movements?

Answer. I do not know as I understood that it was especially to prevent him from joining Beauregard. Our conversation with our superior officers led us to suppose that we were to attack Johnston and whip him. I knew nothing about Johnston joining the enemy at Manassas, except, when we left Bunker Hill, we were then told that our object was to take this side road and prevent Johnston from coming down to Manassas on the railroad.

Question. You knew nothing, then, about the expectation of a battle being fought at Manassas at that time?

Answer. Yes, sir; the reason I knew was this: I called upon General Patterson about that time. General Cadwalader, who was our brigade general, referred me to General Patterson. We called to represent to him the state of our regiment, and he told me that he expected that a battle had been fought at Manassas on Tuesday, and thought he should hear of that battle on that day, and that we were to attack Winchester.

Question. In your judgment, as a military man, while you were at Bunker Hill would it have been in your power to have detained Johnston in the valley of Winchester, if that had been your purpose and object? Could you have prevented him from coming down to Manassas?

Answer. That is rather a difficult question to answer. I do not know what I would have thought then, if I had had the information that General Patterson had. But I think now, knowing the strength of the two parties, that we could have done it. That opinion is, however, based upon my present knowledge of the situation of the two parties, and not upon the knowledge that General Patterson and all the officers may have had at that time.

Question. How strong did you take the enemy to be at that time? Did you estimate his strength to be superior to your army?

Answer. He was not generally thought by the officers composing our army to be superior. There was a great deal of indignation among men and officers that we were marched and countermarched so much. There was great anxiety to march on—to get on. It was very difficult for those of us commanding regiments to make our men satisfied. We were there without tents—only four tents to a company—and when it rained the men were exposed. We had supposed that we were going to be marched on to fight. And the men were marched and countermarched until they became very tired of it.

Question. At what time did you first discover that it was not the intention to bring on a battle?

Answer. At Charlestown.

Question. Was there any dissatisfaction among the men until it was found that there was no probability of their being led to battle?

Answer. There was not in our brigade—in the 21st, the 6th, and the 23d Pennsylvania regiments, composing our brigade.

Question. Did the men refuse to go further or stay longer after their time should expire, at any time before they ascertained that they were not going to be led against the enemy?

Answer. I can speak better of my own regiment. At Charlestown there was some dissatisfaction in the regiment about the marching and countermarching, and the retreat; for they considered this march to Charlestown a retreat.

Question. It was a retreat in fact, was it not?

Answer. Yes, sir; they so considered it when we did not take this side road, as we expected. When we came to Charlestown their three months' time was out, and about 300 of my men were without shoes. My regiment had offered again for the war under myself—had offered to remain before that—but the offer had not been accepted at Washington. The time had come to go home, and a great many of them were without shoes, and they felt discouraged. I went to see General Patterson, and told him that if shoes were furnished my men to march, and there was any prospect of any fighting—if they were going to march on to Winchester—the regiment would to a man go on to Winchester and fight their way to Manassas, and so come on through Washington home. But if they were to be kept there marching and countermarching, it would be almost impossible to detain them much longer than their term of enlistment.

Question. At what time did you ascertain that Johnston had left Winchester?

Answer. I did not hear of it until the 21st or 22d of July.

Question. You were not near enough to him to ascertain when he did leave, I suppose?

Answer. No, sir.

Question. How far is Charlestown from Winchester?

Answer. I think it was some fifteen or sixteen miles. We were about eight miles from Winchester while we were at Bunker Hill, and this was a side movement that took us away some seven or eight miles further. I think it was about fifteen miles, though I do not know how far it was.

Question. You have already said that you considered this march to Charlestown a retreat?

Answer. Yes, sir; when we passed through the little town about half-way to Charlestown, and passed the little road down which we expected to turn towards Winchester—when we passed that, we understood that we were retreating.

Question. And then the dissatisfaction among the troops commenced?

Answer. Yes, sir; when we got to Charlestown.

Question. You had not heard the dissatisfaction before in your own brigade?

Answer. No dissatisfaction; some feeling at marching and counter-marching so much.

Question. While they were expecting to be led to battle they did not reckon upon quitting the service?

Answer. No, sir. If the men had been told that they were to be led to battle, I think they would have gone. I think there would have been no dissatisfaction if there had been any certainty that they would be led to battle.

Question. I am thus particular in asking about this matter, because that has sometimes been assigned as a cause for the retreat.

Answer. There was a great deal of dissatisfaction at Charlestown—that is, these regiments did not want to be retained if they were going to be marched and countermarched as they had been.

Question. That is, after all prospect of fighting was over?

Answer. Yes, sir. There was no such dissatisfaction at Martinsburg or Bunker Hill that I saw. I never saw men more rejoiced, who seemed to feel more like being led into action, than our men at Bunker Hill.

Question. They were enthusiastic and anxious to be led on?

Answer. Yes, sir, until we began to go back.

By Mr. Chandler:

Question. Are you aware of the fact of Captain William McMullin, of the Rangers, having been sent out to ascertain the number of troops at Winchester?

Answer. Yes, sir.

Question. What was his report?

Answer. I heard from others that he reported the enemy to have forty thousand men.

Question. Did you solicit the privilege of taking some of your men, and heading a reconnoissance, to ascertain the exact force of the enemy?

Answer. I told General Thomas that I had very little confidence in Captain McMullin; that I considered him a very disreputable character; and that I had in my regiment men who would make excellent scouts, and that I should be very happy to take a few of them, and try myself to ascertain the strength of the enemy.

Question. The permission was not granted to you?

Answer. No, sir; but the general said he would mention it.

Question. You did not believe McMullin's report at all?

Answer. Well, sir, it was just in this way: You probably know McMullin's reputation. He has always been a noted character in Philadelphia—a bully, a kind of a character there. He is a fellow of courage, and all that, but he is not a man in whom I would place the most implicit confidence.

By Mr. Odell:

Question. Do you mean his judgment?

Answer. His judgment is good enough. But I would not place the utmost confidence in his statements. He is a man of courage, and of fighting propensities, and all that. He is that strong enough.

By Mr. Chandler:

Question. He would report according to circumstances, not according to the fact? That is about the amount of it, is it?

Answer. Yes, sir; that is, I would not have that amount of confidence in his statements that I would have in the statements of others who felt more interest in the cause.

By Mr. Covode:

Question. Was he sent out to reconnoitre before you came back to Charlestown or after?

Answer. He was used for that purpose. There was a company raised at the request of General Patterson—not exactly as a body guard, but he used them as scouts and in matters of that kind.

By Mr. Chandler:

Question. Did he not make this report, that Johnston had 40,000 men at Winchester, after Johnston had left Winchester entirely?

Answer. I think so. We left Winchester on Sunday, and marched back to Harper's Ferry. I did not think there was any knowledge then—at least we did not know—that Johnston had left Winchester.

By Mr. Covode:

Question. Was it after you came back to Charleston that you proposed to reconnoitre?

Answer. That was merely in the way of conversation with General Thomas. I merely stated to him, as we were talking about the fire in the evening, that I had very little confidence in McMullin, and that I had some men in my regiment whom I had the most implicit confidence in; and I would even go with them and see that this information was obtained. That was before we went to Charlestown; that was when we were at Martinsburg.

By the chairman:

Question. Had you any reason to believe that Johnston's army had been re-enforced?

Answer. No, sir.

Question. You knew that Beauregard was to be attacked at Manassas?

Answer. I heard so.

Question. They would not, of course, under those circumstances, re-enforce Johnston from Manassas. And where was there any probability of his army being re-enforced?

Answer. I do not know.

By Mr. Odell:

Question. When did the time of your regiment expire?

Answer. On the 21st of July.

Question. What was the spirit of your men at Bunker Hill, in reference to marching against the enemy?

Answer. They were perfectly willing to go; they were anxious to march on Winchester.

Question. From Bunker Hill?

Answer. Yes, sir. We had the idea that we were to go home by way of Manassas, through Washington, and so on home that way. There was a rumor that we were to go home that way.

Question. How was it with the men when they were at Charlestown?

Answer. There was great dissatisfaction there.

Question. Do you think, as a military man, that Johnston could have been held or fought better from Bunker Hill than from Charlestown?

Answer. We were then seven miles nearer to him.

Question. Seven miles nearer at Bunker Hill than at Charlestown?

Answer. Yes, sir. We supposed the idea in the movement to Charlestown was to take this side road, and thus avoid the intrenched turnpike.

Question. Did not you and your officers understand that your business at Bunker Hill was to hold or fight Johnston while General McDowell engaged Beauregard at Manassas?

Answer. Yes, sir; I was told we were to prevent the junction.

By Mr. Chandler:

Question. That was the general understanding, so far as you knew, of all the officers there?

Answer. Yes, sir; we supposed we were to attack him.

By Mr. Covode:

Question. Did you not believe that efforts were being made by McMullin and others to magnify the size and strength of Johnston's army?

Answer. Not exactly that; I only judged from my knowledge of the man. I did not feel that I could depend upon his statements.

WASHINGTON, *January* 14, 1862.

Captain CHARLES GRIFFIN sworn and examined.

By the chairman:

Question. What is your rank and position in the army?

Answer. I am a captain in the 5th regiment of artillery, in the regular service.

Question. Under what colonel?

Answer. Colonel Brown is the colonel of the regiment.

Question. Were you at Bull Run at the time of the battle there in July last?

Answer. Yes, sir.

Question. Under whose command?

Answer. I was attached to General Andrew Porter's brigade, which belonged to General Hunter's division.

Question. Will you please inform us what, according to your best judgment, led to the disasters of that day?

Answer. I can tell you what occurred on the right, where I was. I was brought into battery about half past 11, and opened on the enemy's artillery. I should suppose it maintained its position for about a half an hour, when it retired. I changed position two or three times, and opened upon their infantry. It also retired, and as far as my observation went, we were successful in all parts of the field. There was a lull; we had nothing to fire at. Then Major Barry (now General Barry) approached me and said that it was General McDowell's order for us to move on a hill about a thousand yards distant, where the enemy's battery was that I had fired at. I hesitated about going there, because I had no support. I was told the Fire Zouaves would support us. We started for the hill, and halted once or twice. Once I went to Major Barry and told him I had no support; that it was impossible to go there without a support. He told me that the Fire Zouaves would support us; that they were just ready to take the double-quick and follow us. I told him if such was the case, I wished he would permit them to go and get into position on the hill—let the batteries

(Captain Ricketts's and mine) come into position behind them, and then let them fall back. And I told him the better place for our battery was on a hill about 500 yards in the rear of the one to which we were then ordered. He said that General McDowell's order was to go to the other hill; and he also refused to let the Fire Zouaves go on the hill first and form into line. I told him they would not support us. He said they would. He said, "Yes, they will: at any rate, it is General McDowell's order to go there." I said, "I will go; but mark my words, they will not support us." In going to the hill my first lieutenant went towards another place, and I had to give the order to countermarch, and go on the hill indicated. The turning off there by my first lieutenant threw Ricketts's battery to the front. We got on the hill and fired about half an hour, when I moved two of my pieces to the right of Ricketts's battery. We were then firing upon the enemy's battery, which was not certainly over 300, if it was 250, yards from us. I had only five pieces there. One of my pieces had had a ball lodged in the bore so that it could not be got in or out. I had five pieces there, and Ricketts had six, making eleven pieces side by side. As I said, I moved these two pieces to the right of Ricketts's battery, and commenced firing. After I had been there about five minutes, a regiment of confederates got over a fence on my front, and some officer (I took it to be the colonel) stepped out in front of the regiment, between it and my battery, and commenced making a speech to them. I gave the command to one of my officers to fire upon them. He loaded the cannon with canister, and was just ready to fire upon them, when Major Barry rode up to me and said, "Captain, don't fire there; those are your battery support." I said, "They are confederates; as certain as the world, they are confederates." He replied, "I know they are your battery support." I sprang to my pieces and told my officer not to fire there. He threw down the canister, and commenced firing again in the former direction. After the officer who had been talking to the regiment had got through, he faced them to the left, and marched them about fifty yards to the woods, then faced them to the right again, and marched them about forty yards towards us, and then opened fire upon us, and that was the last of us. I had about fifty horses killed that day. I had had several horses and some men killed before. Before this occurred I started to limber up my pieces, so thoroughly convinced was I that they were the confederates. But as the chief of artillery told me they were my battery support, I was afraid to fire upon them. Major Barry said, "I know it is the battery support; it is the regiment taken there by Colonel ——." "Very well," said I, and gave the command to fire in another direction with the battery. But I never delivered the fire, for we were all cut down. The Zouaves were about twenty yards to the rear of us; they were sitting down. I begged them to come up and give them a volley, and then try the bayonet. They did not run at first, but stood as if panic-stricken. I do not believe they fired fifty shots, certainly not over one hundred. And after they had received three, perhaps four, volleys from this regiment of confederates, they broke and ran. I went down the hill and found Major Barry at the stream watering his horse. I stopped to water my horse also. Said I, "Major, do you think the Zouaves will support us?" Said he, "I was mistaken." Said, I "Do you think that was our support?" "I was mistaken," he said. "Yes," said I, "you were mistaken all around." I can substantiate all this if anything is said to the contrary. There are living witnesses to support it. Lieutenant Read stood by my side and heard the conversation about the battery support.

By Mr. Chandler:

Question. Could you have cut up that regiment with a charge of canister so that they would not have charged upon you?

Answer. I could have staggered them terribly. While the colonel was making his speech to them we had plenty of time to have passed word along the whole line, and if the whole eleven guns had been turned upon them, they could not have touched us.

Question. Was that the commencement of the repulse?

Answer. Yes, sir; the first I saw of it. We had been advancing gradually before that. The report of General Andrew Porter is the best testimony of that.

By the chairman:

Question. What time was that?

Answer. About 3 o'clock, earlier or later—later if anything. I should suppose it was not far from that time.

Question. What happened after that?

Answer. Well, sir, I got off the field with one piece, there being one wheel horse and one lead horse to the piece. That piece I only got off about a thousand yards. I got off the field two pieces—two Parrott guns—the one that the ball was lodged in, and one with the horses attached to it. I went to the rear to get some horses to get my third piece off. There were several of our regiments that attempted to retake our batteries, and the enemy was driven back twice, if not three times, to my certain knowledge, by the brigade of General Franklin. I do not know what regiments he had. I know very few of the regiments. I knew the Fire Zouaves and the New York 14th, and I knew the battalion of regular infantry; that is about all, I believe. I met the 71st regiment, but they were not in our brigade. I also knew the Rhode Island troops when I saw them, but they were not in our brigade.

Question. You attribute the disaster in that part of the field where you were principally to a mistake in the place where you were to be posted, to having no support of infantry, and to a mistake as to the character of the regiment that appeared there?

Answer. I thought we ought to have gone on a different hill, and I thought Ricketts ought to stand still. But then I was but a subaltern there, and complied with the orders. I think we would not have lost our batteries if we had done so.

Question. Suppose you had been supported, what would then have been the consequence?

Answer. If we had been properly supported, we would not have lost our batteries.

Question. Supported by the Zouaves?

Answer. The Zouaves could not have supported us. They were not support enough. Five hundred men are not enough to support eleven pieces of artillery.

Question. What number do you think attacked you there?

Answer. There must have been 5,000 or 6,000, because there was regiment after regiment came on the field during the fight. The fight must have lasted half or three-quarters of an hour between our infantry and theirs—different troops coming up. A great many of our regiments turned right off the field as they delivered their fire, turning even as they delivered their volleys. They did not go off in any system at all, but went right off as a crowd would walking the street—every man for himself, with no organization whatever. The officers lost control of them. It is to be remarked that the men were very tired. I can readily see that if our men had been fresh when this thing occurred, with the success we had before, it might have been different.

Question. Do you understand this to be the first repulse of that day, or the first repulse where you were?

Answer. I understand it to be the first repulse of that day. I understand that is the only repulse we received that day.

Question. Suppose that reserve brigade at Centreville had been brought forward to support you, what, in your judgment, would have been the effect?

Answer. That would have had great influence. It might have been different; it might have been the same. I think the mistake was in sending our batteries so far ahead without support; and then I think the disaster was probably the result of numbers.

By Mr. Gooch:

Question. You say that you thought you should have gone to a hill five hundred yards in the rear. Do you mean in the rear of the position you occupied when the order was given to move forward to the other hill, or five hundred yards in the rear of the hill to which you were ordered to move?

Answer. I mean five hundred yards in the rear of the hill where we lost our batteries—the hill to which we were ordered.

Question. How far were you ordered to advance from the position you had been occupying?

Answer. About one thousand yards.

Question. You say that the Zouaves did not exceed five hundred at that time?

Answer. I do not think they did; I think that is a large number.

Question. What was their condition at that time?

Answer. I thought them in a disorganized state when they were ordered to support us.

Question. What support did Ricketts's battery have?

Answer. Just the same as I did.

Question. Do you mean that they were supported also by the Zouaves?

Answer. The Zouaves were in the rear to support the two batteries.

Question. Do you mean to be understood that these five hundred men were all the support both batteries had?

Answer. All the support I saw when I went on the hill, and all that I believe any of the officers saw.

Question. I suppose there is some rule in relation to the proper number of infantry to support batteries?

Answer. Yes, sir; there ought to have been at least 1,000 men to every gun, or at least there ought to have been not less than 4,000 men to support those batteries. It seems, from the reports of other officers, that there were other regiments brought up afterwards to support us. I find in General Barry's report that he met Colonel Heintzelman taking up the New York 14th. But if he meant that the New York 14th was in front of us supporting us, it certainly is not to be explained, because the New York 14th had red pants on, while the regiment in front of us had blue pants on, blue shirts, and straw hats. It can be established beyond a doubt, I think, that the New York 14th never came on the ground until after the batteries were lost. There were officers present who saw this, and can probably tell more about it than I can. Captain Averill, now in General Fitz-John Porter's division, certainly can tell more than I can. He was assistant adjutant general to General Porter, and can tell you exactly how these batteries were lost.

Question. I will ask you, as an artillery officer, in relation to the efficiency of artillery. Must it not always be accompanied by an infantry support?

Answer. Certainly; it is helpless by itself—perfectly helpless. Artillery must be supported, or you better not have it on the field.

Question. And you say that four thousand men at least were required to support our batteries at that time?

Answer. Yes, sir. If either one of those batteries had been by itself, there should have been at least a brigade to support it. But they were side by side, and I have therefore reduced the number required to four thousand good troops as the least we should have had.

Question. And your judgment is that if the batteries had been supported by four thousand men, they could not have been driven from their position?

Answer. Yes, sir; I have no idea they could.

Question. And if your batteries had retained their position there, would there have been any repulse at that time in that part of the field?

Answer. I do not believe there would. I believe if I had been allowed to take the position I wanted to go, and to which Captain Kensel wanted to go, we would not have lost our batteries. Captain Ricketts is living, and I understand that he refused to move forward. When Lieutenant Snyder, of the engineers, who died a few weeks ago, came up to him, Captain Ricketts said to him, " Snyder, I have such an order to move forward." Lieutenant Snyder said, " You have the best position in the world ; stand fast, and I will go and see General McDowell." He went, and came back and said that General McDowell would comply with Major Barry's orders. That was very proper and polite in General McDowell, for Major Barry was the chief of his staff ; but it shows that the officers of my battery were not the only ones who thought we should not have been moved forward. General Andrew Porter came to me after the battle, and spoke very severely. Said he, " Sir, I want to know how you got into such a situation." I said, " I went in accordance with the order of General Barry, from General McDowell." General Porter had told me that he relied upon me, as I was his only battery. He said, " When I found you had gone a thousand yards in advance, I cannot tell you my feelings. I was afraid I had allowed you to go there upon my order." He felt, perhaps, that I had gone there upon my discretion.

Question. When this confederate regiment came up in front of you, was there a fence intervening between you and them?

Answer. No, sir ; but there was a four or five rail fence about two hundred yards in front of me. This regiment got over that fence, and its colonel came out between the regiment and myself and made a speech. The regiment was standing still when I gave the order to fire. There was some kind of grass there, in which the men stood, I should say a little above their knees.

Question. I do not suppose you know certainly, but do you suppose now that that could have been one of Johnston's regiments, part of Johnston's reserves?

Answer. From what I have learned since, it was a North Carolina regiment.

Question. Are they supposed to have been in Johnston's reserves?

Answer. My impression is that that regiment was in Johnston's force.

Question. Was the attack of Johnston that day at that point?

Answer. I have always so understood.

Question. How many of your horses were killed by the fire of this regiment?

Answer. I should suppose there were thirty or forty killed.

By the chairman :

Question. Were the enemy all infantry that attacked you?

Answer. Yes, sir. There was a regiment of cavalry that charged through the Zouaves, as it appears from some of the reports ; but that was before we lost our battery. That cavalry I never saw.

Question. How far were you followed off the field?

Answer. We were followed certainly to Cub Run.

Question. Why did they leave you there?

Answer. I do not know. It was almost dark when we got there. It must have been dark in ten or fifteen minutes after I crossed Cub Run. It was then between seven and eight o'clock.

Question. You say this attack was made about three o'clock, or a little after?

Answer. Yes, sir.

Question. Then it took you about four hours in your retreat to get from where you were attacked to Cub Run?

Answer. We had troops to cover our retreat; for instance, Arnold's battery covered our retreat, and the regular infantry and cavalry covered their retreat; and the men went very slowly in a dense mass, probably not more than two or two and a half miles an hour.

By Mr. Gooch:

Question. Were there any other batteries besides yours and Ricketts's on that part of the field?

Answer. The Rhode Island, I should say, was some 500 or 600 yards to my left in battery, and firing when I first came on the field in the morning. The position where I first opened my battery was not more than 1,000 to 1,500 yards from where I lost my battery.

Question. Did that battery change its position during the day?

Answer. No, sir; when I came back I found that battery limbered up with the horses turned towards Centreville. They were a mile or a mile and a half from where my battery was lost.

Question. You have supposed that the principal attack was on our right?

Answer. I have always supposed so.

Question. You say if your battery and Ricketts's had been properly supported, it could not have been taken?

Answer. If those eleven guns had been properly supported, I think the day would have been different; and I think if we had not been moved on that point, and the captains of the batteries had been allowed to exercise their own judgment, the day would have resulted differently.

By Mr. Chandler:

Question. Probably if you had cut up that one regiment in front of you, it might have changed the fate of the day?

Answer. I think it would probably have done so.

Question. They would then have retired in disorder if you had fired canister upon them?

Answer. They would have been cut to pieces.

Question. It is not expected that raw troops will stand point blank range of canister and advance afterwards?

Answer. No troops can stand it long; for we could certainly have cut them all to pieces.

Question. Was it not possible to ascertain, during this time, whether they were or not confederate troops? Could not Major Barry have sent an aid or gone himself and ascertained in time to have saved you?

Answer. Of that I think the committee can best judge. Every man is capable of judging that. For instance, if one who is the chief states to another, "There stands your support," and he wants to convince another of that fact, he can easily do so if he is on a horse. He might have gone right down in the woods to see where the support was. That is a question that every man is capable of judging about. It would merely be my opinion any way.

By Mr. Covode:

Question. You have fixed a definite number necessary to support your battery. Does it not depend entirely upon the advanced position the battery occupies as to the number of infantry necessary to support it?

Answer. Yes, sir; it might. But a battery, if thrown forward at all, to be properly supported, should have certainly a thousand men to a gun.

Question. If you had occupied a position 500 yards further in the rear of where you were, would not a less number of men have been necessary to support it than you think should have supported you where you were?

Answer. We could have got support easier, and we could have known what the enemy were doing. If I had had 500 yards more space in front of me then, I could have seen what was coming.

Question. Was it not necessary, in your advanced position, that you should have had the largest requisite number to support you?

Answer. Yes, sir. In the first place, a battery should never have been sent forward to reconnoitre. That is a military mistake. Of course, I am only a captain, and a great many would censure me for saying this; but it is so. It was the duty of the infantry to have gone forward and found out what the enemy were doing, and not have sent the battery forward to find that out.

By Mr. Odell:

Question. You spoke of a conversation you had with Major Barry in reference to the character of the regiment that came out in front of you?

Answer. Yes, sir.

Question. How near were you and he to each other when you had that conversation?

Answer. Side by side almost, as two gentlemen who would meet each other and talk to each other would naturally be.

Question. There could be no mistake between you?

Answer. No, sir. There could be no mistake about it, because we had two or three conversations in reference to the support—in reference to the Zouaves more immediately. When I countermarched my pieces, after they had turned off, and moved up on the hill, my last words were, "These Zouaves will never support us."

Question. Why did you think that?

Answer. I had seen them on the field in a state of disorganization, and I did not think they had the moral courage to fight. I do not think that any troops that will go through the country in a disorganized state, thieving and robbing, are brave men. They were all running around the field in any way. They were in no kind of order. We got them collected together in some kind of order when we moved on the hill; but before that they were in no kind of order. At least, that is my recollection of it.

Question. And it was that that induced you to say they would not support you?

Answer. Yes, sir.

By Mr. Gooch:

Question. You did not consider them sufficient in number?

Answer. No, sir.

By the chairman:

Question. You do not believe in the maxim, "The worse the man the better the soldier?"

Answer. No, sir; I do not. I believe in the maxim that he who is universally cruel to a fallen foe is a coward.

By Mr. Odell:

Question. Did you have more than one conversation with Major Barry about this regiment of confederates?

Answer. I did not. Lieutenant Read was a witness to Major Barry's telling me that those were our troops. I state this that what I say may be established by something beyond my own hearsay. In justice to Major Barry, I will say that before this battle we were never on good terms. We never have been on good terms. But I do not wish to do him a particle of injustice.

Question. Were you in a good position to fire upon this confederate regiment when they presented themselves?

Answer. I could not possibly have been in a better position. They stood about two hundred yards in front of us, with the slightest slope in the world between us and them. All I had to do was to fire right down upon them.

By the chairman:

Question. Could you not tell by the flag they carried what they were?

Answer. I did not see any flag. I saw no flag that day on the field. I do not recollect of seeing a flag the whole day, either with the confederates or our own troops, except after the battle, when I saw a regiment or two going off the field have their flags rolled up. I do not pretend to have seen much on that field. I only know what occurred in reference to my own battery, and those standing by the side of them.

Question. In a battle like that should not the colors be shown, so that there should be no mistake?

Answer. Yes, sir; I have no doubt our troops had their colors; they say they had. But I had a particular duty to perform. I had no support all day long, with the exception that the New York 14th came to me when I was in my second or third position. An officer said, "I have been ordered here to support you; where shall I go?" He went to a fence in rear of the batteries. I said, "Don't go there in rear of us, for you will stand a chance of being hit. If their batteries fire at me, and don't hit me, it will pass over us and hit you." They then went to one side, and when I saw them again they were falling back, every man for himself, about 500 yards from me. That was the last I saw of that regiment that day, excepting a straggling man here and there, or groups of twenty or so.

By Mr. Gooch:

Question. You consider one of the errors—the serious error of that day—was the fact that the artillery was not properly supported by infantry?

Answer. Undoubtedly. I consider that the first great error that was committed that day was the sending these batteries forward without support. And it is my opinion—at any rate, I do not know that I am called upon to express an opinion—but it is my opinion that if an officer received an order from the general to advance those two batteries forward, no matter how peremptory that order was, it was his duty, I think, not to have carried out that order if the batteries could not be supported, especially if he was the chief of the staff. Times may arrive when it is necessary to sacrifice a battery to secure some important result; for instance, Arnold's battery was sacrificed on our retreat to cover that retreat. But this was not one of those desperate cases.

Question. You think that it was a part of Major Barry's duty to see that the batteries were properly supported before they were ordered forward?

Answer. I pretend to say I should not have done it.

By Mr. Covode:

Question. Could Major Barry order this infantry forward without his superior's orders?

Answer. According to his report, he did.

By the chairman:

Question. If the general commanding should order the batteries forward, would not the chief of artillery understand that they were to be properly supported, without any particular orders to do so?

Answer. I should certainly consider it so.

Question. You would consider the order to mean that?

Answer. I think if the chief of a corps has no discretion like that, the general is in a bad situation. He certainly cannot be expected in a time like that to enter into all the details of his orders. He cannot do it. He gives his orders in a general form, and the details are attended to by others.

Question. You do not impeach the order of General McDowell in advancing the artillery forward, because undoubtedly he intended them to be supported properly?

Answer. Yes, sir; I take that for granted.

Question. It would be as unreasonable to expect a battery to go forward without a support as without horses—that is, a support is a necessary accompaniment to a battery?

Answer. I have always supposed so. There may be a time when it is necessary to sacrifice a battery. At Buena Vista General Taylor had lost everything, and was trying to retrieve. He ordered General Bragg to go forward. General Bragg undoubtedly turned to him and said, "I shall lose my battery;" and General Taylor probably said, "You must lose your battery, or all will be lost." And he went forward, and by his fire of grape gained the day.

Question. You were under no such necessity that day?

Answer. No, sir.

Question. You think the battery ought not to have been ordered forward until after the advanced position had been reconnoitred by infantry?

Answer. Or without a sufficiently strong support.

Question. Do you mean to say these two things should have been done: first, to have the advanced position reconnoitred by infantry, so as to have known what there was in advance, and what the position of the enemy was, and what they were doing, as far as possible; and, second, when the batteries did go forward, they should have had a sufficient support of infantry?

Answer. Yes, sir. I contend that as long as the chief of artillery had not the sufficient support for the batteries he should not have moved them forward. If they were to be moved forward on that hill, we should have had a heavy and strong support, for the reason that that was the hill the enemy had occupied. We could see nothing beyond that hill. We could not tell what they were doing. We could not tell whether there were 1,000 or 5,000 beyond the hill. I had occupied about as high a position as any one, and I do not believe any man could see beyond that hill. And then I contend that the next blunder was that Major Barry told me the confederate regiment was our support.

Question. These two errors, you think, led to the first and most important repulse of the day?

Answer. I think these two errors led to the first and *the* repulse of the day. I think General Porter's report will sustain me in that.

By Mr. Covode:

Question. Was Major Barry in a position where he was able to distinguish between our forces and theirs?

Answer. The major stood about 200 yards from them, right by my side. That is, he was on his horse and I was on my horse, and we were side by side.

Question. Was his opportunity a good one, from the position he occupied, for knowing the character of these confederate troops?

Answer. That would be a mere matter of opinion. His opportunity was just as good as mine.

By the chairman:

Question. They seemed like our soldiers?

Answer They may have been dressed like some of our regiments. I went across the river on the 5th of July. The battle was on the 21st. I had not seen all our troops. I knew but four or five regiments.

By Mr. Covode:

Question. Were not cavalry in reach of you at that time?

Answer. I am under the impression that there was a squad of cavalry at my right. But they were in the woods, and might have just as well been at Centreville.

Question. That was not a proper time to use cavalry to reconnoitre?

Answer. No, sir; infantry should have been thrown forward.

By Mr. Gooch:

Question. Had you any cavalry that could be called in to support your battery?

Answer. No, sir. I am told by a cavalry officer that he received an order to charge right down through the woods. In the first place, he could not do it. Even if there was no enemy there, the cavalry could not charge through the woods.

WASHINGTON, *January* 14, 1862.

Colonel THOMAS A. DAVIES sworn and examined.

By the chairman:

Question. What is your position in the army?

Answer. My present position is colonel of the 16th New York volunteers.

Question. Were you present at the battle of Bull Run?

Answer. I was not present at what is called the battle of Bull Run, but I was six miles from that, upon the left wing.

Question. What position did you occupy there?

Answer. I left Alexandria in command of the 2d brigade, 5th division of the army of the Potomac.

Question. Acting as brigadier general?

Answer. Yes, sir.

Question. Will you, in your own way, go on and tell us what you know about the causes of the disaster of that day, what was done, and what you think might have been done?

Answer. Shall I tell what I did?

Question. Give us a general idea, without any great minuteness.

Answer. The fifth division, together with Runyon's division, was marked upon our programme when we started as the reserve—I mean in the card that was issued by General McDowell. Colonel Miles, of the infantry, was in command of the fifth division, and Brigadier General Runyon was in command of his part of the reserve. There were two commanders to the reserve. We went by the way of the old Braddock road to Fairfax Court-House the second night, driving the enemy before us, and capturing some few things; skirmishing all the way through the woods about six miles. On the third day we arrived at Centreville, and camped about a mile from Centreville. The part we took in the battle of Sunday was decided upon in a military conference held the night before the battle, at which the division and brigade commanders were present. General McDowell read off the programme, and as soon as we found that our position was to be in the reserve and remain at Centreville, we left the council very early, and I heard nothing more said in respect to the plan of campaign than what was read there. Early the next morning we got our troops up—very early, for they were awake pretty much all night, or half asleep and half awake all night. We started in the morning, I with instructions to go down to the position that was occupied as a battle-field on the afternoon of the 18th, what was then called the battle of Blackburn's Ford.

By Mr. Chandler:

Question. You were not in the affair at Blackburn's Ford?

Answer. No, sir; I lay at Centreville that day. Instead of stopping where he ought to have stopped, as I understood it, General Tyler went on there. The bringing on of that battle, as I understand it, was an accidental affair altogether. This division of Miles, on Sunday, was to occupy a position at Centreville Heights, and also at Blackburn's Ford, which was two miles further towards Bull Run. The road from Centreville to Blackburn's Ford runs directly to Manassas Junction. The Warrenton turnpike that led up to where the battle of Bull Run was fought made an angle with the Blackburn's Ford road of about thirty degrees, and bore off to the right, went on to the Stone Bridge, and so on across where the balance of the army went. All the army, excepting Miles's division, moved up the Warrenton road, while that division moved off to the left to Blackburn's Ford with my brigade, leaving Blenker's brigade on Centreville Heights, with instructions to intrench the heights that day. Lieutenant Prime was to furnish the tools for that purpose. We went off to the left and were to make a feint at Blackburn's Ford to attract the attention of the enemy and draw their troops there.

Richardson's brigade, I found, was up there. But Colonel Miles told me to go down and compare notes with him, and find out which ranked, the one ranking to take command of the two brigades. I met Colonel Richardson, compared notes with him, and found that I ranked him. I then took command of the troops, and stationed him on the road directly to Blackburn's Ford, and exactly on the battle-ground of the 18th. I took a road that led off further south from this road, and went into an open wheatfield and took possession of the brow of a hill, where I could annoy the enemy by shell during the day, and make a demonstration. My position was about eighty rods, I should think, from Colonel Richardson's. I had brought into the field two regiments of infantry and Hunt's battery. Green's battery was behind, but by mistake Green's battery, belonging to my brigade, got into Richardson's brigade, and Hunt's battery, belonging to Richardson's brigade, got into my brigade. We went on making a demonstration, and at 10 o'clock I found that our ammunition was running short. I sent back word to Colonel Miles, at Centreville Heights, that our ammunition was running short, and I wanted to slacken my fire. He sent me back word to fire on. I did fire on very slowly, and kept up the fire till about 11 o'clock, when Colonel Miles came himself. He made some new disposition of the troops. I suppose, however, that is not important.

Question. Unless it led to important results.

Answer. It did. I had stationed two of my regiments on a road that led around from Centreville Heights off in the rear of my position entirely. I happened to find it out from the guide who went along with me down there to show me the way. He mentioned casually, saying, "There is a road that leads around to the enemy's camp direct." Said I, "Can they get through that road?" "Oh, yes," said he, "they can." I gave the word of command to halt immediately, and put two of my regiments on this road, and two pieces of artillery, and went on with my other two regiments into the open field with the battery. When Colonel Miles came down in the morning he was in a terrible passion because I had put these two regiments there. He gave me a very severe dressing down in no very measured language, and ordered the two regiments and the artillery forward, without knowing what they had been put there for. I complied with the order, and said nothing. But when he left me, about an hour afterwards, I immediately sent back pioneers who cut down about a quarter of a mile of trees and filled the road up. As I expected, the enemy made an attempt to go up that road, but finding it obstructed by trees, and protected by a few pickets, they went back. We did not see them coming up, but when they were going back we shelled them pretty severely.

We continued the firing by degrees all day, until I got a line from some one in the advance. I could not read the whole of it. It said something about being beaten, but I did not understand which side was beaten; but I knew one or the other was. The firing about six miles to the right had ceased when this line came to me. I afterwards learned it was from Colonel Richardson, and I could see that the enemy or we were beaten, but I could not tell which. And there was something else about it, but I do not remember now, for I have lost the note. I saw unmistakable evidence that we were going to be attacked on our left wing. I got all ready for the attack, but did not change my front. About 5 o'clock, I think, the enemy made their appearance back upon this very road up which they had gone before; but instead of keeping up the road, they turned past a farm-house, went through the farm-yard, and came down and formed right in front of me in a hollow out of my sight. Well, I let them all come down there, keeping a watch upon their movements. I told the artillery not to fire any shots at them until they saw the rear column go down, so as to get them all down in the little hollow or basin there. There was a little basin there, probably a quarter of a mile every way. I should think that, may-be, 3,000 men filed down before I changed front. We lay there with two regiments back, and the artillery in front, facing Bull Run. As soon as about 3,000 of the enemy got down in this basin I changed the front of the artillery around to the left in face of the enemy, and put a company of infantry between each of the pieces of artillery, and then deployed the balance of the regiments right and left, and made my line of battle. I gave directions to the infantry not to fire a shot under any circumstances until they got the word of command from me. I furthermore said I would shoot the first man that fired a shot before I gave the command to do so. I gave them orders all to lie down on their faces. They were just over the brow of the hill, so that if they came up in front of us they could not hit a man. As soon as I saw the rear column, I told whom I thought to be Lieutenant Edwards to fire. It proved to be Lieutenant Benjamin, because in placing the companies between the artillery they had got displaced. Lieutenant Benjamin fired the first shot at them when the rear column presented itself. It just went over the tops of their heads, and hit a horse and rider in the rear. As soon as the first shot was fired, I gave the order for the whole six pieces of artillery to open with grape and canister. The effect was terrible. They were all there right before us, about 450 yards off, and had not suspected that we were going to fire at all, though they did not know what the reason was. Hunt's battery performed so well that in 30 minutes we dispersed every one of them. I do not know how many were killed, but we so crippled their entire force that they never came after us an inch. A man who saw the effect of the firing in the valley said that it was just like firing into a wheatfield: the column gave way at once before the grape and canister; they were just within available distance. I knew very well that if they but got into that basin the first fire would cut them all in pieces; and it did. We continued the fire for 30 minutes, when there was nothing more to fire at, and no more shots were returned.

About the time this firing commenced, or a little before that, I received this note from Colonel Richardson. It seems that Colonel Miles, instead of sending the order through me, as the ranking colonel in command, to Richardson to retire on Centreville Heights, sent it, or his aid gave it, directly to Colonel Richardson himself, and also gave orders directly to my two regiments, which lay back as a reserve for me, to move back on Centreville Heights, leaving me in this open field with two regiments and six pieces of artillery, and no reserve to support me. As luck would have it, however, I was successful in the manner of making the fight there, and I did not require any support.

When I got through, and the order came to me to retire on Centreville Heights, I retired my own brigade first, because I was the ranking brigade. I went over to give the order for Colonel Richardson to retire, but I found he had been gone about an hour. I then went to find my other two regiments, which I had had in reserve, and found that they had already been ordered back to Centreville Heights. And when I retired my force, which I did in perfect order, I found my two regiments there on Centreville Heights, and Richardson's brigade all formed on the heights; rather, they were all there, but running about in a great deal of confusion, for Colonel Miles was not in a condition to be very accurate that afternoon. But for the defence which Hunt's battery made there, and the little arrangement to keep the men from firing, I think we should have been broken through by the enemy.

By Mr. Chandler:

Question. You have referred to Colonel Miles. Did you see him frequently during the day?

Answer. I saw him two or three times during the day.

Question. What time in the afternoon did you last see him on the field?

Answer. He left me about three o'clock in the afternoon, with instructions to encamp on the ground.

Question. Did you see him after that?

Answer. I did, at Centreville Heights, when I first got back with these two regiments. He had thrown forward the balance of the division and Richardson's brigade on Centreville Heights.

Question. Did you consider him in a fit condition to give orders at three o'clock in the afternoon.

Answer. Well, sir, I do not want to be the accuser of Colonel Miles here; I will give my testimony at the proper time; but I would prefer not to answer the question now, unless it be deemed essential as eliciting information in regard to the conduct of the war.

Mr. Chandler: We want to know what causes might have led to the disasters of that day. We want to find out, if we can, all the causes.

The chairman: We have some testimony to that effect already, and perhaps, in justice to those who have testified about it, we should have all of it.

The witness: Well, sir, I do not think the colonel was exactly fitted for duty much of the day. I did not see him drink, but I pretty well understood what his condition was.

By the chairman:

Question. You consider that the portion of the army you led were victorious throughout?

Answer. Entirely so. I claim that 13,000 of our men were victorious in that battle, and I never want it written down in any other way.

By Mr. Gooch:

Question. That is, our left wing.

Answer. Yes, sir. We are entitled to that, and we should have a report made so; and the 18,000 on the right were victorious, too, until a very late hour; but the left wing were entirely victorious, and have a right to claim such to be the case.

By the chairman:

Question. What led to the final defeat, as near as you could ascertain on the ground?

Answer. I can tell you what I think is the cause of the whole defeat of that day. The troops were raw; the men had been accustomed to look to their colonels as the only men to give them commands. They had never been taught the succession of officers, which is necessary to understand upon the battle-field. They did not understand the command devolving in succession upon the colonel, lieutenant colonel, major, and the captains, in their order of rank. The officers did not themselves know what to do; they were themselves raw and green. Every man went in to do his duty, and knew nothing about anybody else. When the colonels were killed or wounded, the subordinate officers did not know what to do, or the men did not know whether to obey them or not. When they lost their commanding officers, or those to whom they had alone been instructed to look for commands, they supposed they had a right to leave the field. That, I think, was the cause of many of the regiments retiring from the field; not from any cowardice, or fear of fighting, but because, having lost their colonels, they supposed they were out of the battle. I consider that the great cause of our army being put in rout on the right wing.

Question. Were you in a position to observe about the arrival of Johnston's re-enforcements at that time?

Answer. No, sir; I know nothing about that; I was too far to the left. I was going on to give my reasons for what I suppose caused our defeat that day. There were two, probably three things, which, though they may not have controlled the matter, are, in my judgment, to be considered as some of the reasons why we were not as successful as we might have been. But every general has his own plan of campaign, and my ideas may run counter to those of our general, as he may have had, doubtless did have, reasons and considerations for his plan which I am ignorant of. But judging from what I knew, if I had been in command there I should have harassed the enemy for the three nights before the battle that we were there. I would not have allowed them to lay there quiet all that time, when, with a half a regiment or a regiment, we could have kept them awake all night and worried them exceedingly. We had the power to do it. If we had done that we should have fought them to great advantage.

Question. You spoke of a council of war the night before the battle?

Answer. Yes, sir.

Question. What was understood there as to Patterson's holding Johnston from that battle? Was that an element taken into consideration in that council?

Answer. I did not hear it mentioned, that I am aware of. It might have been mentioned there, but I did not hear it. I was on the outside, and did not enter much into the inside of the discussion. There were two tents there, and most of the officers were a great way inside, while I was on the outside.

Question. Was not that a fact of so much importance that it should have been known and acted upon in planning the battle?

Answer. I think it should have been considered, and it may have been. I know it was understood by all the officers there that Johnston was to be held by Patterson. That matter was talked over among the officers, and it was so understood.

Question. If it had been known the day before the battle that the next morning Johnston would be down there with re-enforcements, would it have been prudent to hazard a battle until you had also obtained re-enforcements, or until Patterson's army had followed Johnston down?

Answer. I should not have risked it, though my reasons for not risking it may be different from those of the one in command. He may have supposed that he had good grounds for fighting the battle.

Question. Would it be according to military prudence to fight a battle that must be uncertain, when you can make it all but certain by waiting a day or two?

Answer. That is very clear, according to my view of things.

Question. What would have been the effect had you waited there on Centreville Heights and rested your men a day or two—seeing Johnston was down there—until Patterson's army had followed him there, and been ordered to turn their left?

Answer. We should undoubtedly have won the battle.

Question. Was there anything to prevent that?

Answer. I know of nothing that could. I was going to mention three things which seems to me ought to have been done. One was to harass the enemy all we could. Another was to have intrenched Centreville Heights during the three days we lay there. The men would have fought better after working all day and sleeping well all night, than to have gone into the field as they did. And another thing was this: Now, I do not know the facts, I am only telling you my opinion of what should have been done, if the circumstances of the case had all been as I suppose they were. Not that I find the least fault with General McDowell, for I believe he is a splendid soldier; but if I had been in command of the right wing I should have intrenched after I got to the first run, and allowed them to attack me; we had the sure thing; we had the game there, and they might have got it back the best way they could. After the first run, after their first line broke and retired, then we should have intrenched and let them attack, and we would have had the victory. We had a sure thing, and there was no use in throwing it away.

Question. How was it about the men coming on the ground fatigued with marching? Had they marched any considerable distance, many of them?

Answer. No, sir, I do not think they had marched a great deal. But they had been loafing around a great deal; had been out a great deal of nights, and had been broken of their rest, and had not had full rations. They were not altogether in a prime condition for fighting.

Question. There was a brigade or a division in reserve on Centreville Heights most of the day, was there not?

Answer. Yes, sir; Blenker's brigade lay there the whole day.

Question. Could not they have strengthened our centre if they had taken their position on the field of battle?

Answer. The object of leaving that force there was to intrench Centreville Heights so that in case any accident occurred we could have retired there. But instead of that being done as was designed, there was some difficulty about getting intrenching tools forward, and on that account they never broke ground there. There were 3,000 men there, and in one day they could have thrown up a pretty fair intrenchment. If those intrenchments had been prepared there when we got back we need not have gone back any further.

Question. After the repulse of our army, the enemy did not follow up their victory?

Answer. No, sir; not at all. There were only a few who came running after the right wing, firing random shots.

Question. They did not pursue?

Answer. No, sir; they did not pursue at all. Some cavalry came down, I believe, and made one or two charges which amounted to nothing.

Question. What necessity was there for bringing our army back to Washington? Why not have taken position on the heights and intrenched there at Centreville?

Answer. I did take position there. General McDowell, after the suspension of Colonel Miles, wrote an order on a visiting card, putting me in command of the left wing of the army as it stood; and I was going to stay there, and should have stayed there, except that I got an order between 11 and 12 o'clock, first to retire to Fairfax Court-House, and then to Washington. My brigade was the last to leave the heights at Centreville, which we did between 12 and 1 o'clock. There was no enemy there then.

Question. Would there have been any difficulty in rallying your whole forces and holding your position on Centreville Heights, while you sent for Patterson, or for re-enforcements from here and Fortress Monroe? Would you not have worsted the enemy in that way?

Answer. We never should have been compelled to leave the place with what troops I had under my command. I could have held my position there with the troops I had, which were my brigade, Richardson's brigade, Blenker's brigade, and some batteries that came down from the point above.

Question. Was it not a terrible military blunder to come back to Washington in disorder?

Answer. That is putting it rather strong. I should not like to say it was a military blunder.

Question. Well, it was a mistake, then?

Answer. I think this: that we could have held our position there; there is no doubt about that.

Question. Then you ought to have held it, ought you not?

Answer. That is a matter I am not responsible for. That is a matter which rests with the other powers, for I do not know all that combined to make up their judgment.

Question. Would it not have been easier to have defended Washington on Centreville Heights than to have come pell-mell here to do it?

Answer. I can answer that very readily: I think it would; there is no doubt about that.

By Mr. Gooch:

Question. I understand you to say that our left wing was victorious that day?

Answer. Yes, sir.

Question. Have you stated precisely what the left wing did?

Answer. Not in every respect, for Runyon's division lay behind us as part of the left wing.

Question. Was that engagement you have referred to the only one of the left wing that day?

Answer. Yes, sir.

Question. Did our left wing make any attack that day?

Answer. No, sir; not at all; we only defended ourselves. We were the reserve; we were to maintain our position.

Question. When you say you were victorious, you mean to say that you maintained the position assigned you?

Answer. Yes, sir; that is always a victory. When one is attacked in a position, and is successful in repelling that attack, that is as complete a victory as can be; and I think that all those troops which have been, in the accounts, submerged with a defeated body of troops, ought to have the credit of being victorious. It ought to have read that we were victorious with the 13,000 troops of the left wing, and defeated in the 18,000 of the right wing. That is all that Bull Run amounts to. The attack upon the left wing was repulsed, and the enemy never attacked there again. I have understood from the secession accounts of that battle that we killed there about one-third of all that we killed at the battle of Bull Run. And neither of my two regiments there fired a shot; if they had, we probably should have been defeated.

Question. What was the number of the enemy that came around the first time upon the road you speak of?

Answer. As near as we could judge, there were about 3,000—that is, judging from the time it took them to pass a given point; we could see the dust, but we could not see the troops; there was a light growth of bushes that separated them from us; we fired shell into the bushes.

Question. The force left at Centreville and the force under your command were both necessary, in your opinion, to prevent the enemy coming around and attacking the main body of our army in the rear?

Answer. Certainly: entirely so.

Question. Then you cannot strictly call that a reserve?

Answer. No, sir; not strictly so. We were put down upon the programme, as I stated in the forepart of my testimony, as a reserve. But we, in truth, expected to make an attack upon the enemy, as well as the right wing. We, however, made an attack simply upon a body of troops that lay in the woods waiting for us. There were about 10,000 of the enemy's troops concentrated upon our position all day long, hoping to take our army in the rear.

Question. So that it would not have been safe at any hour of the day to have taken our troops from Centreville and moved them forward to the main body of the army?

Answer. I think, as it turned out, that Blenker's brigade, which was expected to have intrenched Centreville Heights, might have been spared. Yet, after all, we might not have been able to have maintained our position. We might have been broken, and then Blenker's brigade would have been necessary for us to have fallen back upon. If the failure had taken place on our left wing, nothing in the world could have saved our army or Washington. When I got here to the city I could have taken the place with a thousand men, or even a less number. I never saw such an excited condition of things as there was here.

By the chairman:

Question. At what time did you get back and form on Centreville Heights?

Answer. The last two regiments got on Centreville Heights about 7 o'clock in the evening.

Washington, *January* 18, 1862.

Colonel R. Butler Price sworn and examined.

By the chairman.

Question. Did you serve with General Patterson during his expedition into Virginia; and if so, about what time?

Answer. I served with him from his first orders from the President, some time in April. He left Philadelphia on the 2d of June, and I remained with him until he was discharged from the service.

Question. What was your rank and position?

Answer. I was senior aid under General Patterson, with the rank of major.

Question. You accompanied him on his march from Martinsburg to Charlestown?

Answer. Yes, sir.

Question. About what was his force at that time?

Answer. He had about 19,000 men with him—that is, for all purposes. A portion of those men were detailed for special duty, guarding wagon trains, &c. He had probably 15,000 or 16,000 fighting men—not over 19,000 men in all.

Question. What was the object of that expedition? What particular purpose was it intended to accomplish?

Answer. From Martinsburg over to Charlestown?

Question. Yes, sir.

Answer. There were two reasons, I think, which prompted General Patterson to make that movement from Martinsburg to Charlestown: one was partly the condition of the quartermaster's and commissary's departments in relation to the supply of the army; and another was to make Charlestown as a more favorable base of operations, either to the front, or to fall back to Harper's Ferry. Charlestown was considered safer than Martinsburg; Harper's Ferry being within six miles of Charlestown.

Question. You were with him on the march from Martinsburg to Bunker Hill?

Answer. Yes, sir.

Question. What was the distance?

Answer. About twelve miles.

Question. How far is Bunker Hill from Winchester?

Answer. I think about sixteen miles; I am not positive about that; but I think the distance is in the neighborhood of sixteen miles.

Question. Was one great object of General Patterson's expedition to prevent Johnston from joining Beauregard at Manassas?

Answer. Yes, sir.

Question. That was the principal object?

Answer. That was one of the motives; yes, sir. To place General Patterson in a position where he could do that to the most advantage. As I said before, Charlestown is a point which would have facilitated either in making a forward movement, or falling back upon Harper's Ferry.

Question. When he was at Bunker Hill, was he not then in as good a position to have prevented Johnston from joining Beauregard as from any other point?

Answer. No, sir; he was not in so good a position as at Charlestown. And under the circumstances it would have been impossible for him to have remained at Bunker Hill.

Question. For what reason?

Answer. The difficulty of provisioning his army; getting forage forward. There was no nearer point there than Maryland.

Question. How came he to go to Bunker Hill, then?

Answer. He did not go there with the intention of staying there.

Question. Was it on the direct road to Charlestown?

Answer. No, sir; but he went to Bunker Hill because he was ordered to keep Johnston in check, and always keep a force in front of him. He went there for the purpose of offering Johnston battle.

Question. Johnston was not at Bunker Hill, was he?

Answer. He was there while we were at Winchester. As we approached him he fell back.

Question. And Johnston having fallen back to Winchester, General Patterson approached him no further?

Answer. No, sir; not towards Winchester.

Question. Why not?

Answer. Because he heard while at Bunker Hill that the force of General Johnston was very much greater than his own, both in number and in artillery force.

Question. Had he any intelligence that Johnston's army had been increased during this period?

Answer. Yes, sir; very materially increased.

Question. Where from?

Answer. Somewhere between Winchester and Manassas; it was not known where. He got positive information at Bunker Hill that Johnston had 42,000 men at Winchester, and, I think, sixty-three pieces of artillery.

Question. From whom did he get that information?

Answer. It was given to him by General Cadwalader, who obtained it through private parties; I do not know who they were.

Question. Where did these re-enforcements come from?

Answer. From towards Manassas.

Question. At what time were these re-enforcements supposed to have joined Johnston?

Answer. Between the time of our leaving Martinsburg and leaving Bunker Hill, which was a period of two and a half days.

Question. Was it not very singular that he should have retreated to Winchester with this great increase of force?

Answer. He was re-enforced while he was at Winchester, after he left Bunker Hill. From the best knowledge we could obtain while at Martinsburg, General Johnston had in the neighborhood of 25,000 or 26,000 men.

Question. Was it not very singular that Johnston should be re-enforced from Manassas when they knew they were about to be assailed by the central army, under General McDowell?

Answer. I can give no opinion in reference to their motives.

Question. Had you any authentic information of re-enforcements joining Johnston during this period?

Answer. It was information that was given to General Cadwalader from what he considered a reliable source, and he so reported to General Patterson. The information proved to be correct, as we learned from various sources afterwards.

Question. That he received a very large re-enforcement at this period from Manassas?

Answer. Yes, sir; making his whole force over 42,000 men.

Question. How did you learn that afterwards?

Answer. By information from various persons. One was a gentleman, whose name I forget. His *soubriquet* is "Porte Crayon." He was in Winchester at the time General Johnston left with 35,000 men, leaving 7,000 at Winchester. There were two or three other persons, who were at Winchester at that time, who reported the same thing, thus verifying the report Cadwalader made to General Patterson.

Question. Had it not been for this supposed re-enforcement, would he have advanced upon Winchester from Bunker Hill?

Answer. Yes, sir.

Question. That was his intention?

Answer. Yes, sir; provided he thought proper to do so after arriving at Bunker Hill.

Question. Where was he when he heard of this re-enforcement?

Answer. At Bunker Hill.

Question. And then he retreated from the enemy to go to Charlestown?

Answer. No, sir; he did not. It was not a retreating movement. It was merely a movement across the country to Charlestown.

Question. He gave up all idea of encountering Johnston?

Answer. Yes, sir.

Question. Then, when he left Bunker Hill, he knew he could no longer hold Johnston in check, did he not?

Answer. Yes, sir; he gave up the idea of attacking Johnston. But then he was under the impression that the necessity of his holding Johnston in that part of Virginia had passed away, from the fact that he supposed the battle at Manassas had at that time been fought.

Question. What made him think that?

Answer. From despatches he received from General Scott, and letters fixing the date of the attack.

Question Did General Scott ever send him any despatch that he would fight at Manassas on any particular day?

Answer. Yes, sir.

Question. Where is that despatch?

Answer. I suppose it is among the papers of General Patterson. It was either a despatch or letter; I did not know which.

Question. Did you learn the date of that despatch?

Answer. I do not recollect now.

Question. Do you know what time was stated when the battle would be fought at Manassas?

Answer. Yes, sir; on the Tuesday previous to the Sunday on which it was fought.

Question. Do you suppose, as a military man—I ask your opinion as a military man—that General Scott could fix, beyond a doubt, upon a day when he could attack the enemy with such an army, the two being so far apart? Could he fix with certainty that he would fight on a particular day?

Answer. I think he could, having the control of his operations.

Question. He did not fight on the day he proposed?

Answer. No, sir; he did not.

Question. Then it is possible for a military man to be mistaken about that?

Answer. Yes, sir.

Question. And a military man would know that there would not be any certainty about such a thing?

Answer. Yes, sir.

Question. General Patterson, if I understand it, had the means of communicating by telegraph with General Scott?

Answer. The facilities were not great from Bunker Hill. There was no telegraph nearer there than Hagerstown.

Question. How far was that?

Answer. About 42 miles. All the despatches received from and sent to General Scott were carried by carriers from any position in which the army happened to be to Hagerstown.

Question. Would it not have been well for General Patterson, when he had ascertained that Johnston had received re-enforcements, that rendered it impossible for him to detain him—would it not have been well to have sent General Scott the earliest information of that?

Answer. He did.

Question. What was the import of that communication?

Answer. The import of that information was that Johnston's force was then estimated at 42,000 men, and was much larger than what General Patterson had.

Question. And when he turned off to Charlestown, and found he could no longer detain him, did he notify General Scott of that?

Answer. No, sir; I do not know as he sent any despatch that he could no longer detain him, but General Patterson was under the belief he could not detain him there any longer. When he discovered that Johnston's force was moving he telegraphed to General Scott.

Question. As the matter stood, suppose he had, the moment he received that information, and had made up his mind that he could no longer detain him—for you have said already that it was the object of this expedition to detain him there, and prevent his joining Beauregard—had he communicated that immediately to General Scott, would it not have been a military fact that would have had a controlling effect upon planning and carrying out the battle of Manassas?

Answer. I think it ought to have been.

Question. And if he did not give General Scott the earliest information of that, would it not have been a negligence and unmilitary act?

Answer. So I should have considered it.

Question. But you think he did give him that information?

Answer. I am under that impression—yes, sir.

Question. How long did you remain at Charlestown?

Answer. I think we stayed there, at Charlestown, five days.

Question. Was there any order from General Scott to General Patterson, that if he could not detain Johnston, he should follow him down to Manassas?

Answer. No, sir.

Question. No such arrangement?

Answer. None that I have ever heard

Question. When he turned off from Bunker Hill to Charlestown, had you heard any dissatisfaction manifested among the officers and troops?

Answer. Nothing of the kind—not the slightest; nothing but the most unqualified approbation.

Question. Was there any period when the troops whose time was expiring refused to go further?

Answer. Yes, sir.

Question. What time was that?

Answer. That was at Charlestown.

Question. You did not hear anything of that before?

Answer. No, sir. I heard of the circumstance, but it was not within my own positive knowledge.

Question. Charlestown was the first?

Answer. Yes, sir; the first open exhibition of it.

Question. Then, in brief, the Pennsylvanians, when they supposed he was advancing upon the enemy, did not wish to take advantage of their time being out?

Answer. They did not grumble about there being no fight, because General Patterson, in the appeal he made to them at Charlestown, begged them to stay for ten days in case he might have to fight with the enemy.

Question. Did he expect to have a fight with the enemy?

Answer. He thought he might have a fight, and in the mean time he had sent to General Scott for orders, and did not know what orders he would get.

Question. After Johnston had been re-enforced, he had double your force; would he have fought him then?

Answer. He would not follow him up, but he would have fought if Johnston had attacked him.

Question. Why not throw himself across Johnston's path, and detain him in that way?

Answer. It was impossible for him to do that while at Bunker Hill or at Charlestown.

Question. Was it not possible to do that?

Answer. It was totally impossible.

Question. What was the impossibility?

Answer. It was that he could not reach the track that Johnston took before Johnston could reach it; for he could march his men to a point below Strasburg, and then take his men to Manassas, and it was impossible that General Patterson could reach that point to intercept him. I do not think he would have made an attempt to do that.

Question. If it was an object to detain him, how did he expect to detain him?

Answer. He did not expect to do it after he left Bunker Hill.

Question. If he was willing to fight double his force in the open field, why not follow him up?

Answer. He was intrenched there; not in the open field.

Question. You say he could not get to the railroad without attacking Johnston at Winchester. Now I want to know this: I find from the testimony that General Patterson turned from Bunker Hill, and gave up the original intention of detaining Johnston, because Johnston had been greatly re-enforced.

Answer. Yes, sir, that was one reason; and another reason was that he thought the necessity had passed.

Question. Now I understand you to say that he would have fought Johnston even after he had been re-enforced, perhaps at Charlestown, and expected to do it, and wanted to keep his troops there.

Answer. Yes, sir. He would have fought him, if he had attacked him.

Question. If so, and his main purpose being to detain him in the valley there, why did he relinquish his original position?

Answer. The design no longer existed after he left Bunker Hill; and if he had been so disposed, he could not have thrown himself across the track of Johnston after he left Winchester.

Question. Suppose that, before Johnston left Winchester, Patterson had taken a position between Manassas and Winchester upon that railroad, could he not have done that?

Answer. No, sir; not before Johnston.

Question. Not before Johnston left?

Answer. No, sir.

Question. Then he could not have prevented Johnston from going to Manassas, whether he was re-enforced or not?

Answer. No, sir. He could not have prevented Johnston from going to Manassas, whether he was re-enforced or not. But he would have attacked him at Winchester, if he had not been re-enforced. He offered him battle on two or three different occasions. Johnston was between Martinsburg and Bunker Hill when we marched to Martinsburg. He then fell back to Bunker Hill, and then he fell back to Winchester, laying a trap for us all the time.

Johnston would not have fought before he got to Winchester, and there he had a great advantage over us.

Question. You think General Scott was apprised of this right off.

Answer. Yes, sir.

By Mr. Gooch:

Question. General Patterson moved from Martinsburg to Bunker Hill because there he more directly threatened Johnston?

Answer. Yes, sir; he marched there for the purpose of offering him battle.

Question. For the purpose of threatening him?

Answer. Yes, sir, to threaten him, and to hold him there and give him battle. From the best information we had, Johnston's force was from 22,000 or 23,000 to 26,000.

Question. The great object you deemed to be to hold Johnston, and you moved to Bunker Hill so as to threaten him and hold him?

Answer. Yes, sir; and fight him there.

Question. And Johnston fortified himself at Winchester?

Answer. Yes, sir.

Question. You moved to Bunker Hill and sent out some pickets?

Answer. There was a reconnoissance made from Bunker Hill on the day we arrived there, I think, with probably 800 or 1,000 men. They marched on the road to Winchester, a distance of four or five miles. There they found the cavalry pickets of Johnston, which they dispersed. They found the road obstructed.

Question. The object of the reconnoissance was successful?

Answer. Yes, sir. To find the condition of the road from there to Winchester, and to find out the preparations to prevent General Patterson from marching to Winchester.

Question. You found no indication to show that Johnston intended to attack you at Bunker Hill?

Answer. No, sir.

Question. The indications were that he wanted to fight you behind his intrenchments at Winchester, and not to come out to attack you?

Answer. Yes, sir.

Question. Did you send some of your baggage trains directly from Martinsburg to Charlestown?

Answer. No, sir. They all came down by the way of Bunker Hill. We marched on two roads from Martinsburg to Bunker Hill.

Question. During all this time you were following up Johnston, there was no time that he offered you battle, or proposed to do so in any way in the open field?

Answer. No, sir. Not upon any occasion.

Question. He wanted to fight you upon unequal terms at Winchester?

Answer. Yes, sir.

Question. You did not believe when you reached Bunker Hill that Johnston intended to fight you at Bunker Hill?

Answer. No, sir. We found no such indication.

Question. When you were at Bunker Hill, I suppose that you felt that, during that time, you were threatening that position of Johnston, instead of his threatening you?

Answer. Yes, sir.

Question. Then, when you moved from Bunker Hill, you moved to a point, Charlestown, which was further from Winchester than Bunker Hill?

Answer. I think Charlestown is rather further from Winchester than Bunker Hill is: probably five or six miles further.

Question. You moved down from Martinsburg to Bunker Hill in two columns. Did you propose to move forward upon Winchester in two columns?

Answer. No, sir. I do not know that we did.

Question. General Sanford had a column there, had he not?

Answer. We marched in two columns from Martinsburg, but they were all concentrated in the vicinity of Bunker Hill.

Question. Was it not the intention to move from Bunker Hill to Winchester?

Answer. Yes, sir. At one time General Patterson had given an order to move from Bunker Hill to Winchester. He was very unwilling to leave Johnston even at Winchester without attacking him; and on the afternoon before we left Bunker Hill he decided to attack him, notwithstanding his strong force.

Question. Behind his intrenchments?

Answer. Yes, sir; it went so far that his order was written by his adjutant, General Porter. It was very much against the wishes of General Porter; and he asked General Patterson if he would send for Colonel Abercrombie and Colonel Thomas and consult them on the movement. General Patterson replied: "No, sir; for I know they will attempt to dissuade me from it, and I have made up my mind to fight Johnston under all circumstances." That was the day before we left Bunker Hill. Then Colonel Porter asked to have Colonel Abercrombie and Colonel Thomas sent for and consulted as to the best manner to carry out his wishes. He consented, and they came, and after half an hour they dissuaded him from it.

Question. At that time General Patterson felt it was so important to attack Johnston that he had determined to do it?.

Answer. Yes, sir; the order was not published, but it was written.

Question. You understood General Patterson to be influenced to make that attempt because he felt there was a necessity for detaining Johnston?

Answer. Yes, sir; to detain him as long as he possibly could.

Question. That order was not countermanded until late on Tuesday, the 16th, was it?

Answer. That order never was published. It was written; but at the earnest solicitation of Colonel Porter it was withheld until he could have a consultation with Colonel Abercrombie and Colonel Thomas.

Question. It remained the intention of General Patterson to make the attempt to move on Winchester from Bunker Hill?

Answer. Yes, sir.

Question. And the order to move on Charlestown was not promulgated until 12 o'clock that night?

Answer. It was later than that; it was between 1 and 2 o'clock in the morning.

Question. Your position on the staff of General Patterson was such as to enable you to know of the telegraphic despatches passing between him and General Scott?

Answer. Yes, sir.

Question. If I understand you, after you moved from Bunker Hill to Charlestown, you were then no longer directly threatening Johnston?

Answer. No, sir; the movement towards Charlestown was a flank movement, not one threatening General Johnston.

Question. So that Johnson at that time would not have felt that his force at Winchester was in danger of being attacked by your force?

Answer. No, sir.

By the chairman:

Question. If I have understood you, I am not able to see how at any time you could have prevented Johnston from going to Manassas, if he saw fit to go?

Answer. We never could have prevented Johnston from going to Manassas if he had chosen to do so. He retreated before us all the time. His cavalry force, under Colonel Steuart was hanging around us all the time.

Question. So that you knew all the time that if he saw fit to retreat from Winchester, and so on down to Manassas, he could have done so?

Answer. Yes, sir, at any time.

Question. You have been asked if you thought General Scott, the commanding general, would positively fix the time upon which a battle could be fought?

Answer. I thought he could fix upon the time when he decided to have the attack, unless circumstances arose to prevent it.

Question. As a military man, do you not know that there are numerous contingencies to render it very uncertain when two armies shall meet?

Answer. There is always an uncertainty. But I think an officer with a large army could fix upon the day when he should commence his attack. That was not done in this case.

Question. You mentioned that the roads were barricaded in front of you at Bunker Hill, what was the character of those barricades?

Answer. From the reports of officers, I understand there were trees cut down and thrown across the roads there.

Question. Would you, as a military man, consider that a formidable obstacle in the way of an army 20,000 strong?

Answer. No, sir, not by any means. There were fences built across the road, stone walls built across the road; and they became more numerous as we approached Winchester, and more formidable. And it was reported that the road was defended all the way from that point to Winchester. They would not retard the progress of an army, but they would give great advantage to a foe lurking in the neighborhood. I should not think it was a serious obstacle in the way by any means. I only mention this to show that there was no disposition on the part of General Johnston to attack General Patterson at that point.

Question. Were you not cognizant of the fact that General Patterson had a positive order from General Scott to hold Johnston in the valley of Winchester?

Answer. Yes, sir; those were General Scott's orders all the time.

Question Was not that with direct reference to the battle that was expected to take place at Manassas?

Answer. Yes, sir.

By the chairman:

Question. Was not the order a little more than that? Was it not that if he could not detain Johnston he should follow him down by way of Leesburg?

Answer. No, sir; the Leesburg proposition was made by General Patterson, but not consented to by General Scott. That was before we left Martinsburg.

By Mr. Odell:

Question. Do you think your position at Bunker Hill was a success so far as holding General Johnston was concerned, in accordance with the order received from General Scott?

Answer. Yes, sir; but the position of General Patterson, at Bunker Hill, could not have prevented Johnston from leaving Winchester any moment he pleased.

Question. Your army, while at Bunker Hill, was successful in holding Johnston in the valley of Winchester, in accordance with the orders of General Scott.

Answer. Yes, sir.

By the chairman:

Question. Is there anything else that occurs to you which you wish to state ?

Answer. In reference to the forward move from Martinsburg, there was a council of war held there, at which I was present, and heard all the opinions given. They were unanimous against a forward movement any further than Bunker Hill. In reference to the discontent shown by officers and soldiers, I never saw anything of the kind. After the army left Bunker Hill, on the march to Charlestown, every regiment that we passed were halted and faced to the front, and by the command of their officers, they cheered General Patterson, without a single exception. There was not the slightest sign of disapprobation shown by officers or men, that I saw.

By Mr. Covode:

Question. You had no information that Johnston was reinforced at the time you held your council at Martinsburg ?

Answer. No, sir. The supposition when we left Martinsburg was that Johnston would fight us at Bunker Hill.

By Mr. Gooch:

Question. What do you now understand to have been Johnston's force at Winchester on the day you commenced your movement to Charlestown ?

Answer. 42,000 men. I am as certain of that as I can be of anything I do not know of my own knowledge.

Question. I suppose there is always great uncertainty in the movements of large bodies of men ?

Answer. Yes, sir.

Question. And it is impossible almost for a commander to say a week beforehand that he will be with 20,000, 30,000, or 40,000 men at a given point on any given day ?

Answer. Certainly.

Question. Because contingencies may arise to prevent his getting there, even if he meets with no foe ?

Answer. Yes, sir.

Answer. And of course there is always great uncertainty in fixing the time when you will attack the enemy?

Answer. Yes, sir ; most undoubtedly.

Question. And, as a military man, I suppose you would not be willing to base any important military operations upon the assumption that there had been an engagement, simply because it had been fixed upon a week beforehand for a certain day ?

Answer. That is true. But under the circumstances under which General Patterson was at the time, and from the various letters and telegraphic despatches between Washington and himself, I would have drawn the conclusion that the battle of Manassas would be fought on Tuesday. Because General Scott was positive in his despatch in fixing Tuesday as the day. I would not have been certain the battle would have taken place on that day. But I would certainly have expected it in twenty-four hours of that time, although it might have been delayed, as it was in that case.

Question. Still you would not have based any important military operation on the assumption that it did take place that day ?

Answer. Although I would not suppose it was a certain thing that the battle would take place that day, yet at Bunker Hill General Patterson's column was very much exposed ; there was difficulty in getting forage and provisions for it. His army was some thirty-two miles from the Potomac, and anything but a friendly country and people in his rear, and he might have placed himself in a very precarious and dangerous position. I would have taken these things into consideration, with the supposition that there was no longer any necessity to remain there. I should have been governed by those considerations.

WASHINGTON, *January* 18, 1862.

Colonel CRAIG BIDDLE sworn and examined.

By the chairman:

Question. Did you serve under General Patterson in his campaign into Virginia?

Answer. Yes, sir; I was his aide-de-camp.

Question. We desire a statement, in as brief yet comprehensive a manner as occurs to you, of the military incidents of that campaign, beginning with your movement from Martinsburg to Charlestown. That probably is the most of the military part that we care to inquire into. What number of men did you have at Martinsburg?

Answer. I do not recollect precisely the number. I would not like to state that except from the documents.

Question. About how many do you suppose?

Answer. I suppose we had about 18,000 men; that is, after Colonel Stone came up with his command.

Question. You marched from Martinsburg with about that number?

Answer. I think so.

Question. Where did you go?

Answer. To a place called Bunker Hill, and then diverged to Charlestown.

Question. What was your object in going to Bunker Hill?

Answer. To make a demonstration against Johnston, who was supposed to be at Winchester, and to create the impression that we were going to Winchester.

Question. Was he at Winchester while you were at Martinsburg?

Answer. We supposed so; or rather he remained at Bunker Hill a day, and then fell back on Winchester.

Question. You advanced to Bunker Hill with the intention of giving him battle?

Answer. If he was there, that was the idea. The idea was either to attack him there—it was estimated that the column was not strong enough to attack him, and therefore we meant by demonstration to hold him there as long as we could.

Question. Was not the object of your army to hold Johnston in the valley of Winchester until after the battle at Manassas?

Answer. We hoped to do so. I understood that was the object.

Question. You went to Bunker Hill?

Answer. Yes, sir.

Question. That was on the road from Martinsburg to Winchester, was it?

Answer. Yes, sir.

Question. How long did you remain at Bunker Hill?

Answer. I think we were there only a day.

Question. One day?

Answer. I think so; we went on the 16th, which was Tuesday, and stayed there until Thursday or Friday, I think. No, sir; we got to Charlestown on Sunday morning, and we must have left Bunker Hill on Saturday.

Question. From Bunker Hill you made a reconnoissance still further towards Winchester?

Answer. Yes, sir.

Question. With a view of advancing the army still further?

Answer. Yes, sir. I ought to say to you that I am not a military man. This was my first experience in military matters. I voted for Mr. Lincoln, and I thought it my duty to set an example and go in the field, if necessary, and I joined General Patterson's staff; but upon questions relating to the military conduct of the campaign I do not feel my judgment sufficiently good for the committee to take.

Question. You came here at the instance of General Patterson to give us, I suppose, such information as he desires to have stated. I do not know precisely what he wants. We have a pretty full account of that transaction. But he wanted us to examine you. I do not know exactly to what points, and therefore I wish you to testify to anything material which occurs to you.

Answer. Anything I should say would, of course, be very much like the observations of any other person who was not a military man.

Answer. Very well; state any facts that may occur to you as material to General Patterson or to the government.

Answer. The point I have always understood to be in controversy was the propriety of General Patterson's going on to Winchester.

By Mr. Odell:

Question. We are not discussing or examining any controversy here; we merely want the facts.

Answer. I do not speak of what is said or thought here, but of what is said by others.

By the chairman:

Question. If we had summoned you I should know what it was for; but I do not know. I want General Patterson to have a fair hearing, and to let his witnesses who were with him state what they may know in relation to the matter.

Answer. I was present, of course, at all the discussions. The discussion at Martinsburg was as to whether or not General Patterson should go on to Winchester. General Patterson was very full of that himself. He was determined to go to Winchester; but the opinions of all the regular officers who were with him were against it. The opinions of all the men in whose judgment I had any confidence were against it. They seemed to have the notion that General Patterson had got his Irish blood up by the fight we had had at Falling Waters, and was bound to go ahead. He decided upon going ahead against the remonstrances of General Porter, who advised against it. He told me he considered he had done his duty, and said no more. The movement was delayed in consequence of General Stone's command not being able to move right away. It was then evident that there was so much opposition to it that the general was induced to call a council of the general officers in his command, at which I was present. They were unanimously opposed to the advance. That was at Martinsburg.

Question. You did advance to Bunker Hill?

Answer. The order of General Scott was, that if he thought he was not strong enough to attack Johnston he was to make a demonstration and endeavor to hold him there as long as he could. General Scott had fixed Tuesday, the 16th, as the day on which this was to be done. Those de-

spatches I saw. General Patterson advanced on Tuesday, and held him
there until Thursday afternoon; and we were all as confident as possible
that the battle at Manassas had been fought, and that General Patterson
had succeeded in doing all he could; and the flank movement down to
Charlestown was considered judicious by everybody, especially as we considered that our utility there was at an end.

Question. You say that before that, at Martinsburg, it was not thought
best to attack Johnston?

Answer. It was thought by all the officers there that a forward movement
was not advisable; that our troops were entirely undisciplined. Although
it was thought perfectly proper to attack in the open field, as General Patterson had been trying to do ever since he started, yet it was perfectly idle
to attack the intrenchments at Winchester. Everybody represented the
force of General Johnston as from 30,000 to 40,000.

Question. Where were you when you heard that he had been re-enforced?
Answer. At Martinsburg, I think.

Question. Was it not at Bunker Hill that you first heard that?
Answer. No, sir; I do not think so.

Question. Do you think it was before the council of war was held at Martinsburg?

Answer. I think so.

Question. It is your opinion, then, that General Patterson could not have
prevented General Johnston from going to Manassas?

Answer. I do not think he could possibly have done any more than he did.
As I say, my opinion is founded upon the opinions of all those gentlemen in
whom I have the utmost confidence. I consider General Porter one of the
most accomplished officers I ever had the pleasure to meet with.

Question. When did you first hear any complaints there that the regiments wanted to go home?

Answer. I think there was no question about their going until they got
to Charlestown. The time of none of them expired until then. They all
expected to go home at the end of their three months. There was no appeal
made to them until we got to Charlestown.

Question. They manifested no dissatisfaction before that time?

Answer. No, sir; I do not know as they did until at Charlestown, when
they expected to go home. I recollect perfectly the discussions that took
place in regard to those troops. The regular officers said the troops would
not stay a day after their time had expired. The general said: "Well, you
will see." They said: "We know, because we saw it in Mexico." I said:
"This is entirely a different matter; this is a fight for the existence of our
government, and the men will not dare go home, I think." General Patterson took it up and went out and made a direct appeal to the men. The
general speaks very well under all circumstances, and he made remarkably
good speeches then, as I thought, and as all thought. The general went to
his son's regiment, which was a very fine regiment, and which we understood was willing to remain. The general made a speech to them, but to
our surprise a considerable number of them refused to put up their muskets
when the question was put to them. The officers were very much mortified
at this, and spoke to the men, and finally they got them, with few exceptions, to put up their muskets. But still it was a sort of touch-and-go with
them. That was the first time the fear crossed my mind that there would
be trouble. The general then went to the other regiments, but found that
it was not feasible at all; from one-half to two-thirds refused to go. He
finally got to an Irish regiment and made a very powerful appeal to them,
knowing the Irish character very well. He carried them with a sort of
shout, and they all said they would remain. They all lifted up their mus-

kets. But he had hardly turned his back when they hallooed out, " Shoes and pants!" " Shoes and pants!"

Question. And it was evident, then, that you could do no more ?

Answer. Yes, sir.

Question. You did not expect after you turned off to Charlestown that there would be any fighting ?

Answer. It was supposed that if it were necessary to advance we could advance better from Charlestown than from Bunker Hill. We had not such a long line to protect; Bunker Hill was clear in the enemy's country, where it was not possible to do anything with the supplies we had.

Question. Then you knew very well it was no longer possible to hold Johnston from going to Manassas ?

Answer. We thought he had gone.

Question. And if he had gone you supposed you could not have prevented his going ?

Answer. We thought we could do it better if we should advance from Charlestown than from the other place, because we could get supplies. It was the opinion of the quartermaster, commissary, and engineers, that we were on a false line at Bunker Hill, and that the enemy would get in our rear.

Question. Of course you did not know whether he had gone or not ?

Answer. We heard he had gone on Thursday afternoon.

Question. That was the first you heard of it ?

Answer. Yes, sir.

Question. If he had gone why did you not go to Winchester ?

Answer. We thought we should do no good, for if we went there we would have to come back again ; we could not hold it.

By Mr. Odell:

Question. Where did General Sanford join you ; was he with you at Martinsburg with his re-enforcements ?

Answer. I think he joined us at Martinsburg.

Question. Did you include his men in the 18,000 you said you had there ?

Answer. Yes, sir ; I think we did.

Question. The understanding among your officers, I think you said, was to fight or to hold Johnston in the valley of Winchester ?

Answer. We understood that that was what was desired; to fight him if we could, or, if not, to hold him there as long as we could; that is, for this fixed time; to hold him there on the 16th, which was the day that General Patterson was directed to hold him there.

Question. Was that all that he was directed to do; to hold him there one day ?

Answer. That was the day on which he was to make an advance, to pretend to attack him, or rally to attack him, in order to hold him there. General Scott was to let General Patterson know on what day he wanted him to advance, or to make an attack, whichever he was able to do; and General Scott intimated to him, or telegraphed him directly, that it was on the 16th that he wanted him to do so; and having held the enemy there until Thursday afternoon, he conceived that he had done all that General Scott desired him to do. It was impossible to hold him any longer time there, for the time of the men was expiring then. There is an impression abroad in regard to General Patterson's popularity among the men. I believe General Patterson was always an extremely popular commander, and that all this dissatisfaction with him was got up afterwards ; it was entirely an afterthought.

Question. While at Bunker Hill, the night before you left there, were any orders issued to march on the enemy?

Answer. I think there were such orders.

Question. Did not General Patterson issue orders at Bunker Hill, the night before you marched to Charlestown, for an attack on the enemy?

Answer. I think such orders were written. I do not think they were issued. I think General Patterson was again persuaded not to made an advance. General Patterson was extremely popular with the army until after those men got home. They all expected to be received at home with great homage; but General Patterson having asked them to stay, and they having refused, the first question asked of them after they got home was, "Why did you not stay? why did you refuse to remain?" And in order to answer that question they had to get up some excuse, and it took the form very often of abuse of General Patterson.

Question. Were not the men in good spirits and ready to fight while at Bunker Hill.

Answer. Yes, sir; the men were ready to fight at any time. I always conceived that the spirit of the men was broken when they were ordered back across the Potomac. They had been hanging on week after week, and had got the impression that there was to be no fight at all; and they did not want to be kept there on the borders for no purpose at all. And the men had got the idea that their time was out, and there would be no fight at all. When this order was given everybody was in the highest possible spirits. They dashed across the river, and the whole army was aroused to go forward. We got two orders from Washington. The general did not mind the first order; then there was another one which said, "I have twice ordered you to send on all the regular troops." And the men came back from over the river, and became greatly disheartened.

By Mr. Covode:

Question. Did you not believe all the time, up to the time when you turned back to Charlestown, that the men would remain over their time if they could have been led forward against the enemy?

Answer. I think, if the thing had been put through in a spirited way from the first, after they had got into it, they would not have backed out. There were various reasons which justified the men. The force had been raised in a great hurry—in a month or two—and a great many of their officers were totally inefficient. They had a perfect dread of going into battle with their officers, and they wanted to go back and enter into new organizations the next day after they got back.

WASHINGTON, *January* 20, 1862.

General DANIEL TYLER sworn and examined.

By the chairman:

Question. Will you please state what is your rank and position in the army, or what it was?

Answer. I was a brigadier general, second in command under General McDowell.

Question. You were present at the battle of Bull Run?

Answer. I was there.

Question. Please give a brief and concise statement of what you saw there, and how the battle was conducted, &c.; do this without questioning at first; I want to get particularly what, in your judgment, caused the disaster of that day.

Answer. The first great trouble was the want of discipline and instruction in the troops. The troops needed that regimental and brigade instruction which would have enabled them to act together in masses with advantage.

Question. Were there any other more proximate causes than that?

Answer. There was a great want of instruction and professional knowledge among the officers—the company and regimental officers.

Question. Well, sir, give a concise history of that battle.

Answer. I will begin back to the occupation of Falls' Church. The first advance made by our troops, after the occupation of Alexandria, Arlington Heights, Fort Corcoran, and Roach's Mill, was to Falls' Church. That was made by me with the Connecticut brigade, about the 5th of June. I remained in that division, commanding the advance of the army, until the advance upon Manassas. When we advanced upon Manassas I was assigned to the command of a division of four brigades. My line of march was by Vienna to Flint Hill, and from there I had authority from General McDowell to take either the route by Fairfax Court-House, or the route by Gormantown, as my judgment should indicate. I took the advance through Gormantown, and arrived there in advance of any other division of the army, on the turnpike to Centreville. We continued our march until about 4 o'clock in the evening, and then bivouacked for the night. I think that was the first misfortune of our movement. I think, if we had gone on to Centreville that night we should have been in much better condition the next day. I was ordered by General McDowell to take my division forward at 7 o'clock on Thursday morning and attack Centreville, he assigning me two twenty-pounders to assist in that attack. On arriving at Centreville, I found that the enemy had evacuated their fortifications, and that Cox's division, as I was told by the people there, had passed over Stone Bridge, and Bonham, with the South Carolina and Georgia troops, had passed down by Blackburn's Ford.

I waited there an hour and a half, getting such information as I could collect, and then, not finding General McDowell, or hearing from him, I took a squadron of cavalry and four companies of light infantry and went forward with General Richardson towards Blackburn's Ford. After passing through the woods there we came out immediately upon Bull Run. From that point we had a very good view of Manassas. We found they had not occupied the left bank of Bull Run at all. There is a distance, along the stream there, of about a thousand yards of perfectly open country. There is not a tree until you get to Bull Run, and then it is covered with trees. I got there in the morning, with merely my staff and this squadron of cavalry and the light infantry. I was perfectly astonished to find they had not occupied that position on the left bank. It had complete control of it, so complete control that, after we got our artillery in position, we had the whole control of that valley. Beauregard, in his official report, complains that we threw shot in his hospital. We did, but we did not know it was his hospital; we thought it was his headquarters. The whole ground there, clear over almost into Manassas, was commanded by that position. This was a chain of heights, extending along the whole of this ford, and completely controlling the bottom of Bull Run.

As soon as I found out the condition of things I sent back for Ayres's battery—Sherman's old battery—and had it brought and put into position. After firing two or three shots they replied to us; but having only smooth-bore guns they could not reach us. After the two twenty-pounders came up we had eight pieces in position, commanding the whole of that run. They could not make a move in front of the woods there without our controlling them. They made no movement at all; we could see no show of force. All we could see was some few around their battery. I then took Richardson's brigade and filed it down there to see what there was in the bottom. This was evidently on the direct road to Manassas. They marched down through in front of the whole of that wood, without bringing any fire upon them. I sent some skirmishers into the woods, and there were some thirty or fifty shots fired from a few men.

I saw an opening where we could have a chance to get in a couple of pieces of artillery, and I ordered Captain Ayres to take a couple of his howitzers and go into that opening and throw some canister shot into the woods. The very moment he came into battery it appeared to me that there were 5,000 muskets fired at once. It appears by Beauregard's report that he had seventeen regiments in front there. They were evidently waiting for our infantry to get into the woods there. Ayres threw some ten or fifteen canister shot in among them, but was forced to come out, which he did very gallantly, with the loss of one man and two horses. We then came on the hill, and the whole eight pieces were placed in position, and we exchanged with them 415 shots in three-quarters of an hour, our shots plunging right in among them. They fired at an angle of elevation, and the consequence was that we lost but one man; whereas our artillery was plunging right into them, and every shot had its effect.

The Rev. Mr. Hinds, who was taken prisoner on Monday after the fight, was taken down to Bonham's camp there. He has lately been exchanged and returned, and represents their loss there at some 300 or 400 men that day. My idea was that that position was stronger than the one above. But that is a mere matter of opinion. But after this affair of Thursday that point was never abandoned. We held that point until after the battle of Sunday. Richardson's brigade was left there, and Davies's brigade supported him. And when General Ewell tried to cut us off at Centreville on Sunday afternoon they repulsed him. We could have made a first-rate artillery fight there on Friday morning before Johnston's force came up. We knew of the arrival of Johnston's forces on Friday afternoon, because we could hear the arrival of the cars up the Winchester road.

My division was stationed on Cub Run from Thursday evening, except Keyes's brigade, which was left back at Centreville. My orders were for my division to move forward on Sunday morning to Stone Bridge, and threaten that bridge. We left our camp at half-past two o'clock in the morning, and arrived there a little past six o'clock. The fire was opened immediately after getting the division posted, say at a quarter past six o'clock. Our first fire was the signal for Richardson to open fire at Blackburn's Ford at the same time. Under the instruction to threaten Stone Bridge, it was contemplated that Hunter and Heintzelman, after passing over by Sedley's Church, would drive the enemy away from the front of the bridge, and enable us to repair the Stone Bridge, which General McDowell assumed to be ruined, and would be destroyed. We had a bridge framed and prepared for that purpose.

Now, at that time, when that should have been done, my division was to pass over the bridge and take part in the action in front of the bridge. About 11 o'clock, seeing that Hunter's column was arrested on the opposite side of Bull Run, and that they were requiring assistance, I ordered over Sherman's brigade, containing the 69th and 79th New York, a Wisconsin, and another regiment, with orders to come into line on the right of the troops that we saw attacked, which we supposed, from the appearance of them, to be Hunter's division. They did so, and Sherman's brigade made a very gallant attack there, and relieved Burnside's brigade from the embarrassment they were in. General Burnside, in his official report, acknowledged that he was taken out of a very tight place.

At that time we supposed the battle to have been won. I had had no opportunity of seeing what had been done on the other side until the moment that I came into line with Keyes's brigade on the left of Sherman's brigade, and at that moment I saw Captain Fry, of General McDowell's staff, standing by the fence, crying out "Victory! victory! We have done it! we have done it!" He supposed, and I supposed, and General McDowell at that time supposed, that the victory was substantially won. That was about half-past 12 o'clock. To show that he had some reason to believe that, we passed from that point with my division clear down to the Canady House on the Warrenton turnpike, driving the enemy without any show of resistance. There was hardly a gun fired. There appeared to be a general flight before us.

It was not until we got to that house that we met the enemy in any force at all. They had occupied a plateau of ground immediately above it with their batteries. Ricketts had his fight further over on the other side, while we attacked them by way of the road. At that point my brigade, after carrying the house twice, were repulsed and fell back under the hill. And at that moment, through General Keyes's aid, who was with me, I sent verbal information to General McDowell that we were going to try to turn the batteries on the plateau by a movement below the Stone Bridge. That movement was subsequently made. We continued under the hill, advancing with the Connecticut brigade, with General Keyes's brigade, until we reached a point considerably below the position of the enemy's batteries on the plateau. And as Keyes faced his brigade to the right, to advance up the hill to attack the batteries, we had the first intimation of the retreat of the army by seeing them pouring over towards Sedley's Church.

By Mr. Gooch:

Question. At what time was that?

Answer. That was, perhaps, nearly three o'clock. Keyes's brigade then faced to the left and took the same route back under the hill by which they had made the advance, recrossed Bull Run at the original point of crossing, went on up the Warrenton turnpike, at or near the hospital, and on the Centreville side of Bull Run, and continued their retreat towards Centreville. I did not see General McDowell on the field, and I did not receive any orders from him during that day.

Question. Have you anything further to state?

Answer. Nothing. I suppose you ask opinions about the panic. It has been very much discussed before military circles.

Question. We have heard various speculations as to the reason why the battle was not commenced earlier on Sunday; will you state the reason why the battle was delayed to so late an hour on that day?

Answer. The impossibility of moving an army of 22,000 men, with their ammunition, ambulances, &c., over a single turnpike.

By Mr. Odell:

Question. Did not the most of the column wait in the road until Keyes's brigade, which was back at Centreville, came up and joined you?

Answer. No, sir. The reason why the battle was delayed was this: The advancing so large an army as I have stated over one common road; and for the further reason that the country between Cub Run and Bull Run was supposed to be occupied by the enemy, and it became indispensable for the leading division, being without cavalry, and with no knowledge of the country, to move slowly, in order to protect themselves against any surprise on the part of the enemy, and force a position we had not the least conception of.

By Mr. Gooch:

Question. Was yours the leading division?

Answer. Yes, sir.

Question. Were the rest of the divisions delayed by your movement?

Answer. They were not more than was absolutely necessary under the circumstances.

Question. What time did your movement commence?

Answer. At half-past two o'clock, as will appear by the official reports of Generals Schenck, Sherman, and Keyes.

Question. You were to advance how far?

Answer. To the Stone Bridge, about two and a half miles.

Question. And the other divisions turned off from the road on which you advanced before they reached Stone Bridge?

Answer. Yes, sir; some two miles from the bridge.

Question. At what time did the rear of your division reach Stone Bridge?

Answer. Keyes's brigade, being delayed to guard the road going down to Manassas, did not reach Stone Bridge until about 11 o'clock. But that brigade was acting under the orders of General McDowell.

Question. At what time did the portion of the division under your command reach Stone Bridge?

Answer. It reached there by six o'clock, perhaps a quarter before six. We opened fire, as General Beauregard states, at six o'clock. Our time said half-past six, but I presume their time was nearer right than ours. I was there more than half an hour, posting my division, before we opened fire.

Question. Then do I understand you to say that none of the other divisions were held back by any portion of your division?

Answer. Yes, sir.

Question. The last part of your division had reached the point where Hunter's and Heintzelman's divisions were to turn off in time so as not to hold them back at all?

Answer. The two leading brigades of my division, Schenck's and Sherman's, arrived at the Stone Bridge in the neighborhood of and before six o'clock. Keyes's brigade, having been detained by General McDowell's order, arrived about eleven o'clock. Keyes's brigade, therefore, is the only brigade that could have interfered with the movement of Hunter's and Heintzelman's divisions. That brigade of Keyes's had no artillery. And so soon as General Schenck got his brigade on the line of the road, I saw the difficulty that there might be in consequence of Keyes's brigade being left back at Centreville, having two miles of road to pass over, that they might interfere with Hunter's column. I then sent an aid back to tell General Keyes that as he had no artillery he should file immediately off the Warrenton turnpike into the fields, and immediately clear the turnpike for the use of the other columns. And I deemed it of so much importance, that after sending my aid, I rode back myself and saw the leading regiment of his brigade file into the fields, and gave him a positive order to put his brigade into the fields entirely out of the way of the other divisions. General Keyes reported to me that he did so, and I have no doubt of the fact, for I saw the leading regiment file off.

Question. Did any of the other divisions, or any portions of the other divisions, pass through a part of your division in order to get forward of them?

Answer. When Keyes's brigade reached the road they occupied it, and Keyes's brigade passed along parallel to the road and entirely out of their way. He was enabled to do that because he had no artillery. The others having artillery, there was no other place for them to pass, except up the road and over the bridge at Cub Run.

Question. At what time did the rear of your division—I do not mean to include Keyes's brigade, but the rear of that which was with you that morning—pass the point where Hunter and Heintzelman turned off to the right?

Answer. We passed there before four o'clock.

Question. Or in two hours after you started?

Answer. Yes, sir.

Question. Then do I understand you to say that the road was clear, so far as your division was concerned, up to the turning-off point after four o'clock, with the exception that Keyes's portion of your division was then on that road?

Answer. Alongside the road, but off it.

Question. Why did you move first, as you were to move the shortest distance over the road?

Answer. That was the order of march by General McDowell. I did not see General McDowell or hear from him after the fight began, until we got back to Centreville.

By Mr. Odell:

Question. Did the fact of Keyes's brigade not joining yours impede the progress of the other columns?

Answer. I do not think it did in the least.

Question. You did not receive an order from General McDowell to hasten your march?

Answer. No, sir; I received no orders from General McDowell after I left him on Saturday night. It was my suggestion to put Keyes's brigade in the field. After seeing the head of his first regiment file into the fields, I did not wait there, but immediately pushed forward to post the other brigades at the Stone Bridge.

Question. Was there any portion of the march, with reference to Centretreville Cross Roads or anything, retarded, so far as you know by your column?

Answer. No, sir; not that I know of.

By Mr. Gooch:

Question. Was it understood that Keyes, with his brigade, should march up and join your division in advance of the movement forward of all the other troops?

Answer. I presume so. That was the understanding—to keep the division together.

Question. I understand you to say that it was expected that Keyes should move up in advance of any other portion of the army, and join your division?

Answer. Certainly; for General McDowell said, " The first division, (Tyler's,) with the exception of Richardson's brigade, will move first."

Question. That was not done, was it?

Answer. Yes, sir.

Question. Why did he not move forward so as to keep out of the way of the remainder of the army?

Answer. He states that he did not interfere with them.

Question. You say he turned off into the field. Why could he not, with the road clear before him, if he was in advance, move forward so as to keep clear of the others?

Answer. He might, if the movements were made with perfect regularity.

Question. He had no artillery, and was first on the road. Why did he not pass over the road so as to offer no obstruction?

Answer. Because, by passing into the field he would have given the rear columns the advantage of two miles and a half of clear track, which there was a possibility might be interfered with, but which was not interfered with.

Question. Were Hunter's and Heintzelman's columns in advance of the position where Keyes turned off the main road?

Answer. No, sir; they moved from behind Centreville on the morning of the 21st.

Question. If he was first on the road, and they were behind him, and he had nothing but infantry, why could he not have moved forward with sufficient celerity to leave the road open to the rest as fast as they advanced?

Answer. He could if the column in advance of him had moved with perfect regularity.

Question. What column was in advance?

Answer. Sherman's brigade and Schenck's brigade.

Question. Then it was your division which obstructed his movement forward:

Answer. We did not obstruct him at all. When I ordered Keyes into the field he had not reached the rear of my division. But seeing the possibility of an interference, I ordered him into the field.

Question. If he had marched up and joined your division, as your division then was, would the rear of his brigade have extended back to the junction of the road where the others turned off?

Answer. At the time he joined us?

Question. Yes, sir.

Answer. I think it would at that moment; but still we were all advancing.

Question. Then did you make the movement into the field with Keyes's brigade in order to prevent that difficulty?

Answer. It was to prevent a circumstance that might occur. It was to prevent difficulty, when I knew there were two brigades in advance of him, and to carry out the instruction to march through the field. It was not that any difficulty had occurred, but to take every precaution against any such occurrence. I had not seen the head of Hunter's and Heintzelman's columns, and I did not know where they were. But foreseeing the difficulty of moving 20,000 men over one turnpike, after getting the artillery and wagons and ammunition into line, I saw that there must be difficulty, and to obviate that as far as possible I rode back and ordered Keyes, who was without artillery, to file out into the field. At that time I did not know where Hunter's and Heintzelman's columns were, and I did not know that they had moved a foot.

Question. Did you see the rear of General Keyes's column?

Answer. I did not. I only saw the leading regiment filed into the field.

Question. You do not know whether Hunter's and Heintzelman's columns was directly in the rear of Keyes's brigade or not?

Answer. No, sir; but I wanted to provide against a contingency.

Question. At that moment you did not know the condition of things in the rear of Keyes's command?

Answer. I did not. I had no idea where Hunter's and Heintzelman's column's were. I supposed they were on the road, however, but I did not know where; but I wanted to do all in my power to remedy any possible difficulty that might occur.

By Mr. Chandler:

Question. The first attack on Thursday, I understood you to say, was made by a single brigade?

Answer. It was made by four companies of a brigade. There were never more than 300 men, except artillery, engaged with the enemy at any time.

Question. Supported by a brigade?

Answer. Yes, sir; by Richardson's brigade.

Question. Should that attack on Thursday have been made at all, unless it was followed up and made successful?

Answer. It was not an attack. It was merely a reconnoissance to ascertain what force they had there on Bull Run. It was not the intention to make an attack. And the very moment the force of the enemy was discovered, which it was important to know, that moment the troops were withdrawn, and merely a cannonade kept up in order to see what effect it would have upon the men in the bottom of Bull Run. The whole affair was over before six o'clock. It was one of those advance engagements that spring up sometimes without any expectation of anything very important coming from it.

Question. It was intended as a mere reconnoissance?

Answer. Yes, sir. After we had ascertained the force of the enemy there, I ordered Richardson to withdraw his brigade. He was very anxious to make an attack at the time, and was very confident that he could repulse them and force them out of the woods. I told him our object was not to bring on an engagement. But there was one thing very significant in that affair. Richardson's brigade moved along the whole front of that wood, and skirted it along without being attacked, though Beauregard says he had seventeen regiments in the woods there. The reason was that Richardson was supported by the artillery on the hill, and the enemy would have suffered very severely if he had made any attack.

Question. Was it your understanding that Patterson was to hold Johnston in the valley of Winchester?

Answer. Yes, sir.

Question. You did not expect Johnston down there?

Answer. No, sir.

Question. Had Patterson held Johnston, what, in your judgment, would have been the result of that battle?

Answer. We should have whipped Beauregard beyond a question.

Question. Then you deem that the real cause of that defeat was the failure of Patterson to hold Johnston back?

Answer. Undoubtedly. From Blackburn's Ford we could have a fair view of Manassas, and could see what they had there; and I have never had the least doubt that if Patterson had kept Johnston's army out of the way we would have whipped Manassas itself.

By Mr. Gooch:

Question. You think if you had driven Beauregard into and upon Manassas, you could have driven him out of it?

Answer. Yes, sir; if Johnston had been kept out of the way. There has been a great deal said about their fortifications there. It was the understanding that, from Flint Hill to Gormantown, we should find a succession of very severe abattis and batteries, which would render it a very difficult passage for our troops. We first fell in with, on advancing from Flint Hill, an abattis, which was so miserably constructed that the axe-men of one of our Maine regiments cut it out in the course of fifteen minutes, so that our brigade passed right on. We found a second one of the same character; and then we found an abandoned battery, which two rifled guns could have knocked to pieces in fifteen minutes. At Centreville all the fortifications were of exactly the same character. They were the meanest, most miserable works ever got up by military men. And I have no reason to believe that, even back as far as Manassas, they were much better constructed than they were on this side the run.

Question. Then you attribute the advantages of the enemy in that fight, and the advantages which they probably would have had at Manassas, so far as they would have had any, to the natural location of the country, rather than to any earthworks or artificial works that had been erected?

Answer. Yes, sir; at Manassas particularly. There they had an elevation in their favor, and we would have been obliged to attack them there to some disadvantage.

Question. I suppose you knew, when you moved forward to make the attack, you were moving forward with undisciplined troops; but you also knew you were to attack undisciplined troops?

Answer. We supposed our men were equal to theirs, and we found them to be so.

Question. You did not expect perfection in our movements any more than you did in theirs?

Answer. There was nothing in their troops that I saw that induced me to believe that their discipline and instruction was in any way superior to ours.

Question. Do you know the particulars of the loss of Griffin's and Ricketts's batteries that day?

Answer. They were on the opposite side of the hill from me, and I did not see them. But I think the loss of those two batteries created the panic.

Question. Do you think it very probable the issue of that battle would have been different if those batteries had not been lost?

Answer. I think if we could have had two good batteries there we could have done a great deal better than we did. I think the loss of those two batteries had a great effect upon us.

By Mr. Odell:

Question. Did you receive from General McDowell, through his aid, Mr. Kingsbury, orders to make a more rapid advance?

Answer. No, sir; I did not.

WASHINGTON, *January* 22, 1862.

General DANIEL TYLER re-examined.

The witness said: I made one mistake in my testimony when before the committee on Monday last. I then stated that I received no orders from General McDowell during the day of the battle of Bull Run. That was an error. I did receive an order from him about 11 o'clock in the morning to press the attack. That was the time when Sherman's brigade advanced and relieved Burnside's brigade.

By Mr. Gooch:

Question. What regiments were engaged in the action at Blackburn's Ford?

Answer. Two Michigan regiments, a regiment from Massachusetts, and one from New York. The skirmishers belonging to those regiments were those who were engaged with the enemy. The others were sustaining the skirmishers in the woods.

Question. What was the conduct of the Massachusetts regiment, Colonel Cowdin?

Answer. Colonel Cowdin's regiment I had immediately under my eye during the whole of that affair. They behaved like gallant, brave men, and had no superiors, as a regiment, in my opinion, on the field.

Question. The regiment was well commanded?

Answer. Yes, sir; it was well led and well commanded. I will say that on Sunday Ayres's battery repulsed the charge of the enemy's cavalry on the Warrenton turnpike, and that was what effectually checked and drove off the pursuit.

By Mr. Covode:

Question. Did you know, before the engagement on Sunday, that Johnston had arrived with his force?

Answer. Yes, sir; we knew that Johnston's forces began to arrive Friday afternoon, for we could hear, at Blackburn's Ford, the trains arrive at Manassas, and we knew they came on the Winchester road. On Saturday afternoon I told General Cameron that, in my opinion, Johnston's army had arrived. At the time we received orders on Saturday evening previous to the battle, I asked General McDowell this question: "General, what force have we to fight to-morrow?" He replied: "You know, general, as well as I do." My reply was, "General, we have got the whole of Joe Johnston's army in our front, and we must fight the two armies." I gave him the reason for that belief, that we had heard the trains coming in. He made no reply.

Question. What, in your judgment, would have been the result if you had fought them the day before?

Answer. I believe we would have whipped them beyond question before Johnston's forces arrived. I never had a doubt that, single-handed, we could have whipped Beauregard's army.

WASHINGTON, *January* 20, 1862.

General DANIEL BUTTERFIELD sworn and examined.

By Mr. Chandler:

Question. What is your rank and position in the army?

Answer. I am a brigadier general of volunteers, and lieutenant colonel of the 12th regiment of infantry in the regular service.

By Mr. Odell:

Question. We want to know something about your connexion with the army under General Patterson's command. Were you colonel of the 12th New York regiment under General Patterson?

Answer. Yes, sir.

Question. You first came to Washington?

Answer. Yes, sir; under orders from the governor of the State.

Question. And you went where from Washington?

Answer. From Washington we led the first advance over the Long Bridge in May into Virginia. About the 6th of July, I think, on a Sunday, we left Washington by rail to Baltimore, and thence to Hagerstown. We remained at Hagerstown one day. Hearing that General Patterson was going to make a fight or an advance the next day, the men were anxious to go ahead. We left Hagerstown at 6 o'clock at night, and came up with the advance guard to Martinsburg at 3 o'clock in the morning, 26 miles, besides fording the Potomac. That shows how anxious the men were to be in at the fight.

Question. How long did you remain at Martinsburg?

Answer. We remained there until Monday, the 15th.

Question. Where did you then go?

Answer. To Bunker Hill.

Question. What was the distance?

Answer. From 9 to 12 miles. I do not remember the exact distance.

Question. What did you understand was the object of that advance?

Answer. I understood the object was to advance on the position of the enemy.

Question. The enemy under General Johnston?

Answer. Yes, sir; at Winchester.

Question. Was that the understanding of the officers generally?

Answer. That was the general impression prevailing among the officers and. troops, that we were going after Johnston at Winchester.

Question. What was the temper of the troops while you were at Bunker Hill?

Answer. They were very anxious for a fight; you might say "spoiling for a fight," some of them. The three regiments under my command were anxious for a fight.

Question. Was there any dissatisfaction in the army there?

Answer. Not any in my brigade. I knew nothing at all about the other regiments at that time. I was assigned, shortly after my arrival at Martinsburg, to the command of a brigade which consisted of the 12th and 5th New York militia and the 19th and 28th New York volunteers. I started from Martinsburg with the command of this brigade. I had had command of it for some time at Martinsburg; I know they were generally very anxious for a fight. With regard to the disposition of the other troops in the army there I knew nothing at that time. My time was fully occupied in taking care of my own men.

Question. In your intercourse with the officers of that force did you hear any dissatisfaction expressed?

Answer. Not the slightest. On the contrary, the general expression of the officers, of my own regiments particularly, was one of the greatest anxiety to get into a fight. They expressed great dissatisfaction in being ordered away from Washington, as they thought they would then see no fighting. I had a personal interview with General Scott, and he told me it was a very important movement indeed, and that we would probably be in a fight sooner than by remaining here, and when I told my officers that they were perfectly willing and anxious to go.

Question. Did you understand that the object of your going from here to Martinsburg, to Patterson's column, was to prevent Johnston from joining Beauregard?

Answer. I did not at the time we moved.

Question. Did you after you got there?

Answer. I did not until after the whole affair was over. I did not understand that that was the particular object for which General Scott designed us. He simply told me that our movement was a very important one, one of great importance. He made that remark to me before we left Washington, on the 6th of July. He said: "I have picked out your regiment as one of the best disciplined, and we calculate that you will lead the way; that you will not disappoint us in the estimate we have made of you." I supposed from that that there was work of some kind cut out for us there.

Question. How long did you remain at Bunker Hill?

Answer. We remained there two days. We left Bunker Hill to go to Charlestown on the 17th of July.

Question. What was the effect of your position at Bunker Hill upon the enemy?

Answer. It was a threatening position upon the enemy. We were twelve miles from Winchester, and we were in close expectation of a fight there; the troops expected it.

Question. Did you make any demonstration forward from Bunker Hill?

Answer. Yes, sir; while at Bunker Hill the Rhode Island battery and some other troops—I think Colonel Wallace's Indiana regiment and some cavalry—

went out to within six miles of Winchester, where they found an abatis constructed across the road, with a cavalry picket, which they drove in. They threw some shells towards Winchester. I afterwards understood that the effect of that demonstration was to draw up the whole of Johnston's army in line of battle behind their intrenchments at Winchester. This I learned from a young officer who was attached to the staff and went out with the expedition.

Question. Was this abatis a serious impediment to the movement of a large body of troops?

Answer. It was simply trees felled across the road—not much of an impediment; this young officer who gave me the account of it stated that a large number of trees had been felled across the road to impede the advance of the army. I supposed it was merely a precaution to enable the force behind to get into line to receive any body of men coming up.

Question. Did you receive any orders while at Bunker Hill to make an attack upon the enemy?

Answer. I do not now remember. I have got copies of all the orders I received. If there are any such orders among them I can send them to the committee. Our orders generally came about 11 o'clock at night, and were promulgated immediately. We oftentimes used to keep the orders sent to us to be sent out by staff officers to be read to the colonels, deeming it necessary to have it done at once.

Question. At what time did you receive your order to go to Charlestown?

Answer. I think we got it at 11 o'clock the night before we moved. We moved to Charlestown on the 17th. I am very positive the order came between 10 and 11 o'clock at night to move the next morning at daylight.

Question. What was the effect of that movement upon the troops?

Answer. Well, sir, it was bad.

Question. Why was it bad?

Answer. Well, sir; one colonel came to me and said that the men said they were retreating; and that if they carry their colors at all they would carry them boxed up.

Question. Was it not a retreat?

Answer. I did not so consider it at the time.

Question. Was it not a retreat, so far as your relative position to the enemy was concerned?

Answer. I did not consider it so at the time, from the nature of the country, as shown by the map. I was not consulted or advised what the nature of the movement was. I simply received the order and obeyed it. I did not know but what it was an attempt to cut off General Johnston from making a junction with Beauregard, by getting our army between him and Manassas.

By the chairman:

Question. Was it not the understanding of the troops when they started that they were merely going down to another road, and then to throw themselves in the rear of Johnston?

Answer. I had that impression, and I think I circulated it as a matter of policy among the troops. If I did not circulate and give currency to it, I explained that we could make such a move when we got to Charlestown as would not bring us in front of the intrenchments prepared for us at Winchester.

Question. Which, in your opinion as a military man, was the better position to prevent Johnston from joining Beauregard—Bunker Hill or Charlestown?

Answer. I should have selected Charlestown if my movements could have been concealed, because I could have attacked Johnston, with his army marching in flank, if he had attempted to move. I would not have attacked him at Winchester, where he was intrenched and prepared to defend himself.

By Mr. Odell:

Question. In leaving Bunker Hill for Charlestown did you not free Johnston from our control?

Answer. No, sir; not if our movements were directed to hold him. The army was in position at Charlestown, if it was determined to cut Johnston off from joining Beauregard, to be thrown in between him and the Shenandoah.

Question. How far is Charlestown from Winchester? More or less than Bunker Hill?

Answer. A greater number of miles. But we would have no further to go to reach the line which Johnston would have to take to Manassas than we would at Bunker Hill?

Question. Do you know what our force was at Bunker Hill?

Answer. I had no positive knowledge. I judged it to be about 20,000.

Question. Did you at any time offer to make a fight with your portion of the army there?

Answer. I stated to General Sanford that we had come there for a fight; that we were ready to fight; and if there was going to be a fight, we wanted to be counted in, and we were willing to lead at any time when the fight was opened.

WASHINGTON, *January* 21, 1862.

General ANDREW PORTER sworn and examined.

By Mr. Chandler:

Question. What is your position and rank in the army?

Answer. I am a brigadier general of volunteers, and at present provost marshal.

Question. Were you at the battle of Bull Run?

Answer. Yes, sir.

Question. What position did you hold there?

Answer. I commanded the first brigade of the second division.

Question. General Hunter's division?

Answer. Yes, sir; General Hunter was cut down almost at the first fire, and I then commanded the division.

Question. Hunter's division was on the extreme right that day?

Answer. Yes, sir.

Question. Will you go on and give as briefly as may be the action which that division took on the day of that battle?

Answer. I would rather refer you to my report, which was made up immediately afterwards from my notes, which I have not since read. It contains accurate details, and if I attempt to state it now I would perhaps not recollect everything.

Question. Was it in your division that the rout commenced?

Answer. I cannot tell.

Question. Were Ricketts' and Griffin's batteries in your division?

Answer. Griffin's battery was in my division. Ricketts' battery came up afterwards. I do not now recollect whose division he was in.

Question. Were you near Griffin's battery at the time it was captured?

Answer. I was within a couple of hundred yards, I suppose. I recollect very distinctly the volley that was fired from the woods. I was far enough off to see that that part of the game was played out after that fire.

Question. You were there when that regiment from the woods opened fire?

Answer. Yes, sir; but some little way off—200 or 300 yards.

Question. Had you seen any confusion or symptoms of a rout previous to that volley?

Answer. Yes, sir. The volunteer regiments were constantly breaking. They would break, and then we would rally two or three regiments and bring them up again. The New York 14th (Brooklyn) that behaved so well was broken nearly all to pieces at the first fire. But they rallied again and went up with Griffin's battery, and stood their ground remarkably well.

Question. Do you consider that Griffin's battery had sufficient support at that time?

Answer. The troops were not at all reliable. If they had been reliable, and could have been kept up to their work, I should think there was sufficient support.

Question. Was the position of that battery a good position with the support it had?

Answer. That is a mere matter of opinion. I would not like to criticise the act of others. I did not put it there.

Question. You stationed it some thousand yards further in the rear, I believe?

Answer. Not a thousand yards. But I put it in a position where it did most murderous execution.

Question. And where you considered it safe?

Answer. Yes, sir; because the enemy could not have got over to it without passing over a thousand yards of ground. I know the fuses were cut for a thousand yards, and they were pretty accurate.

Question. Had these batteries been retained in an effective position and properly supported, do you think it would have made any difference in the result of the day?

Answer. That would be a mere matter of opinion.

Question. We ask your opinion as a military man.

Answer. My experience of military life is not sufficient to warrant me in setting up my opinion against officers senior to me.

Question. You had hardly any seniors upon that field, had you? All the generals in command were brigadiers, were they not?

Answer. The only brigadier there was General McDowell. I was only a colonel. General Hunter was a general officer, but he was cut down almost at the first fire.

Question. Was it the understanding among the officers of the army that General Patterson was to hold Johnston in the valley of Winchester, so that he should not take part in that battle?

Answer. I cannot say; I knew nothing of that at the time, and I do not think that the officers generally had any idea of it one way or another.

Question. Up to the day of the fight?

Answer. Yes, sir; I know that some person told me that Patterson had been ordered down, but that was a mere matter of conversation from some irresponsible person who came out from Washington. I said nothing about it to anybody, for I supposed it was a state secret.

Question. Had Patterson detained Johnston in the valley of Winchester, so that no re-enforcements would have been brought down from Johnston to Beauregard, what in your opinion would have been the result of that battle?

Answer. Well, it might have ended one way or the other. Our troops could not stand the attacking of the enemy; they were played out quite early. The men were exhausted—somehow or other they seemed to have no heart in the matter. The officers were more to blame than the men. We had the enemy whipped up to 3 o'clock. Then their re-enforcements came up. Whether our men would, without that, have retained their success I do not know. The enemy had Manassas to fall back upon. They had skilful generals in command. I think we should have prevented the rout at all events.

Question. You would have prevented the rout but for the last re-enforcements that came down?

Answer. I think so.

Question. Was it not the understanding among the officers of the army that re enforcements from Johnston had arrived during Friday or Saturday night, or prior to the battle on Sunday?

Answer. That I do not recollect. I have an impression that such was the case, but I do not recollect it distinctly. It would have been mere supposition on our part any how, for we gained no information from spies or in any other way in regard to their forces.

Question. Only from the whistling of the locomotives and the movement of the trains?

Answer. I did not hear anything of that. There were two or three hills intervening between my position and that.

Question. Was there any detention Sunday morning in your march?

Answer. Yes, sir. Our orders were to get under way at 2 or half past 2 o'clock in the morning. We got out into the road and were delayed a great while there. We were formed on the road in front of my camp. I had the reserve brigade in the rear. After some delay we then moved on some distance and halted again; and we kept pottering along, pottering along in that way, instead of being fairly on the road. It was intended that we should turn their position at daylight, as we could have done very easily but for the delay. There was a great deal of delay—very vexatious delay. I do not know what was the cause of it. The whole affair was extremely disagreeable to me. I was disgusted with the whole thing, and I asked no questions, and I did not want to know who was to blame.

Question. Suppose you had been on that road by daylight, as you say you might have easily been, and had reached your position and turned their left as early as was intended, what effect do you think it would have had?

Answer. I think it would have had a very beneficial effect.

Question. And all the time you were delayed the enemy were changing their order of battle?

Answer. No, sir; I do not think they knew where we were going to attack them. When we got to Bull Run we were left on a high point, and we could see in the distance two different columns of dust. Captain Griffin and my staff were with me. I remarked upon it. We saw it coming, but did not know whether it was General Heintzelman coming in from above, or whether it was the enemy. We rather thought it was Heintzelman, as we expected him there if he was successful. The enemy came closer while we were staying there three-quarters of an hour, probably more. We could see their guns, and could see some blue pantaloons. We could distinguish this, when Major Woodbury came to me and said we had got now to Bull Run, and suppose we go down and have a consultation. I mentioned what I had seen to them. They had not observed it before. General Hunter moved the column and started them at once forward, threw out skirmishers, but before the skirmishers on the left were deployed they were at work. The enemy had just got there then, for we saw them coming two or three miles off at first. If we had got around there first we probably would have had the position in open ground to fight them. As it was we went right out from the woods. If we had got there a little earlier we could have chosen our position there to meet them.

Question. In that case you would have flanked them?

Answer. Yes, sir; we would have got between them and their re-enforcements. The plan of the battle was admirable; it could not have been better. Every thing was as well looked to and taken care of as could be.

Question. The only fault was this delay?

Answer. It may not have been a fault.

Question. Accident, then.

Answer. The fact existed. If we had gotten off in time, as we might, we would have got in around them.

By Mr. Covode:

Question. Were not Griffin's and Ricketts' batteries moved too far forward to be supported by infantry?

Answer. Not with good infantry.

By Mr. Gooch:

Question. Was the battery properly supported with infantry?

Answer. As well as could be. There were one or two regiments that did as well or better than any other volunteer regiments. As I said, the Brooklyn 14th behaved remarkably well.

By Mr. Covode:

Question. Were you in a position to see the enemy that were mistaken for our troops at the time they opened on the batteries?

Answer. I saw that regiment going by in the distance. I was 200 or 300 yards off.

By Mr. Gooch:

Question. What number of infantry supported those two batteries?

Answer. I cannot tell. The marines were intended for the support of Griffin's battery in the first place. The Brooklyn 14th rallied on the battery in its first position. There was another regiment there; I do not now remember distinctly which it was. There was enough to support it if the troops had been steady. If we had had the same number of such troops as we have now they could have supported it. I know one regiment of the old regulars would have held it.

Question. How many guns were in those two batteries?

Answer. There were twelve. There were four rifled guns and two howitzers in Griffin's battery. I do not recollect exactly about Ricketts' battery, as it was not under my command.

WASHINGTON, *January* 28, 1862.

Colonel WILLIAM W. AVERELL sworn and examined.

By Mr. Gooch:

Question. What is your rank in the army?

Answer. I am lieutenant in the 3d regiment of regular cavalry and colonel of the 3d regiment of Pennsylvania cavalry, now commanding the second cavalry brigade.

Question. Were you at the battle of Bull Run?

Answer. Yes, sir.

Question. In whose division?

Answer. I was in General Hunter's division, acting as assistant adjutant general to Colonel Andrew Porter at that time.

Question. What, in your judgment, caused the disaster of that day?

Answer. They commenced, I presume, almost from the time we started from Arlington, from the other side of the river. There were great many causes that combined to lose the day to us. The most apparent cause, however, at the time we first felt we were beaten, that we had to retire—and that we had felt for some time beforehand—was the want of concentration of the troops; the feeling that we ought to have had more men in action at one time.

Question. The want of concentration on the field?

Answer. Yes, sir. We crossed the run with 18,000 men. I do not believe there were over 6,000 or 8,000 actually engaged at any one time.

Question. There were more than that number engaged during the day?

Answer. Yes, sir.

Question. Was it impossible to bring more men into action, or were not the proper steps taken to do so?

Answer. I am unable to say. I was not present at the council the night before, although I was almost immediately made aware by Colonel Porter of all that had taken place in the council. But as to what orders were given to other commanders of divisions or brigades I do not know.

Question. All you know is in relation to the management of your own division on the field?

Answer. Yes, sir.

Question. Were or not as many men of your own division brought into battle at any one time as could have been brought in?

Answer. I think they were.

Question. Was not the nature of the battle-field such that it was exceedingly difficult to bring a large body of men into action at any one time?

Answer. I think it was about as fine a battle-field as you can find between here and Richmond. I have no idea there was any better.

Question. Was the field favorable for the movement and manœuvering of large bodies of men?

Answer. One or two divisions of the size we had then could have manœuvred very well.

Question. I speak of the field as a whole?

Answer. Well, sir, to come to the causes of the disaster, another cause was perhaps the fall of General Hunter, who was wounded at the beginning of the action. That took Colonel Porter away from his brigade to look after the brigade that Colonel Burnside commanded. It was thrown into confusion, and Burnside was in danger of losing his battery, and came to Colonel Porter for a battalion of regulars to help him. That was diverted from the position it was originally intended for; from the extreme right to the extreme left of our division. They were the flank of the division, thrown out to lash the enemy, as you might say; that battalion being to our extreme right what the knot is to the lash. At the beginning of the action they could have inflicted very severe and telling blows upon the enemy. But as it was they were taken to the extreme left of the division. General Porter went to look after the affairs of that division. The enemy were repulsed and commenced giving way rapidly. In the mean time I had formed the brigade into line, developed it, and deployed it. The report of General Porter will tell you how it was done. The whole line of the centre of the enemy gave way, followed by the wings as far as we could see, and we drove them rapidly back. For the first two or three hours it seemed as though nothing could stop us. At the end of two or three hours, Heintzelman's column came on the same ground; the 2d Minnesota, the 38th New York, and the 5th and 11th Massachusetts. There was a want of a headquarters somewhere on the field. All the staff officers who knew anything about the position of the enemy had to act without orders. I had the command of Colonel Porter's brigade for about an hour and a half or two hours. After standing a half an hour in line, under a severe fire, without venturing to give an order to move, I formed the 8th and fourteenth New York in column, and pushed them down the road right straight to the house where we afterwards lost the batteries and everything. They went down in fine style, perfectly cool and in good order. They were going so rapidly that the enemy could not keep the range—were constantly losing the range; and the column was not cut much—had but very few casualties. When they got down to where the road they were on crossed the turnpike, then, by some misunderstanding, an order was sent to them to turn up that road, instead of keeping on according to the previous purpose, and thus those two regiments were diverted to the left. If they had gone up to that hill at the time the enemy were going away, they could, I believe, have taken that house and held that position, And then Griffin's battery could have gone up there in safety, and they could have cut off the retreat of those rebels who were flying before Burnside's brigade and Sykes's battallion, probably 2,000 or 3,000 of them. Turning up this road kept our troops under the fire of the enemy's batteries, and subjected them to a desultory fire from those running rebels, which broke them up. The eighth New York broke and never afterwards formed to any extent—not over 200. The field officers left the field and went back off the ground. There were only two officers in that regiment who afterwards displayed any courage and coolness at all that was observable—two field officers, the quartermaster and the major, I think. Griffin's battery was then without support; and as I was passing by his battery at that time, he called to me and said he was without support, and asked what he should do. I saw the fourteenth New York collecting in little masses over to the left of the field. I rode as rapidly as possible over to them, collected them, and marched them over to the rear of Griffin's battery.

Question. How many men did the regiment have then?

Answer. It was pretty nearly formed.

Question. Pretty nearly full?

Answer. Yes, sir; I should think that three-fourths of the men were there. They formed very well, did very well, indeed. The officers behaved well; but, as I said before, this feeling was uppermost : want of orders. Lieutenant Whipple, who was acting assistant adjutant general to the division commander, and reported to Colonel Porter after General Hunter fell, and myself met about this time. We talked over the position of affairs, and came to the conclusion that that hill in front of us was the key-point of the enemy's position, and must be taken before the battle would be given up. We felt that we had won the battle; but in order to make it decisive and hold the position, we would have to take that hill. We agreed upon a plan which was to collect the regiments in the centre of the field : the fifth and eleventh Massachusetts, the second Minnesota, the thirty-eighth New York, and, I think, Colonel Coffer's regiment, sixty-ninth, I think—five or six regiments—and to send them up on the hill in line. Put the fourteenth on the right, with the marines and zouaves, and then move them all up together with Griffin's battery in the centre. That would make an embrasure of troops for the battery to fire through, and they never could take the battery as long as these supports were on its flanks, neither could their cavalry ever charge upon the infantry line as long as the battery was there. We went over to the centre and succeeded in getting these five regiments started. I found Colonel Franklin and two or three other officers there who assisted me. Colonel Franklin was conspicuous. Colonel Wadsworth was also conspicuous in starting these regiments. Just about this time I became aware that General McDowell had come on the field from this fact. We saw the battery moving up on the hill. I had gone to Griffin and notified him of this plan, telling him these troops were going to move up, not to mistake them for the enemy and fire upon them. He had necessarily, from his position, to fire over their heads at one point of the movement, if he kept up his fire. A great many incidents occurred along about that time that I presume you have heard many times.

Question. We want the main statement.

Answer. The battery was seen moving up on the hill, and without any support except the marines and zouaves. The New York 14th was then down in a hollow; they had followed Griffin's battery for about half the distance. There were two slopes coming down to each other; Griffin was on one slope and the enemy was on the other, which was a little higher than the one we were on. The 14th went down into the hollow and there waited. The marines and zouaves went up with the battery, and had to cross a deep run with high banks on each side.

Question. Did Ricketts' battery go with Griffin's?

Answer. It joined it in this movement. I immediately rode over to the right of the field and inquired where General McDowell was. I found him on top of a little hill in a little field beyond the turnpike. In going over I had spoken to the 14th, and told them to push up to the woods on the right of Griffin's battery. They went forward finely in line. I followed the 14th, going around the right flank of it, and got up on the hill where General McDowell was. General McDowell called out to the colonel of the 14th to march the regiment by flank. There was probably a delay of two or three minutes in executing that movement. I spoke, then, to the General, and said: "General, if that battery goes up on the hill it will be lost; the woods are full of the enemy, for I have seen them there. I had then been on the ground seven hours watching closely with a glass all the movements. Said I, "For heaven's sake let the 14th go up in the woods." Marching them by the flank, changing the movement, was sending them up in rear of the battery, where they could have no effect upon the enemy on the flank. General McDowell said: "Go and take the 14th where you want it." I immediately went to the 14th, changed its direction to the woods, and told it to take the double quick. The battery was still moving. The general said it was too late to recall the movement. I was so apprehensive that the battery would meet with a disaster there that I rode up to where the battery was. The marines were then sitting down in close column on the ground on the left of the battery. The battery was then getting into position and unlimbering. The fire zouaves were still in rear of the battery. The zouaves immediately commenced a movement, rose up and moved off in rear of the battery, a little to the right. I rode up then to the left of the battery, and there met Colonel Heintzelman. I saw some troops immediately in front of us, not over 75 or 100 yards off. I should say it was at least a regiment; we could see their heads and faces very plainly. I said to Colonel Heintzelman: "What troops are those in front of us?" He was looking off in another direction. I said: "Here, right in front of the battery." I do not remember the reply he made, but I dropped my reins and took up my glasses to look at them, and just at that moment down came their pieces, rifles and muskets, and probably there never was such a destructive fire for a few minutes. It seemed as though every man and horse of that battery just laid right down and died right off. It was half a minute—it seemed longer—before I could get my horse down out of the fire. I then went to the marines and halloed to them to hurry on. Their officers were standing behind them keeping them in ranks; but the destruction of the battery was so complete that the marines and zouaves seemed to be struck with such astonishment, such consternation, that they could not do anything. There were probably 100 muskets fired from the zouaves and marines—not over that; and they, of course, fired too high. They were below the battery, and where the battery was we could not see more than half of the bodies of the rebels, and what they did fire was ineffective. They began to break and run down the hill, and nothing could stop them, and then the enemy rushed right over there like a lowering cloud—right over the hill.

Question. Why did not the batteries open upon those men in front?

Answer. I do not know from actual operation why they did not. The battery was unlimbered, and the men were standing at the guns. In going down the hill, after the general wreck, I saw an officer galloping along a little in front of me. I recognized Major Barry, and cried out, "Halloo, Barry, is that you?" He said, "Yes," Said I, "Where is Griffin?" He said, "I am afraid he is killed." I said, "That battery is lost; I am afraid we are gone up," or some remark to that effect. Barry then said: "I am to blame for the loss of that battery. I put Griffin there myself." Well, the 14th, by this time, had reached the woods on the right, The 38th New York, which led the column on the left, which we intended to support when they got there, had reached this little cross-road, and the 14th and 38th held on very well—indeed, splendidly. The enemy came right over the brow of the hill, and their fire was very deadly. They made a rush over the top of the hill, and their cavalry made their appearance at the same time; this 14th and 38th hung on for fifteen minutes there, while all the officers about there tried to collect these scattered troops and get them back to that position to the assistance of the 14th and 38th, and appealed to them in every way that possibly could be done. But it was of no avail. What there was left of the battery, a few limbers and caissons that had live horses to drag them, came galloping down the hill, right through this mass of running troops, and occasionally a horse would fall, and the whole thing would get all tangled up.

Question. Was or not that the beginning of the panic?

Answer. That was the turning point of the affair, right there.

Question. Did you not look upon that as the turning point upon the field?

Answer. Yes, sir; oh! yes, sir. We had eight regiments marching towards that hill then.

Question. Were those batteries properly supported when they moved up the hill?

Answer. No, sir; that is shown from the fact that they were taken.

Question. If they had been properly supported they would not have been taken?

Answer. No, sir.

Question. Could they have been properly supported?

Answer. Yes, sir; the troops were there to do it.

Question. Then it was a mistake to order those batteries forward without a proper support—a mistake on the part of some one?

Answer. It must have been so.

Question. Do you know why Captain Griffin did not open fire upon the regiment in front of them?

Answer. It was generally understood that these troops were mistaken.

Question. By whom was the mistake made?

Answer. It was understood that these troops were mistaken for our own, and Captain Griffin was ordered not to fire. My impression is that it was the chief of artillery on the field who made the mistake.

Question. Who was the chief of artillery?

Answer. Major Barry.

Question. General Franklin's brigade came on after that, did they?

Answer. Well, sir, they were partially on the field then. I do not know exactly what troops composed his brigade. He was there himself. Then Sykes's battalion moved across and occupied this hill in the middle ground, and held it. Our troops then scattered all over the battle-field, their backs turned towards the enemy, and all going to the rear.

Question. The capture of that battery, and the rapid retreat of the horses and men in the vicinity of the battery, tended to create confusion among all those in the rear?

Answer. Yes, sir; that taken in connexion with the exhaustion of the men. There was no water for the men to drink about there, except in the rear, and a great many were dying of thirst. Everybody wanted water. Well, sir, it was a pretty hot day; and it was probably a little unfortunate for us that the water was in the rear of the field of battle. We then came back to our first position on the field of battle. If we had had a fresh division there, or a fresh brigade there, we could have made a stand. Johnston's forces—that is, I have been told since they were Johnston's forces—made their appearance on the field at that time.

Question. Just at the time of the loss of the batteries?

Answer. Yes, sir. They deployed in several lines on our extreme right, and with the rapidity, apparently, of fresh troops. The moral effect of that deployment had a great deal to do with the panic among our troops.

Question. That happening at the same time with the loss of the batteries?

Answer. Yes, sir. If we had not lost the batteries, and had had a fresh brigade there, we could have made a stand there, because our troops formed very well back on our first position. The 27th New York formed first, and stood steady (though the men were very much exhausted) for nearly half an hour, while the other fragments of regiments gathered in their places about them, the enemy's artillery throwing projectiles right through us all the while. We had no artillery to reply to them, only a section of the battery of Captain Arnold. We had no artillery, no fresh troops, and could not make a stand, but were forced to retire.

Question. Then you attribute the disasters of the day to the loss of Griffin's and Ricketts' batteries, the great exhaustion of the men from the want of water, and the fact that Johnston's troops came on the field fresh just at the time of the loss of the batteries?

Answer. Yes, sir. Those three causes alone would have been sufficient to have defeated us. But there were many other minor causes that had their effect. There was a want of discipline in our troops.

Question. The troops were not familiar with their officers?

Answer. Yes, sir; that was one thing. That they could have stood was shown in the way that Sykes's battalion stood, because they were disciplined, and came off the field in regular order.

WASHINGTON, *January* 28, 1862.

Lieutenant CHARLES E. HAZLITT sworn and examined.

By Mr. Gooch:

Question. What is your rank in the army?

Answer. First lieutenant of artillery.

Question. Where are you now stationed?

Answer. On Minor's Hill, over in Virginia.

Question. Were you at the battle of Bull Run?

Answer. Yes, sir.

Question. Were you in Griffin's battery?

Answer. Yes, sir.

Question. What was your rank then?

Answer. The same as now.

Question. Can you tell what led to the loss of Griffin's and Ricketts' batteries in that battle?

Answer. As far as I am able to judge, it was in consequence of the battery being sent to such an advanced position without any support.

Question. Will you give us the particulars of the loss of that battery—what occurred just previous to the loss of it, and at the time?

Answer. I do not know what occurred just at the moment of the loss, as just before the time the battery was put in position they changed and took up the position where they were lost. Another officer and myself stayed where we were in order to get away two guns that were left there; one had two horses killed, and we had to send for horses; and another one that had a wheel which was broken, and we were engaged in putting on a spare wheel, so that we were not with the battery in the last position. All that I know is that we had been in action some time, and I understood that there was an order for us to move the battery forward up on a little hill where there was a house. I do not know who the order came from. I only knew we were to go there. The officers of the batteries were all averse to going there, as before that we had had no infantry with us that was put there as our support. We were told to go up to this place. We talked about having to go there for some time; and I know it was some time after I was told that we had an order to go that we had not gone. I heard Captain Griffin say that it was no use, and we had to go. We started to go up on this hill. I was in advance of the battery, leading the way, and I had to turn off to a little lane to go to the top of the hill. Just as we turned off the lane in the field, an officer of the enemy on horseback appeared about 100 paces in front. As he saw us turn in, he turned around and beckoned to some one on other side of the hill, and we supposed the enemy were just on the other side of the hill waiting for us, as they had been there just before. An officer hallooed up to me and said we were not to go there, that we had to go to another hill to the right, which was the place we had spoken of going to, where we wished to be sent instead of to the other position. We then started off towards the hill on the right, but I do not think we had got more than half-way up the hill when I was told to go back to the hill we had started for first. We then went back there and came into position. We had been in action there for some time; the fire was exceedingly hot; and being in such close range of the enemy we were losing a great many men and horses. We were in full relief on top of the hill, while they were a little behind the crest of the hill. We presented a better mark for them than they did for us. I do not think there was any order to move the battery around to the right of the little house on the hill. I remember asking Captain Griffin if I could not move the piece I was firing to another place, as it was getting almost too hot there, and I wanted to go to the left. The enemy had just got the range of my gun, and I wanted to move it out of range. The captain said I could do so. And then it is my impression that I asked him if we had better not move the whole battery away from there, as they had got our range so well. And then we started to move. Lieutenant Kensel and myself stayed back to get away the two guns I spoke of. Just after we got them started off we saw the battery in this other place flying all around, and the horses with the caissons running in every direction. That was the time the battery was lost, but we were not there at the time.

Question. Did you see the regiment that fired at the battery when it was lost?

Answer. No, sir.

Question. You know nothing of the loss of the battery further than you have stated?

Answer. That is all.

Question. You do not know who gave Captain Griffin the order to move forward?

Answer. No, sir.

Question. And nothing of any orders given after that?

Answer. No, sir; only what I have stated that we had orders to go up to his place. We put it off for some time and it was repeated.

WASHINGTON, *January* 28, 1862.

Lieutenant HORATIO B. REED sworn and examined.

By Mr. Gooch:

Question. What is your rank in the army?

Answer. I am second lieutenant in the fifth regiment of United States artillery.

Question. Where are you now stationed?

Answer. Minor's Hill, Virginia.

Question. Were you at the battle of Bull Run?

Answer. Yes, sir; I was chief of line of caissons in Griffin's battery.

Question. Can you tell us the movements of the battery just before it was lost, the orders given, and what led to the loss of the battery?

Answer. Our battery was in battery five times. We first came in battery I do not know by whose orders. A had charge of six caissons, a battery wagon, and forge. I left the battery wagon and forge some distance below where we came in battery the first time. Our battery was again ordered in battery—by whose orders I do not know. General Barry—then Major Barry—came to my captain, and I am under the impression my captain made some protest against going forward on account of the want of support. But we then advanced in a field upon the right. We found that was not where we had been ordered, and we then went upon a hill and came in battery for the fourth time. That was on the left of the house there. We then came in battery on the right of the house. I was chief of the line of caissons, and my position was in the rear. As we advanced upon the hill I wanted to go with the battery, and I left the caissons and went forward. I think we came in battery with two pieces; Lieutenant Hasbrouck in command. There was a body of troops coming up, and I know there was something said about those troops being our own, sent by some one to support us. I have heard since that it was said General Heintzelman sent them, but I did not hear the name mentioned then. We did not fire there until the troops advanced so near that they fired upon us and cut us down.

Question. Why did you not fire upon them?

Answer. We had orders not to fire.

Question. Who gave those orders?

Answer. I am under the impression that General Barry gave them.

Question. Did you hear the order given by General Barry?

Answer. I heard the order given by some one to Captain Griffin and Lieutenant Hasbrouck—and I am under the impression that it was General Barry—not to fire upon that body of men, for the reason that they were troops sent up to support us. Just after that they fired upon us and cut us down.

Question. Was General Barry there at that time?

Answer. Yes, sir.

Question. Could you have broken up that body of men by your battery if you had opened on them?

Answer. We could have done so unless they were better troops than we saw that day; I think we could have swept them off with canister; we could have scattered any body of troops, I think, no matter how efficient—that is, to the best of my belief.

Question. Was Ricketts' battery captured at the same time?

Answer. I presume it was. My horse was shot from under me at the time, and I was somewhat stunned by falling on my breast. We advanced together, but I never met Captain Ricketts except on that occasion, and he rode up in advance of his battery, and I was in rear of ours.

Question. Did the panic on the field commence immediately after the capture of those batteries?

Answer. Well, sir, the Ellsworth zouaves were ordered to support us, but they ran away before that.

Question. Did you have any support at that time?

Answer. No, sir; we were ordered there without any support but these zouaves.

Question. Did not the marines support you?

Answer. No, sir; they could not get up there. When we first went into battery, we went ahead of them.

Question. Was your battery without support during the day?

Answer. Yes, sir. I went after the 14th New York, and they went up with us for a little time, and then they left; their officers did all they could.

Question. About what time did the loss of your battery happen?

Answer. I have a very faint idea of time on that day, for I did not exactly know what time we came into battery; I was without a watch. We left our camp about 12 o'clock at night, and I suppose we went into action about 11 o'clock; and if we did, I think this was about 4 o'clock.

WASHINGTON, *February* 18, 1862.

NATHANIEL F. PALMER sworn and examined.

By Mr. Gooch:

Question. Will you state in what capacity you served in the army under General Patterson?

Answer. I was appointed wagon-master in the 8th Pennsylvania regiment by Colonel Lumley.

Question. When did you enter the army?

Answer. On the 15th day of May last.

Question. You were captured by the enemy?

Answer. Yes, sir.

Question. On what day and in what engagement?

Answer. I was taken on the 2d day of July.

Question. At the battle of Falling Waters?

Answer. There were two divisions of the army after we crossed the river; they came to a fork of the road, and one part took the right and the other the left. The 15th Pennsylvania regiment was on the extreme right of the right wing; they had an advance guard thrown out, and Dr. Tripp and myself were taken with it.

Question. Where were you taken after your capture?

Answer. To Winchester.

Question. When did you arrive at Winchester?

Answer. On the morning of the 4th of July.

Question. Can you tell what number of troops Johnston had at the time you were taken—his whole force at Winchester and with him?

Answer. After we were taken we were taken with their retreat through Martinsburg. We came around to Martinsburg from Falling Waters. We were not on the road at Falling Waters, but on the road west of it. But it was all the same engagement. They then retreated three miles out of Martinsburg to a place they called Big Springs. There we lay over night with three regiments of infantry. I do not know how much cavalry they had, for they were scattered, coming in and running out, helter-skelter, and I could not get much idea of them. We then lay there until, perhaps, the next morning at 9 o'clock, when we fell back three miles further towards Bunker Hill, and went into a field, where they drew up in a sort of line of battle. There they were met by two more regiments and six pieces of light artillery. I think four of the guns were brass, and the other two were iron. We lay there in that field until after dark; I do not know what time in the evening it was; and then we were put on their baggage wagons, and everything was sent into Winchester—all their traps.

Question. Did the force there go into Winchester at that time?

Answer. No, sir. We left them on the ground there, but all their wagon trains went into Winchester.

Question. Tell us, as near as you can, the whole number of Johnston's force at that time, what you left behind you, and what you found at Winchester.

Answer. From the best calculations that we could make—and we got our information from very good sources—we concluded that they had about 7,000 men, besides their cavalry. That was scattered about in such confusion that we could not tell anything about it.

Question. How long did you stay at Winchester?

Answer. Until the 18th of July.

Question. Did Johnston's force continue to increase while you remained at Winchester; and if so, to what extent?

Answer. There were squads coming in there every day. I do not think there was a day but what some came in. They would come in two or three companies at a time; no full regiments ever came in while we were there. By counting up the squads and calculating the best we could, we concluded that by the 18th there was but very little over 13,000 there.

Question. Did this increase of force come in from Manassas or from other points?

Answer. They did not come from Manassas. They were reported to us as coming from towns off in Virginia. I cannot remember the names of them. We made inquiries, and they were reported to us as coming in from different places in Virginia; that is, they were volunteers that had been picked up through the country.

Question. What was the condition of the fortifications at Winchester when you arrived there?

Answer. I did not see anything of any fortifications myself. Some of our men were taken out to work on the 5th of July, I think. When they came back they reported that they had been working at a cannon to mount it on a little fortification they had in the edge of the town where the Charlestown railroad comes in at Winchester. They reported that there was a little fortification there, with a sort of rifle-pits or trench dug for some fifteen or twenty rods.

Question. Is that the only fortification you heard of there?

Answer. That is the only one we ever got information about.

Question. How many guns had they there?

Answer. Only this one they tried to mount.

Question. You left Winchester on the 18th of July?

Answer. Yes, sir.

Question. Will you state where you went and what you saw on the road?

Answer. We were taken from Winchester to Strasburg, and arrived there in the evening about nine or ten o'clock. We lay there until the next morning until two o'clock, when we were put in the cars for Manassas. On our way to Manassas, I should think twenty miles from there, we ran a foul of Johnston's men. One of them came into the cars whom I knew, because he stood guard over me while I was at Big Spring. He said they had three regiments then bound for Manassas, and that there were more coming on behind. While we lay there on one side, there were two trains that ran in there and went by us. We got into Manassas about nine o'clock in the morning. In the course of a couple of hours or so these trains came in with these men on and unloaded.

Question. How many regiments were there in all that came in?

Answer. There were three came in there. Whether they brought them all down there is more than I can tell. They had perhaps four or five switches at Manassas, where the headquarters were. They ran in there and ran past us, unloaded the trains, and then they went right back again. They were gone until nearly night, when they ran in again and unloaded some more men there.

Question. How many men were brought into Manassas while you were there?

Answer. We were told that there were 7,000 of them.

Question. Was Johnston there himself?

Answer. That is what we understood that he was there.

Question. Did you hear of any battle when you had got to Manassas?

Answer. We heard before we got there of the battle of the 18th. We heard that at a station called the Plains. There was quite a gathering and hurraing there. Some men had shot guns and threatened to shoot us through the windows of the cars.

Question. When did you leave Manassas?

Answer. On the 19th, about ten o'clock in the evening.

Question. Where did you go?

Answer. We ran down to Culpeper Court-House. I lay there until the next day, the 20th, at one o'clock, when we left.

By Mr. Covode:

Question. Why did you lay there so long?

Answer. To let trains pass coming from the south.

Question. From Richmond?

Answer. I do not know as they all came from Richmond. Some of them came in from Gordonsville.

By Mr. Gooch:

Question. How many troops, according to your estimate, passed you going to Manassas, while you were on your way from Manassas to Richmond?

Answer. We calculated that if Johnston brought 7,000, there were then taken there twenty-two regiments.

Question. Including the 7,000 brought down by Johnston?

Answer. Yes, sir. There were three in Richmond that night; two trains were loaded, and another regiment was at the station, standing and sitting about there.

Question. The whole you think amounted to twenty-two regiments?

Answer. Yes, sir.

Question. You do not know, of your own knowledge, what became of the force Johnston left behind at Winchester?

Answer. No, sir; I could not tell anything about that.

By the chairman:

Question. Were there any large re-enforcements at Winchester at any time?

Answer. No, sir; they came in there in small squads. I do not think there was any number at one time come in higher than perhaps four or five companies.

By Mr. Gooch:

Question. And none of those came from Manassas?

Answer. No, sir; none of them were reported as coming from Manassas.

By the chairman:

Question. And in all they had not more than 13,000 there?

Answer. No, sir; there could not have been more than that.

By Mr. Covode:

Question. Did they get that gun mounted while you were at Winchester?

Answer. We did not know. They were pretty much all young men who were taken out for that work. After they found out that that was the work they had to do, we came to the conclusion that we would not work on their fortifications or their guns. The fact of it was, we thought if we were going to be murdered by them, we might as well have it done first as at last. I protested against going out, and all the other men came up and declared that they would not go out and work on the fortifications, let the consequences be what they might. The result was that they did not come for us again.

By Mr. Gooch:

Question. What time did Johnston start with his men from Winchester?
Answer. He started the 17th, in the night some time. We heard in the evening that he was going to start.

By Mr. Covode:

Question. You started the next day after?
Answer. Yes, sir; the next day at 1 o'clock.
Question. Would there have been any difficulty in Patterson's force coming and taking Winchester when you arrived there?
Answer. No, sir; they never could have made a stand at all. We expected them hourly all the time, and had got the wall of the jail fixed so that we could get out in five minutes. And all over town, at every door almost, there was a horse and wagon hitched, so that they might be ready to get right in and leave the town—standing there day and night.
Question. Looking for Patterson to come in?
Answer. Yes, sir, hourly.
Question. How did you keep the jailer from knowing that you had fixed the wall?
Answer. We hung blankets over it. The fact is, I had a scheme of my own to attend to that jailer. When we were first brought there, he came in, and when he saw me he said: "Damn you, you are the fellow I have been looking for. I am going to hang you on the bars here." As he was not armed, I answered him pretty sharply. While that was going on, Lieutenant Buck, who was a gentleman, came in and chided the jailer for treating a prisoner that way. He was a brute, that jailer, if ever there was one. There was an old man named Martin, over eighty years of age, taken because he was a Union man, and brought there a prisoner from Martinsburg. The way that the old man was treated was shameful. And I had just made up my mind to attend to that jailer if our troops came. I could have got out there in five minutes, and finished with him before our troops could get through the town; but they did not come.

WASHINGTON, *February* 24, 1862.

ALFRED SPATES sworn and examined.

By Mr. Chandler:

Question. You are president of the Chesapeake and Ohio canal?
Answer. Yes, sir.
Question. Were you along upon the line of the canal during the past summer?
Answer. Yes, sir; from May last up to the present time.
Question. Were you there, or in that vicinity, at the time General Patterson crossed the Potomac and went to Martinsburg?
Answer. I was in that vicinity.
Question. Have you any knowledge of the force of the enemy under Johnston at or about that time?

Answer. I have no personal knowledge. I have knowledge from information obtained from those constantly coming from the river—from the section at which this army was then stationed. I have that kind of knowledge.

Question. Please state it.

Answer. From the best information I could obtain—from those said to be familiar with the amount of force there—I should say it was between 8,000 and 10,000 men.

Question. Were you generally acquainted in that vicinity?

Answer. Yes, sir; intimately.

Question. Were you in frequent communication with persons on the Virginia side of the river?

Answer. I frequently saw men from the other side of the river. We were doing some work on the canal about that time, and for a part of our force the work was on the Virginia side, and within five or six miles of Williamsport, Patterson being then at Martinsburg.

Question. The general impression, in that vicinity, was that Johnston's army was between 8,000 and 10,000 men?

Answer. Yes, sir. I never heard any man put it higher than 10,000 men.

WASHINGTON, *February* 24, 1862.

A. K. STAKE sworn and examined.

By Mr. Chandler:

Question. Where do you reside, and what is your present occupation?

Answer. I reside in Williamsport. I am officially connected with the Chesapeake and Ohio canal—as general superintendent of the canal.

Question. Have you any knowledge of the force under Johnston at the time when Patterson was at Martinsburg?

Answer. None except from intercourse with Virginians whom I knew to be refugees. They corroborated all that Mr. Spates has said about it. I know that it was the impression throughout the community, and in the army, that there was not more than 10,000 men under Johnston; and there is this additional fact, ascertained since from perfectly reliable gentlemen, that there never was at any time, in Winchester, as many as 14,000 men, and of these there were, perhaps, 4,000 or 5,000 militia. The gentleman from whom I received this information is perfectly reliable. He is a southern man, and says there was not at any time as many as 14,000 men at Winchester, and of these there were from 3,000 to 5,000 militia, badly armed and equipped. I am not aware what information General Patterson may have had; but I should think he could have had the same information in regard to that matter that outsiders had.

Question. It was obtainable—current information?

Answer. Yes, sir. There was a party about him—McMullin's men, "scouts," as they were called; they were so constantly about him that very few persons could approach him with matters of that kind. I could sometimes get to his headquarters about other matters, but not upon subjects of that kind. General Patterson told Mr. Spates and myself afterwards, at Harper's Ferry, that he had positive information that Johnston had 42,000 men at Winchester. Of course, we believed as much of that as we pleased.

Question. Were you at Martinsburg when Patterson moved his force to Bunker Hill?

Answer. Yes, sir.

Question. Do you know the feeling of the troops at that time?

Answer. When he moved from Martinsburg to Bunker Hill the supposition was that he was going out to attack Johnston, and the troops were in fine spirits

Part ii——15

about it. They had laid there at Martinsburg four or five days, and were tired of that, and were anxious to meet the enemy, and when they turned off towards Charlestown they became very much dissatisfied; but the officers allayed a great deal of that feeling by asserting that they were going down to Wizard's Cliff, (a place on the road between Charlestown and Winchester,) from which they were to approach Winchester, so as to avoid the masked batteries that would be in their way if they went direct from Bunker Hill. But when they came to Wizard's Cliff and passed on towards Charlestown there was a great deal of dissatisfaction; and at Charlestown, as I learned afterwards—I did not go there myself—was the first distinct refusal on the part of the three months' men to follow General Patterson any longer. They declared that they had no disposition to be bamboozled any longer in that way, and as their time was up they would go home, unless he was disposed to go out and attack the enemy. He rode up before two regiments at Charlestown and announced to them that their time was up, and he had no further claim upon them; but he desired them to remain with him, as he hoped to meet the enemy in the field. My opinion is that there was not a word of dissent at that time; but when they retreated still further, to Harper's Ferry, they became still more dissatisfied, and determined to go home. I had this from those who had official positions about him at that time. I heard General Cadwalader say, at Martinsburg, that the enemy had from 25,000 to 30,000 men. I do not know where he got his information, for there was no man outside of headquarters that estimated Johnston's force at over 10,000 or 15,000 men.

WASHINGTON, *February* 26, 1862.

Dr. IRA TRIPP sworn and examined.

By Mr. Covode:

Question. What has been your connexion with the army?

Answer. My position was hospital steward.

Question. In the three months' service?

Answer. Yes, sir; under General Patterson, in the 8th Pennsylvania regiment. I was taken prisoner on the 2d of July, near Falling Waters.

Question. Well, go on and state about that.

Answer. We were captured near Falling Waters on the second day of July, and taken to Martinsburg that day. There our horses were taken away from us.

Question. By whom?

Answer. By a rebel captain; I forget his name now. That evening we were taken about three miles beyond Martinsburg, and encamped there during the night.

Question. What force had the enemy at that time?

Answer. As near as we could judge, Johnston had about 5,000 men at that time. We were with them but one day there. The next day we were taken to Winchester, where they had about 2,000 more troops, as near as we could ascertain, making their entire force at that time about 7,000.

Question. What day were you taken to Winchester?

Answer. The 4th of July.

Question. What was done with you there?

Answer. We were kept in jail there two weeks.

Question. How many of you were there?

Answer. I think there were 45. During that time the enemy received reenforcements of men, varying from perhaps a regiment down to a company, coming into Winchester at different times during the two weeks we were there.

As near as we could calculate, their re-enforcements might amount in all to 5,000 or 6,000 men.

Question. Do you know from what direction these re-enforcements came?

Answer. I should judge, from the way they came into Winchester, that they were from Strasburg and in that direction.

Question. They did not come from Manassas?

Answer. No, sir; I do not think any of them came from Manassas.

Question. What was the condition of their fortifications at Winchester at the time you went there?

Answer. They were very light. They fortified a little, not a great deal, during the time we were there. After we had been there about a week, some of our men were taken out to the fortifications and made to work to try to mount a gun, as they told us when they came back. That was the only gun they saw; they saw some little intrenchments on each side of the road, not to exceed twenty rods altogether.

Question. Rifle-pits?

Answer. No, sir; not rifle-pits. They had some empty barrels there and a trench thrown up. There was no fortification of any strength at that time.

Question. You only knew of one gun there?

Answer. That was all at that time—one large gun; they had some seven or eight pieces of light artillery that we saw. They got a few after that—some four or five that we saw come in. They never had at the outside over 13,000 men at Winchester, I think, before the battle of Bull Run.

Question. Would there, in your judgment, have been any difficulty in Patterson's taking Winchester?

Answer. No, sir; not at all. I do not think there would have been any trouble in his doing it.

Question. Did they appear to expect an attack from Patterson?

Answer. Yes, sir; daily.

Question. What do you know of any preparation to leave in case of an attack?

Answer. We hardly knew of any preparation they had to leave. They expected an attack. We had that from the jailer there and from the officers themselves. A great many of them left the day we did. I have no doubt that they expected that Patterson would come on and take Winchester after their troops left. I judge so from seeing so many going away the day we did; we saw their carriages, &c., on the road to Strasburg.

Question. What day did their army leave?

Answer. On the 18th of July.

Question. What number left?

Answer. As near as we could calculate, about 10,000 men in all left for Manassas.

Question. That would leave how many at Winchester?

Answer. Perhaps 2,000.

Question. Did they all leave at one time?

Answer. They left during the night of the 17th and the morning of the 18th, as near as we could get at it. We left on the 18th.

Question. By what route did they go to Manassas?

Answer. I do not know the route. I am not acquainted with that country. We got to Manassas in the morning on the 19th, about nine o'clock, I should judge.

Question. What time did you leave Winchester?

Answer. At noon of the 18th, in a great hurry.

Question. By what route did you go?

Answer. We went to Strasburg, about eighteen miles from Winchester, and there we took the cars to Manassas.

Question. What did you see of these troops after you left Winchester?

Answer. We saw some of the cavalry at Manassas on the 19th, and saw

General Johnston himself there. We knew three of the cavalry, because they were of those who captured us.

Question. How long did you remain at Manassas?

Answer. From nine in the morning until nine or ten o'clock at night.

Question. Do you know whether these troops came into Manassas before you left?

Answer. Only a portion of them. All I know of their being there was seeing a portion of the cavalry and General Johnston himself. There were large re-enforcements coming in that day from the direction of Richmond. That is what I suppose kept us there; we could not get away because the track was occupied by these troops coming in. I should judge that that day and the day following there were 15,000 of re-enforcements from between Manassas and Richmond, coming in from the south on different roads. We had to guess at it, but that is about as near as we could get at it. Heavy trains were coming in constantly all the day long.

Question. Did you, on your way to Winchester, see any strong fortifications anywhere, after you were captured?

Answer. No, sir; we did not see any anywhere. There were no strong fortifications made after that I am certain. I do not think they ever expected to stand a battle at all against Patterson.

Question. Did you, while at Winchester, look for Patterson to come there?

Answer. We looked for him every day. We just as much expected he would come as we were living. We expected to be taken out by our own men or hurried off by the rebels.

Question. Our force was double theirs?

Answer. Yes, sir; nearly so. I calculated that Johnston had not more than 12,000 at the outside. And knowing the difference between the strength of the two armies, we constantly expected Patterson would take the place.

Question. What was the character of the re-enforcements that came into Winchester? Were they well armed and equipped?

Answer. All had arms; not very good arms. They looked like old muskets. Some came in in the night, and we could not tell what they had. Some of them were not very well uniformed, such as we saw. Some had citizens' clothes on—no uniform at all. They looked like they had just been gathered up right out of the fields, with no uniform at all. There was in the jail yard a big pile of stone that had been pounded up for pavement, and getting on that pile we could see their encampment, and all over the country there.

Question. Did you see any fortifications at Winchester, except the small one at the terminus of the railroad from Charlestown?

Answer. That is all that we saw.

WASHINGTON, *March* 5, 1862.

Major WILLIAM W. RUSSELL sworn and examined.

By Mr. Chandler:

Question. What is your rank and position in the army?

Answer. I am major and paymaster of the marine corps.

Question. Were you attached to the staff of General Patterson during his advance into Virginia; and if so, how did you become so attached, being an officer of the marine corps?

Answer. From current reports and rumors I became convinced that General Patterson's column would be engaged in the valley of Virginia, and I sought leave of absence from the Secretary of the Navy to endeavor to join General Patterson's staff, where I thought I could be useful. I held a semi-civil position here as paymaster of the marine corps at the time. Having a great many friends south, and being a southern man myself, when my brother officers were resigning all around me, I thought it my duty to endeavor to do something for the government which had supported me for eighteen years, and something outside of my ordinary semi-civil duties. I obtained permission from my department and authority from the commandant of my corps to transact my business during my absence. General Cameron gave me a letter to General Patterson. General Scott, finding that I was going, also gave me a letter, though I made no application to him for it. I went up and joined General Patterson at Martinsburg, and he immediately placed me on his staff as one of his aids.

Question. What movements did General Patterson make after you joined him?

Answer. On the 15th of July he moved from Martinsburg on Bunker Hill with about 18,000 men and took possession of that place. He remained there until Wednesday morning, the 17th, when he marched to Charlestown. The only rebel force we observed on the march was a detachment of cavalry, said to be commanded by Colonel Stuart. The Rhode Island battery, on the right of our column, expended several shots in dispersing them.

Question. Were you aware of any reconnoissance being made from Bunker Hill towards Winchester?

Answer. No, sir; I was not. I heard some rumors of a reconnoissance made by some of General Sanford's staff, but there were so many stories told I did not rely upon them. Colonel Thomas advanced several miles on the road with a portion of the cavalry under his command. I do not think any extended reconnoissance was made.

Question. What information had you relative to the force of the enemy?

Answer. A deserter presented himself at the headquarters of General Patterson at Bunker Hill, who seemed to be of a very communicative disposition. From his statement, the captain of engineers made a diagram of the works and defences of Winchester. I have it here. It reads "Defences of Winchester, obtained from a deserter from the confederate army, and believed to be reliable. J. H. Simpson, captain of engineers." The deserter was so very communicative that I had some curiosity to find out something about him. I asked him where he was from, and he told me he was from the neighborhood of Bunker Hill. A son of a merchant whose house we occupied there was a smart, bright little fellow of some thirteen or fourteen years of age. We were very careful to protect the property left in his charge, and at my request sentinels were posted about his father's store. He had every confidence we would protect the property and pay for what we got there. I asked him about this man. In the first place, as a deserter I did not believe him, because he was a perjured man, and had deserted the flag he had sworn to support. This boy stated that this man and his brother were worthless characters, who resided within two miles of Bunker Hill; that he would work a few days and then loaf about the drinking establishments; that he had no character or reputation in the community in which he lived. I stated the information I had thus gained.

Question. Did you state it to General Patterson?

Answer. I think I stated it in his presence. I said that on general principles I would not believe a deserter, because a man who would be false to his oath would be false in his statements.

Question. What was your opinion at that time relative to the force of the enemy?

Answer. I had no opinion about it. I did not believe a word that I heard. We had no positive means of getting information. They were all idle rumors, that I did not think were reliable at all. On the 17th we marched to Charlestown, not seeing any rebel force on that march, and encamped in and around that place with the whole of our army.

Question. During your service with General Patterson, were you aware of the receipt by him of any despatches from General Scott, relative to the movement of his column? If so, state what they were.

Answer. On the night of the 17th, General Patterson and his staff having all retired, I was sitting on the porch of the house we occupied as headquarters. Between twelve and one o'clock at night a special messenger arrived with a despatch for General Patterson. He was accompanied by one of General Sanford's aids; I do not now recollect who it was. That despatch I took up to the adjutant general of the column, Colonel Fitz-John Porter. I woke him up, and he read it in his bed, I reading it at the same time. Colonel Porter arose from his bed, and exhibited it to Captain Newton, the chief of the engineer corps of that army. After some little discussion, of which I do not recollect the particulars, (it did not amount to much,) Colonel Porter requested me to take the despatch to General Patterson and wake him up. I suggested that I had but lately joined his staff, and would prefer his doing it. I thought it was a despatch of very great importance. He said, "You better take it." I replied, "I will do so," and proceeded to General Patterson's room, where I aroused him from his sleep, and handed the despatch to him. It was as follows:

"HEADQUARTERS OF THE ARMY,
"*July* 17, 1861—9.30 *p. m.*

"I have nothing official from you since Sunday, but I am glad to learn from the Philadelphia papers that you have advanced. Do not let the enemy amuse and delay you with a small force in front, whilst he re-enforces the Junction with his main body. McDowell's first day's work has driven the enemy beyond Fairfax Court-House. The Junction will probably be taken to-morrow.

"Major General PATTERSON,
"*United States Forces, Harper's Ferry.*"

I read from a copy which I got at the War Department, and I believe it a true copy of that despatch. After General Patterson had read it twice over he turned to me and asked me if I had read it. I told him that I had. He then asked me what I thought of it. I replied that I had lately joined his staff, and would beg that he would ask Colonel Porter, or some other officer who had been with him longer than I had, as I did not like to give him an opinion. He said, "I desire your opinion, sir." I then replied, "I will give you my opinion, honestly and without hesitation. I look upon that despatch as a positive order from General Scott to attack Johnston wherever you can find him; and if you do not do it, I think you will be a ruined man. It will be impossible to meet the public sentiment of the country if you fail to carry out this order. And in the event of ⅍ misfortune in front of Washington, the whole blame will be laid to your charge." Those were as nearly the words as I can now recollect. He said, "Do you think so, sir?" I repeated that that was my honest conviction. He then said, "I will advance to-morrow. But how can we make a forced march with our trains?" I said, "Sir, if you cannot send them across the river into Maryland, we can make a bonfire of them." I then said, "General, have you positively made up your mind to this advance?" He said, "I have." "Then," said I, "I hope you will allow no one to influence you to-morrow in relation to it. The next morning orders were sent to the different brigades and divisions to cook three days' rations, and to be ready to march at a moment's notice. I had no conversation with any one in relation to my interview with General Patterson up to 9 o'clock in the morning. About 9 o'clock I was in the room occupied as an office, when several prominent officers of the column appeared. I think they had been summoned there by the general. General Patterson entered and said, "Gentlemen, I have sent for you, not for the purpose of consulting you as to the propriety of the movement I intend to make, but as to the best mode of making it." I then left the room. After these officers had separated I was told by the general that he did not think the

Pennsylvania troops would march, and that an order had been issued for them to be assembled on their parade grounds that afternoon, that he might consult them in person. He did so. He appealed to them in very strong terms to remain with him a week or ten days; that they had promised him that in the event of a battle taking place they would stand by him, and he desired them to intimate, when the command "shoulder arms" was given to each regiment, whether they would comply with his wish. Several of the Pennsylvania regiments came to a shoulder when the order was given—one (Colonel Patterson's) with but one exception; but the majority in the others failed to respond. I was near General Patterson during the whole time, and heard his speech to them. The advance was not made.

By Mr. Covode:

Question. Did General Patterson, at any time when he was addressing the troops, propose to march on to Winchester?

Answer. No, sir; not to my knowledge. General Patterson did not ask the troops whether they would advance against the enemy at Winchester. He asked them if they would remain with him. I think it due to those troops to state their condition as to clothing. They were very poorly clothed, indeed. Many of the men had their pantaloons patched with canvas from the flies of the tents, and their garments were particolored. They had received very hard treatment; were very badly clad, and many of them were without shoes. I did not hear General Patterson, before any regiment of Pennsylvania troops, ask them if they would advance against the enemy.

By Mr. Chandler:

Question. Had you any conversation with any of the officers in relation to this advance?

Answer. After I left the room, which I did while this discussion was going on, and which I had no curiosity to hear, Colonel Abercrombie, who commanded one of the brigades, came to me and asked me what I thought of the proposed movement of General Patterson. From the relations that existed between Colonel Abercrombie and General Patterson, I felt satisfied that he already knew my views about the proposed movement. When conversing in reference to the movement of the trains, and the suggestion that if they could not be saved, I thought that, under the circumstances, they should be burned, Colonel Abercrombie desired to know how the men could get along without their cooking utensils. I suggested that there were plenty of trees and bushes between Charlestown and Winchester, and the men could cook their meat as they did in California, by holding it before the fire. Then he remarked, "You would place everything on the hazard of the die; sacrifice our line of communication, and in all probability cause the command to be cut off." I told him that I thought General Patterson was just in the position to place everything at that hazard; that if he failed to move, I was satisfied that, no matter how pure his intentions might be, he would be overwhelmed by public sentiment. I told him that as to cutting off our communication, I felt perfectly satisfied that the people of this country would open the line of communication if he took the risk suggested. The colonel did not agree with me, and our conversation ceased.

Question. You spoke some time ago about some information furnished by a deserter. Had General Patterson, that you know of, any reliable information in regard to the enemy?

Answer. Not that I know of. I think I should have heard it if he had had any.

By Mr. Odell:

Question. You deemed Bunker Hill an important position for the purpose of holding the enemy?

Answer. Well, sir, Bunker Hill was, I think, 10 miles from Winchester, and at Charlestown we were 22 miles in another direction.

By Mr. Chandler:

Question. Did you not at Bunker Hill directly threaten Johnston?

Answer. By our advance from Martinsburg to Bunker Hill we threatened him.

Question. When you turned off to Charlestown from Bunker Hill, did you not intimate to the enemy that you were leaving him, and that he was free to move where he pleased?

Answer. If putting more miles between us and the enemy was such an intimation, we made it.

By the chairman:

Question. As a military man, in your judgment, was there any insuperable obstacle or barrier to your detaining Johnston there, if you had pursued him vigorously from Bunker Hill?

Answer. I think if we had advanced on Johnston, our men could, in all probability, have marched as fast as he could. Having only 10 miles the start of us, he could not have got to Manassas much before we could. If he had attempted to pull up the railroad as he passed along, we should then have overhauled him.

By Mr. Chandler:

Question. Did General Patterson send you to Washington with despatches for General Scott? If so, what took place at that interview?

Answer. General Patterson sent me to Washington to explain to General Scott the reason of his not moving against Winchester. He sent me on Friday, the 19th, and I arrived here on Saturday morning. I immediately called upon General Scott at his private quarters, and found him there with several of his staff. I stated to him what General Patterson had directed me to say to him, as nearly as I could. I exhibited to him the sketch made by the captain of engineers, giving the plan of the fortifications at Winchester, and the forces that occupied them, as stated by the deserter. General Scott seemed very much annoyed at the failure of the troops to advance, and said to me, "Why did not General Patterson advance?" I said, "Sir, General Patterson directed me to say to you that he understood your orders to him were to make demonstrations; to hold Johnston, not to drive him." The general turned in his chair very fiercely on me, and said very excitedly, "I will sacrifice my commission if my despatches will bear any such interpretation." Seeing the excited manner of the general, I begged to be excused for the present, and said I would call on him again at 12 o'clock, at his office. I then left him. I called at 12 o'clock, and he informed me that the Secretary of War had the day before relieved General Patterson from the command of that column, and had ordered General Banks to succeed him. I will state, also, that at this time I urged upon General Scott the request of General Patterson that re-enforcements should be sent him to enable him to make the movement on Winchester. And after my return my impression was that if they would give General Banks 25,000 men, and let him force his way through and take possession of Winchester and Strasburg, it would be an important movement at that time. That same movement seems now to be taking place under General Banks, other troops being placed in position at his old camps. On Monday morning, the 22d of July, I left this place on my return. On my arrival at Sandy Hook, a mile this side of Harper's Ferry, I observed some officers I had left at Charlestown, and a number of troops. I called to them and asked them what they were doing there. They said that the whole army was at Harper's Ferry. That was the first knowledge I had of any contemplated movement from Charlestown to Harper's Ferry.

Question. Did you not understand when you advanced from Martinsburg to Bunker Hill that your object was to whip Johnston, or at least to hold him there?

Answer. To hold him; not to allow him to re-enforce Manassas. There is another thing that convinced me that my view of the despatch to which I have referred was correct. Another despatch was received by General Patterson from General Scott, on the 18th, as follows:

"Sir: I have certainly been expecting you to beat the enemy; if not, to hear that you had felt him strongly, or at least had occupied him by threats and demonstrations. You have been at least his equal, and I suppose his superior, in numbers. Has he not stolen a march, and sent re-enforcements towards Manassas Junction? A week is enough to win victories. The time of volunteers counts from the day of mustering into the service of the United States. You must not retreat across the Potomac. If necessary, when abandoned by the short-term volunteers, intrench somewhere and wait for re-enforcements."

By Mr. Odell:

Question. What was the temper of the troops on the receipt of orders to move from Martinsburg to Bunker Hill, and while at Bunker Hill?

Answer. The march from Martinsburg to Bunker Hill was made in admirable order. I rode along the line several times to convey orders from the right to the left, and there did not seem to be any dissatisfaction that I could observe. The men preserved the order of march, and seemed to be in very good spirits.

Question. Did any dissatisfaction manifest itself at Bunker Hill?

Answer. I heard of none. The men violated the regulations somewhat, by foraging around, as all soldiers will.

Question. Did you hear of any expression of opinion to the effect that the men did not want to make an advance?

Answer. I heard some of the officers speak of the certainty of the Pennsylvania troops claiming their discharge at the expiration of their term of service.

By Mr. Chandler:

Question. Where was that?

Answer. I do not know. It was a general rumor.

Question. At Charlestown you heard of great dissatisfaction?

Answer. Yes, sir.

By Mr. Odell:

Question. Was there any dissatisfaction among the troops at going to meet the enemy?

Answer. I do not know that the men ever had that point—that they were going against the enemy—presented to them. Many of the men were in very bad condition as to clothing, &c. There was a regiment there from Indiana that was in as bad, if not a worse, condition than any regiment I have seen. General Patterson did not address that regiment. But they volunteered through their colonel to remain, without the suggestion of any one. Many of the men had no shoes, and the feet of some of them were so cut and injured by the flinty roads over which they marched that their officers had to order them to be carried in the wagons. Yet they volunteered through Colonel Wallace, their commander, to advance on Winchester, or against the enemy.

By Mr. Covode:

Question. Did the troops know they were retreating when they left Bunker Hill?

Answer. I do not think that either the officers or the men were aware that they were retreating, except from the direction that they took. After General Patterson was relieved, General Banks invited me to remain and occupy the same position on his staff that I had on General Patterson's. I did so until after he moved across the Potomac with the main body of his army and encamped on this side. The movement across the river was made by General Banks after full consultation with all the highest officers in his command, who voted each separately that it would be highly imprudent and dangerous to attempt to continue the occupancy of Harper's Ferry with the small force left under his command; and that it could be held by means of guns mounted on the Maryland side, and without risk to his troops. On their advice he acted. He never surrendered, during the time I was up there, the place of Harper's Ferry, but always kept a guard there for its protection.

By Mr. Covode:

Question. Did you, before you went up there, have any conversation with General Scott; and if so, what did he tell you as to what he wanted done?

Answer. After receiving permission, and the order from General Cameron to proceed to join General Patterson, I called on Colonel Townsend, the assistant adjutant general, and offered to convey any despatches he might have for General Patterson's column. While there General Scott heard my voice and called me into his room, and inquired when I was going. I told him. He then asked why I did not come to him for a letter to General Patterson. I told him I knew he was very much engaged, and I was almost afraid to ask to see him. He then directed Colonel Townsend to write a letter and bring it to him to sign. I think he remarked that we were in the same boat, meaning that we were both southern men, he from Virginia and I from Maryland. I said to him, "General, I have made up my mind that the column of General Patterson will be engaged by Sunday." He replied, "It may be before that, but it cannot be long before it is." I told him then that I would hurry and try to join General Patterson as soon as possible, which I did. I will remark here, that what I have stated in my testimony are entirely impressions of my own. And my advice, if it may be so called, to General Patterson as to an advance, was to meet the sentiment of the country, and what I conceived to be the first wish of the people—the defeat of the army of the rebels in front of Washington.

By Mr. Odell:

Question. What were your relations with General Patterson while with him and subsequently?

Answer. The first time I ever met General Patterson was at Martinsburg, when I presented the letters of General Cameron and General Scott, recommending me to his notice. General Patterson's bearing towards me was exceedingly kind; he extended to me every courtesy and confidence during the time I was with him, and, in consequence, I have always felt the liveliest feelings of gratitude towards him. His impressions of my services may be obtained from this letter:

"HEADQUARTERS DEPARTMENT OF PENNSYLVANIA,
"Harper's Ferry, July 25, 1861.

"MAJOR: I regret that in relinquishing the command of this department I can no longer avail myself of your services on my personal staff. For the promptness and gallantry with which those services were tendered at a critical moment, and the zeal and fidelity with which they have been discharged throughout, I can only offer you my cordial thanks.

"I remain, with great regard, very sincerely, yours,
"R. PATTERSON,
"Major General Commanding.

"Major W. W. RUSSELL,
"United States Marine Corps, &c."

WASHINGTON, *March* 19, 1862.

General GEORGE CADWALADER sworn and examined.

By the chairman:

Question. What has been your rank and position in the army?

Answer. I hold a commission of brigadier general in the State of Pennsylvania, under which, upon the call of the President last spring, I came into the service for three months. I also held a commission as major general by brevet in the army of the United States, conferred upon me after my commission as brigadier general had terminated. I state that, as it is considered material by General Scott.

Question. When did you commence service last year, and where did you serve?

Answer. I was mustered into service on the 19th of April, 1861, for three months.

Question. Under General Patterson?

Answer. Not at that time. I was assigned to the command of the department of Annapolis, my headquarters being at Baltimore. I succeeded General Butler in that command. I subsequently joined General Patterson's column, where I commanded the first division of the column, consisting of the three brigades then commanded by General Williams, Colonel Thomas, and Colonel Miles.

Question. Did you accompany General Patterson in that campaign until he returned?

Answer. I joined him at Chambersburg, and remained with him until the army returned to Harper's Ferry.

Question. What was his force at Martinsburg, Virginia?

Answer. My official position only gave me official knowledge of my own division, and perhaps I can only give an estimate.

Question. Give your estimate, according to the best light you had upon the subject.

Answer. I should say, according to the general knowledge I had, that he had from 18,000 to 22,000 men; perhaps from 18,000 to 20,000 men for duty.

Question. What was the object of that expedition, as you understood it?

Answer. I never was informed there, and never was officially consulted in regard to it by General Patterson. General Scott told me when I left here, and I also knew from the Secretary of War and the President, that the object was to drive General Johnston and the rebel force under him out of Harper's Ferry. That was the object for which I went there, and I expected to be relieved and to return here the moment that was accomplished. I was so promised by the Secretary of War, but it was not done.

Question. General Patterson followed General Johnston from Harper's Ferry for a while, did he not?

Answer. My division, as a part of General Patterson's column, was in the advance. I crossed the Potomac from Williamsport; and when Johnston retreated as we advanced upon Harper's Ferry, we went down as far as Falling Waters, on the Virginia side. I was there met with an order to send to Washington all the regular troops—they were all under my command—as it was thought that Johnston had fallen back to re-enforce Beauregard, and that Washington was in danger. All the regular troops being ordered to Washington, and the object of dislodging the enemy from Harper's Ferry having been accomplished, General Patterson was compelled, or rather induced, to give me the order to fall back. I was then on the way to Martinsburg, and had got as far as Falling Waters, some miles on the other side of the Potomac. General Patterson was still at Hagerstown. A great misfortune, by the by, was that recall.

Question. Did you accompany his army into Virginia?

Answer. Yes, sir; I remained with the army until we went on up to Martinsburg, and on to Bunker Hill, which is ten miles from Winchester.

Question. What was Johnston's force at Falling Waters, as near as you could estimate it?

Answer. My information was so uncertain, so vague, that I never had any very definite idea upon the subject.

Question. He retreated before you after the battle of Falling Waters, did he not?

Answer. Yes, sir. He fell back first upon Bunker Hill, and then upon Winchester, which is due south about ten miles from Bunker Hill.

Question. Your position at Bunker Hill threatened Winchester, did it not?

Answer. Yes, sir.

Question. Do you know the orders General Patterson received from headquarters here?

Answer. I know now; I did not know then. When I returned here General Scott expressed great astonishment that I had been kept in ignorance of everything of that kind, and directed Colonel Townsend, his adjutant general, to furnish me with copies of everything that had passed between him and General Patterson.

Question. When Patterson was at Bunker Hill with his army, was there any difficulty in his detaining Johnston in the valley of Winchester, and preventing his going down to join Beauregard?

Answer. I always considered our position a false one from the time that Johnston retreated from Bunker Hill. I could see that no movement we could make from there could accomplish the purpose of holding Johnston at Winchester one moment longer than he chose to stay. To the south of him he had the whole country open, while we were directly north of him. I always thought we should have moved more in a southeasterly direction, where we could have been more within supporting distance of a column moving from here, and also in a position more threatening upon Johnston's right flank—our left upon his right. On the only occasion I ever was consulted, which was at Martinsburg, where the commanding officers of divisions and brigades, and the officers of the engineer corps on duty with our column, were summoned together by General Patterson, I expressed my opinion that, as we were not holding Johnston at Winchester one moment longer than he chose to stay there, we ought to attack him, and move in this direction at once, and unite with the forces that we supposed were about to attack Manassas. That was the advice I gave before all the officers present.

By Mr. Wright:

Question. When did you advise that?

Answer. It was within two days before we left Martinsburg for Bunker Hill. It was at the only meeting of the officers that was held during the campaign. It was a large meeting, and all the principal officers and the engineer officers were present.

By the chairman:

Question. What was the reason given for not attacking Johnston?

Answer. General Patterson gave no reason. He summoned these officers, myself among others, and asked our opinion as to what, under existing circumstances, we would advise being done. And, according to military usage, beginning with the junior in rank, it came to me last. Major General Sanford, of New York, and Major General Keim, of Pennsylvania, among others, were there. I at last gave my opinion, stated it briefly, as I have stated it here. We were not holding Johnston, because, as we were ten miles north of him, he could leave whenever he chose. He could get information much more rapidly from Beauregard than we could get it from Washington, and he knew exactly what the movements over in this direction were. If the intention was to hold Johnston there, we were not accomplishing the purpose; and we could not do it where we then were.

Question. Would it not have been easy to have placed yourself in a position where you could have done so?

Answer. Certainly. If we had moved upon Berryville and got upon his right flank, and he could not have moved one foot without our being upon his flank, we could have been at Manassas sooner than he could, and could have attacked him at any moment. Some of the officers thought that, as our army moved from here under General McDowell, Beauregard might retreat, falling back upon the whole of Patterson's army, General Johnston uniting with him for that purpose. It was the opinion of two or three of the officers that Johnston might advance and cut us off while Beauregard came with his whole army upon Patterson's column.

Question. Suppose that Patterson had orders from General Scott to hold Johnston in the valley of Winchester?

Answer. Which, I say, he could not have done without attacking him.

Question. Then, with such orders, he should have attacked him?

Answer. That was what I thought; either to have attacked him or to have come down here, as we were doing no good there.

Question. You were at Bunker Hill when Johnston turned off to Charlestown?

Answer. Yes, sir; my division was in the advance from Bunker Hill in the direction of Winchester; and I marched with that column from Bunker Hill to Charlestown through Smithfield.

Question If you threatened Winchester while at Bunker Hill, did you not relinquish your threatening attitude when you turned off towards Charlestown?

Answer. Of course, for we then went away from Winchester.

Question. So, from the time you turned off from Bunker Hill to Charlestown, all hope of detaining Johnston must have entirely vanished?

Answer. Certainly; we were marching away from him. In other words, we were on our way to Harper's Ferry through Charlestown.

Question. Do you know whether General Patterson, when he resigned all hope of detaining Johnston, immediately informed General Scott of that fact?

Answer. I never was consulted about any such thing. Until I came back here I never saw a line from General Scott to General Patterson, or from General Patterson to General Scott. When I so informed General Scott he expressed great dissatisfaction, saying, "General Patterson knew that my communications to him were intended as much for you as for himself." And it was then that he turned to Colonel Townsend and ordered him to make out and furnish to me copies of everything that had passed between General Patterson and himself.

Question. Is there anything more that you deem material which you would like to state? If so, please go on and state it in your own way.

Answer. I have no desire, nor do I know that there is anything of public utility for me to state, other than I have already stated. There are matters personal to myself; that, of course, I have no right to bring before this committee.

Question. You can state anything that you think best. We are endeavoring to find out how this war has been conducted, and you can state anything in that connexion that is material for us to know.

Answer. I should like to state some things on my own account ; and they are historical, too, so far as anybody may deem them of public importance. You asked me what my rank and position in the army were. When I was in command at Baltimore I was sent for by General Scott to come here. General Cameron was at General Scott's headquarters, and General Scott handed me my commission as major general by brevet in the army, saying, "That commission of General Cadwalader's as a major general of the army is a perfectly valid one at this time." The question was whether I should rank as major general with General Patterson, and whether I was to be assigned to duty under my major general's commission. Upon that General Cameron promised to assign me to duty under my brevet commission as a major general. He offered me a commission as major general of volunteers, or a commission of brigadier general in the regular service, which was what I had held during the Mexican war. I accepted the commission of brigadier general in the regular service, with the promise of the President, through the Secretary of War, that I was to be assigned to duty under my commission as major general by brevet, with the promise of promotion as major general, when they heard from General Frémont, which they expected to do in two weeks ; under the expectation and with the conviction, as they told me, that he would decline the commission tendered to him. With that promise I took the commission of brigadier general, with the understanding that I was to be assigned to duty under my commission as major general by brevet, in preference to the commission of major general of volunteers.

Question. When was that ?

Answer. That was the 8th of June. I addressed a letter to the Secretary of War before I left here, reminding him of the promise so as to avoid all mistakes, and which he perfectly remembers. General Frémont, unexpectedly to them, returned and accepted the commission offered him, which prevented their being able to give me that. For some reason General McClellan was brought here, and had I been commissioned major general, I would have ranked him. That prevented their being able to do one thing or the other. In the mean time they made major generals of volunteers, whom I would have ranked, that ranked me. They could not comply with their promise to me, and I went home, as they did not want me. That was the military position I occupied, and those are the reasons I am not now in service.

Question. You say they were convinced that General Frémont would decline. Upon what did they found that conviction ?

Answer. I do not know. That was what General Cameron told me.

By Mr. Gooch :

Question. Did they desire that General Frémont should decline ?

Answer. That I do not know ; I merely tell you what passed. They told me that I was to have that commission ; that they knew he would decline. That was the offer to me. I certainly would not otherwise have accepted the commission of brigadier general in the regular army, when I had the commission offered me of a major general in the volunteers. My commission of major general by brevet dates back to 1847, and ranks all except General Wool. They were unable to do what they had promised. They had appointed as major generals of volunteers General Banks, General Butler, General Dix, &c., and to come in then would have placed me very differently from what their own proposition was. I had not asked for that ; they had sent for me and asked me to take it. I considered it a very complimentary and a very handsome thing ; but, as I have said, they were unable to give it to me, for it interfered with other places. I told the President that if it deranged any of their plans, I was perfectly willing to exonerate him from any promise ; if the interest of the service required it, I was perfectly willing and ready to serve ; and it was not my fault that I went home.

Question. To come back to the other subject. You have not stated yet what you supposed Johnston's force at Winchester to be.

Answer. I desire my remark about his force at Falling Waters to apply to his force at Winchester. I had no reliable information upon which to base an opinion.

By the chairman :

Question. Had you any reason to believe that Johnston's army was materially increased after he reached Winchester ?

Answer. By general rumor it was said to have been greatly increased.

Question. From where was it supposed the troops came ?

Answer. From the south ; we did not know from where.

Question. From Manassas ?

Answer. We did not know. It was just the sort of rumor that would be current among the people of the country, entirely unreliable.

By Mr. Gooch :

Question. Have you ever made any written statement of the force under Johnston at Winchester ? If so, please state when and under what circumstances you did so.

Answer. I never made any official statement of any kind of the forces under Johnston at Winchester, having no knowledge of my own in regard to it. After many of our regiments had started on their march home, their term of service having expired while we were at Harper's Ferry, a Mr. McDaniel, a civilian, came to me on the 23d of July, with a statement of some information which he said he had obtained in regard to the force under Johnston, at Winchester. I asked him to let me copy it, which I did as he read it to me. I put no date to it, merely writing down what he read. I was about leaving, but before I went I showed it to General Patterson, as something that might be of interest to him. I did not give it as information obtained by myself, or express any opinion in regard to its reliability, giving it merely as information which McDaniel said he had obtained—not as information of my own General Patterson asked me to allow him to take a copy of it, promising to return me the original. He, however, did not return me the original, but sent me a copy of it.

By the chairman :

Question. Did you attach any importance to the paper as containing reliable information ?

Answer. Not the slightest ; and if I had, it could not have influenced General Patterson in what he had done, for he had got back to Harper's Ferry, and the troops had crossed the river on their way home, before either of us knew anything about this.

By Mr. Gooch:

Question. When you were at Bunker Hill, if it had been known that General McDowell was about to attack Manassas, and that it was expected that the army under General Patterson would detain Johnston so as to prevent his forming a junction with Beauregard and taking part in the action at Manassas, what should have been done by Patterson's army to have accomplished that object ?

Answer. I do not think he could have detained him in any other way than by attacking him. He could have prevented his taking the route by which he did go to Manassas, by taking up a position on his right flank, that is, to the eastward of Winchester. Johnston, however, would have had open to him the route by the way of Strasburg, which was the one they had always received and sent troops by. The way he actually did go was east, over the mountains to Piedmont, Strasburg lying west of south of him. If we had not attacked him, but had taken a position to the east of Winchester, Johnston could have gone by the way of Strasburg, but could not have gone the way he did go, over the mountains to Piedmont. Believing that we were not holding him where we then were, and that the object of any such instructions or suggestions, if any such existed, as I subsequently learned they did exist, could not be accomplished except by attacking Johnston, I advised that we should attack him, or if that was not done, that we should unite with the main body of our troops here in the attack upon Manassas. The expression used by General Scott, in one of his letters to General Patterson, which I saw afterwards, was "to consider the route by the way of Leesburg." It is true that in the telegrams that came from General Scott it was indicated that General Patterson was to hold General Johnston if he did not attack him. But there was no possibility of holding him if we did not attack. To use General Johnston's own expression in his report, he was merely waiting there looking at us.

By the chairman:

Question. Then if he was to hold him, and attacking him was the only way to hold him, it meant that he should attack him?

Answer. Attack him or consider the route by way of Leesburg.

By Mr. Gooch:

Question. Could Patterson have come down that route in time to have taken part in the battle here?

Answer. Yes, sir; if he had moved on Berryville, we would have been on Johnston's flank all the way.

Question. And you could have reached Manassas before Johnston could?

Answer. Certainly, if we had moved in time. According to McDaniel's memorandum, Johnston started from Winchester at one o'clock on the day we left Bunker Hill. It was more with a view to the time when Johnston started than for any other purpose that I showed that memorandum to General Patterson. We started from Bunker Hill at daylight, and if you take the official report of Johnston, recently published, you will see that on that very day he got his instructions to go to Manassas, and that at one o'clock on the day we left Bunker Hill for Charlestown, Johnston left Winchester for Manassas.

Question. And you should have gone from Bunker Hill to Berryville, so as to have prevented Johnston from going to Manassas by the route he did go?

Answer. If we had done that, we could have gone to Manassas also. We had but 10 miles further than Johnston to go if we had gone by the way of Winchester; and we had not much further to go if we had gone by the way of Berryville, for we were almost as near Berryville as he was.

Question. So that you could have prevented his going the route he did?

Answer. We could have attacked him, which I think would have prevented him. I think he knew that, because he would not fight us in the open ground. He showed that his object was to elude us, according to his own expression.

By the chairman:

Question. And General Scott's idea was to detain him by fighting or in any other way?

Answer. Yes, sir.

By Mr. Gooch:

Question. Then Johnston could have been prevented from forming a junction with Beauregard, and the force under Patterson might have been ready to have taken part in the attack upon Manassas?

Answer. We might have attacked Johnston, and if we had been successful, which I think we would have been, we could have prevented the junction. And if we did not attack him, if we had marched in due time, we could certainly have been at Manassas in time to have taken part in the battle. The way was open to us, and the suggestion of General Scott was "to consider the route by way of Leesburg." If I had had any discretion, I should have gone at once to Leesburg, which was half-way to Manassas, and on a good turnpike road directly there.

Question. Will you furnish the committee with the copies of the telegraphic despatches you received from General Scott?

Answer. I will.

LIEUTENANT GENERAL WINFIELD SCOTT.

NEW YORK, *March* 31, 1862.

On the statement of Major General Patterson, submitted by him as evidence to the honorable the committee of the House of Representatives on the conduct of the war, I beg leave to remark:

1. That his statement, 148 long pages, closely and indistinctly written, has been before me about 48 hours, including a Sunday when I was too much indisposed to work or to go to church; that I cannot write or read at night, nor at any time, except by short efforts, and that I have been entirely without help.

2. That, consequently, I have read but little of the statement and voluminous documents appended, and have but about two hours left for comments on that little.

3. The documents (mainly correspondence between General Patterson and myself) are badly copied, being hardly intelligible in some places from the omission and change of words.

4. General Patterson was never ordered by me, as he seems to allege, to attack the enemy without a probability of success; but on several occasions he wrote as if he were assured of victory. For example, June 12th he says: he is "resolved to conquer, and will risk nothing;" and July 4th, expecting supplies the next day, he adds: as soon as they "arrive I shall advance to Winchester to drive the enemy from that place;" accordingly he issued orders for the movement on the 8th; next called a council of war, and stood fast at Martinsburg.

5. But although General Patterson was never specifically ordered to attack the enemy, he was certainly told, and expected, even if with inferior numbers, to hold the rebel army in his front on the alert, and to prevent it from re-enforcing Manassas Junction, by means of threatening manœuvres and demonstrations—results often obtained in war with half numbers.

6. After a time General P. moved upon Bunker Hill, and then fell off upon Charlestown, whence he seems to have made no other demonstration that did not look like a retreat out of Virginia. From that movement Johnston was at liberty to join Beauregard with any part of the army of Winchester.

7. General P. alludes, with feeling, to my recall from him back to Washington, after the enemy had evacuated Harper's Ferry, of certain troops sent to enable him to take that place; but the recall was necessary to prevent

the government and capital from falling into the enemy's hands. His inactivity, however, from that cause need not to have been more than temporary; for he was soon re-enforced up to, at least, the enemy's maximum number in the Winchester valley, without leading to a battle, or even a reconnoissance in force.

8. He also often called for batteries and rifled cannon beyond our capacity to supply at the moment, and so in respect to regular troops, one or more regiments. He might as well have asked for a brigade of elephants. Till some time later we had for the defence of the government in its capital but a few companies of regular foot and horse, and not half the number of troops, including all descriptions, if the enemy had chosen to attack us.

9. As connected with this subject, I hope I may be permitted to notice the charge made against me on the floors of Congress that I did not stop Brigadier General McDowell's movement upon Manassas Junction after I had been informed of the re-enforcement sent thither from Winchester, though urged to do so by one or more members of the cabinet. Now, it was, at the reception of that news, too late to call off the troops from the attack; and besides, though opposed to the movement at first, we had all become animated and sanguine of success ; and it is not true that I was urged by anybody in authority to stop the attack, which was commenced as early, I think, as the 18th of July.

10. I have but time to say that among the disadvantages under which I have been writing are these : I have not had within reach one of my own papers; and not an officer who was with me at the period in question.

Respectfully submitted to the committee.

WINFIELD SCOTT.

New York, *March* 31, 1862.

Washington, *April* 3, 1862.

General James B. Ricketts sworn and examined.

By the chairman:

Question. What rank and position do you hold in the army ?

Answer. I am at present a brigadier general of volunteers.

Question. What was your rank on the 21st of July last, the day of the battle of Bull Run ?

Answer. I was a captain of the first regiment of artillery.

Question. In whose brigade ?

Answer. General Franklin's brigade.

Question. Will you please give us an account, in your own way, of what you saw of the battle ?

Answer. I saw very little except what concerned myself. You must know that any one who has charge of six pieces of artillery has as much as he can attend to to manage them and obey orders. I went on the field at Sudley's Spring, in General Heintzelman's division, General Franklin's brigade. After crossing the stream, where I watered my horses, my first order was to take to the right into an open field, to effect which I had to take down the fences. I then came into action about a thousand yards from the enemy, I should judge. There was a battery of smooth-bores opposed against me, doing some damage to us; it killed some horses and wounded some few of my men; I myself saw one man struck on the arm. My battery consisted of six rifled Parrott guns, consequently I was more than a match at that distance for the smooth-bore battery. It is difficult to judge of the passage of time under such circumstances, as we never look at our watches then.

But after firing, I should judge, twenty minutes or a half an hour, I had orders to advance a certain distance. I moved forward, and was about to come into battery again, when I was ordered to proceed further on, up on a hill near the Henry House.

By Mr. Chandler:

Question. About what time was it when you first came into action?

Answer. We had marched twelve miles. I should judge my first coming into action must have been somewhere about noon. That, of course, is a mere guess. I received this order to move forward. I told the officer that he must indicate the spot, so that there should be no mistake about it. I saw at a glance, as I thought, that I was going into great peril for my horses and men. But I did not hesitate to obey the order, merely asking to name the spot clearly indicated to me. The ground had not been reconnoitred at all, and there was a little ravine in front that I had to pass. As I marched at the head of my company with Lieutenant Ramsay, he said to me, "We cannot pass that ravine." I told him that we must pass it. As we were under fire, to countermarch there would be fatal. The confusion consequent upon turning around there would expose us to great danger. As it was, we dashed across, breaking one wheel in the effort, which we immediately replaced. I called off the cannoniers and took down the fence and ascended the hill near the Henry House, which was at that time filled with sharpshooters. I had scarcely got into battery before I saw some of my horses fall and some of my men wounded by the sharpshooters. I turned my guns upon the house and literally riddled it. It has been said that there was a woman killed there by our guns. It was in that house that she was killed at the time I turned my battery on it and shelled out the sharpshooters there. We did not move from that position—that is, we made no important movement. We moved a piece one way or the other, perhaps, in order to take advantage of the enemy's appearance at one point or another. But our guns were not again limbered up. In fact, in a very short time we were not in a position or a condition to move, on account of the number of our horses that were disabled. I know it was the hottest place I ever saw in my life, and I had seen some fighting before. The enemy had taken advantage of the woods and the natural slope of the ground, and delivered a terrible fire upon us.

Question. Was that the place where your battery was lost?

Answer. Yes, sir.

Question. And where you yourself was wounded and fell?

Answer. Yes, sir.

Question. Who gave you the order to march forward there?

Answer. Lieutenant Kingsbury, of General McDowell's staff, brought me the order. Lieutenant Snyder was also near, and I told him I wanted him to bear in mind that I had received that order, although no point was indicated.

Question. Had you a sufficient infantry support for your battery?

Answer. At that time I knew of no support. I was told a support was ordered. One regiment, the Fire Zouaves, I know came up to support me, and, when I saw them in confusion, I rode up to them and said something cheering to them. I had not much time to speak to them, but I thought I would say a little something cheering to them, as it might have some effect upon them.

Question. How long did you continue to operate your guns after you took that position?

Answer. Somewhere between a half an hour and an hour, I should judge.

Question. Was Griffin's battery near you?

Answer. I do not know, except from what I have heard. I know there was a battery a little to the rear on my right, and from all accounts I suppose that to be Griffin's battery. They were on my right in my first position, and moved up with me and took a position a little on my right.

By the chairman:

Question. How came they to order you to advance without infantry to support you? Is not that unusual?

Answer. The infantry came up directly afterwards. I do not know where the position of the infantry was. All I saw were the Fire Zouaves, who came up on my right to support me.

Question. In what number?

Answer. I should suppose, when my attention was called to them, that there were from two hundred to three hundred men.

Question. What number of infantry is supposed to be sufficient to support a battery?

Answer. To go into such a place as that, I should say there should have been two full regiments to have supported my battery.

By Mr. Odell:

Question. Was the smooth-bore battery of the enemy supported?

Answer. Yes, sir; and we drove them away. They retired some distance as we advanced. They must have had a heavy support, judging from the amount of lead they threw from their muskets, for long after I was down the hail was tremendous. The ground was torn up all around me, and some bullets went through my clothes. I never expected to get off at all.

By Mr. Chandler:

Question. How many of your men were hit?

Answer. I do not know. I was five months in Richmond as a prisoner. I, of course, made no report, and have made none yet. No report has been made, though I think it should have been made by the next officer, as I was virtually lost; was away from the battery, and knew nothing of what occurred to the men.

By Mr. Odell:

Question. Who was in command of the artillery—the chief of artillery?

Answer. Major Barry—now General Barry.

By Mr. Chandler:

Question. Did he direct the movements of the artillery?

Answer. I did not see him.

By the chairman:

Question. Was the place where you were posted before you were ordered to advance more advantageous than the one to which you did advance?

Answer. I think it was, up to the time that I left it; and I think it would have been for a little longer time, considering that I had longer range guns than the enemy had.

Question. Could you have sustained yourself in your first position?

Answer. I think so. Yes, sir.

Question. From whom did the order to advance emanate?

Answer. General McDowell's aid brought it to me. Major Barry had no aid. Whether it was Major Barry's order or not, I could not tell. He had charge of the artillery, and was supposed to have directed its movements.

Question. Was it good generalship to order you to advance with your battery without more support than you had?

Answer. Do you mean the one regiment?

Question. Yes, sir; the Fire Zouaves you speak of.

Answer. No, sir; I do not think it was. I desire to state here that I have seen it mentioned that I made some mistake as to the enemy. Captain Griffin and myself are coupled together as having made some mistake on the field as to the character of the enemy. I wish to say that I made no mistake in regard to the enemy.

By Mr. Chandler:

Question. You refer to mistaking a regiment of the enemy for one of our own troops?

Answer. Yes, sir.

Question. You are not connected with that in our testimony.

Answer. I am very glad to hear it. I had noticed that, among other things, in the papers; and when I came back from Richmond, I saw the President, and he said to me: "You thought you were going to certain destruction in going up there, so you said," referring to our last position. I replied, "That is a mistake, I made no remark at all, except that I wanted the place clearly indicated to which I was to move."

By the chairman:

Question. Were you present at the council of war the evening prior to the battle?

Answer. No, sir.

Question. At what time on the day of the battle did you learn that Johnston's troops were coming down from Winchester?

Answer. Well, sir, I heard before we left little Rocky Run, this side of Centreville, that there was danger of meeting Johnston's men on that day. I cannot tell you who told me.

Question. In your judgment, as a military man, after it was ascertained that Johnston would be down, was it prudent to fight that battle, unless you could have, for instance, Patterson's army to follow Johnston's down?

Answer. Yes, sir, I think so. I think we could have fought with the army we had. We had apparently as good men as ever were.

Question. Suppose that battle could have been fought two weeks before it was fought, what would have been the probable result?

Answer. I believe if we had fought it even two days before we would have walked over the field. I saw on the field of battle a number of officers who had resigned from our army, whom I had known; and while I was at Richmond some of them told me that at one time they were giving away, and that our panic was perfectly unaccountable to them. We gained the battle with the force we had. I believe there was a time when we had really won that battle, if we had only kept at it a little longer.

Question. As a military man, to what circumstances do you attribute our disaster on that day?

Answer. I impute it to the want of proper officers among the volunteers.

By Mr. Wright:

Question. Do you mean the colonels and generals?

Answer. I mean throughout. I cannot say particular colonels and particular captains, because some of them were excellent. But, as a general rule, many of the officers were inferior to the men themselves. The men were of as good material as any in the world, and they fought well until they became confused on account of their officers not knowing what to do.

By the chairman :

Question. Were you present and able to know the last charge of the enemy which was decisive ?

Answer. Which charge was that?

Question. The same one that captured your battery, I believe. All the witnesses speak of a certain charge that was made there by the enemy.

Answer. My battery was taken and retaken three times. For a part of the time the struggle was going on over my body ; and I think that for a part of the time I must have been insensible, for I bled very freely.

By Mr. Chandler :

Question. Which of our regiments fought over your body for the battery ? Not the zouaves ?

Answer. I did not know which regiment it was. It was not the zouaves. I saw a regiment, after I was down, move very near my battery, and I saw a shell explode among them, somewhere, I should judge, about the color company; and in speaking of it to Dr. Swan afterwards, the surgeon of the 14th New York regiment, who went over the field the next day, I concluded it was the 14th regiment, because he said he saw a great many of his regiment killed there. I therefore supposed that that was the regiment engaged in that struggle for the battery.

Question. Were you captured with your guns ?

Answer. Yes, sir; I suppose I may say I was taken with my guns. When I was found I was asked my name, and I told them my name was Captain Ricketts. They asked if I was captain of that battery, pointing to one that was moving towards them, and I told them I was.

Question. Your guns were turned upon our troops after they were captured, were they not ?

Answer. They say they were turned upon us; and I remember hearing one or two explosions.

By Mr. Julian:

Question. What kind of support did you receive from the Fire Zouaves ?

Answer. Well, sir, these Fire Zouaves came up to the ground, but they soon got into confusion and left.

By Mr. Odell:

Question. Was that in consequence of want of proper directions from their officers ?

Answer. I should judge, from the manner in which the men stood there, and from their not being properly in line, that it was from want of officers; either that their officers were ignorant of their duty at that time, or that they were not there. I cannot say how that was. Our men really behaved very gallantly up to a certain time.

Question. Did the 14th New York regiment support you at all while you were in position ?

Answer. That I cannot tell you. They were in the woods on my right, I know ; because a number of officers told me about them, though they took them for the Fire Zouaves on account of their red uniform.

WASHINGTON, *July* 14, 1862.

General M. C. MEIGS recalled and examined.

By Mr. Chandler:

Question. It would appear from some of the testimony we have taken in regard to the circumstances attending the battle of Bull Run, that one of the causes of the delay of our army at Centreville from Thursday until Sunday was occasioned by a lack of supplies. Do you remember anything in regard to that?

Answer. This is the first I have heard of it. I was called upon to supply a certain number of wagons and horses, the most of which I had to purchase after I was called upon for them. I did all I could. I do not think I supplied them quite as early as I had hoped to do, or as was desired. But my impression has been that before General McDowell moved we could see where were the means of transportation that had been asked for. I may be mistaken about that. I did all that I could, and I think that General McDowell was quite satisfied; at least I never heard any complaint from him in regard to it. We supplied all the wagons that could be obtained, and I think we supplied all that were asked for. The army that moved was larger than it was first intended to move.

Question. Do you recollect the number of troops that were moved out to Centreville?

Answer. My recollection is, that it was first intended that 30,000 men should go, but that some 33,000 or 34,000 actually marched.

Analysis of Beauregard's reports, showing the number of troops in the actions at Blackburn's Ford, July 18, and Bull Run, July 21, 1861.

[The troops occupied a line of eight (8) miles, from Union Mills Ford, on Bull Run, to Stone Bridge.]

	Estimated strength.	Reported.
Ewell's brigade, consisting of—		
5th regiment Alabama volunteers............	600	
6th....do..........do....................	600	
6th regiment Louisiana volunteers	600	
4 guns, Walton's battery, 12th howitzers	60	
3 companies Virginia cavalry	180	
	2,040	
Holmes's brigade, (re-enforcements added on 20th of July, as reported)—		
Infantry......	1,265	1,265
6 guns......................................	90	90
1 company of cavalry......................	90	90
2d regiment Tennessee volunteers	600	
1st Arkansas volunteers....................	600	
	2,645	
D. R. Jones's brigade—		
5th regiment South Carolina volunteers.......	600	
15th...do.. Mississippi........do	600	
18th...do......do ....do	600	
2 guns, Walton's battery, 6-pounders.........	30	
1 company cavalry........................	60	
	1,890	

	Estimated strength.	Reported.

Early's brigade—
7th regiment Virginia volunteers 600
24th....do........do 600
7th regiment Louisiana volunteers 600
3 guns, rifled, Walton's battery.............. 45
          —— 1,845

Longstreet's brigade—
1st regiment Virginia volunteers.............. 600
11th....do........do 600
17th....do........do 600
2 guns, Walton's battery..................... 30
          —— 1,830

Jackson's brigade, (re-enforcements added on 20th of July)—
4th regiment Virginia volunteers.............. 600
5th.....do........do 600
2d .....do........do 600
27th....do........do 600
33d ....do........do 600
13th regiment Mississippi volunteers 600
          —— 3,600   1,261

Part of Bee's and Bartow's brigades, all that had arrived; new regiments, estimated fuller than the others—
2 companies 11th Mississippi volunteers....... 150
2d regiment............do............... 700
1st regiment Alabama volunteers.............. 700
7th regiment Georgia ....do.............. 700
8th.......do..........do.............. 700
          —— 2,950   2,732

Bonham's brigade—
2d regiment South Carolina volunteers 600
3d ....do ....do................. 600
7th....do ....do................. 600
8th....do ....do................. 600
6 guns, Shields's battery 90
6 guns, Delkemper's battery................. 90
6 companies Virginia cavalry 360
          —— 2,940

Cocke's brigade—
18th regiment Virginia volunteers............ 600
19th....do........do 600
28th....do........do 600
6 guns, Latham's battery.................... 90
1 company cavalry......................... 60
    Re-enforcements added on 20th July :
7 companies 8th Virginia volunteers.......... 420
3.... .. 49th......do 180
2.....do.. cavalry 120
4 guns, Rogers's battery 60
          —— 2,730

	Estimated strength.	Reported.
Evans's demi-brigade—		
4th regiment South Carolina volunteers.......	600	
1 battalion Louisiana volunteers	600	
4 guns, 6-pounders.........................	60	
2 companies cavalry........................	120	
Added on 20th:		
Stuart's cavalry, (army of Shenandoah)......	300	
2 companies Bradford cavalry..............	120	
8 guns, (Pendleton's,) reserve...............	120	
5 guns, (Walton's,) reserve	75	
6 companies Hampton's legion, (arrived from		
Richmond)	600	
		2,595
Add, also, army of Shenandoah, not in position on the morning of the 21st, but came up during the day as re-enforcements.............................	2,334	
	27,399	5,338

RECAPITULATION OF BRIGADES.

Ewell's brigade...	2,040
Holmes's brigade	2,645
D. R. Jones's brigade...	1,890
Early's brigade...	1,845
Longstreet's brigade..	1,830
Jackson's brigade...	3,600
Bee's and Bartow's brigade	2,950
Bonham's brigade...	2,940
Cocke's brigade...	2,730
Evans's demi-brigade	2,595
	25,065

This is as the army was posted in the morning, including the army of the Shenandoah, then in the field.

To this is to be added the garrison of Camp Pickens, Manassas, say..		2,000
Also the remainder of the army of the Shenandoah, which came up during the day	2,334	
And Hill's regiment....................................	550	
Making...		2,884
Aggregate...		29,949

ANOTHER VIEW.

Regiments and companies, by States, mentioned in Beauregard's report.

	Estimated.	Effective strength.
Virginia, 1st, 2d, 4th, 5th, 7th, 10th, 11th, 17th, 18th, 24th, 27th, 28th, 19th, and 33d, being 14 regiments, estimated at................	600	8, 400
6 companies of 8th regiment, 3 companies 49th regiment, and 6 companies Hampton's legion	60	900
23 companies cavalry..................	60	1, 380
		10, 680
Tennessee, 1st regiment, (1)		600
North Carolina, 5th, 6th, and 11th regiments, (3)...	600	1, 800
South Carolina, 2d, 3d, 4th, 5th, 7th, and 8th regiments, (6)	600	3, 600
Georgia, 7th and 8th regiments, (2)	600	1, 200
Alabama, 1st, 4th, 5th, and 6th regiments, (4)	600	2, 400
Mississippi, 2d, 15th, and 18th regiments, (3)......	600	1, 800
2 companies of the 11th regiment......	60	120
Louisiana, 6th and 7th regiments, (2)..............	600	1, 200
Wheat's battalion, 4 companies, and 6 companies of 8th regiment...........	60	600
Arkansas, 1st regiment, (1)......................	600	600
Maryland, 1st regiment, (1).....................	600	600

Add 50 guns, manned by 15 men each—		
Walton's battery	16 guns.	
Pendleton's .do	8 "	
Imboden's ..do	6 "	
Shields's....do	4 "	
Latham's ...do	4 "	
Alburtis's...do	4 "	
Kemper's ...do	4 "	
Rogers's ....do	4 "	

50 guns.	15	750	
			15, 270
Aggregate			25, 950

It will be seen that, whether the estimate be taken by brigades or by regiments and corps from States, we come to nearly the same result, and we are warranted in believing the assertion of Beauregard in his official report that the whole number of the army at Manassas was less than 30,000 after the junction of Johnston.

Suppose the whole number of regiments to be filled up, taking the highest number from each State, then the whole army raised by the Confederate States, wherever situated, would be, on that day, as follows:

South Carolina,	8 regiments, at 600............................	4, 800
North Carolina,	11....do......600................................	6, 600
Georgia	8....do......600................................	4, 800
Alabama	6....do......600................................	3, 600
Mississippi....	18....do......600................................	10, 800

Louisiana.....	7 regiments, at 600..........................	4,200
Tennessee....	1....do......600...........................	600
Arkansas.....	1....do......600...........................	600
Maryland	1....do......600...........................	600
		36,600

Add Virginia, 49 regiments, but we know that these are "*militia numbers*," and it is impossible for her to have had more than all the other Confederate States; so we will say 20 regiments of infantry, at 600.. 12,000

Total infantry..	48,600
Add 20 batteries artillery, at 90	1,800
Add 6 regiments cavalry, at 600................................	3,600
Grand total	54,000

This must have been the entire force of the confederate army, as we know that the Mississippi numbers are militia numbers, and that the North Carolina numbers are also militia, because I captured the 7th North Carolina volunteers at Hatteras, on the 28th of the following August, and had been organized but a week.

But it may be asked, how do we know that these were not the earlier regiments, and others of much higher numbers had been raised and in service elsewhere; or that large reserves were not left at Manassas, and not brought up.

Beauregard says the whole army of the Potomac was, on the morning of the 21st July .... 21,833 and 29 guns.
The army of the Shenandoah was .... 8,334 and 20 guns.

Total.................................... 30,167

Beauregard also says, in his report of the battle of Blackburn's Ford, July 18, Rebellion Record, Part 10, page 339:

"On the morning of the 18th, finding that the enemy was assuming a threatening attitude, in addition to the regiments whose positions have already been stated, I ordered up from Camp Pickens, (Manassas,) as a reserve, in rear of Bonham's brigade, the *effective men of six companies* of Kelly's 8th regiment Louisiana volunteers, and Kirkland's *eleventh regiment* North Carolina volunteers, which, having *arrived the night before en route for Winchester,* I had halted in view of the *existing necessities of the service.*"

With any considerable force at "Camp Pickens," (Manassas,) would this regiment either have been stopped *en route,* or the effective men of *six companies only* ordered up as a reserve?

In his report of Bull Run, July 21, Beauregard also speaks of the "intrenched batteries at Manassas" being under the command of Colonel Terret.

Is it possible that the rebels have been able to more than quadruple their forces in the last six months, with the whole world shut out from them, over what they did in the first six months?

All which is respectfully submitted.

BENJ. F. BUTLER.

BOSTON, *February* 11, 1862.